Dialogues
and
Discoveries

James Levine: His Life and His Music

Robert C. Marsh

A LISA DREW BOOK

SCRIBNER

A LISA DREW BOOK / SCRIBNER
1230 Avenue of the Americas
New York, NY 10020

DESIGNED BY COLIN JOH

Set in Bembo

Manufactured in the United States of America

1 3 5 7 9 10 8 6 4 2

Library of Congress Cataloging-in-Publication Data
Marsh, Robert C. (Robert Charles)
Dialogues and discoveries : James Levine: his life
and his music / Robert C Marsh.
p.   cm.
"A Lisa Drew Book"
Includes bibliographical references and index.
1. Levine, Lames, 1943– . 2. Conductors (Music)—
United States—Biography. I. Title.
ML422.L67M37   1998
784.2'092—dc21
[B]   97-44503
CIP

ISBN 0-684-83159-7

In memory of
GEORGE SZELL
Teacher Friend

Contents

Foreword by Jessye Norman   9

Preface   11

PART ONE: Life   15

PART TWO: Dialogues 1973–1996   61

PART THREE: Man at Work   151

PART FOUR: The Recordings   251

Epilogue   277

The Levine Discography 1970–1998   283

The Levine Met Repertory   311

Index   313

Foreword

In a world that rejoices in its superficiality, it is as the proverbial drop of water in the desert to experience the depth of musical commitment, energetic intelligence, and just plain exuberance of James Levine. That he is a master of his art is evident in everything he does.

It is a pleasure to work again and again with Jim; the enthusiasm never falters. The desire to convey the essence of every piece of music he touches lifts music-making far beyond the carelessness of routine to a plane where art, creativity, and soul meet and intertwine. I love him.

On a perfect California day, over twenty years ago, at the Hollywood Bowl, Jim and I met and worked together for the first time, and our journey through Verdi, Mozart, Strauss, Wagner, Mahler, Berlioz, Ravel, Schoenberg, Berg, Schubert, Brahms, Debussy, and Wolf began. We are still traveling. He is as excited about it now as he was then.

Since we know each other well and the years have provided innumerable experiences, one of my fondest exercises is to list the titles of books that Jim could write easily.

1. *Orchestral Conducting for Beginners (First, Steal a Baton . . .)*
2. *Singers: A Psychological Study*
3. *The Rewards of Musical Preparedness (Before the First Rehearsal)*
4. *Handbook for Would-Be Piano Accompanists (Listening Helps)*
5. *Tab Versus Coke: My Thoughts*

In all seriousness, though, let us praise him while he can feel and see our devotion, while we wait for the downbeat that takes us out of ourselves and into a realm where music happens as it should.

I feel a particular pride in having him as a friend and collaborator; he is earnest and true to his amity and his art. I feel a person need have no higher aspiration.

Jessye Norman
London, 9 July 1997

Preface

This is a long and steady look at the most important American conductor, a man who, at fifty-five, can take pride in more than thirty years of steadily growing success and look forward to what may well be thirty or more years of further artistic achievement. James Levine is the international symbol of the stature of American talent, American musical education, and American musical institutions, enthusiastically welcomed in the citadels of European musical culture because their guardians are fully aware that, in his generation, Europe has not produced his equal.

This study is critical in the sense that it is analytic and evaluative. Some of that analysis and evaluation comes from Levine in his own words. The book is not called *Interviews and Discoveries,* and for the best of reasons. The dialogues are genuine interchanges in which Levine has had an equal voice in establishing the final text.

This is not, however, an authorized study of Levine's career. In Parts One, Three, and Four the judgments are those of the author, and although, as a matter of courtesy, Levine has read and been invited to comment upon the text, the author alone is responsible for what the reader encounters. Anyone who knows Levine will realize that he is aware of the value of his work, but is far too modest to describe himself in superlatives. The critic has the right to evaluate him in those terms. But the critic also has the right to tell the story as he sees it, even if Levine or his colleagues do not agree with him. (And they often do not.) If we are to put Levine and his career in a proper perspective in the international world of music, there is room for a range of opinion.

Levine is an intensely private, professional, dedicated, hard-working musician. On even short acquaintance, one must be impressed by his selflessness. He is convinced his efforts can always be improved, and he strives endlessly to achieve this. His work has consistently been well received by the public and the press because his standards have been uncompromising. His finest achievements serve to define the highest level of musical performance today, but it is clear he does not think of them in those terms. They are phases in a process of growth, the end of which is not in sight. He may well be viewed, in time, as the most important conductor of the final decades of this century.

The author has known Levine from his Cleveland apprenticeship and has followed his career with close interest and high regard from those beginnings. For two decades our relationship was that of a professional music critic and a performer, both of whom held important musical posts in the Chicago metropolitan area.

This book is evidence that performers and critics can become friends. What is required is mutual respect and a sense of common goals. Nothing in the author's experience in the past thirty years has been more exciting than Levine's evolving career and maturing talent. And nothing has been more rewarding on a personal level than the fact that through those three decades we were always able to talk to one another, forcefully and candidly, without friction. Both of us were far more interested in music than in our egos, and both accepted fully the idea that the obligation of the musician is to serve music, not himself. We might disagree about details but never long-term goals or fundamental values.

Basic to our friendship is the fact that as professionals we can deal objectively with one another. Each has a sound intuition of how the other person works. Levine is highly verbal. He knows what is required to be a writer, and, as this collaboration proved, he is a skilled and sensitive editor. I was a vocal student a half century ago and have studied conducting formally, in the classroom and in rehearsals. Both Levine and I were deeply influenced by Arturo Toscanini, and, each one in his own way owes an enormous debt to George Szell as a teacher and friend.

I know what it is like to walk onstage and sing an aria. On occasion I have conducted both student and professional orchestras, and I know what it is like to give a downbeat and hear a Mozart phrase take shape in sound. But to think of me as a frustrated performer (a frequent calumny against critics) would be absurd. If Levine, from childhood, saw himself as a conductor, I always knew that my primary career would be as a writer.

This is an independent piece of work by a senior critic who was always free to write as he pleased. It draws on recorded interviews accumulated over more than twenty years, recent conversations specifically focused on this project, and Levine material, published and unpublished, which has been made available to me.

Apparently there is a common but mistaken view that the public is more interested in a celebrated musician's personality and private life than the artistic process that produces the performances we find so exciting. Or there is a feeling that this process cannot be described in words, or that such a description would be so technical that only musicians might understand it. For thirty-five years as music editor of a large metropolitan newspaper I was often sent for review music books that reflected this opinion.

This book is based on the opposite viewpoint. The basic questions confronted in these pages are: How does the performer make music? What is the source of the performance that seizes our attention so firmly? How does the creative process work? This book has been written with these priorities foremost and the belief that these questions can be answered in a way anyone concerned with music will find informative.

Obviously this book would not exist without the cooperation of James Levine, for which I am grateful beyond any descriptive phrase that might come to mind. He was a true collaborator. It is always a satisfaction to work with him. His mother, Helen Levine, and his brother, Tom, both wonderful human beings, also provided essential assistance.

Kenneth Hunt, Levine's asssistant in the artistic department of the Met, was another indispensable person, a constant source of perceptive commentary and most generous support. Mary Ann Martini, Levine's secretary, was also very helpful. The Met press department was most cooperative. Patrick Smith, editor of *Opera News,* was a friendly source of needed information.

Lisa Drew, my editor at Scribner, and Blythe Grossberg, her assistant, are to be commended for their patience, skill, and understanding. Finally, the book would never exist without Marshall De Bruhl, who was involved with it from beginning to end. He was the source of admirable suggestions for the improvement of the text and a wonderfully supportive colleague in every way. The old curmudgeon author has nonetheless insisted on calling his own shots, and in the best tradition of Chicago journalism takes full responsibility for the consequences.

Robert C. Marsh
New Glarus, Wisconsin, 1998

PART ONE

Life

I

James Levine comes from Cincinnati, Ohio. He is the kind of person one might expect from a city that combines a rich European cultural legacy with an influential role in the growth of the nation. These things come together in a remarkable counterpoint of values, ideas, and events that shaped the world in which he lived into early manhood.

Levine is not especially interested in family history. He sees himself as an American, and although he is aware of his roots to central Europe, his family was thoroughly Americanized in the nineteenth century. In his household there was never talk of the old country. He was an Ohio boy, a Buckeye, enriched by the life of the city in which he lived. But in a very real way he symbolizes the fulfillment of the aspirations that brought his ancestors to the United States.

Levine was not born in a city that was striving to develop musical culture. On the contrary, its musical achievements already rivaled many a city in the East. The rivers were the great natural highways of the young American republic, and Cincinnati was a river town. It was closely bound to the Atlantic seaboard. Never was this more forcefully asserted than in 1851, when Jenny Lind, the most powerful musical symbol to be lured from Europe in the early nineteenth century, sang there. She arrived in a comfortable steamboat on the broad Ohio. Chicago, which had no direct rail link to the East until later in the decade, never heard her voice, nor did Cleveland, Cincinnati's rival in northern Ohio.

Secure on its seven hills, Cincinnati fancied itself a little Rome where patrician tastes might be cultivated. It was settled in 1788 and was the first capital of the Northwest Territory. By 1840, before the flood of immigration that was to change its character, it was already the sixth largest city in the nation.

It was first a river town and then a German town. Germans had been an important part of life in the United States from the beginning, but their numbers increased with the influx of Forty-Eighters, liberal thinkers of all social classes who had left Europe after revolutionary efforts at reform failed. In 1850 half the population of Cincinnati was European-born and 30 percent of the citizenry was German. A German-Swiss choral society, with an annual *Sängerfest,* had grown to two thousand members by 1870.

The end of the Civil War in 1865 created a mood of jubilation in which music thrived. The arrival of Theodore Thomas and his touring New York orchestra in 1869 proved a monumental inspiration. Four years later, with Thomas's support, the first May Festival of choral music was heard. A century later James Levine would become its conductor.

During the *Sängerfest*, beer flowed as freely as melody. There was, in fact, a *Bierstube* conveniently located under the stage. Thomas would have none of that, and the serious character of the event was firmly defined. So great was its success that it needed a suitable home, and Cincinnati's Music Hall, still an attractive center for the arts in the city, was ready for the third May Festival in 1878, the year in which the city opened the Cincinnati College of Music.

A small symphonic ensemble was established in 1872. Under the leadership of the wife of a future president, Mrs. William Howard Taft, it gave way to the existing Cincinnati Symphony in 1895. The symphony had an American conductor, Frank Van der Stucken. He was (his name notwithstanding) a Texan educated in Europe—the first American-born conductor of an American symphony orchestra. In 1909 the orchestra went, for three years, to the twenty-seven-year-old Leopold Stokowski, who called for the construction of a music shell that in 1920 became the basis of the city's unique Zoo Opera. In 1922 Fritz Reiner began nine years as conductor of the Cincinnati Symphony. James Levine grew up in a city where Stokowski and Reiner were legendary figures, never suspecting that in Chicago he would someday inherit Reiner's greatest orchestra or record the soundtrack for the sequel to a history-making Stokowski film.

In the years following the Civil War, the expanding city attracted, in addition to Germans, immigrants from the Austro-Hungarian Empire. Among them were one of James Levine's great-grandparents. The conductor's maternal great-grandfather, Morris Goldstein, born in 1840 in a small city south of Budapest, had been a cantor in the synagogue there. He came to America in 1869 with a shipload of cantors looking for opportunities in the young nation. He found a place in Cincinnati, where he married an American-born woman of German descent. In addition to his music he was a painter of stature. His portrait of Isaac Mayer Wise, founder of Reform Judaism in the United States, is in the collection of the National Gallery of Art in Washington, D.C. Their son married a woman whose parents were born in Germany.

On the paternal side of the family were great-grandparents born in Latvia and Germany and a second couple born in Cincinnati of European ancestry. Helen Levine, James's mother, is uncertain of the national origin of the families already settled in Cincinnati or the date of their immigration. All of James's grandparents, however, were born in the

United States in a geographical range from Albany, New York, to Appleton, Wisconsin.

It is not unusual that Levine and two of his most significant teachers should bear a name with the same root. The Levines are Levites, members of the tribe of Levi, the priestly caste in Israel who bore the Ark of the Covenant and made music in the Temple. The pronunciation of Levi traditionally determined the family name.

James Levine is the son of a conductor, but not a conductor of the repertory he represents. In the big band era of the 1930s, visitors to the Beverly Wilshire Hotel in Los Angeles danced to the music of Larry Lee, who as a bandleader and crooner (School of Bing Crosby) was a successful purveyor of the popular music of the day. When many of the good sidemen were called into service after the United States went to war in 1941, the twenty-eight-year-old bandleader turned back into Larry (Lawrence) Levine and returned to his birthplace, Cincinnati, to join his father in the clothing business and to start a family, with his wife, whom he had married two years earlier. A scar on one lung made him ineligible for military duty.

No one called him Lawrence, just as his son James was always Jim in the household. While Larry Levine's children were growing up, he spent considerable time on the road, but the family bonds remained close. He was perfectly suited to be a salesman, and the success of the family business owed much to these skills. One of the immediate impressions on meeting him, even after his sons and daughter were grown, was his dedication and complete loyalty to his children. He followed their lives as avidly as any stage mother, especially after his retirement in 1961. He died in 1994.

Helen Levine, a lively, charming octogenarian, was born Helen Goldstein in Chicago in 1915. Her acting career (as Helen Golden) began in New York at the Neighborhood Playhouse. "My great success," she recalls, "was at the Lyceum Theater on Forty-fifth Street. The show opened in 1937. It was a play by Arthur Kober called *Having Wonderful Time*. I started out in a bit part and after several months was promoted to the leading part. I felt like the heroine of *Forty-second Street*. My leading man was John Garfield. I knew him, since we had been at the Neighborhood Playhouse together.

"I first met Larry Levine under the clock at the New Yorker Hotel on May 4, 1939. We knocked each other's socks off the night we met. It was love at first sight. We were married six months later. The fourth time I saw him was at our wedding."

When James Lawrence Levine was born June 23, 1943, the nation was at war. Europe was a distant, hostile place. He was the beloved first son of a prosperous family, with a lovely house on a lovely street in a lovely neighborhood. His parents represented a strong Jewish tradition that valued culture. Serious music was cultivated in the home. Larry Levine had kept his violin and still played from time to time for his own enjoyment. The environment was loving and encouraging for a child with musical talent, and young Jim was to make good use of it.

A second son, Tom, was born two years later. Here artistic genes expressed themselves in visual sensitivity. Tom Levine is a skilled painter, but for many years he has orbited his elder brother, playing a supportive role essentially the same as Walter Toscanini played for his father.

"Jim has to brush his own teeth," Helen Levine observes, "but since his Cleveland days he has concentrated on the things that only he can do." There are always mundane chores that must be done, but others take care of them. "One of the reasons that his success was so early," his mother believes, "is that he always concentrated his vital energy on the most important things. And for years he has had a support system that makes this possible." Levine himself puts it more simply. "My work comes first," he says.

A daughter, Janet, completed the family five years after the birth of James. A clinical psychologist, she now lives in Massachusetts and tries to be part of her brother's life, but, as her mother puts it, "Nobody who doesn't work with Jim sees an awful lot of him."

From all appearances, young James was a perfectly normal wunderkind. He had a cocker spaniel and a bicycle, and so many electric trains in the basement that a special table had to be built to hold them. He went to public school and grew up doing all the things that American boys normally do, but as he grew older his interest became more and more tightly focused on things musical.

"Jim rarely played with toys," his mother recalls. "Tom had them all pretty much to himself. Jim had a portable windup phonograph he could carry around and about fifty records. Long before he learned how to read, he always managed to get the record he wanted, and even as a little boy he could keep busy for hours playing music to himself.

"I doubt if he has ever had a golf club or tennis racquet in his hand," his mother says, "and he rarely was involved in ball games. But he has always enjoyed swimming."

From the age of three, when he began picking out themes on the piano, it was clear that music was the central interest in his life and that he was a keyboard player. Formal piano lessons began in 1947. There was never an interest in playing the violin, although little Jim could pick up wind instruments and, after some experimentation, find the notes he wanted. The piano was central to his life. Everything else had to be balanced with it. This did not prevent him, early in his school career, from flunking a music course. It was not serious enough, he thought, to deserve his attention.

Levine played his first piano recital at six. Everyone felt he was astonishingly gifted. As a result of this success, his piano teacher, Gertrude Englander, arranged for him to play for Thor Johnson, conductor of the Cincinnati Symphony. As Helen Levine puts it, "She was always a little concerned whether he was really as good as she—and we—thought he was." I knew Johnson well, and can easily see that he and young James were made for each other. Johnson was one of the first Americans to lead a major orchestra in the United States. He was a dedicated teacher, innovator, and champion of American talent. Although Johnson saw conducting as an adult job, he respected young Levine as a pianist and presented him to the public. For Levine, Johnson was an example of an American who, through dedicated hard work and musicianship, could be a successful conductor. The Levine beat was developed, probably with some informal instruction from Johnson, conducting records.

Johnson was interested and began to follow Levine's progress, but he and Jim's parents were conservative and did not want a child exploited or forced into a role for which he was unprepared. When James was ten he appeared as soloist in the Second Mendelssohn Concerto at a neighborhood concert of the Cincinnati Symphony. (The work has not figured in his later repertory.) The debut came as he was changing piano teachers, and everyone in the family rallied to his cause. He later played the Beethoven Third Piano Concerto with Johnson at the Transylvania Music Camp, a summer festival in Brevard, North Carolina. In the 1960s, when Johnson directed a remarkable little summer festival in Fish Creek, Wisconsin, he invited Levine to appear there, but commitments to the Aspen Festival made this impossible.

"The thing that impressed Johnson," Helen Levine says, "is that Jimmy seemed instinctively to know how to play in different styles for different composers. Thor said, 'You are too young to have been taught that. Where do you get that?' " Genes, I suggest. There must be a Mozart gene.

Even as a child young James had many things on his mind. School, especially math and science, often bored him, and his grades reflected this. A quick study from the very start, he once announced to his mother with pride that he had learned two scenes of a Verdi opera during math class, which may explain in part why his grades were not spectacular.

There were times, his mother recalls, when she felt he ought to stop what he was doing and go out of the house. "One afternoon," she says, "I insisted he go outside and get some fresh air. 'For how long?' he asked. 'Fifteen minutes,' I replied. He stood out in the yard looking at his watch for fifteen minutes, came back inside, and returned to whatever he was studying."

Levine's strong foundation was a secure and happy family—lively, intelligent children lived together in an atmosphere of mutual love and respect. With Larry Levine absent much of the time, Helen Levine became the strongest day-to-day influence on the children.

"Jim and I were always, somehow, on the same beam," she recalls. "You know, it sometimes just happens, and sometimes it doesn't, and at other times you work at it, but I always felt we had a sort of natural affinity. We were interested in the same things when he was a child. We would read plays together. I would take all the women's parts; he would take all the men's. And he loved that." The idea that performance was a worthy means of self-expression and self-realization was taught by both parents at an early age.

"His character formation was very early," Helen Levine says. "He began to be the Jimmy that he is very young. He would go to movies beyond his years and come home and discuss them with me. People would come to me and say, 'Where did he get this? From whom in your family did he get this?' And I would say, 'He brought it with him!' We were with him all the way, but it was always less what we did than what he had within himself. We did everything we could to make his success possible, but I am certain if things had been different he would have managed it by himself. He is just that sort of person.

"Jimmy, actually, is built like his father. His complexion, his blue eyes, and his general facial appearance are my side of the family, me and my mother. He has my disposition. I love him for that! One thing we have in common is that we never cry over spilt milk. If something goes wrong, instead of making a fuss, we turn at once to fixing it. The emphasis is going on and getting it right."

Larry Levine was extroverted, outgoing. His son, although blessed with a delightful sense of humor, had an introspective quality his father did not share. James was chubby as a child, but not fat, and as an adolescent he was strong and lean. His increasing girth as he has grown older reflects a lifestyle that makes it difficult for him to stress diet and conventional exercise as much as might be desirable.

"When he was ten, we took him to New York for an evaluation at the Juilliard School of Music. This was on the suggestion of his piano teacher, who was very good for a place the size of Cincinnati. But we were wondering what would happen when our son was compared with the Jimmy Levine from Pittsburgh and the Jimmy Levine from St. Louis. We felt we needed a solid professional opinion of his talent. That was his first meeting with Rosina Lhévinne (who was head of the jury) and his first visit to the Metropolitan Opera House. We saw a new production of *Faust* conducted by Pierre Monteux and several other works."

After the evaluation, Helen Levine remembers, "We were asked to come back to the dean's office for the report. The dean said, 'I don't usually do this, but I want to give you Rosina's report.' We read, 'I must have this boy. How do we get him away from the parents?'

"They were offering him all kinds of scholarships to move to New York to be in their preparatory department. They would put him in some kind of dormitory with overseers. And that's when my maternal feelings arose and I said, 'Absolutely not. This boy has more to learn than how to wiggle his fingers on a keyboard. He has to learn to live with his brother and sister. He has to learn there are many things in this world.' We were delighted he should go to Juilliard full-time, but not until after his graduation from high school.

"When we confronted Rosina with this, her funny little face fell and she said, 'Well, perhaps you are right; after all, you have developed this young man I admire so much.' She was willing to wait a few years before he became a full-time student.

"That's when he began flying to New York for study on weekends. He would leave after school on Friday and return Sunday night. At the beginning I would put him on the plane and his father, who spent a lot of time in New York on business, would meet him. But Jim got the hang of New York very quickly, and if his father was not there, we were confident that he could get a cab and go to the Astor Hotel, where the manager, one of Larry's friends, let Jim practice in the ballroom.

"There were some variations in the pattern over the years, but Jim was so confident and so clearly in command of the situation that we didn't worry. When I went to New York in this period, he was clearly taking care of me."

It was, of course, a blessing for young James that the family's circumstances made this commutation possible. But it was necessary for him to have a teacher in Cincinnati as well, someone who could go beyond the piano to teach him theory, instrumentation, and other basic musical subjects. Walter Levin was the German-born first violinist of the LaSalle

Quartet, which had been founded at Juilliard some years earlier. He had recently moved to Cincinnati, and it was suggested that he become James's mentor. His initial objection to teaching an eleven-year-old vanished when he met his future pupil, and for the next seven years he and his wife, Evi, who was an amateur musician, gave Jim a comprehensive mastery of humanistic subjects as well as music theory. Evi Levin, a professional linguist, taught Levine French and German. This complemented his schoolwork, where he had excelled in history and literature.

"What I found," Walter Levin said, "was a natively talented, undisciplined, slightly overbearing kid who was in serious need of a teacher who could teach him what music was all about." Discipline was enforced. Once when young James showed up unprepared for his lesson, he was summarily thrown out of the house and had to wait in the yard until his mother came to get him.

Recalling the incident, Levine says, "I realized at that point that you had to work your way through the frustrating, boring phases of study, and that unless you got on with it, you didn't get to the treasure at the end."

Even before the New York trip, young James had attended opera. The Cincinnati Zoo Opera made extensive use of Metropolitan personnel as well as young American singers, and Fausto Cleva, a veteran of the Met pit, conducted many of the performances. Young James attended his first opera there when he was eight, and when he learned that prior to the performances there were rehearsals which he might hear, the opera at the Zoo became his summer base. He arrived baton in hand—a knitting needle he had borrowed from his grandmother. "That was his real introduction to opera," his mother says.

As part of its annual tour, the Met visited nearby Bloomington, Indiana, in the spring of 1951, with *Die Fledermaus* and *Don Carlo*. It was back the following year with *Aida* and returned in 1953 with *Rigoletto* and *Tristan und Isolde*. The Levines went to them all, preferring opera in Bloomington to attending Met performances in Cleveland because the distance was shorter and Indiana University had a better hall. After 1953 there were regular visits to the opera in New York, for example a *Carmen* with Risë Stevens and Mario Del Monaco in 1955. Asked by an interviewer in 1996 when he began to consider the Met his home, James Levine responded that he had felt close to the Met all his life and, thus, it seemed perfectly natural that someday he should work there.

During that first New York trip, when he was ten, he visited the F.A.O. Schwarz toy store, where James discovered a toy theater that became a central element in his life. He wanted sets for all the operas he knew, and he scrounged for them when necessary. Act 1 of *Madama But-terfly* had been a drugstore display.

In 1956, at thirteen, he was sent to study with Rudolf Serkin at the pianist's Marlboro (Vermont) summer festival and music school. One of the projects for the summer was a production of *Così fan tutte.* A chorus master was needed for the brief choral scenes, and James took the job. He considers it the beginning of both his career in opera and long attachment to that score.

The Levines attended a Reform synagogue and observed the high holidays as an opportunity for the family, in its larger sense, to come together. As an adolescent, Tom Levine was confirmed in his faith. James did not have a Bar Mitzvah. Yiddish was not part of the family tradition, and neither son learned Hebrew beyond two or three simple blessings. James stopped attending Jewish Sunday school so that he could spend more time with his father. They made music together, talked about what they had been reading, and did such chores as taking the dog to the vet. James Levine plays a mean game of gin rummy, thanks to years of instruction from his father, who was an expert.

Everything that has happened in Levine's life has prepared him for what he is doing today. There was no search for identity or purpose, no sidetracks into other lines of professional interest. One reads with astonishment that even a man as gifted as Reiner was briefly diverted to the study of law as a youth. There are no dead-end streets in Levine's past. He is a prime example of a person whose primary interests were quickly discovered and whose main activities focused on his proper goal early in childhood.

Levine was born to be a conductor, and he followed that path with the conviction that it was his proper objective. His play with a toy opera house was training for the years when he would have a real opera house to run. As a child he was working to make it happen. He has always defined his own priorities. No one can change them because he is not going to change. To live and work with him, you must share his values and join him with a sense of common purpose.

As he sees it: "I had parents who really cared and gave me the background I needed. It was all positive. In this situation I was able to develop. Everything that was different from me interested me. We must respect that every person is responsible for himself, for his own life. If you see a person seeking a goal that you can help him achieve, this creates a possibility of accomplishing something together."

II

A decisive year in Levine's life was 1957, his first of fourteen summers at the Aspen (Colorado) Festival and School of Music. For the first three years he was a student, but from 1960 onward he was a performer as well. In 1961, freshly graduated from Walnut Hills High School in Cincinnati and just barely eighteen, he conducted his first opera, Bizet's *The Pearl Fishers.*

Recalling the situation many years later, he writes: "A festival has always meant something very significant to me—an atmosphere of excitement, a special working relationship among the artists, a sense of community between artist and audience so that the interchange between the creative effort and the audience is very strong—a listening, learning, working, rejuvenating experience."

The early years at Aspen were especially stimulating. "One doesn't encounter this special atmosphere often," Levine recalls, "but it is something I grew up with at the Aspen Festival in the late fifties and early sixties. The whole town seemed given over to the music festival: students, teachers, performers practicing and rehearsing all over town. Shopkeepers knew all the students, many by name. Everybody lived, worked, and relaxed together in this most unusual environment. A lot of unfamiliar music by familiar composers, familiar music by unfamiliar composers, and music for every conceivable combination of instruments and voices was performed. This kind of summer—studying, sharing, and performing, a highly concentrated and closely related program of great music in a uniquely beautiful natural setting—was an indescribable pleasure."

In a 1962 *Life* magazine issue on "The Take-Over Generation," Levine is seen rehearsing the Aspen orchestra. "A conductor," he says, "must know everything—languages, style, repertory, theory, technique. I hate a lazy approach to anything." The interesting thing is that he could have said this last week.

At Aspen Levine conducted *Così fan tutte* for the first time in a wide-ranging repertory that included three twentieth-century works, Strauss's *Ariadne auf Naxos,* Stravinsky's *Mavra,* and Britten's *Albert Herring,* with the composer in attendance. His realizations of these operas, as well as symphonic works, brought consistently fine reviews. From the Aspen experience Levine was prepared to offer firm artistic leadership when he came to the Ravinia Festival, where he emphasized the need for the expanded educational program that he achieved in his final years there.

Also in 1961, he had moved to New York City and enrolled at Juilliard full-time. He completed the undergraduate requirements in a year, remained as a graduate student to work with Lhévinne (he studied with him for fifteen years), and began the systematic study of conducting with one of the great mentors of the day, Jean Morel. This led, in 1964, to participation in the American Conductor's Project of the Baltimore Symphony, where he worked with Alfred Wallenstein, Fausto Cleva, and Max Rudolf.

On the jury was one of Rudolf's closest colleagues, George Szell, music director of the Cleveland Orchestra, who was running his own school for conductors based roughly on the apprenticeship he had served with Richard Strauss at the Berlin Opera in the early years of the century. He invited Levine to become an apprentice in Cleveland with the lure, "You're already a very good conductor and maybe we can make you a great one."

In the autumn of 1964, Levine left Juilliard without formally completing any degree program to begin six years in Cleveland. For most of the period he was assistant conductor of the orchestra. Szell had also been a wunderkind pianist and composer, but chose a conductor's career, and Levine at twenty-one felt much the same way. "I had never been attracted to the big solo pieces," he says, "and I was perfectly aware that the amount of technical work I would have to do to play the Tchaikovsky concerto would be better spent on a different repertory."

I was part of the Cleveland scene at that time, preparing a history of the orchestra for its fiftieth season in 1967. It was obvious, when you caught him off guard, that Szell cherished Levine the way a great teacher delights in the prize pupil he had always dreamed of finding. In his customary manner, to preserve protocol, he kept Levine at a certain distance (Szell's conversation suggested that Strauss had treated him in the same manner), but Szell saw this young man (rightly) as the continuation of everything for which he stood in music. He gave him his love without qualification.

Szell was a much misunderstood musician. One of the most warmhearted persons I have ever known, he was terrified that if he expressed his feelings too openly he would be exploited. Early in a relationship he might test you by giving you a chance to exploit him. If you declined the opportunity, you were safe and he warmed up considerably. With most people he protected himself with a cloak of formal good manners and cool professionalism that caused many to regard him, mistakenly, as a coldhearted authoritarian. Levine's relationships with other artists, although reflecting his warmhearted approach to life, are still clearly influenced by Szell's desire to define roles and maintain a certain protective distance.

My relationship with Szell, which grew steadily closer with time, was completely different from his relationship with Levine, partly because I am nearly twenty years Levine's senior. Szell, in his rehearsals, gave me the ultimate graduate course in how to listen to an orchestra, and it was easy to see how, in working with his junior colleagues, he tried to offer them all he had learned in a lifetime of distinguished music-making. A central element in Szell's instruction, which had a lasting influence on Levine, was the constant pursuit of good texts.

"I am more or less convinced," Szell once observed, "that every standard edition of every standard work contains at least one horrible mistake." To prove this, a wall in his dressing room/office was covered with photocopies of pages from composers' manuscript scores in which there was something of importance missing from the editions currently in use. (This was thirty years ago, and it must be noted that things have improved.)

Characteristic of Szell was that one of the highest priority items when he first took his orchestra to Moscow was to see the manuscript of the First Tchaikovsky Piano Concerto to check one note that had long bothered him. He returned triumphant to his hotel shouting, "It's a B-flat!" The emendation he had made for years was correct.

For a time a standard exercise in what Szell called "skull sessions" was for the apprentices to be shown a single page of orchestral music. One was to identify its probable period, then the form (symphony, concerto, etc.), and finally, if possible, the composer and the work. After a few months Levine and his colleagues had had enough of this, and one afternoon they asked Szell if he would look at a page of music.

"My God," he exclaimed, "it's my second symphony." There were no further quizzes of this type.

Szell, like Toscanini, started conducting in a period in which singers were often very poor musicians. He delighted in telling of a performance of *Rigoletto* in his early years in which a leading singer, who could not read music, had a memory slip and jumped thirty-seven bars ahead in his part. It was the task of the conductor to get everything together as quickly as possible, and Szell, by shouting the new bar number, managed it. But the young conductors Szell was training would rarely encounter a situation of this sort, so being tested in problems of this type was unnecessary. Singers who can work from music at piano rehearsals achieve a type of security uncommon in the past.

Levine made his official debut with the Cleveland Orchestra in a subscription concert in the spring of 1967. He directed Strauss's *Don Juan*. The next day Szell was eager to have my opinion. It was excellent, I thought—propulsive, exciting, and extremely well played—but, I feared, a little inflexible. "He will loosen up!" Szell proclaimed. And, of course, he was right.

In the summer of 1967, Szell was preparing for what was to be his last European tour with the Cleveland Orchestra. He returned to Cleveland from the Swiss golf resort where he spent part of every summer (always in the same room) to go through the programs. Since he was rarely in Cleveland in the summertime, the only air-conditioned space in his house was the wine cellar. He would not have his prize Bordeaux ruined by the Ohio climate. On this occasion he stayed in a hotel.

All the repertory had been heard in concerts of the previous season, and Szell felt if they simply played through the tour programs, all would be well. But he was acutely conscious that what he heard on the stage was not always what the audience heard in the center of the hall, and he wanted trustworthy ears positioned there to deal with questions of balance and texture. The situation was complicated by the fact that new seats were being installed on the main floor, and the space was temporarily empty except for three large chairs. The open floor space improved the resonance of the hall considerably.

"Let's leave it like that," he remarked laconically to the orchestra manager. The chairs were for associate conductor Louis Lane, assistant conductor Levine, and myself. No one had a note of printed music. If the work had appeared in the subscription concerts, Szell's colleagues had to know it well enough to conduct it on short notice if required. At one point Szell turned and asked us, "Is the second bassoon too loud?" He expected a prompt and accurate reply from someone fully aware of what the second bassoon was supposed to be doing at that moment. Lane and Levine managed to deal with these queries while holding an intense conversation on some musical matter. Like Szell, they had learned to do more than one thing at a time.

The rehearsal closed with the Brahms Second Symphony. It went beautifully. There were a few pauses, one or two questions to the orchestra, and after the final bar, a question for us.

"Well, gentlemen, have you anything to suggest?"

"No, Dr. Szell," was the unison reply.

"Well," he said to the orchestra, "if there is nothing more for us to do, I shall see you in Salzburg."

He was releasing the orchestra twenty minutes before the close of a rehearsal, an unknown thing. Lane and Levine disappeared as fast as the players. I walked over to the stairs coming down from the stage and met Szell as he descended.

"Was it really that good?" he asked. "Nothing to do?"

"Dr. Szell," I replied, "I thought it was a perfect realization of what you wanted to do in that work."

He paused and then permitted himself a smile of satisfaction. "I thought so too," he said.

One of the decisive events of Levine's life took place that same year. "I was asked by Bob Shaw [Robert Shaw, Szell's other associate conductor and chorus master] to go to to the summer festival he was starting in a Detroit suburb, Meadowbrook," he remembers. "In the first year we had auditions for the student orchestra I was to lead. Suzanne Thomson is from Detroit, so she was one of the local auditioners. She played the oboe like an angel. She had this unusual feeling for whatever she was doing. Shaw and I took her into the orchestra right away. We've been together ever since, nearly thirty years. She was amazing. So lovely."

Helen Levine observes, "I consider Suzanne my daughter-in-law. James was a young man in the sixties, and this is a sixties type of relationship. They tell me they see so many married couples who are unhappy. Part of Jim and Sue's happiness may come from the fact that they feel free."

While serving as Szell's assistant, in 1966 Levine founded the University Circle Orchestra using students at the Cleveland Institute of Music, where he had become a member of the faculty. He was now able to make music with his own players. He conducted opera in concert form for the Cleveland Concert Association. Creating opportunities for himself to work, Levine gave himself the kind of apprenticeship that European conductors of an earlier generation served in provincial theaters.

It was inevitable that with Szell's death in 1970, Levine, at twenty-seven, would begin extending his formidable Cleveland reputation into the larger world of music by guest conducting. He gave a concert performance of *Rigoletto* at Meadowbrook and directed the Philadelphia Orchestra in its summer concerts of 1970. That year he also conducted *Aida* and *The Barber of Seville* with the Welsh National Opera.

During autumn seasons in San Francisco (1970–71), he conducted two Puccini staples, *Tosca* and *Madama Butterfly*. In 1971–72, he made his debut at the Hollywood Bowl, substituting for an indisposed Zubin Mehta. His first appearances in Los Angeles included performances of *La Traviata* with Beverly Sills, Plácido Domingo, and Sherill Milnes, as well as *Don Giovanni* and *Rigoletto*. There was also a Wagner program with Jess Thomas and Ingrid Bjoerner and numerous symphonic programs, including a performance of the Beethoven Piano Concerto No. 1, with

Martha Argerich as soloist. Jessye Norman's made her American opera debut as Aida under Levine's direction at the Hollywood Bowl and he also conducted a performance of Bernstein's *Trouble in Tahiti*. At the Los Angeles Greek Theater, he led *Tosca* with Dorothy Kirsten.

However, another, more momentous, debut came in the summer of 1971. But when great opportunities were given him, Levine was prepared. On June 5, 1971, two weeks short of his twenty-eighth birthday, he conducted, with great success, *Tosca* at the Metropolitan Opera.

III

Until his death in 1957, Arturo Toscanini, embittered by his years at the Metropolitan early in the century, referred to it as the "casino" ("whorehouse"). It was a place where a certain celebrity could be achieved and money could be made—but only through compromising artistic standards to please businessmen. A year after the maestro's death, Irving Kolodin, a veteran New York critic and respected historian of the Met, tried to get to the root of the matter. In his classic history of the opera company Kolodin discussed the issue. He asked general manager Rudolf Bing whether he felt he was anywhere nearer to the solution of the Met's basic problem.

"What problem?" Bing inquired.

"The problem," said Kolodin, "of maintaining the day-to-day repertory on a level of performance comparable to, or within a reasonable range of, the level of the first performance, new productions, etc."

"Oh," Bing said, "that is simple. Merely a matter of money."

If the Met had unlimited funds, he could have Tebaldi for twenty weeks, not ten, or Björling or Tucker, or whomever. Opera performers, he went on, go where the money is, unlike those concerned with "art."

"If this reply did not beg the question," Kolodin felt, "it certainly did not answer it. Clearly the presence of a Tebaldi or a Björling, or their mezzo and baritone equivalents, would not alter the performance level of an otherwise poorly conducted *Aida* or of a *Carmen* with disreputable stage direction. Nor was the question merely one of money. . . . It was, rather, a question of how one allocated the money one had."

Bing, it must be noted, felt constant pressure from his board to economize. This was partly because the company had evolved into a national artistic institution without ever securing an appropriate endowment or a strong subscription base. In the absence of financial reserves, constant pressure to avoid deficits was inevitable.

As Kolodin saw it, in the existing situation, the responsibility for maintaining quality belonged to one person, the general manager, while properly it should go to (or be shared with) "a sound and responsible group of conductors who would merit respect as well as demand it." Bing did not agree. In his memoirs he says a music director was "a post I frankly avoided because it seemed to me to divide responsibility that I thought should be the general manager's alone." The problem was his apparent indifference to undertaking the continuous supervision without which a high-quality standard could never be achieved.

If, as in 1958–59, he could sell out 110 of 164 performances—67 percent of the season—he felt he had a secure foundation of public support. Bing, in this period, was especially vulnerable to the fickle taste of single-ticket buyers. He had some 8,000 subscribers. (The Met today has more than 30,000.) For Bing, if the money problem was solved, the artistic problem could be ignored. This is the essential difference between managers and musicians. For the manager, money is always the primary consideration.

Bing's attitude does not appear to have changed significantly after the company moved to its new theater in Lincoln Center in 1966. For the twenty-two years he occupied the front office, he was boss, although there were conductors—Erich Leinsdorf is a good example—who had his confidence and whose contribution to the administration of the theater was probably more substantial than the public appreciated.

Leinsdorf, it must be added, viewed Bing's position as an impossible job. In 1970, when speculation about Bing's successor was rife, Leinsdorf, who had left the musical directorship of the Boston Symphony the year before, was frequently suggested as a prime candidate. I asked him about it.

"If you should ever pick up the *New York Times,*" he said, "and read that your old friend Erich has become general manager of the Met, sigh and face the fact that, as the English put it, he has finally gone round the bend. No sensible person can take that job because as it is presently structured, it is impossible to do it right."

Levine first appeared at the Met in Bing's penultimate season, 1970–71. As Bing described it, ". . . the most important debuts of my later years were those of conductors." In addition to Karajan and Bernstein, there were Zubin Mehta, Colin Davis, Alain Lombard, and two very young Americans, Christopher Keene and James Levine, who revitalized the *Luisa Miller,* which was "probably the most successful of all my efforts to restore neglected Verdi operas to the Metropolitan repertory."

One wonders if Bing saw the possibility that ten years after writing these lines, both Keene and Levine would be at work full-time at Lincoln Center. Levine had remained at the Met. Keene, after establishing himself as a conductor with the New York City Opera, became artistic supervisor of that company in 1982. At the time of his tragically early death (at forty-eight in 1995), he had been general director for six years.

Bing observed that the American singer has far more generous opportunities to find training than the American conductor. "The Metropolitan Opera Auditions have become a bore of little productivity for the company," he noted. But the Met auditions were screening talent that had previously been discovered and trained by others. Bing apparently never saw the Met as an educational institution operating on a large scale, although the Metropolitan Opera Studio, which functioned in the later Bing seasons, was an important gesture in an area that called for more intensive cultivation. This was to come, in time, with Levine's Young Artist Development Program.

In Europe, Bing noted, the young conductor could serve an apprenticeship. "Karajan worked two years at Ulm and two years at Aachen, conducting everything at a German repertory house, and then he was Karajan; he knew. Today talent is found too soon and sent off to conduct difficult operas at international festivals. Instead these boys should go two years to Magdeburg and two years to Stuttgart, and then they would be great conductors. Someone [in America] ought to start paying attention to the training of conductors."

He failed to note that, among others, his old adversary Szell had paid attention. Levine was a product of that program and, in terms of existing opportunities, had put in a reasonable apprenticeship.

Levine's Met debut, a matinee performance of *Tosca* (without stage rehearsal with orchestra), June 5, 1971, was part of "June Festival." Grace Bumbry sang the title role at the Met for the first time with Franco Corelli, Peter Glossop, and twenty-nine-year-old Paul Plishka in the cast. (Twenty-five years later Plishka was singing Falstaff for Levine, the fruition of long and productive seasons together.) A week later there was a repeat, an evening performance this time.

Concertmaster Raymond Gniewek recalls that he went to Levine after his debut and said, "That was the most exciting performance I have played since Karajan conducted us." The absence of rehearsal had not been a drawback, since Levine had done the opera before. It was securely in his stick.

"As the weeks passed into months," Gniewek continues, "a lingering thought kept recurring. Can he be this talented and also so gentle, considerate, and patient? But the day of the old-school autocratic conductors has indeed ended. Here was a young man who could coax, cajole, inspire, yet never compromise the discipline or concentration so essential to unifying a hundred instrumentalists into a powerful musical force.

"Jimmy's formidable intelligence and awesome memory, enviable as they are, do not necessarily ensure greatness as a conductor. For me the special ingredient in that recipe for success is Jim's uncanny knack of personal communication and the incredible support he gives even under conditions of enormous stress. He radiates a feeling of warmth, integrity, and purpose that inspires our team to play more gloriously and eloquently than we ever believed possible."

Two weeks later Levine made his debut at the Ravinia Festival in Highland Park, Illinois, directing the Chicago Symphony Orchestra and Chorus in Mahler's Second (the *Resurrection*) Symphony. The day before the performance, Levine had marked his twenty-eighth birthday. Whether he sensed it or not, through the success of both performances he established important musical bases in which he was to concentrate his work for more than twenty years—the Met for opera and suburban Chicago for symphonic music.

During 1971–72, Bing's final season, Levine's appearances increased from two to nineteen and he participated in the gala for the retiring general manager. There were seven performances of *Tosca* between early November and mid-December. There were four Toscas, four Cavaradossis, and three Scarpias, a classic example of the manner in which Bing passed singers through standard operas with little or no rehearsal. I suspect the most exciting night was November 6, when Bumbry (in the second of her four performances) was joined by Plácido Domingo and the greatest Scarpia of his day, Tito Gobbi.

Domingo and Levine had first appeared together at the Met on November 4, 1971, when the tenor replaced Richard Tucker in *Luisa Miller*. Stability in the nine performances of the Verdi tragedy was provided by Plishka as Wurm, a villainous role he played with extraordinary force. Adriana Maliponte and Gabriella Tucci alternated in the title role. The opening night, October 15, marked the first Met collaboration of Levine and Sherrill Milnes, another professional relationship that was to produce remarkable results. Again Levine was back for the post-tour weeks, this time two performances of *Falstaff*.

The new leadership for the Met, as initially set forth, was Goeran Gentele as general manager and Schuyler Chapin as assistant manager.

Rafael Kubelik was to conduct in the 1973–74 season and become music director in 1974–75. Levine remained firmly in place on the conducting staff, with his duties extended to twenty-one opera performances and two programs for children, one of which, a telecast with Danny Kaye, won an Emmy Award. But Bing had scarcely cleaned out his office when, in July 1972, Gentele died in Europe in an automobile accident. Chapin took over the direction of the company, and plans for 1972–73 had to be revised quickly.

Levine's schedule for 1972–73 had, in fact, been negotiated with Gentele before his death. The original plans called for Levine to conduct *The Barber of Seville, La Bohème,* and *Faust.* He saw problems.

"I don't like the *Faust* production, it's a disaster," he calmly told Gentele. "If I'm going to be a representative of the Metropolitan Opera, if suddenly I am going to appear to endorse what the Met does, then I have to be able to subscribe to my own performances."

With that statement, the demise of the casino was inevitable. Within a decade, Levine had become the central figure in the creation of an artistically renewed Met that Toscanini could have viewed with pride.

Gentele was too fine a theater man to fail to see the necessity for Levine's position. He replied that if Levine couldn't stand looking at the Met's *Faust,* he could do *Otello* instead.

"Later," Levine told an interviewer, "I went to him on the same kind of issue for another reason. I had been assigned *Bohème* because Gentele wanted it revitalized. Then I got a look at the casting, which was done subsequently. Nothing wrong with any individual singers, but so many cast changes were impossible. Furthermore the production is older than God, and while you might be able to revitalize *Bohème* with a new conductor and a stable, well-integrated cast, you sure as hell can't do it with a smorgasbord cast. *Rigoletto* was open; I looked at the casting and it was very stable. So I tried it." The introduction of stable casting was high on Kubelik's list of priorities, and Levine supported it thoroughly.

Viewed from the perspective of a quarter century, in 1972–73 Levine gave the greatest part of his time to the opera he was to conduct more than any other at the Met, *Otello.* There were ten performances from early December to early January and two more in the June series. Jon Vickers sang the title role eight times, and James McCracken did the remaining performances, an alternation of two outstanding performers. The lyric Desdemona of Renata Tebaldi contrasted with the dramatic force of McCracken and Milnes in January performances that brought the Met some of its greatest moments of the season.

The Met's six *Barber* performances of the spring of 1973 probably followed the traditions of the house with respect to cuts and staging. However, Levine had Marilyn Horne as Rosina, Fernando Corena as Bartolo, Cesare Siepi as Basilio, and Hermann Prey as Figaro. The conductor returned to the opera only once more, to record it in London in 1975. The album set a new standard of taste in the work and permitted us, for once, to hear all the music associated with the score. There were six *Rigolettos* in the winter months. In that work, on February 6, Levine appeared for the first time with Luciano Pavarotti, who was delighted with the young maestro.

Levine's operatic activities in the early 1970s were not confined to New York. In 1972 he did a concert version of *Rigoletto* in the Robin Hood Dell concerts of the Philadelphia Orchestra, and in 1974 he gave *Le Nozze di Figaro* in a concert version with the Atlanta Symphony and his old Cleveland friend, Robert Shaw. He returned to Cincinnati from 1974 to 1978 to conduct the May Festival, where (in concert form) he gave *Parsifal* for the first time. Other May Festival repertory closely associated with his career were *Porgy and Bess, Les Troyens, Oedipus Rex, Tannhäuser,* and *Lohengrin.* His 1978 *Barber of Seville* was the final performance of the Cincinnatl summer opera at the Zoo. In 1976 the University of Cincinnati gave him an honorary doctorate.

Levine's career on the Continent began in 1975 with *Otello* in Hamburg. He repeated the work in Vienna in 1982. Two primary European bonds were soon established. In 1976 he was invited to conduct at the Salzburg Festival, beginning a long association—seventeen consecutive seasons—with that distinguished music center, and he was invited to conduct the centennial production of *Parsifal* at Bayreuth in 1982. In 1973–74 Kubelik was resident at the Met. At the beginning of the season Levine had been named principal conductor, the first in the eighty-eight years the Met had existed, and was in residence seven months of the year, assisting Kubelik when he was present and seeing that his policies were enforced when he was not.

Asked about his duties at the time, he said, prophetically: "A music director has to see to the problems of orchestra and chorus personnel, rehearsals, assistant conductors who are assigned to musical preparation, casting, cancellations, understudies, all of this. Somebody has to do this from the musical side of the general manager's office when Kubelik isn't there. That's my administrative job. I work with Kubelik when he's here and report to him when he isn't, because the final decisions are his.

"I do not want the responsibility of having to act for the music director because I'm not the music director. Someday I hope to be head of a symphony orchestra and/or an opera house. But I do not want the headaches of being the music director here without the rewards. Furthermore, I do not think it is fair for the major opera company in the United States to have someone making these decisions who is thirty. This is not true where my functioning as a conductor is concerned. There I have as much control over casting as is feasible."

The season was to have contained Verdi's *Un Ballo in Maschera,* in Gentele's much-acclaimed Stockholm production, but with his death it was felt another work should be found. Levine was recording *I Vespri Siciliani* in London in August with essentially the same cast that had been engaged for *Ballo.* In an inspired switch of repertory it was brought to the Met in January 1974, produced by a brilliant English director, John Dexter.

Levine's appearances were now almost double those of the previous season. He continued to conduct "look in" programs for children, and offered five operas from a Mozart, Verdi, Strauss repertory for a total of forty-two performances. This was the year when *Salome* arrived and departed from his repertory. (Bumbry was the princess of Judea for all ten performances, stable casting triumphant.) *Otello* continued with Vickers and McCracken alternating as the moor and Kiri Te Kanawa (in her Met debut) and Teresa Stratas, two glamorous prima donnas, as his ill-fated spouse.

In the spring of 1974, Kubelik resigned. As Chapin suddenly moved from number two man in the front office to number one in 1972, Levine had to accept the fact that the Met now had a thirty-one-year-old music director, although the title was not officially bestowed until 1976. He conducted thirty-eight operatic performances in 1974–75.

Chapin's 1974 plan for the administration of the house was that Levine should be music director and John Dexter should be in charge of production. Chapin was to dominate this troika, and there was every hope it would pull together. In 1976 Dexter acerbically wrote a friend, "I am having a wonderful time at the Met. I don't know if Levine and I can do anything about dragging the place into the twentieth century or even, for that matter, into the nineteenth. But the challenges it opens up and the occasions it provides for experiment are fascinating."

But if Chapin had Dexter and Levine, he lacked other talented people needed to sustain a season. His difficulties in retaining senior conductors were a factor that led to the termination of his duties as general manager early in 1975. Thomas Schippers, who had opened the new house in

1966, was dying. Leinsdorf, William Steinberg, and Max Rudolf, one of Bing's long-standing artistic advisors, had made their exit.

Chapin was told by William Rockefeller (chairman of the Metropolitan Opera Association) that the ninety-one-year-old post of general manager was being abolished: "The Metropolitan is too complicated to be run by one man any longer. We must never have an impresario again. We've outgrown the need." This was particularly true if the manager was not a musician and thus unable to make decisions that required the specialized knowledge of a musical professional. Out of this crisis came a reorganization of the company that, with our present perspective, resulted in the Met of today, one that honors Toscanini's standards of artistic integrity.

Chapin felt a general manager of the type Bing had represented was still an artistic necessity, but a far better pattern had been established at the major American symphony orchestras where, in Chicago, for example, Fritz Reiner as music director was in charge of the artistic side of the operation and a skilled musical administrator, George Kuyper, handled the business matters.

In the summer of 1975, Anthony A. Bliss, who had been on the Met board since 1949, retired from his law practice to come to the Met as executive director. A patrician who had long evidenced the deepest commitment to the performing arts, he had the wisdom, experience, and influence in the community to reshape the company successfully.

Let us hear him describe this moment. "In many respects, because of close family associations, the Met has been my life. For over twenty years my father, Cornelius N. Bliss, served on the Met's board, and, as a result, I can hardly think of a day I did not have some thought or task involving opera. Often famous names of Met history would visit our home. When I was only seven, my father took me to hear Caruso in *Pagliacci*. He felt it would be Caruso's last year, and he wanted me to have heard him."

Bliss saw the need for significant change. One no longer balanced the books at the close of the season, he observed ironically, by "asking Mr. Rockefeller out to lunch." There had to be a more solid and businesslike approach, based on long-term planning. Media and marketing departments were to be strengthened and revitalized, and the Met was to make a maximum impact on the nation through the *Live from the Met* television series, inaugurated on PBS in 1977. (It is now *The Metropolitan Opera Presents* since the shows are now taped for later presentation.)

In 1984 Bliss happily offered the world the first two laserdiscs (and video cassettes) of Met productions. The company was not merely creating excellence, it was preserving it and making it permanently available to the world of music. Moreover, it was offering real documentation of actual events, not an artificial product made perfect by editing and retakes. Levine had defined that policy in 1982 when RCA issued a recording of the Leontyne Price/Marilyn Horne concert as heard in the *Live from the Met* series.

"This recording," Levine states in the album notes, "embodies the entire concert of March 28, 1982, exactly as it occurred on the stage of the Metropolitan Opera House. No material was taken from rehearsals; no remake recording sessions took place. As with all of the *Live from the Met* presentations, the principle of documenting the truly live performance guided us, and in our view ultimately carried a more sincere and significant artistic statement to our audience."

In fact, Levine had thrown down the gauntlet. The public was to hear the live event, and the quality of the live event was to be such that no corrections would be necessary. It was to be done right, without compromises, without anything that might ever occasion the need for an apology. One thinks of Reiner who, when once asked, "Doesn't the Chicago Symphony ever make mistakes?" replied, "No."

Standards of this level were not achieved easily. Money was tight. But men of vision can solve problems that ordinary souls find overwhelming. Bliss and Levine were united in the idea that excellence would triumph, that the solution was not to economize but boldly to raise standards, to challenge the city and the nation with an opera-producing organization so fine that it was unconscionable that it should not be adequately supported. For a start the Met deserved a real—rather than a token—endowment. And, in the early 1980s under Bliss's leadership, the Met raised $100 million. Excellence was now affordable.

"There is an evolutionary process at work inside the Met," Bliss stated, "and I hope it never stops. We are always changing, yet always the same. Our goal is the next performance, but we build on our past. All we do today and in the future is the part of one great tradition. The Metropolitan Opera is justifiably proud of its history. Still, we are keenly aware of the job yet to be done. The highest standards must be maintained, and our loyal public must be served."

Levine, the de facto music director, was soon to hold the post de jure. Dexter remained as director of production. But his successes reflected his primary interests. He and Levine could work together with extraordinary effect in planning innovative projects. The day-to-day requirements of the job produced difficulties. In 1976–77, Levine conducted seventy-six performances from a repertory of ten scores. He was learning how to run a big, international theater, and he was putting his mark on the house. Of a half-dozen new productions in 1976–77, only one was a work Met audiences had heard before.

Igor Stravinsky's bitter quip of 1964, that there was a place at the Met for Menotti's *The Last Savage* but not Berg's *Lulu,* might be laid to rest. *Lulu* arrived in 1976 and stayed for seven remarkable performances. Dexter attempted to make the maximum dramatic sense of the incomplete text then in use. Four years later *Lulu* was back, this time in its full three-act dimension. Teresa Stratas, who had introduced the work to the world in this form, sang the title role. Dexter skillfully integrated the now-complete score into his critically acclaimed production, which had been designed by Jocelyn Herbert with this eventually in mind.

Bliss was in favor of offering more twentieth-century music and budgeted these projects as generously as possible. Dexter, it proved, was not especially concerned with the necessity of bringing basic scores back to the stage in a fresh and convincing manner consistent with the company's budget requirements. But there were *Aidas* and *Rigolettos* to be staged, and Levine shared with Bliss increasing concern that they receive their due. The troika was now an unstable team. In 1980 the production staff was reorganized and Dexter left his post in management to become a staff director, working on his own shows.

During the Bing years every operatic revival was controlled by a prompt book based on the instructions of the director of the original production. Levine saw these documents as a form of bondage, the implicit demand that the weaknesses or failings of the first performances be preserved indefinitely. Dexter agreed. Henceforth, revivals would be seen as an opportunity to reconsider the production in a new light.

Dexter took his leave with two of his most successful works, the first a triple bill evoking French music of the early part of the century. Called *Parade,* it opened with Satie's ballet of that name, went on to Poulenc's *Les Mamelles de Tirésias,* and concluded with Ravel's *L'Enfant et les sortilèges* in a production Levine particularly admired. Manuel Rosenthal was the conductor. Dexter's final Met production was an equally memorable Stravinsky triple bill (*Le Sacre du Printemps, Le Rossignol,* and *Oedipus Rex*), conducted by Levine in the 1981–82 season. Dexter died in 1990.

In his book *The Met,* Martin Mayer, a seasoned observer of musical life and historian of the Met's first century, says of this period, "What cannot be skipped is the significance of James Levine, who assumed the role of Music Director and Principal Conductor in 1976 and whose steady, rapid growth through the decade was the source of the company's impressive artistic dignity as its first century came to a close [in 1983]. . . . The story of the Met as it moves into its second century will be, in large part, the story of the mid-life of James Levine . . . a prodigious protégé of Max Rudolf, and a pupil of Fausto Cleva and George Szell, [Levine] was the most significant conductor to commit himself full-time to the Met since Toscanini. Levine had arrived at the Met in 1971, a technician of the first order, who could maintain rhythmic tension at any tempo, follow singers when they deserved that tribute, and lead them when the arch of a work required a conductor's architectonic discipline.

"The striking aspect of Levine's work at the Met, however, was something else: his visible, fully communicative delight in making music. There was never a routine evening, for performers or listeners, when Levine was on the podium: he was always 'up.' And there was not a glimmer of self-satisfaction in . . . his delight, for he took it as given that every performance could be better than it was—and should be better than the last time the same forces offered the same work." With the establishment of this attitude at the top of the chain of command, the problem Kolodin set for Bing was solved.

The Met centennial was marked by an issue of *Time* with Levine on the cover. "Every year my life gets better," he says in the text. "It's all sort of like a dream. It's so nice."

In my years as a newspaper critic I insisted that an evaluation of an opera season could not be based on the limited experience of a series of first nights. If a production was exciting, I might see it as many as five times. From this you learn that every opera changes as it passes through a series of performances, and it was the critic's business to know what those changes were. This was especially true of the Met in this period, when it might be claimed that Levine never conducted a repeat performance. There were always changes, places where he saw improvements that might be made, and he made a maximum effort to achieve them.

He now had greater control than ever before over casting, and he was assisted in these responsibilities by a new assistant manager, Joan Ingpen, who arrived in the late seventies. Her vast knowledge of singers and their resources ensured that the Met would henceforth engage individuals who had a special gift for projecting the roles they were to play. There resulted a closer bond between the audience and the stage. Levine's Met became a home for singing actors.

This was a major change from the Met of the 1940s, the Met of what Levine called "stand up and sing" singers, artists who often had magnificent voices (For me, Kirsten Flagstad is a paradigm of the type), but limited acting ability and a minimal sense of theater. Flagstad's Isolde, probably her most important role, was, in the experience of this listener, exciting for the beauty of her voice but static, and without passion in the physical expression of its drama.

Nothing is more distinctive of the revitalized Met than high morale. *A Year at the Met,* another book published in the centennial period by Patrick J. Smith, a writer close to the company (Smith now edits *Opera News*), defines the cause. "Levine, because of his infectious enthusiasm, boosts morale in the house and that leads to better performances."

It also raises money. One of the reasons the Met is secure is the strong sense that in New York there is a Met family, people whose bonds to the company go far beyond buying tickets or making an occasional contribution. "Levine's ubiquitousness and seeming approachability have transformed the once austere Met."

Bing, an arrogant Viennese filled with British class consciousness, thrived on austere relationships. In contrast, Levine's warmth creates a situation in which subscribers will accept more innovation than was possible in the past. It is the responsibility of the artistic director of a major opera house to lead the public, but this requires creating a situation in which the public will permit itself to be led.

Nowhere were the performances better than in the orchestra pit. For Smith, "the vitality and accomplishment of the orchestra is the brightest area of improvement at the Met." Artur Rodzinski, who put the Cleveland Orchestra on the musical map, insisted that conducting was 75 percent psychology. Levine's formulation is "This job is part psychiatrist."

Levine realized that the Met Orchestra needed to perceive itself as a star performer among other star performers. The best way to do this was to put the orchestra on the stage, to make it the center of interest. Orchestral concerts became an established part of the Met's activities beginning in December 1980. Levine opened the Met season, which had been delayed by a strike, with the Mahler Second Symphony. This new and demanding repertory that traditionally belongs to symphonic ensembles but requires opera house forces.

The 1981 tour contained seven performances of the Verdi Requiem, the last two in Cleveland and Boston, where critical comparisons with the resident symphony orchestra were inevitable. A decade later Levine was ready to begin a concert series in New York's temple of symphonic music, Carnegie Hall, and a series of records of both symphonic and operatic repertory.

Smith concludes, "Whatever one may feel about James Levine's work in the pit, he has transformed those who must play seven times a week for thirty weeks." Again, enthusiasm, well-applied psychology, and comprehensive musicianship are keys to Levine's success.

One of Levine's strongest supporters for many years has been Michael Ouzounian, his principal viola, who joined the orchestra in 1972 and stayed because of Levine. "I don't think I could have survived in the orchestra more than four years as it was when I arrived," he told Smith. "Everyone played for themselves, and there wasn't that collective pride that I find indispensable for my work. . . . Levine is never negative, and he often lets pass mistakes that someone else might stop and correct, simply because he knows the player is aware of them." In this, he emulates his mentor, Szell, who followed much the same practice.

"Some conductors," said Ouzounian, "like to instill a negative competitiveness in an orchestra to get results, but I find that if this is done I tend to get negative myself and downgrade the playing of others instead of trying to build up an ensemble sense."

By 1973 Levine had a solid grasp of the things the orchestra did well and the things it needed to do better, and he began a systematic program of concentrating each year on an area that had to be improved. It worked. One may still debate whether the Met Orchestra plays Mozart better than the Vienna Philharmonic, but the ensembles are peers today and they were not in the early eighties. Is Verdi better at La Scala? Perhaps on some nights. Is Wagner finer at Bayreuth? No. Is there a comparable opera orchestra anywhere else in the United States? Certainly not.

Szell taught Levine that if a music director is to maintain high standards, he must be a constant presence in the house. "It doesn't matter how carefully you select guests," he once announced, "you go away for two weeks and when you return something has slipped."

"I don't spend much time on planes," Levine remarked in the early eighties, "and I'm proud of that." His hours of flying have increased, but only after he imprinted his presence on the theater, first by conducting a hundred or more times each season, and second by making the Met more competitive in the constant international rivalry for the most celebrated singers by ensuring it would be a pleasant place to work.

There was no question that heavily subsidized European theaters could pay several thousand dollars more per performance than the Met could offer, especially as the dollar weakened against the Deutsche mark or the lira, but the great ones want to be not merely well paid but happy. "I could go where they pay four or five times what I get at the Met," Domingo says. "But the other places do not offer the opportunity to work with Jim."

In 1983, as Mayer saw it, the Met had become "more dependent on one man than it had been at any time since the days of Toscanini." Levine wanted to increase that dependence, not decrease it; he saw the day coming when the musical conception of the work and its realization on the stage would reflect a single point of view. "The separation of the musical and the dramatic," Mayer quotes Levine, recalling exchanges between Toscanini and Gatti (Giulio Gatti-Casazza, general director of the Metropolitan Opera, 1908–35), "has become for me intolerable."

It is clear from these documents of some fifteen years ago that what Levine has done in his later years is implement decisions and policies that were perfectly well formulated in his mind when he became principal conductor. There has been no vacillation, no sign of doubt; his vision of the new Met was clear, and he has pursued it resolutely with all his skill.

Bliss led the Met for what may well prove to be the most important eleven years in its history. At the close of the 1984–85 season (six years before his death) he retired at seventy-two and was succeeded as general manager by Bruce Crawford, the current president of the Metropolitan Opera Association. Crawford served four years, resigning at the close of the 1988–89 season.

Hugh Southern moved from acting chairman of the National Endowment for the Arts to become general manager of the Met in November 1989. He served until August 1, 1990, when Joseph Volpe, who had been assistant manager of the Met for a decade, became general director. In the 1992–93 season he became general manager.

The Met of the 1990s can work to Levine's standards because it has the financial resources to do so. As a beginning, with its recordings, Saturday broadcasts, and televised performances, it has become the American national opera company. Its potential base for fund-raising is fifty states, and that base is effectively utilized by a large and energetic development department.

In the financial report for 1995–96, the company reported a balanced budget, the fourth consecutive year in which the financial goals had been achieved—a spectacular success in the American performing arts in this decade. In 1995–96, an impressive 62 percent of the Met's budget came from operating revenues and box-office receipts. The shortfall was made up by the contributions of more than 200,000 loyal friends and subscribers, bequests, and grants. An opera company that can operate on the Met's artistic level and earn its way is doing exceedingly well.

Levine has faced criticism for insisting on a high level of musical scholarship, demanding good new editions of standard works, eliminating cuts, and seeing tradition as, in many ways, an excuse for question-able musical practices. "Tradition," Mahler said, "is the last bad perfor-mance." Maria Callas thought the second act of *La Traviata* was too long. How to shorten it? Cut the baritone aria. Who wants to hear a baritone aria? Levine would be horrified.

In Levine's Met, *La Forza del Destino* is about an hour longer than it was in the Bing years. *Don Carlo* has its first act. When Levine conducted *Tristan und Isolde* in 1980–81 and 1983–84 in all probability Met audiences heard the complete opera for the first time. The "Night and Day" cut in Act 2, made in virtually every theater in the world except Bayreuth, was no longer observed. Bayreuth has hour-long intermissions that permit tenors to recover after demanding Wagnerian duets. "It's a stamina cut," Erich Leinsdorf once explained. "If you want to make sure you still have a tenor for Act 3, you make that cut in Act 2." Levine counted on his tenors and won most of the time.

A season at the Met, as characterized by the 1996–97 schedule, involved thirty weeks of production from late September to late April. Twenty-four operas made up the subscription repertory, to which the four operas of Wagner's *Ring* cycle were added in the final two weeks of the season. These scores can be divided into three groups.

Four operas (all of them works produced previously by the company) were heard in new productions. Six operas, half of them new produc-tions heard in the 1995–96 season, returned. Eighteen operas the Met has offered in years prior to 1995–96 were revived. In this group the new productions, as a matter of course, would receive the greatest rehearsal time—about a month of preparation. (This means that, for functional purposes, the Met's working season begins early in September.) The revivals were all to be given ample rehearsal time, especially if the casting was substantially different from the most recent staging of the work—as nearly always proves to be the case.

The surprise is that the new productions of the previous year, which in some celebrated European houses would be carried over with little or no additional rehearsal, get nearly as much preparation time as works revived after a much longer absence from the Met stage. There were to be some 220 performances in the course of the season, six evenings and one matinee a week, with the house dark on Sunday and at Christmas and Thanksgiving.

In 1983 Levine complained to Martin Mayer, "People don't digest what it means to do seven performances every bloody week. This is not like Covent Garden, where they do only two operas for six weeks, or Vienna, where the only thing that ever gets rehearsed at all is the new production. We don't have the relief of ballet evenings, or the relief of a small house [as an alternate venue]. Of the twenty to twenty-four operas we do, twenty are on a *stagione* basis." That is, a cast is rehearsed and kept intact, as much as possible, for a series of performances.

Thus the remarkable *Così fan tutte* of 1995–96 opened February 8 and was heard ten times before it left the repertory March 14. In contrast, *La Bohème* entered the repertory December 11 and was still running, with several changes in personnel, April 27.

Illuminating contrast is provided by the 1996–97 season of the most important regional opera company in the United States, the Lyric Opera of Chicago. Its comparable season ran twenty-five weeks, September 21 to March 8, but the repertory consists of only eight operas, and over the holidays the house is dark for as long as sixteen days. There are seventy-nine performances, which makes the twenty-five-week season equal, in terms of operas staged, to a little over eleven weeks at the Met.

Everything is on a *stagione* basis. *Don Carlo,* the opening night production, entered the repertory September 21 and departed October 18 after nine performances. There was a change of conductor the final week, but the cast remained intact.

The Lyric can be applauded for its consistency. With rare exceptions, the quality of the opening night performance can be sustained or even improved as the opera runs, a phenomenon that accounts in large part for the success of the company in consistently achieving maximum box-office income in recent seasons. One may plausibly argue from this that Chicago could support more opera than it is offered, but the company takes a conservative view of the ability of the community to subsidize opera. It is reluctant to risk large deficits in order to increase its services. Having discovered a formula that works with reasonable assurance of financial stability, it chooses a safe course.

The Lyric has advantages the Met does not share. The orchestra has a good summer job playing free concerts in Grant Park. The chorus and stage crews also have off-season work, and the Lyric has successfully evaded the responsibility of sustaining a large ballet company. The Met, to keep its organization together in high-cost-of-living New York, has to provide weekly paychecks throughout the year.

Accepting that growth demands challenges, the Met looks to further expansion, a steady repertory growth to an annual level of twenty-five operas. Important operas from this century that have not been produced at the Met, or have been out of repertory many years, will be heard. Most important, the lesson of history, that fine operas are written when there are theaters prepared to stage them, will be respected. Every few seasons should contain a new score written at the company's behest.

Part of the problem is the size of the house. Some operas that invite revival would appear to be better suited to a smaller, more intimate theater. When Bliss retired, he told an interviewer: "My greatest regret is that we couldn't develop a small theater to be used as a creative space for Mozart- and Rossini-sized productions." Talk of a mini-Met has gone on through the thirty years since the move to Lincoln Center, but the day may be approaching when the talk could yield something real in terms of a performance space. A smaller theater is on Levine's agenda, and that, too, will come in time.

IV

For more than two decades, from 1971 to 1993, James Levine lived a double life, divided largely between the two largest American cities. In New York, where he spent most of his time, he was perceived primarily as a theater conductor, the youthful master of the Met who was leading the company to ever greater heights. In Chicago he was seen as a symphony conductor of exceptional eloquence and vitality, music director of the summer concerts of the Chicago Symphony at the suburban Ravinia Festival.

Although his residence at Ravinia was commonly three or four weeks, in that time he might prepare and play as many different programs as the downtown music director, Sir Georg Solti, offered in a winter season. Solti was in the city for a longer period, but he played repeat performances. Levine never repeated anything in a given year. There was no need to do so. Solti functioned in a concert hall that seats 2,500. Levine worked in a park that can easily accommodate 10,000 listeners. In theory, anyway, Levine could reach as many in a week as Solti could in a month.

Summer music in Chicago differs from the usual American pattern in that the Ravinia Festival is completely separate from the governing body of the Chicago Symphony. Organized as a music festival in 1905, from 1912 to 1931 Ravinia was home to a remarkable opera company that fell victim to bad management and the Depression. Reorganized in 1936 as a festival of symphonic music, Ravinia has engaged the orchestra for two months each year and produced its own series, independent of anything that happened downtown the previous winter. It has had its own artistic director since 1959.

The seventies were a wondrously exciting time to hear a superlative orchestra dividing its time between a senior European conductor and an incredibly talented young American. No group was more excited than the members of the orchestra. The transition from Solti to Levine and back to Solti was an easy one. Both men were Toscanini disciples and wanted the same kind of clear, clean, energetic playing. Both understood that with the Chicago Symphony the only limits were those of the conductor's imagination. Neither would settle for anything less than excellence.

Summer concerts, which musicians may come to regard as a chore— indifferent music-making justified by the need for a weekly paycheck— became a challenge, an opportunity to achieve (and, through recording preserve) something as valuable as anything the winter season might offer.

Toscanini used to complain that he physically suffered when he did not hear the performance he had in his mind, and I am sure this is true. The NBC Symphony, in its final years, had become a high-quality ensemble that could meet his expectations on most occasions, but in its early seasons it was a second-rate orchestra. Even at its best it was not equal to the Reiner-trained Chicago Symphony that Solti inherited in 1969 or the Boston and Philadelphia orchestras of Toscanini's day. Solti and Levine did not suffer. If the rehearsal time permitted, they had the resources to do whatever they wished.

Of course there was a crossover between Chicagoans who attended opera in New York and were well aware of Levine's achievements there, and New Yorkers who bought records or turned up at Ravinia and realized his successes in this very different milieu. In a New York series, *Music from Ravinia,* Levine was able to show what the festival offered in terms of recitals and music for smaller groups. But Levine at 74 degrees west longitude and at 88 degrees west longitude still presented distinctively different aspects to his respective publics.

For those who think of him primarily as a theater man, one must recall that his training by Szell was in the symphonic tradition. In the 1960s, Szell, by choice, was no longer a theater conductor. Early in his American career, from 1942 to 1954, he had conducted a total of ninety performances of a repertory of eleven works at the old Met. There was friction with Bing over standards, and this time the general manager, confronted with another formidable Viennese, was unable to dominate the situation. Secure with the Cleveland Orchestra, Szell departed.

Levine's arrival at Ravinia sounds like something from a screenwriter at MGM. In June 1971 the festival was to open with the Mahler Second

Symphony conducted by Eugene Ormandy. But shortly before opening night, the maestro became ill and canceled. István Kertész, then principal conductor of the series, agreed to step in, and then *he* became indisposed. Edward Gordon, manager of the festival, was desperately searching for a conductor.

Opening night at Ravinia was then the most important social and artistic event of the Chicago summer. It is a sumptuous lawn party and a fashion show in addition to being a major musical event. If premium-priced tickets are to sell, a celebrity conductor was considered essential. Levine's name was proposed. Gordon knew his reputation, particularly the success he had just achieved at the Met. They talked.

"Do you really know the score?" Gordon asked.

"I've been studying this music for sixteen years" was the reply, "and if you wish, I'll conduct both the rehearsals and the concert without a score."

Levine, who had learned most of the Mahler symphonies when he was a teenager, got the job. The first rehearsal proclaimed that all was well and a historic moment was at hand. It was a classic case of a major American talent being discovered, not in Europe, but by a perceptive American public and management. Levine turned a possible disaster into one of the great nights in the history of the festival.

After more than a quarter century, it is still easy to recall the impact of the performance. It came as no surprise to this listener. Levine was part of my Cleveland connection. But to most of those present he had arrived straight out of the blue.

He was instantly reengaged for the next summer, but there was more than that afoot. Kertész's contract was running out. He had succeeded Seiji Ozawa as head of the concerts, but had proved unsuccessful in sustaining the level of excitement characteristic of the Ozawa seasons. Gordon wanted to plug into a big electrical generator with the kilowatt capacity of Solti downtown. Levine was the ideal choice. He lit up the park like a truckload of floodlights.

In his second summer Levine conducted a concert version of *Tosca* he had inherited from Kertész and (also in concert format) the first act of *Die Walküre*. He was his own piano soloist in the Bach D Minor Concerto, and he proved he was worthy of the noble instrument Reiner had perfected in a performance of the *Great* C Major Symphony of Schubert. Gordon knew he did not have to search any further. Thus began one of the most influential and productive collaborations in the history of American summer music.

This was the kind of moment that comes from almost perfect harmony, unusually close rapport between Levine and Gordon, and an equally strong relationship between Levine and the members of the Chicago Symphony Orchestra. Everyone sensed that the opportunity for great achievement was there, and everyone was ready to seize the moment.

Levine's first summers at the park were wonderfully innovative. He seemed to be an example of perpetual motion—Figaro here, Figaro there, the vital force that was transforming Ravinia from a rather conventional summer music series into something truly festive. He gave the early part of the week to recitals and chamber programs and turned to the orchestra as the weekend approached. At the keyboard and on the podium, he provided one occasion after another for rejoicing.

In those early years every summer had a theme, a group of composers whose works were emphasized. This gave the series a desirable sense of continuity and, at the same time, allowed Levine the opportunity to quickly build a foundation of rapport and repertory with the orchestra over the widest possible variety of styles. The foundation thus established, the later years could be devoted to delving deeper into many of the same masterpieces while continuing to increase the stylistic range. It proved to be a clever and inspired plan that overcame many of the inherent difficulties of American summer concerts. Looking back at the repertory presented, I think the achievement was formidable.

For his first opening night as music director Levine chose the Beethoven *Missa Solemnis*. Other big inaugural pieces followed—the Mahler Eighth Symphony in 1974, Schoenberg's *Gurrelieder* in 1976, and a concert version of *La Forza del Destino* with Leontyne Price in 1979. Ravinia lacked the facilities for fully staged operatic performances, but Levine expanded the role of operatic music in the festival and offered repertory new to the city. Never was this more dramatic than in 1978, when Berlioz's *Les Troyens* was heard in concert form five years before Levine staged it at the Met.

Projects of this type were possible because Gordon was a musician first and a manager second. In 1985 he wrote, "One might think that two musical personalities working together so closely on programming would have frequent differences of opinion. But Jim Levine and I have very few. On the rare occasions when we do not fully agree, we strive for and eventually reach a decision that is in harmony with Jim's artistic need and my particular sensitivity to the response of Ravinia's public. Our discussions are invariably spirited and gratifying to both of us."

Let us hear Levine on the subject of Gordon: "I find in the Executive

Director Edward Gordon someone who understands my point of view, who understands what kind of a festival I am trying to achieve, and who helps me every step of the way and stimulates me in directions which I don't generate on my own. For one thing, he is such a fabulous and experienced pianist [Gordon had been a soloist with the Chicago Symphony both downtown and at Ravinia] that he has gained respect from his colleagues as a first-class performer.

"This makes an enormous difference. The orchestra members and soloists feel he can understand the problems and appreciate the difficulties. He can smell potential crises before they happen, and improve the conditions and eliminate the distractions as cleverly as has ever been done. Ours is a wonderful relationship and, as I've said before, the chance to work on this kind of level in a summer festival is extraordinary."

Part of the problem, it should be noted, was that the orchestra had an unusually militant and aggressive union organization that was at war with the downtown management, the press, and anyone else it felt it couldn't dominate. The success of Levine and Gordon in avoiding confrontations and getting the orchestra to work as long and hard as it did reveals true mastery in human relations. The key to it is that both were really admirable human beings, not the most common quality in the music business.

In May 1995, following Gordon's death from cancer at sixty-five, Levine added: "It is impossible for me to characterize with words, in any meaningful way, my twenty-five-year relationship with Ed Gordon. Certainly we enjoyed an immediate and lasting rapport stemming from similar musical interests. The fact that he was a gifted administrator who was also a talented musician meant that he understood, instinctively, the full spectrum of considerations from both the artistic and practical points of view—every music director's dream, I should think. He knew a huge repertoire and had a world of experience to draw upon. He reveled in solving musical problems creatively. He had the nerve to take risks. And he was the only administrator I ever knew who could, and was trusted to, pick the right piano for virtually every pianist who came to Ravinia!

"But just as important, Ed was lots of fun. We managed a good many years of productive, often exciting, sometimes exhilarating music-making, and we had a great time doing it. Ed's take on things, the particular way he would express an opinion, the specific choice of words coupled with his midwestern background and sophisticated musical training, was a combination that kept us laughing for years. He thoroughly enjoyed making me laugh, and his own zest for life increased our energies. When I picture Ed in my mind's eye, he has a smile on his face. That's a gift, and a wonderful way to remember this great friend and colleague. I will miss him."

They excelled at problem solving. For example, in 1980, the issue was where to place the tenor soloist in the opening night performance of the Berlioz Requiem. Berlioz had a very special effect in mind, one that would be totally lost if the singer was simply center stage or seated in the chorus, where he might be buried. Placing him at the rear of the Pavilion made him too remote.

Gordon had an inspired thought. "We have a spotlight booth in the ceiling, so I proposed putting him there and Jim agreed. While precon-cert picnickers enjoyed their suppers, tenor Philip Creech put on tennis shoes and climbed to his overhead post, where, as darkness enveloped the park, he awaited his cue. That moment of a pure single voice singing 'Sanctus, sanctus, sanctus' brought a unison intake of breath from the audience—followed by utter silence except for the music and the rustling of leaves in the night breeze."

Levine wanted to attract major soloists to the festival by giving them an opportunity to do something more interesting than the usual summer music program. One artist to accept the challenge was Alfred Brendel, who played the Schoenberg Piano Concerto with Levine in 1974. In 1977 Levine and Brendel decided not to do just one Beethoven concerto but to do all five in the course of two evenings. Levine wanted it to be fresh.

He later recalled the event. " 'Now look, I said to the orchestra. You play the Beethoven concerti all the time. You've known the Beethoven concerti since before I was born. Some of you played with Stock and Schnabel [in 1942] for crying out loud! OK, but now we want to try to do something. Alfred has a concept of these pieces. It is important to me that we share it and develop a unity with it, so I want to try to work a cer-tain way.'

"And what was the result? The result was they all got interested, they all thought Alfred was marvelous. I don't mean they *all thought*—I don't know, maybe eight of them thought the result was lousy: That's OK too—but the point is they did it. And then two years after they did it a second time, and then another few years later they prepared it yet a third time, this time for recording.

"Imagine an orchestra of the caliber of the Chicago Symphony care-fully and conscientiously rehearsing music as familiar as the Beethoven concerti in the heat of the summer for an outdoor concert. And doing it three times without losing their energy and spontaneity! Now that is typical of the kind of extraordinary work this Ravinia relationship can produce, and will continue to produce, I think, in a variety of styles."

Let us hear from Brendel. In May 1996 he wrote me that his "collaboration with James Levine was always a particularly happy one. In works by Mozart, Beethoven, Brahms, and Schoenberg, mostly at Ravinia and Chicago, but also in Berlin, Vienna, and Salzburg, I knew already before the rehearsals that I would find an open ear and mind, and the readiness to set up a performance instead of just improvising one. Even with the very limited rehearsal time at Ravinia, the results were remarkable.

"I remember a performance of Schoenberg's Op. 42 with no more than two hours rehearsal spread over two days which, thanks to Jimmy's knowledge of the score, and everybody's concentration, turned out to be outstanding. I also remember playing three Beethoven concertos in one evening in a climate of 100 degrees Fahrenheit and 95 percent humidity, in short sleeves.

"Before doing our live recordings of Beethoven's concertos at Orchestra Hall [in 1983] we had done two Ravinia cycles. At Orchestra Hall the public gracefully cooperated and stayed away from coughing. The LPs won several awards although the sound left something to be desired. The release of these recordings had been announced, and my Philips producer had to do the editing and balancing without being able to use the required Soundstream machine. These were the early days of digital recording and the needed equipment was not always available." (The recordings have since been reissued in remastered sound.)

When Levine conducted his first concert as music director in June 1973 the audience and the orchestra were all solidly behind him. He was not an upstart thirty-year-old kid from Cincinnati with the hubris to challenge the sixty-year-old Solti. He was loved, respected, and supported artistically because of the proven quality of his work. You looked to him for great things, and you were not disappointed.

Ozawa had done some splendid things at Ravinia, but he worried a lot. There was often, to some degree, a nagging fear—that he was overextending himself, and, indeed, in the programming of difficult twentieth-century works, he took significant risks. More than anything else, Levine radiated joy. There was no greater joy for him than to lead the Chicago Symphony. But it was joy mixed with confidence, determination, and, above all else, a sense of obligation to music. It would be presumptuous to say Szell taught this to him. These things are basic Levine. But Szell surely reinforced these commitments since they were such a fundamental part of his own nature.

Gordon's retirement did not change Levine's role at Ravinia. He quickly established a warm and fully cooperative relationship with the new executive director, Zarin Mehta, who continued to implement and expand innovative changes. But even though Solti's periods of residence in Chicago grew shorter in his final years, the orchestra that came to Ravinia through the summer of 1991 was an ensemble accustomed to playing to Solti's standards.

In 1991–92, Solti had become laureate music director in Chicago. Primary responsibility for the ensemble had passed to Daniel Barenboim. Leinsdorf, who had been a guest conductor downtown that season, commented after his final concert in March: "If an orchestra becomes accustomed to playing to 80 percent of its capacity, it is like pulling teeth to get it back to the 100 percent level. Fortunately," he added with a wicked Viennese smile, "I am a very experienced dentist."

But when Leinsdorf returned in October 1992 he complained bitterly to management that he had not been given an ensemble that could play the program he had selected to his satisfaction, something that had never happened to him in Chicago since he first led the orchestra in 1945. It was the close of a long and distinguished relationship. Leinsdorf died in Switzerland in 1993.

With a major commitment to Bayreuth for 1994–98, to do the *Ring,* Levine announced that he would appear at Ravinia only once in 1993, for a farewell concert. Mehta took his departure philosophically: "Whether it's James Levine at the Met, Salzburg, or Bayreuth, Ravinia is proud to say he was here first."

Levine and Ravinia had proved to be, as Solti said of his relationship with the orchestra downtown, a happy marriage. At Ravinia, Levine first affirmed his artistic range in the most unequivocal terms. And the festival yielded great nights that will not soon be surpassed. Unfortunately, his influence on the festival eroded quickly after his departure.

V

James Levine offered a key to himself some twenty years ago when he told an interviewer: "One of the big fights of my life has been to make people understand that I don't have time for a lot of stuff they have time for. My parents could never understand why I couldn't sit for two hours lingering over dinner. It was difficult for them to realize that they had interrupted me from a problem that was on my mind all the way through dinner."

Thirty years of familiarity with Levine and his work have only strengthened my first impressions of him. He is, first and foremost, a thinker. He has no time for trivia. Always a remarkably mature and stable personality, he would be delighted if he could go through life radiating a smile of love for music and humanity. His artistic principles were firmly established in his teens. He does not question them, or the objectives they define, but runs on rails toward his goals. It quickly becomes apparent that those are very different goals from the self-obsessed, glamour-boy conductors who vie for public attention. Like Toscanini, who, after all, was possibly the greatest glamour-boy of all, Levine is content to be what the great maestro called himself, "Only an honest musician."

What is the source of that honesty? It is a constant awareness of the proper relationship of the performer to the composer and his music. The performer exists to serve the composer by offering the most scrupulous realization of his artistic intentions.

Levine's life is music. Other conductors give themselves long vacations. He is rarely free for more than two weeks, and the usual pattern is several short breaks in the course of a year. In the classic division of interest between mountain people and ocean people, Levine is an ocean person. Look for him at Antibes, not Zermatt. But while on vacation he rarely spends his time on what most people might consider recreational activities. Szell was an avid alpine golfer, playing in snow with red balls. ("At high altitudes I can actually break seventy," he announced with delight.) Suzanne Thomson enjoys tennis. James rejoices in a sunny pool, but he may also see the terrace as a great place to study an unfamiliar score.

"When the situation is right, I can relax and enjoy a good meal with wine and the usual amenities," he told me recently. Given the choice, the meal will be French or North Italian. A pleasant Italian restaurant just up the road from the Bayreuth Festspielhaus knows him as a frequent customer. (He has an account.) The steady expansion of his waistline over the past thirty years attests to a respect for good cooking—and its availability. Suzanne's achievements in the kitchen have equaled her mastery of the oboe.

"I have always resented the idea," Levine says, "that an artist's nonmusical life is anybody's business any more that that of any other person. But the public is curious about you, and there will be individuals who try to tell them what they want to know.

"When I see some Woody Allen films, I instinctively take his side. We are living in a society in which everybody, to some degree or other, thinks it's their business to say how other people should live. Why is it my business on any level what other people do with their lives?"

In 1974 he told Stephen S. Rubin, author of *The New Met in Profile,* "I want to make myself obsolete in the concert itself. I want to be able to have the conception seem to emanate from the orchestra members, who are, after all, the ones with the instruments, instead of the crazy magician with a stick who is making all the gestures and telling the audience what they ought to be feeling and hearing. I would like to get to the point where the audience would have the feeling they don't see me."

Recent conversations confirm that he still feels this way, and finds the Bayreuth orchestra pit, in which both conductor and musicians are unseen by the audience, an ideal place in which to vanish.

In realistic terms it is quite unlikely he will ever become as invisible as he might like. If a large orchestra is to play in a fluid and flexible manner, there has to be someone center stage to hold things together. But, as Levine proved in his Ravinia years, the conviction and intensity of his performance can be such that the listener's attention goes so completely to the music that Levine becomes simply one of some ninety musicians arrayed before the audience.

"I really think this shift of focus from the conductor to the players could be done a lot more methodically than it has been," he continued. "I've had experience with student orchestras that technically weren't up to professional ones, and that worked on a piece from scratch without any of the inhibitions the profession puts on you, and we got a performance that was unbelievably communicative. Something very like this happened in a concert that the NBC Symphony played without a conductor after Toscanini's retirement. They did Dvořák's *New World,* and it was more intensely communicative than the one they recorded with the Old Man, although that one is neater."

Levine argues whether the often-cited dichotomy between Toscanini and Furtwängler was as rigid as it might first appear. One need not attend many of Levine's Met performances to appreciate how skillfully he can mix passion with precision in effects that are no less grand and moving for the faultless synchronization of orchestra and stage.

"I find myself totally disinterested in the question nowadays of technical proficiency, which literally seems to be the basis for evaluating an orchestra's performance up one side and down the other," he told his interviewer. "You can read the words of composers from Bach to Stravinsky, what you find them screaming into the night about is not the technical execution but the conception, the spirit, the purpose, what was supposed to be conveyed. To read Berlioz on this subject is so eye-opening you can't believe it. He performed in situations so primitive they would curl your hair today. We now must have fifteen to twenty orchestras in this country which Berlioz would have thought a dream technically. But where is the piece? It gets lost.

"I have one visionary dream, and I feel that everything I do draws me a little closer to it. Once in a while I hear a performance that is the kind of incredible thing that must have driven composers to go on writing music despite unbelievable personal adversities. It seems to me there is a way to this which, so far, our system has not provided. I want to try and provide it."

As he grows older Levine seems to be withdrawing more and more into the circle of things for which he has time. The vanity and glitz have no real interest for him. In his early years at the Met, Levine offstage might catch the eye with a zesty sports coat, but as he grows older he has become increasingly indifferent to clothes. Albert Einstein on his arrival at the Institute for Advanced Study in Princeton decided that a sweatshirt, sweatpants, and tennis shoes were the ideal outfit in which to do theoretical physics. Levine has long functioned on the same level. His brother, Tom, sees that he always has what he needs to wear. At work, his clothes are always completely comfortable and functional.

His involvements with other people can reflect the current state of his involvement with music. "When I am musically frustrated, unhappy, unproductive, then my personal involvements are miserable," he told Rubin. "When my music-making is good, they are marvelous. I've been into all kinds of living, including communal ones, and I found them quite satisfying. Being able to relate to people freely, without legal structure, produces various gradations in the way you feel about them and affects the kind of rapport you establish."

In his Cleveland years Levine, his mother says, was the leading figure in a commune of about fifteen young musicians that included Suzanne Thomson. "Jim and some of the others had jobs, and those who were without an income performed services for the group like cooking. They occupied a house and some other spaces—Jim had a hotel room—but they functioned together in a spirit of mutual support. Many of them went on to successful careers, and I think that most of them look back on this as a rewarding experience."

Levine, in part, one suspects, because of experiences such as this, has become skilled in dealing with musicians. "One of the problems one has artistically," he recently stated, "is when you make a judgment against what an artist thinks are his or her interests. Invariably there will be a personal reaction lacking objectivity. I have come to accept that artists will never see things from my point of view. When you exercise your artistic responsibilities you better not do it with a baseball bat. There's a lot of psychology involved. I never do anything I feel might create difficulties in an artistic relationship I value highly."

The point of Levine's life is making music. His primary job is running an opera house from September to May, and he is happy, productive, and fulfilled giving himself completely to these things. After a time it dawns on you that for Levine the Met is a workaholic's paradise. Given the choice of making music or taking a day off, he would prefer to work on the music.

Levine wants to feel that he is in control of his life. Eugene Ormandy used to plan his schedule—where he would be, what he would play, possibly what he would have for dinner—for years ahead. Levine works in flexible time frames. If he must secure the services of a singer long in advance, he will, of course, do so; but if he is making a short trip out of New York, he may not decide just when he is leaving, or how he is traveling, or exactly where to stay, until the last minute. He likes to have options.

Naturally gregarious, Levine sincerely enjoys people who accept him on his terms. He hates confrontations, and those with whom he works on a daily basis are individuals who are prepared to keep things moving smoothly and effectively with minimal friction. The key to everything is to understand his priorities. His private life is very public. There is hardly a day when he is not on view somewhere. Therefore, he has always protected what he sees as his right to close a door and enter a place that is his and his alone. Here he recalls Szell, who always wanted a certain personal distance between himself and others, especially coworkers. Musically, his social relationships were limited to soloists whom he admired and first desk players, people he felt had no private axes to grind.

"Jim is nearly always attending to some kind of business," Helen Levine observes. He welcomes opportunities to relax and think. He delights in old films. (He was extremely pleased when I gave him a copy of *One Hundred Men and a Girl,* starring Leopold Stokowski and Deanna Durbin.) When he can, Levine goes to the theater. Home is a place to read serious books, study scores, play the piano for pleasure, and listen to other people's recordings.

Basically nocturnal, he prefers to go to bed late, sleep in, and begin the working day in the late morning. Met rehearsals customarily begin at 11 a.m. When a performance ends, the first priority is to change into something dry, but he may want to take some time to wind down.

"He cannot resist an opportunity to make music," says Helen Levine. "I think he suffers from something a weekly magazine found a few years ago when they were going to write a feature on him. They abandoned it because the writer they assigned came back and said, 'He's too nice. I can't get anything that makes a colorful story.'"

Compared to conductors like Leonard Bernstein or Herbert von Karajan, who were often featured in the gossip columns as much as the musical pages, Levine has never been a source of hot copy or been featured in the tabloid press.

Levine lives in a large but unpretentious apartment in one of the classic old buildings on the Upper West Side of Manhattan not far from Lincoln Center. He permits himself the luxury of lots of space, and the apartment has high ceilings and big rooms. Coincidentally, his windows look directly into the apartment across the street where Leonard Bernstein lived for many years. The two conductors often waved to each other and Levine dined frequently at the Bernstein apartment, particularly on the Jewish holidays.

The artistic chief of an organization made up of orchestral musicians and opera singers cannot avoid being a target for envy and the subject of gossip. Hardly had I begun work on this book when I was informed, through a mutual friend, by some anonymous backstage source that Levine had ceased to grow artistically and secretly lived a wicked life. Both statements are patent nonsense, symptomatic of what Toscanini called "the primordial jungle we call the world of music."

It is no surprise that Levine excels in the operas of Mozart and Wagner because of the moral themes they develop so movingly. In *Parsifal* the simple goodness of the protagonist is the key to a moral victory. I find no difficulty understanding Levine's great attachment to this work. Wagner ends the *Ring* cycle with the affirmation of redemption by love.

Levine's life is based on love—the love of his parents, his teachers, and those closest to him in his work. This has sustained and energized him, and, of course, the energy is returned. When a singer comes onstage and looks to the maestro, a welcoming smile is there. If the singer is to sing of love, love is flowing from the pit.

If it looks as if James is really tired, hurting, drained, vulnerable, protective curtains instantly descend and he is whisked to a quiet place of safety and serenity. The way it is done does not suggest the protection of valuable property but the most sincere kind of caring on the deepest human level. Needs are sensed and met. Everyone, deep in the psyche, wants caring of this type, but few experience it as adults. But Levine does not inspire envy. Whatever others give him, he returns to the world multiplied tenfold.

Tom Levine, while in many ways his brother's keeper, has not sacrificed his own career to do so. He combines these responsibilities with his painting and has had frequent one-man shows of his work in both the United States and Europe.

For the clearest vision of James Levine we must go to the roots. Here is the Levite making music in the temple, the temple of music called the Metropolitan Opera House. There he continues his unceasing search for beauty and artistic truth, which is itself an act of worship.

PART TWO

Dialogues

1973–1996

July 15, 1973. Dialogue at Ravinia.

RCM: You have completed your first summer as music director of the Ravinia Festival. Anything you say about it has to come off the top of your head since you clearly have no perspective yet. Your final performance was only last night. But, at the same time, there must be some clear impressions of how the series has gone.

JL: Basically, my point of view at this moment is very positive. We both know the problems of summer concerts in the out-of-doors, but I feel if I work on them they can be reduced. The weather is a central factor, the ability to make maximum use of rehearsal time another. If you have a really lousy night and the rain pours down and the trains pass at all the wrong times [Ravinia in 1973 was on the northern line of Chicago and NorthWestern (now Union Pacific) railway] it might be best if you were playing something that demands minimal concentration. But you can't plan evenings of this type in advance, and to put a program requiring minimal concentration on a really glorious night is a wasted opportunity.

I grew up studying at the Aspen Festival, fourteen summers starting when I was fourteen. It is different now, but in those days Aspen was a unique festival and a real musical community, a group of people who played, taught, and interrelated, and the audience was responsive. The music was well rehearsed and well played and, for the most part, not the most standard works. It was music that was interesting and at the same time broadening and deepening.

There is this conflict between those who think that in the summer the music should be light and those who think it should be adventurous. Obviously there is a limit to the concentrated, heavy repertory one can bring to a public. A change of pace is desirable.

RCM: The long successful history of the Boston Pops has shown us that. You could have the highest regard for Serge Koussevitzky and his programs with the Boston Symphony and still have wonderful evenings in the spring at a table in Symphony Hall drinking claret punch and listening to Arthur Fiedler. The key, of course, was that Fiedler was a superb musician and he played good music. He had the budget to secure attractive arrangements from talented people. If the Pops programs had been on a lower artistic level it would have been another matter.

JL: Summer is an ideal time to play lighter repertory, but it also gives you a chance to try some things that you might not normally do in the winter series. Some of these can be contemporary works, some can be pieces in older styles that for one or another reason are rarely performed, like Schoenberg's *Gurrelieder*.

On the other hand, on a summer rehearsal schedule it is very difficult to get the best possible performances of works that are not played all the time. I have learned that when you play a piece that is relatively standard, if you pick out the spots that are really difficult and give the orchestra a set of marked parts, you can accomplish a lot in short order. The more my rapport with the orchestra increases, the more I can accomplish. The more it is understood what will "go" in concert without rehearsing, what will go from the stick, the more we can concentrate our time on what needs attention.

[Levine conducted Gurrelieder *at Ravinia in 1976 and 1987. Although Sir Georg Solti talked about doing it, it still awaits a complete performance downtown.]*

RCM: Hans Knappertsbusch, the great old Wagnerian, once said to a Munich orchestra at the start of a rehearsal, "I know this music. You know this music. What are we doing here? See you tonight." And, of course, they could play it, at a certain level, without preparation. Many older conductors liked to work that way. Tommy Beecham was a perfect example.

JL: But in things that come up less frequently, say the Berg *Altenberg Lieder* we did last week, rehearsal is necessary. This was music the orchestra had never seen before. The musicians could not have been more cooperative. They worked like lightning, but still it was not comparable to having two or three evenly spaced rehearsals preparing for a concert in the winter season. In the summer you have one try at the piece, and you stand or fall on what you accomplish then. Even so, I feel it is valid to do what we are doing, more valid than to keep on playing, say, the Shostakovich Fifth and pretend we are fulfilling our debt to this century's music that way.

[Shostakovich never figured in Levine's Ravinia repertory.]

I really felt that, for the most part, the results this summer were on a high level. We had a remarkable number of performances that compare favorably with the orchestra playing in a closed hall with any number of rehearsals. I would expect in the winter concerts there is room for a lot of subtlety and refinement in balance that I can't attempt, but I am uncertain, even if we managed some of these things, that the acoustics and the sound system would carry them.

RCM: One mark of a good conductor for summer music is that he knows what to do preparing a week's music in four rehearsals with an orchestra as fine as this. Some, Europeans especially, will come in, play the concert through, and then be totally at a loss what to do next.

JL: This orchestra understands very quickly what you're getting at, why it requires a repetition to fix this point but not that. When I consider the programs that I would have wanted to improve, now that I have been through a season, I see how to make these things work, balancing programs and rehearsal schedules. I think we have every reason to think that things will get better every year.

RCM: I agree.

[And they did.]

JL: I am often asked if when I conduct a piece I am being original. What you hear when I conduct a piece is me and is there because I'm me. But I spend every iota of concentration trying to project what I think the composer wanted to communicate to the listener. If original means departing from the composer's score to insert something that comes from me, not him, that is something I make every effort to avoid, not to cultivate. If my sense of rhythm is this way now and different when I'm sixty-five, that is me changing with experience, not searching for originality. I never feel I must do something which is my invention for the sake of being different.

When I was young, I would never attempt to play a piece on the piano until I had memorized it. I carried the music of the Berg piano sonata around Aspen all one summer. There had to be absolute concept contact before there was technical contact with the keys. But working with Szell I had to do a lot of sight-reading of unfamiliar music, and I discovered this was a completely different way to start to study a piece. I was getting it into my mind and my fingers at the same time, working out the technicalities and absorbing it into myself.

RCM: Much twentieth-century music cannot be learned from the score alone. It is full of things that the imagination often cannot produce accurately in terms of sound.

JL: I *never* learn new music from recordings. But this is a case where a good recording can be helpful, especially one in which the composer has taken part in some way—it can give you a general impression.

I need to ask you something. What could we artists do, if anything, to promote more intelligent criticism? Or is there no way? Is it just a silly question?

Good criticism is writing that tells a musician something he will find of interest in terms that make sense to him. If he agrees with the critic, he will be glad his opinion is shared. If the critic disagrees with him, the critic will do so in terms that may cause the musician to ask himself, "Am I wrong?"

But so much criticism that one reads is simply boring and/or useless. It says little or nothing about the music. It may reflect no previous experience with the work and little or no real perception of its content. Whether it's favorable or unfavorable is unimportant. It's just not in any contact with the subject.

A story on the sports page about a baseball game tells you what happened in the game. A concert review may never give a real account of what happened in the concert.

RCM: It always helps, for a start, to know the pieces! [Both laugh.] I spent years learning pieces before I wrote a word of criticism. But, you know, the readers usually know if you're faking. The public generally is a lot smarter than you think.

JL: Not than I think. I'm right with you on that one.

RCM: If someone is writing bullshit. . . .

JL: They take it as bullshit. So help me God, I was once asked, did I think a critic had to be a trained musician? I said, "I do not think it possible for them to know too much." But some people apparently think that all it takes to be a critic is to find some way to get into print. How are critics trained?

RCM: For many years everyone interested in criticism had to devise his own training process. The Rockefeller Foundation has just completed a seven-year project based at USC that was rather similar to Szell's school for conductors. It also involved apprenticeship. I had some systematic training in criticism under the music faculty at the University of Cambridge, but at Northwestern University, as an undergraduate at the Medill School of Journalism, music criticism belonged under women's features. It was an effete, la-de-dah sort of thing. Any really red-blooded "Amurican" boy would prefer to write about sports or politics. Such training as I received at Northwestern was, not unexpectedly, in the music school. In fact, the NU music school has produced more important critics than the journalism faculty.

JL: That's a really encouraging sign.

RCM: The root of the problem is that music critics are hired by editors, and most editors began their newspaper careers as political reporters. They are no more into music than is the average American politician, which is to say they probably are not into it at all. I had a publisher, Marshall Field IV, who understood and valued my work, and I carry on years after his death doing the job to honor his memory. And, praise be, the front office lets me alone so I can do it.

I don't think I ever had an editor who believed that anyone would buy a newspaper because of a music critic. The public expected the paper to cover cultural events, so there had to be a critic on the staff, but his or her potential contribution was so inconsequential that there could be no rewards for doing the job well and, by inference, no punishment for doing it badly. The main thing was to avoid lawsuits, which I always succeeded in doing. In fact, since the editor probably never read a word a critic wrote except when there was a protest from some indignant reader, there was a wonderful kind of freedom that made up for other things like never getting a pay raise.

JL: But it's not true that critics don't sell papers. Claudia Cassidy, I understand, sold lots of papers in Chicago.

RCM: Her position at the *Tribune* was assured nearly thirty years ago when in one week she drew a barrage of letters protesting what she was writing. Her boss, Bertie McCormick, could not imagine that a music critic had that many readers, let alone that many sufficiently steamed up to write letters. So she got a contract that made her a tremendous force in the city's musical life. The fact was, Cassidy knew very little about music. Some of her reviews—Reiner's performance of the Webern Op. 6, for example—were so totally uncomprehending as to be highly embarrassing. It was all completely subjective, and when she couldn't relate to something or someone, she could go completely haywire.

But she was an Irish bard (female gender) with a wonderful gift for words. People read her to see what outrageous things she would say, whether they had any relation to reality or not. That sold papers and made her a valued employee. There is a kind of Gresham's Law in journalism. But instead of bad money driving out good, the people who have nothing important to say drive out the people who have something serious on their minds. A music critic who refuses to become an entertainer has to accept that management will see the entertainers as more valued writers.

JL: And there is no way for artists to reply to unfair or uninformed criticism?

RCM: Artists can do very little, I fear, because they are not considered disinterested parties.

JL: They're not.

RCM: The only hope I see is for management to open a conversation with editors in which management is, heaven bless us, candid. If a bad performance gets a negative review and management agrees that the opinion is justified, then it is in a position to come back and get attention when something good gets unfair treatment. But if you have the familiar self-serving attitude that everything we do is wonderful, there is no basis of credibility on which to open a discussion.

Szell once said of Cassidy, "I always thought she was a gossip columnist." That was being ironic, of course, but I appreciate ruefully that my editor would find my columns greatly improved if they contained a certain amount of gossip.

JL: My lips are sealed!

July 26, 1975. *Dialogue at Ravinia.*

RCM: It is my feeling that Ravinia is finally turning into the kind of festival that many of us have always wanted it to be. This is due in large measure to you, and also to Ed Gordon and a board that has offered you these opportunities.

JL: We have the only group of American summer concerts where, if you call them a festival, you are using the right word. I look at the programs of other summer music series, and most of them are so boring, one terribly familiar work after another. Of course you have to have a certain amount of basic repertory, we all know that. But there must be contrast.

RCM: When you plan programs you have to assume a level of taste, a level of involvement, and select appropriate works. Needless to say, I would much prefer that you set your sights too high than too low. I read last week, "You never go wrong underestimating the taste of the American people."

JL: I can't operate that way. I cannot believe there is not a large enough public to support serious, high-quality work. And if that public exists, we must not betray it by directing our efforts to a lower level.

RCM: Some of your programs this summer have assumed an unusually high level of musical sophistication. They drew large audiences but not capacity audiences. Stravinsky's *Variations for Orchestra* is music that ought to be heard at Ravinia, and Ravinia is honored by it being there, but you will sell more tickets for the Brahms B-flat Concerto with Misha Dichter.

JL: But the Brahms is also distinguished music. No apologies are needed for playing it. You have to respect differences in taste. Listeners have a right to prefer Brahms to Stravinsky. Where things go wrong at other summer concert series is that it is not Brahms or Stravinsky but Brahms instead of Stravinsky.

There were a number of nights with favorable weather when we had between 4,500 and 5,000 people. I consider that a good turnout. This is not a resort area like the Berkshires. Tanglewood draws a lot of people who are on vacation, away from home, looking for things to do. Ravinia presents the Chicago Symphony in the same area in which it plays winter concerts, and 5,000 people—twice the capacity of Orchestra Hall—is a good crowd.

RCM: Of course.

JL: The Stravinsky *Variations* were possible because the orchestra knew them from performances downtown. We repeated and recorded the Mahler Third, which we did two years ago and is now familiar to us. The summer choice is clear, playing concerts with music like this and trusting the public will support us or playing the Liszt E-flat Piano Concerto until everyone is screaming for mercy. I didn't come here to go that route, and no one is suggesting that I should.

RCM: Listening to the Mahler Third I couldn't help remembering that Dimitri Mitropoulos dropped dead on the stage of La Scala while rehearsing it.

JL: Do you agree that in the years after Toscanini's death, when there was an abundance of superlative conductors, Mitropoulos was one of the most exciting?

RCM: He was most exciting in terms of the range of things he was doing.

JL: He always seemed to me to be one of those conductors who, in music he found congenial, understood intuitively the intention of the composer and got closer to the heart of the composer than others who may have stressed faultless execution of the notes. He was wonderful in Mahler, Strauss, Berg, the entire modern school. Perhaps he was not as successful in older music—the classical school. But others brought that to us.

RCM: I remember one morning when he called and said I must come to his rehearsal with the Philharmonic. He was playing a wonderful piece by a talented young man who played horn in the Met Orchestra.

JL: Gunther Schuller.

RCM: Right. And it was a wonderful piece. Mitropoulos felt an overwhelming urge to communicate, and he wanted to communicate to warm bodies, not to an abstraction like a microphone. He is usually better in live recordings than studio work. In fact, he hated studio work. "Studio recording," he once announced to me, "is artistic masturbation."

JL: Szell, on the other hand, excelled in the studio.

RCM: I once asked him after a rehearsal of the Mozart G Minor, "How can you pour a performance like that into an empty hall?" "Mozart is listening," he replied.

JL: And that was not just a fantasy. He really felt that in some way it was true.

RCM: Szell's father was Jewish, but his mother raised him as a Roman Catholic. I suspect that implanted deep in his mind in childhood was the idea that there was a transcendent level of being and communication between us and that level was possible. This produced a certain attitude that had no relation to the frequency or, more properly, infrequency with which he attended Mass. The attitude I have in mind is the essence of prayer. A seraphic performance of the Mozart G Minor is very like a prayer, or a hymn to the glory of all things beautiful.

I wonder how objectively a performer can evaluate his success on that level. When you look back at a performance the morning after, with what confidence can you say, This was marvelous, this did not go, take flight as much as I might have liked.

JL: During the summer I sometimes make a checklist for myself, which performances were really good, which ones were OK, and which misfired. There were seven misfires this year, which is not a lot out of a total of nearly thirty events. On the other hand, there were quite a few evenings that I thought were quite good, that fairly represented the orchestra and the level of what I might call my musical self. It's the just OK performances that are puzzling. There is no way I can tell you why some things simply did not come up to my expectations. It wasn't something obvious like the weather.

You know that rehearsal time isn't everything. It's ephemeral. You have frequently commented on the way in which musicians begin to interact with one another and set a performance going with one fantastic moment after another. Sometimes you hope you have created a situation in which it might happen, but it doesn't. The fuse fizzles and the rocket never flies. In every phase of my life there have been great performances and relatively lousy performances, and I have never been able to find a relationship between these results and the amount of rehearsal time. It just doesn't work that way.

RCM: There is an element of magic.

JL: You can call it that. If I could make it concrete I might be able to control it better, but I can't. I don't think it is *one* thing. It's a combination of things, how many times I have played the work lately, how many times the orchestra has played the score (and what it is carrying over from those previous performances), the atmosphere, the vibes that may be coming out of the audience—a lot of things that have a distinct psychic and unpredictable effect. After all, we are not machines.

July 8, 1978. *Dialogue at Ravinia.*

RCM: How do things look after six summers as headman at Ravinia?

JL: It may not last forever, but for the time being I love the orchestra, I love working with it. The sound for me on the stage is excellent. It's a very good stage. Ed [Gordon, manager of Ravinia] breaks his back to give me conditions that will stimulate me. We managed to improve the concept of the programs this year that, barring the crummy weather, might even have been a financial success.

RCM: After last weekend, when rains made the lawns uninhabitable and Berlioz's *Les Troyens*—incredibly fine music—was thus heard by such a small public, something has to be done to make the festival more weatherproof. And after all the work you put into that project, the rain must have been a real frustration. When you go to Salzburg you go to a real theater.

JL: Oh yes, of course. I certainly do. But then there is the other frustration. I can only do a certain number of not-quite-rehearsed-enough performances of standard repertory before the whole thing becomes meaningless. If it ever comes to that, I have to go.

RCM: Soon after Seiji Ozawa began conducting at Ravinia, he appeared with the orchestra downtown and demonstrated what he could do in that situation. So people come to me and ask, What would Levine bring us in a normal winter rehearsal situation that he can't do now?

JL: The difference is that with an orchestra as responsive as this in matters of detail there is no limit to what you can do. Just no limit. What they give you off the stick under disturbing weather conditions outdoors is quite astonishing sometimes. I agree there is no point in producing effects that may not be heard past the first twelve rows and certainly are below the threshold of reproduction of the sound system. In a good concert hall they will be heard by everyone.

I hope that in Chicago, eventually, I will be able to do a carefully rehearsed indoor performance with the orchestra.

[It happened in 1983 in four pension-fund concerts in Orchestra Hall, Chicago, devoted to the Beethoven piano concertos with Alfred Brendel.]

When you work seriously and carefully with people with whom you have very strong rapport, things happen in rehearsal that represent the peak, or the greatest intense concentration, of the things that give a rehearsal meaning in the first place. You are trying to get to the ultimate levels of musical issues. And there are things about most performance atmospheres that take you a little bit away from that.

Sometimes there are magic concerts; things go in your favor and all the things you have worked on in the rehearsal click. In the six years I spent with Szell I would hear him do a dozen Brahms Fourths in a season and there seemed to be no explanation why one of them was the performance in which it all happened. The tempi were about the same. He was always working for the same nuances. The orchestra sounded marvelous. But a moment came when what he exuded and they got was like all those rehearsals paying off. There was never any way to predict where those performances would happen. It could be in Carnegie Hall, or a matinee in a college town. So help me. He would just come out relaxed and conduct them with all of the assets of their intimate collaborative knowledge but with a freshness as if he were new to them and they should concentrate in some extra way. And that's the thing that happens in rehearsal that is very hard to capture in concerts.

I have the experience of rehearsing an opera in New York knowing we are going to do, say, a dozen performances. And they may all be at a certain level. But it never fails, there is one when we all come up onstage and we all know that performance had *it*. All the elements coalesced. And it has absolutely nothing to do with whether it was or was not a night when the horns made a crack or two, it is purely on a plane where what you were rehearsing *happened*.

RCM: All your expectations were fulfilled.

JL: We feel we all did as well as we could do.

RCM: You are making quite a few records.

JL: One funny quirk of life is that you go around and try to convince a recording company to do something fairly low key, and they aren't interested. For the umpteenth complete Beethoven symphony cycle, they're interested. And these are records I don't want to make. I was driving in my car in New York recently and heard a broadcast of my Pastoral Symphony from here in 1976. It was a perfectly good performance, and all I could think of was, If you like the Toscanini listen to that one, if you like the Reiner listen to that, or if you prefer the Szell, take that, but you don't need one from me. I'm not going to be more perceptive than these men. Maybe someday if I have a certain group of musicians who are in my orchestra I will reach a point when I feel it is finally valid for me to make a Beethoven symphony recording. But I have absolutely no interest in quantitative recording for its own sake.

[Fifteen years later, in 1993, Levine finally recorded a Beethoven symphony, the Third, with the Met Orchestra.]

RCM: Your first Beethoven Ninth with this orchestra [in 1976] you approached with certain attitudes, certain emotions, certain psychological things that produced a performance I found extraordinarily gratifying. But when you did it again the following year, maybe simply because you were doing it again after such a short interval, the circumstances were different, the vibes weren't quite right, and the second performance was not as successful as the first.

JL: You're right. You know what it is, in a situation like this you always have to gamble. One of two things can happen. It can lose impact, or the rapport can somehow continue and you go on to a higher level. We did the complete *Brandenburg* Concertos three years in a row [1975–77] and every year they improved. We started where we left off the summer before and were able to make it better. That Beethoven performance, no. The second time the weather was hotter, we had less time, and details I wanted to get right weren't always well fixed. It's a much harder piece than they would have you think if you really want to do it well.

RCM: Ravinia has a wonderful tradition that allows the performers to dress for the weather. Jackets, ties, even shoes can go. The first time you led the Ninth you wore sandals. Never before had the Chicago Symphony beheld the conductor's naked toes while playing. I am not sure that was decisive, but you never can tell which variables are significant. [*Both laugh.*]

You know I'm not saying that you should never take risks. Quite the contrary. My point is, when you do, we have to be prepared to accept a few good ideas that don't work out.

JL: That's right. It's the nature of the beast.

RCM: I can see the day coming at Ravinia when you will ask yourself, What am I doing here when I could be in Salzburg or doing nothing?

JL: There is truth to what you say. I can certainly agree that there will come a time, I surmise it is coming between the next five and ten years [1983–88] when I want to work noticeably less. If somewhere between now and the time I'm forty-five I could get a situation doing festival work one month a year and symphonic work with my own orchestra, or with one orchestra, four months in the year, and I was doing opera two or three months in the year, I would be working seven or eight months annually, and I would be taking four or five unbooked months. If a project came along that interested me, I would be free. Or maybe I could just go back to the piano and get in shape so that I could record the Mozart concerti and sonatas on the level I would wish to do them. I still play enough that the fingers stay in shape, but there are certain piano projects I would like to do that require a different continuity of piano work.

[This change in schedule never took place. Nearly twenty years later Levine was working harder than ever with an even more crowded calendar. Asked why, he says, "The situation at the Metropolitan was just too exciting to consider spending less time there."]

I used to have inactive time in which I could just reflect and have visions. OK, I accepted that over a period of time when there was a great deal of challenging work to do I would have to go at it a different way. There is no question that taking more time off is in the cards. There is no question that there is a great appeal in places like Salzburg that don't have Ravinia's problems.

Yet Ravinia offers a concentrated working period with one orchestra that I don't have anywhere else. I feel I have a winter relationship in Philadelphia that is similar to the summer relationship in Chicago.

[Unfortunately it was short-lived.]

I direct the Vienna Philharmonic, the Berlin Philharmonic and London orchestras, but for someone who is not able to make symphonic recordings with his own orchestra, the Chicago and Philadelphia relationships are extraordinarily stimulating and satisfying.

[Significantly, Levine's final recordings with the Chicago Symphony and his first symphonic recordings with the Met Orchestra date from the same year, 1992.]

You have to understand another thing about my life at present. I am getting a very major gratification at the Met. Now if you walk into the Met any old night you are much more likely to get a good performance than a bad one. Apparently Karajan said it took ten years to make any major changes in an opera house. That might be extreme, though even I thought it would take three years before we got a noticeable change, but in a year and a half the orchestra and chorus had reached a different level. It's an absolute artistic turnaround.

At the Met I work indoors with a lot of time spent on one piece, I am in the city in which I live seven months a year. I love living in New York these days. There is a real resurgence of quality. The itinerant, outdoor part of my life is limited to Ravinia, and is really too short. Still, my schedule balances out well, all told. In Salzburg, of course, everything is indoors, but the environs are gorgeous when you can drive around.

I've done the wild Beethoven piece, *Wellington's Victory,* with cannons in the Hollywood Bowl for 17,000 people. By being away from Ravinia at the close of the summer, I've so far successfully avoided ever having to conduct the *1812* Overture, but I may not be lucky forever.

You know, looking back, I've only conducted one Beethoven Fifth in my life—the one this summer.

RCM: It's a good piece, Jim. You'll get to like it.

[*Great laughter.*]

[As of 1996 he still hadn't rescheduled it.]

JL: We were talking about the first Beethoven Ninth I did here?

RCM: Yes, of course.

JL: That was the first Beethoven Ninth I ever did. I've always been careful about repeating standard pieces, especially if it wasn't necessary. Szell once said to me, "You are the only young American I have ever come across who really had a lot of repertory."

But the more music you know, the more information you have, the more insight you've got into other pieces you may be doing by the same composer. I have avoided being stuck into the wrong sort of cliché repertory, Beethoven for instance. He is, I find, a composer with whom an orchestra is very responsive to the interpretive ideas of its music director. I didn't want to do Beethoven as a guest and get back a lot of Solti and Karajan. The orchestra is caught in the middle. It can't do what it does with him, and in limited time it can't quite do what I want, so the musicians would just be reading notes without anyone making a firm impression on the performance. I normally choose music in which this is unlikely to happen. To this day I have never conducted a performance of the Tchaikovsky Fifth.

RCM: You're in good company. Toscanini never played it either.

JL: But it's crazy, isn't it, to have conducted *Lulu* and *Gurrelieder* but never a Tchaikovsky Fifth? And I *like* the Tchaikovsky Fifth.

[But by 1996 he still had never done it despite lots of Onegins, the Sixth and Fourth Symphonies, piano and violin concertos, ballet suites, etc.]

July 14, 1981. *Dialogue at Ravinia.*

RCM: When you took over Ravinia in 1973 it was your primary summer job. For the past five years Chicago has shared you with Salzburg. You will be an annual visitor to Bayreuth after 1982. It looks as if your European commitments are going to increase. When you have wonderful indoor facilities with which to work and the Vienna Philharmonic to lead, what keeps you braving the rain and mosquitoes at Ravinia?

JL: Ravinia provides me with three things that make up for all the problems of weather and limited rehearsal and summer stress. First, it has been of inestimable artistic value to me to have a relationship with this orchestra. I love not only our work together, but this is an orchestra whose qualities are parallel to my musical priorities in a lot of ways.

Second, we now have ten years of growing rapport and a lot of music, some of which was rehearsed well, some of which was quick, but they know me, I know them. The management has brought in a tremendous number of players since I came, but they are well assimilated into the ensemble. I've had ten years of exposure to some genius musicians, like Frank Miller and Bud Herseth, from whom I never stop learning.

[Miller was Toscanini's principal cellist in the NBC Symphony; Herseth has been principal trumpet since 1948.]

Third, I simply feel as long as I can construct programs here, we can do some high-quality recording of things that have been rehearsed well, and I can do a certain number of things for myself for the first time. I can repeat certain pieces with them that I feel we can do better, and that I now can work on and realize with a different, finer sort of detail using the schedule's change of pace to artistic advantage.

Finally, so long as this relationship here in the park has this kind of vitality, the musicians and I realize we have built something together that we all view with great pleasure.

November 19, 1983. Dialogue at the Met.

RCM: We are both aware of what you have said over the years about the Ravinia programs having a theme, concentrating each summer on one or more composers, and avoiding the usual summer concert stereotypes. You are now going into your twelfth season. How would you define your artistic policy?

JL: Let's face it. We are playing at Ravinia with the Chicago Symphony, one of the world's great orchestras, in an outdoor pavilion with good acoustics and a wonderful stage that is nonetheless subject to weather. We are playing three programs a week on four or five rehearsals, roughly the same amount of rehearsal time given to a single concert in the downtown series. We have our Murray Theater evenings for smaller works.

I feel it would be completely wrong for Ravinia to attempt to enter the same artistic province as the winter season concerts in an enclosed hall. Which is to say, if I had been the music director of a symphony orchestra during the Webern anniversary [1983 was the centennial of Webern's birth], I would have played the complete works of Webern over a whole year's concert season. There is not a single work that takes longer than fifteen minutes. Every single one of them will fit into a symphonic context, a chamber context, or an orchestra with chorus program. To have scattered those pieces on minimal rehearsal through our summer schedule with the inevitable weather hazards struck me as simply a losing gamble. I went a different way. I had a chamber preview in the Murray Theater where we had relative control. And I played one work on an evening concert.

The 1984–85 season is a Berg anniversary. He was born in 1885. Here at the Met we will play both *Wozzeck* and *Lulu* in the same season. I don't mean that people should pat me on the back and give me a medal and tell me how revolutionary I am. I only mean that *Wozzeck* and *Lulu* take an enormous amount of rehearsal time for what they can possibly earn at the box office. We do this out of a profound artistic necessity and love of these works. It is advantageous that we have done both operas before, but these performances will be different, improvements on their predecessors. This is what the music director of an opera house can do for a major anniversary. If I were music director of a symphony orchestra then my way of honoring a great composer's anniversary would again be different.

My point is that one cannot ignore the fact that, in order for Ravinia to function, its artistic concepts, its artistic purposes, its artistic points of view must all be, in some sense, different from what is appropriate in an enclosed concert hall. You cannot do things that are perfectly feasible in a thirty-week season.

RCM: And no one should expect that.

JL: There is a search for balance in all this. Let's assume you decide to play the Verdi Requiem or the Brahms Requiem. I mention those two pieces because they are very often played, and they certainly are in the CSO repertory. The Verdi Requiem had not been played in seventeen years at Ravinia before I did it last summer and the Brahms Requiem was a Ravinia premiere. So both works were new for me with the CSO. Maybe it's not a good enough raison d'être, but from my point of view if there is a big work on the schedule and the orchestra already knows the notes, we have rehearsal time we can use for something else. Without these opportunities we would never have a chance to counterbalance that programming with something unfamiliar.

The one thing that is frustrating, and I cannot find a ready-made solution, is I simply wish to play new music. My problem with playing new music is that I have to have enough rehearsal. I have to have music with which there is a minimal gamble that it will be scattered to the four winds on a noisy, rainy night. This balance is difficult. And the one thing I wish people would understand is we don't plan everything on the basis that the artistic approach will either hinder or help us financially. We are literally in a position where the single, overriding financial factor is not programming but the weather. Whether we plan slightly more or slightly fewer nights that are artistic or financial gambles has no relation at all to whether we end up with a black figure or a red figure at the end of the concerts. The weather is vastly more important than the program content. And when we make programming decisions, no one has the remotest idea of what the summer weather will be like.

RCM: And summer at Ravinia is unpredictable, to put it graciously!

JL: There will be years when everything is glorious from my first concert to my last. Then there will be a summer when the big project of the year draws the wettest and windiest weather imaginable. There is no way of knowing.

RCM: Some patrons apparently feel, however, that as you have grown older, you have become somewhat more conservative.

JL: In some sense I may have somewhat less reckless abandon than I did in my early years. But there are two reasons for this: First is I feel that some of those early innovations were not so good, and second is that I like being able to work in some kind of depth, and you can't get that without repetition. This is the way a performance grows. You and the musicians keep returning to a score and every time you come back you can work on things that need to be improved.

I gather that in the early years of Ravinia, with four programs a week and a constant change of conductors, the audience heard a lot of what critics used to call standard readings. Everyone played it pretty safe. If the notes were right and the ensemble held together, the results were considered satisfactory. A high level of refinement was not expected. What we need now is to build a foundation based on an educated audience that is supportive of today's artistic policies as the old Ravinia public was loyal to the performers it heard forty years ago. I don't see a way to do that in some sort of slapdash, radical manner. But I offer this comment with the utter awareness that it may not be true. There may be an alternative approach I haven't found yet.

RCM: In the 1960s, as you know, Seiji Ozawa added Sunday programs that a lot of Ravinia people regarded as terribly avant-garde. I saw them as a ghetto for new music, but that was better than nothing. Since rehearsal time was limited, he took horrible risks, but fortunately nothing really bad ever happened. The orchestra knew he was risking his reputation and was very supportive. As I look back, those programs do not appear especially radical today, but they introduced a great deal of music and a number of important composers who had never been heard at Ravinia before.

While he was doing this Ozawa told me what he really wanted was to introduce what he called mixed programming, an example being a regular evening performance when the Berg Violin Concerto prefaced a Beethoven symphony. At the Ravinia of those years, the Berg had to be assigned to a dreadful modern music concert, and you prefaced a Beethoven symphony with nothing more adventurous than a Mendelssohn concerto. Without a lot of hoopla this change has quietly come to pass in your time. Today no one would raise an eyebrow seeing Berg and Beethoven on the same program.

JL: We do it all the time. People come to me and say, "Isn't it wonderful that last season Abbado did the Stockhausen *Gruppen* in Orchestra Hall." I have two reactions. Abbado *should* do the *Gruppen* at the downtown concerts. That's where such a work belongs. He has a setup with enough control that he can manage it.

RCM: No one in their right mind should think that *Gruppen* is appropriate for Ravinia. Quite apart from the way the audience would respond to it, the sheer difficulties in presenting it would be insurmountable.

JL: What bothers me is that the first CSO performances of pieces like Schoenberg's *Gurrelieder* and Piano Concerto, the Berg *Altenberg Lieder,* and even older works like the Berlioz Requiem, and Mahler's complete *Rückert Lieder* were my Ravinia performances. These are major scores, masterpieces that must be heard, that were not played downtown once every ten years, or even every twenty years, but never at all. How could an orchestra established in 1891 go season after season ignoring this music? Probably because one can never address *all* the great music. Fortunately there is too much of it!

In a winter schedule a greater density of twentieth-century music can be successfully performed than will ever be possible in the summer. But in the summer, although it may be regarded as a matter of lesser urgency, long-neglected scores from the past can be performed effectively.

A perfect example of my philosophy is the fact that since 1976 we have done the first Met productions ever of *Les Dialogues des Carmélites, Lulu, Billy Budd, Mahagonny, Les Mamelles de Tirésias, L'Enfant et les sortilèges, Oedipus Rex,* et cetera. That number of twentieth-century works, classic or no, was not done in the preceding thirty years—not since Gatti, who kept trying to present American works whether they faded into obscurity afterwards or not. I suppose if someone were to observe that my programming concept at Ravinia does not get more adventurous, or may in some respects get less adventurous, I can only say you are probably right. But one of the reasons is that, knowing the orchestra so well, and having worked with them for such a long time, I have this longing to work on detail, which you cannot do when you are doing something for the first time. You can only do it when you are doing something *again,* returning to music you have played before where the basics of the performance are already securely in place.

RCM: I think we both agree that the element of contrast in a program is highly important. Hans Rosbaud . . .

JL: Such a great conductor!

RCM: You know how we came to love him in Chicago. He did some extraordinary innovations in his years as a guest conductor of the CSO downtown. He used to insist that you can play *anything* with a good audience response if you put it in an appropriate context.

JL: Programming facinates me. We have both heard examples of bad programs. Managers are stuck with the fact that the conductor wants to play a piece like Varèse's *Arcana,* so they convince him to couple it with a warhorse romantic concerto. The people who want to hear the Varèse may gladly accept a contrasting romantic work, but probably not something that has been so overplayed, while the people who want the Tchaikovsky B-flat will regard the Varèse as an imposition. So it is not a good compromise at all. Everyone is unhappy.

RCM: It seems to me with the present skills of yourself and the Chicago Symphony that there are certain pieces of American music—the Ives Second Symphony is a prime example—which are perfectly acceptable in the repertory. There isn't a reason in the world that you could not get them prepared in the time available and stylistically they would be perfectly accessible to the audience. No one is going to yell and scream over a symphony that so often sounds like Brahms. It seems to me, in terms of the overall picture we are describing, that there are quite a few pieces you could play.

JL: I think you will see that. I think that turnover is in the cards.

[In July 1984, Levine directed the Ives Second at Ravinia with great success. It had been added to the downtown repertory in May 1981 by Michael Tilson Thomas. When the Vienna Philharmonic saw Ives listed in the Ravinia brochure, the orchestra asked Levine to do some Ives with them, too, and in 1985 he played the first VPO performances of Three Places in New England *in Vienna and repeated the work at Ravinia.]*

RCM: As I see it, the Ravinia concerts have an enormous potential for mixing the new and the old, the familiar and the unfamiliar, along the lines Rosbaud suggested.

JL: I agree.

RCM: How well do you feel this is being realized?

JL: It's a constant balancing act. You have to toss your hat in the ring and try something. Invariably there are seasons in which you end up feeling there was too much of one thing and not enough of another. And don't forget, you can only do what you find convincing. That you *ought* to do something is not enough. Mere obligation of that type produces a dead performance. Any program that is done out of duty and not love has failed before it starts. In my case, I can't conduct works that I don't love and/or respect in some way.

RCM: I don't think we should look at Ravinia seasons as isolated groups of events. What we need to do is examine what is happening over a longer period of time, three or four summers in a row.

JL: Absolutely. In the opera house there may be something you want to do, but it has to be postponed because you can't put an appropriate cast together. What happens in the long run corresponds to what is happening to me.

RCM: Like all good politicians you can run on your record.

JL: [*Loud laugh.*] Despite unusually hot weather last summer, for the second year in a row Ravinia broke its attendance record. The financial base is completely secure. Clearly we are doing something right because this wonderful public support is there. We are not inhibited by a fearful conservatism. That feeling simply is not there. The main thing is to develop the possibilities the festival provides. But I am programming less densely so I can rehearse more. The orchestra members and I have talked about this. There is a strain working in a situation where you can feel certain weekends that nothing is really prepared, nothing truly digested. These musicians are not on the stage doing a job. They are realizing a performance, and at the end of the evening they want to feel, not that they have played several thousand notes, but that a performance has taken place.

We have to accept a certain number of gambles.

RCM: But what matters most for the public is the final product, what comes out of the kitchen. I have told you of the afternoon when Ozawa, in a real bind, rehearsed both the Beethoven Fifth and the Schubert *Unfinished* in twenty minutes. And two days later he was to record these scores. Of course the concert became the real rehearsal, and the playback of the first take demonstrated where more work had to be done, but by the close of the session he managed to produce effective recorded performances that one might argue gained in freshness and energy what they lacked in refined detail.

I have been listening with care to three of your recent CSO recordings, the Dvořák *New World* Symphony and the Mozart K. 550 and K. 551, and no one can fault them for lack of refinement, even though they came from a summer concert situation.

JL: They were prepared pretty carefully. They took a lot of time. To spend that time I had to pay the price of surrounding them with other music the orchestra already knew. I don't accept the idea of recordings reflecting the different expectations of summer and winter music seasons. The standards of excellence don't change with the seasons.

RCM: Don't you see this as a part of your growing maturity? In the beginning you were in your twenties and the sheer excitement of making music with the Chicago Symphony had an exhilarating effect. You were carried along by that. But the more you worked with the CSO, the more acutely you saw the possibilities of the situation, and now, at forty, the exhilaration has worn off. Now you want to hear the best performance that you can imagine.

JL: You are absolutely right. And for that best performance I need the time.

July 4, 1987. Dialogue at Ravinia.

RCM: You have just brought us this miraculous realization of *Ariadne auf Naxos*. And what a cast! Margaret Price, Kathleen Battle, Susanne Mentzer, Dawn Upshaw, Gary Lakes, and Hermann Prey are not the sort of combination that normally turns up at American music festivals. On nights like this Ravinia's claim to be the American Salzburg has some validity. I found Dawn Upshaw a real discovery, even though she had a small role.

JL: There was a time when it was said that to do an opera like this in an idiomatic manner you had to have German singers. Maybe it never was true, but it certainly isn't true today.

RCM: National origin means less and less, but the character and the level of training mean a great deal. I think we are agreed that although historically European opera houses since World War II have assumed a great deal of responsibility for providing American singers with early professional training, it is ridiculous for us to assume that training of that sort should inevitably happen abroad.

JL: Indeed.

RCM: There must be more opportunities here, and the ability to follow a career should not depend on the ability to get a job in Stuttgart.

JL: I couldn't agree more. The question always used to be, Why do American singers have to go to Europe blah, blah, blah. I think this impression is wrong. American singers don't *have* to go to Europe. There have always been opportunities in this country. In fact, most singers want to go to Europe, should go to Europe. There is no question that there is some kind of cultural, historical, language-absorption process that can go on there and that a certain kind of singer will find that enormously valuable. One must not disregard that. On the other hand, one should not *have* to do that and there should be ways in America, like the Young Artist Development Program, for musicians of all sorts to get proper training and proper experience in the no-man's-land of music that often exists outside big cities.

A part of proper training is seeing things as wholes. Neophytes, especially singers, are always trying to separate voice and technique. To them technique sometimes means high notes, or runs, or something like that.

RCM: It's rather like a sauce that you add before serving.

JL: But, of course, as they grow they realize that technique encompasses all the tools for communicating the content of the music. It is the means to the end.

RCM: It's two aspects of the same thing. The technique is in the music and the music is in the technique. You can't separate them.

March 25, 1993. Chicago. Ravinia in Retrospect. A Farewell. Extemporaneous Spoken Remarks.

Little did I know when I started what kind of partnership this would become, and what kind of development it would stimulate both in my artistic growth and in the chance to give to the musical community in Chicago something that really continued growing in depth and detail during the entire time. In our time, twenty-year partnerships are becoming so very rare. For me, this development of having a symphonic base at Ravinia ran parallel to my establishing an operatic base at the Metropolitan Opera.

I hope everyone is aware that Ravinia is really a unique set of circumstances which allows all of its participants—the audience, the great Chicago Symphony Orchestra and Chorus, the administration, all the volunteers, everybody that makes this work—to have always a stimulating experience.

I remember thinking back in the old days that the prototype for summer music in America was Tanglewood, which is two hours from

Boston and is really a resort area. Ravinia, though, relies essentially on the same community as the downtown winter season.

Also, in the winter season, one performs a different program every week, rehearsing very carefully, making some repetitions of a program, sometimes touring. At Ravinia, we play a program once, prepare three programs a week, and solve a very stimulating configuration of how to rehearse all that music—three programs in four or five rehearsals. At the same time, we have this wonderful balance between bringing in well-known, established artists, versus beginning to work with young artists. All this happened because when Ed [Gordon] and I started to work together, Ed said, "I want you to be music director."

At first I said, "What do you want a music director for?"

He said, "I think now is the time that I really need an artistic collaborator, now that we have a facility I can put to this kind of use."

There was the beautiful Pavilion, there was the Murray Theater, in the back of our heads was the idea that one day we would get an institute program going for young artists at the same time, as has now taken place. The idea was not just to have a disconnected series of concerts but to have a *real festival*.

In my mind, the Aspen Festival, where I grew up, was the prototypical summer festival, but this, again, was not an area where people worked all winter. I tried to think, What was it about Aspen? Then I realized in a flash what it was: Musicians love to play music in a relationship to nature and natural surroundings, in a relationship to some of the things that stimulated the composers to write the music in the first place, and in relation to each other.

The stories of the great composers writing music in the country or in non-city circumstances—and then going to the city to have it played—are, of course, legion. So many masterpieces were brought into being that way. It seemed we could find some way to use this feeling you get when you play music close to nature, to get the feeling of using the open Pavilion and the smaller chamber hall to make music of all different sizes and proportions.

A summer festival also afforded the possibility of hearing the lesser-known works of great composers or the greatest works of some not-so-well-known composers. Or works for unusual groups of instruments. In short, something other than a format of the regular symphony concert on the regular subscription day. Or the regular string quartet series. Stimulating as they are, that's not what summer music really is.

Not only is the Chicago Symphony Orchestra a great orchestra—one of the few—but it's a unique orchestra. Where else could you find an orchestra on such a high level that plays such a huge array of music that is not only undaunted by the idea of playing a program once or playing it in cold or hot weather, or rehearsing it in a completely different configuration from winter, but is actually stimulated by it? So many of them used to say to me, "This is really fun to do, if you can do it in continuity with a music director so that eventually your rapport is so strong that you don't have to talk about it too much."

I tried to maintain a standard rather than let something random happen here all these years. Let it be said that everything about this whole experience was beautiful and challenging and helped me more with my artistic development than I will ever be able to say.

Maybe we can be proud of one thing more than anything else: Ravinia feels like a communicative community. If it weren't, you'd never be able to play three programs a week and draw an audience. Where would they come from if the same people weren't coming back several times a week?

None of this would have been possible without *all* these elements: without these facilities, without my collaborator [Zarin Mehta] and his predecessor [Ed Gordon], who, with such singular dedication and understanding of all the things that have to be solved, really were the greatest possible partners for me. And, of course, now when I think about it, I swallow very hard because the Chicago Symphony has been an extraordinary, a singular partner in all this.

You know, the orchestra has had a great history of playing with very great conductors, and when you're twenty-seven years old and you conduct the Chicago Symphony and come back year after year, inevitably you are teaching yourself, and the orchestra knows you're teaching yourself. Presumably the orchestra would never put up with it if they didn't think it was worth their while to help you—to respect your talent despite youth and inexperience.

I appreciate very much over the whole time, certainly, Margaret [Hillis] and her extraordinary chorus, but also what every member of this orchestra gave to this situation in order to have its special esprit de corps.

I'm very sorry it comes to an end. You can tell I wouldn't have continued for twenty-two years if I wasn't happy to return each year. I would gladly have continued forever, but there came a time when necessary and organic developments became pressing and served to take me away from the continuity of these summers. I only hope that I'll be able to come back to Ravinia frequently in the future, even if not very often in the years I see immediately ahead.

I could hardly thank everybody involved with these summers enough. There would not be the right words to express what the whole of this large piece of my life means to me. I thank all of you, everybody who ever had anything to do with these memorable years.

January 31, 1996. Dialogue at the Met.

RCM: Neither of us underestimates for a moment what Szell gave to you, but, in fact, you came to him with a well-developed conducting technique which you had acquired at Juilliard.

JL: I got a great deal from Jean Morel. He taught me one of the basic precepts to which we keep returning: that there is never such a thing as too much rehearsal time. He taught me that the more time you have, and the more sophisticated your concept is, the more things you will find to work on and develop in the performance. I saw this once when Szell, with a luxury of time I had never imagined possible, conducted the Cleveland Orchestra at the peak of its powers, in the *Freischütz* Overture, a Mozart piano concerto with Serkin, and the Beethoven Sixth. He had five rehearsals, yet he could still find things to do with the time and lifted that music to unbelievable heights—which is where it belongs, of course, but so rarely arrives.

Morel's career was limited by two big factors: One, he had a spiteful, short-tempered, irritable side to his personality; and two, he did not conduct the classic German repertory well, which is rough if you're going to be the music director of an orchestra. But he was an exceptional teacher, full of all the important knowledge, and he gave fabulous performances of a lot of music, especially romantic French and early twentieth-century scores. But the important thing about him—all the Juilliard Orchestra graduates will attest to this—he had the most persuasive body language. His entire pattern of movement was telling you what to do. He and Carlos Kleiber.

I had an experience in Berlin, in a program with two very familiar pieces—Schumann Two and Three, I believe—when I don't think I talked a total of ten minutes in the entire rehearsal period. It is an orchestra with incredible discipline, and they are so responsive to the stick, and to every other gesture you make, that it got to be really fun to see how much I could accomplish without speaking. This is particularly true when you are dealing with an orchestra in what it regards as home repertory. Do a Mozart opera with the Vienna Philharmonic and they barely have to look at the music. There is nothing to explain except the smallest subtleties, and even these could probably be conveyed with the body or the stick if one had the skill and they knew you well enough.

I noticed when Szell conducted his own orchestra, which knew him as well as he knew them, he was about 50 percent conductor and 50 percent teacher. For example, he could give time to matters of style, so the musicians automatically played trills and other ornaments in the correct manner for the work in front of them.

But when he went to guest conduct and knew he had to get the concert prepared in three or four rehearsals (or whatever it was), there was so much more to his gesture. He tried to communicate so much in the beat because they did not know him as well, he did not know them as well, and therefore he felt he had to overcome that problem to get his kind of results.

RCM: As conductors you and Szell are direct descendants of Wagner, who broke with tradition and conducted phrases, not bar lines.

JL: If you have an orchestra that understands the rudimentary elements of conducting, and all you beat is bar lines, the next thing you know, that's all you're getting—bar lines. But you must know where the bar lines are, even if they're not what you're showing. The biggest beast of a piece to do from memory is something like Stravinsky's Symphonies of Winds, because this score, although only twelve minutes long, recycles the same music again and again but barred differently each time. If I conduct that piece and take my eye away from connecting what is in the score to the pattern of the beat I will make a mistake and we will have a train wreck.

One thing that the intelligent critic always gets right, and the dumb one doesn't (just as the dumb conductor doesn't), is realizing an artist is growing all the time and trying in some way to retain whatever is good and work over what needs to be improved. And this can't be done always in a straight line.

One of the most fascinating things is the way your technique evolves, because the more the orchestra understands, and the less you have to show the conventional things, the more you can look for ways to show the singular, the exceptional things. That presents a completely different—and much more interesting—set of problems than those that arise when you have to work in short rehearsal time.

RCM: I had a difficult moment or two with Szell when he came to Chicago as a guest for what turned out to be the final time in March 1968. Of course, he had been conducting the orchestra for more than twenty-five years, but he had been absent for a long time. It was an all-Beethoven program with the Fifth and Sixth symphonies, both works the orchestra had recorded with Reiner. And they still tried to play the Reiner performances even though Jean Martinon had succeeded him. This was the Chicago Symphony's transitional period between two music directors, Martinon departing and Georg Solti arriving, and knowing the mood the orchestra was in, I feared that if Szell played the teacher and concentrated on detail in such familiar works, the musicians would go stale on him. So I persuaded him to *cancel* one rehearsal. This was great for morale. He could not have made himself more popular. In rehearsal he had all the essentials of the performance firmly in the stick, and they responded with strength, accuracy, and lots of vitality.

I congratulated one of the musicians on how well they sounded, and he replied, "Who could sound bad with conducting like that?" So Szell made a very forceful impression with a concert that, as Toscanini would have said, "had a lot of blood in it." But the cost of that energy was a certain loss of polish in a few places. He was unhappy about that. I atoned for my sin, if I had sinned, by taking him and his wife to the Tavern Club for a superlative dinner enhanced by a marvelous burgundy I had been saving for him. By the time we reached the cognac, I knew I was forgiven.

JL: I know what you mean! I find myself, after all the years I have been at the Met, understanding that kind of situation from the inside. If I go to an orchestra with which I have not had a long, continuing, in-depth relationship, I go back to the principle that the gesture has to show as much as possible. But don't forget that a gesture is useless unless the musicians mostly understand what you want and it is already part of their vocabulary.

The fascinating things happen when you really have a chance to work with an orchestra in the same close, concentrated way that you would be working as part of a string quartet with the same three colleagues. I watched this all through my years with Walter Levin and his colleagues in the LaSalle. In that context, ironically, you end up talking your way through the rehearsal. Instead of using a sort of gesture shorthand, you talk about what the issues are. And that's a completely different thing from having to hurry and, in a short time, give a pragmatic correction for everything you dislike.

RCM: Bernard Haitink once told me, I *think* facetiously, that you could rehearse any piece with four phrases, "Too loud, too soft, too fast, too slow. Except," he added, "they never are too soft, so it is really only three." That is real pragmatic shorthand, and we both have attended plenty of rehearsals that were done on that level.

JL: And, unfortunately, it always shows! This subject fascinates me because now I find that people notice when I am conducting Met Orchestra concerts at Carnegie Hall, how few big gestures I make. When I was younger several things made me try to get as much in the gesture as possible. First of all I was working with the great Chicago Symphony and had five rehearsals in which to prepare three different programs. Clearly if you are working on a piece they know, they can look at you and play what you show them to play. But, on the other hand, you know them, and their predilections in that score, or that style, and you must decide whether to go along with those, and let them follow their natural impulses, or to insist on something different. If you agree with them, fundamentally, you say very little: Let them play.

I remember the first time we read the *Great* C Major Schubert symphony. This was a sensation that was so striking for me, as if someone had given me an instrument that knew exactly what I wished it to do. All I had to do was show it what I wanted and there it was. It was their collective discipline, style, the timbre of their sound . . .

RCM: The legacy of Fritz Reiner.

JL: Exactly.

RCM: I would assume that working with the orchestras of Berlin and Vienna you now feel that through long association you have a freedom not normally associated with guest conducting.

JL: Absolutely.

RCM: But these orchestras have very different traditions.

The Berlin Philharmonic was established in 1882 to play symphony concerts on a regular basis. Hans von Bülow, as I need not tell you, was the first conductor, and in a century he had only three successors, Arthur Nikisch, Wilhelm Furtwängler, and Herbert von Karajan. Talk about continuity, there you have it.

The Vienna Philharmonic is older, 1842—the same age as the New York Philharmonic—and both these orchestras drew on musicians who spent most of their time in a theater orchestra pit and wanted an opportunity to play a different repertory. Hans Richter, who conducted the first *Ring* at Bayreuth, was conductor at Vienna from 1875 to 1898. His most important successor—just barely in the nineteenth century—was Mahler. In this century it has been led at one time or another by nearly every conductor of reputation in central Europe. But this is an orchestra that has always come from the pit of an opera house. It offers about a dozen programs a season, and because of the schedule at the Staatsoper, these concerts are on Saturday afternoons and Sunday mornings.

You can't possibly treat the two ensembles alike.

JL: Of course I know and respect the two traditions, and I work within those traditions to try to produce the best possible results, to create a situation in which the musicians do not hesitate to follow their natural impulses and make music in the most spontaneous and expressive manner they can. I enjoy immensely working in Berlin and Vienna, but I also really enjoy going to orchestras like Boston or the Philadelphia, where the players have not encountered me for some years. And they will come to me and say, "Hey, you aren't the same conductor you were when you were here last. You're working in a whole different sphere." And I say, "I hope so, because conductors are supposed to get better instead of worse as they grow older."

RCM: Szell, of course, went to New York for a season as musical advisor. I met him on the street in Chicago in 1969—the end of Bernstein's last season—and he was really angry as only Szell could be angry.

"That damned Bernstein," he said. "He wanted to go out smelling like roses, so he has not fired anyone, or retired anyone, or reauditioned the strings, or rearranged the seating for several seasons. So to start my job, I must do all that, and that means I come in being the son of a bitch for moving this man back a stand, or suggesting that someone think of retirement."

Szell felt, I discovered, that the orchestra should have been offered to him in the fifties, when Bernstein arrived, and he never seemed to grasp that the decision was not made on the basis of musicianship but on the fact that what New York wanted was a conductor who would attract attention. Bernstein was charismatic, and Szell didn't appeal to the public on that level.

It was thought that Boulez might have that charismatic quality, and, in a rather different way, he did. But he tried to lead a conservative audience too quickly, and the money people, the old guard, got him. I shall never stop wondering what it might have been like if he had had another five years in New York.

JL: It is the constant problem, whether major cultural institutions are going to lead or follow!

RCM: Morel's problems with German literature were shared by Jean Martinon as conductor of the Chicago Symphony. He conned us for fair. His supporters felt that as a composer he would expand the repertory further into the present century, but apparently he lost his adventurous spirit the minute the ink on his contract was dry. Martinon dealt with his insecurities by insisting that the CSO played for him better than for any previous conductor—pure hubris. He studied the Reiner records and insisted they were stylistically incorrect, which, I surmise, translated into "not French." But his correct, Frenchified versions of Brahms and Strauss were very sad to hear, and, of course, the musicians hated being required to play music they knew so well in this manner.

He maintained this self-deception by being out of town when the orchestra had guest conductors, but one week he was caught. Leopold Stokowski was the guest, and protocol demanded that Martinon attend one of his concerts. He sneaked in on Friday afternoon. The symphony was the Shostakovich No. 10. Stokowski had given it the most convincing performance I had ever heard Thursday night, so, naturally, I took advantage of the opportunity to hear it a second time. I was backstage, walking to the conductor's dressing room, when I heard slow steps behind me. It was Martinon.

Looking at his face, I imagined a scenario. He was walking in the Bois de Boulogne and in the distance he saw a couple on the grass. Growing closer, he observed and admired the passion and intensity with which they were making love. And growing even closer, he saw that the woman was his wife.

Martinon had heard Stokowski produce sounds from his orchestra unlike anything it had ever produced for him, and he obviously did not have the slightest idea how Stokowski had achieved this.

I stood aside as Martinon entered the dressing room and he muttered a few polite phrases. The good Leopold Stanislaus could not have been more gracious. Had he wished to be rude, he might have said what I am sure he thought, You French fink, don't you realize what you have here? Instead, he said how happy he was to return and work with this marvelous ensemble. Martinon retired quickly, his honor intact.

On the way out I met an old friend from the cello section, Mr. Greenbaum. "What does Stokowski do to get playing like that?" I asked.

"Easy," was the reply. "He doesn't get in our way."

JL: That's wonderful. Members of the Vienna Philharmonic said the same things about Karajan conducting the New Year's concert.

RCM: And this coincided with Stokowski's own explanation of a few years before, that he made it a point to know the distinctive character of every orchestra he led, the way a violinist would know the distinctive qualities of a number of instruments, and to play on the ensemble as a large instrument. You go with the flow, not against it. Martinon spent five years swimming upstream, and although he did some good things, the close bonds many of us hoped he would achieve never materialized.

JL: Some fascinating things happened to me as I was developing the Met Orchestra. After a certain amount of time of making essentially technical corrections, you reach a point where you want these people to be inspired by what inspires you. You wind up saying things like, "Here for me the problem is . . . ," and you are letting them in on your conception so they are part of the process of developing a performance—as if we were playing large chamber music. Szell used to do that all the time. I find the result is that they know where I am going. It's become essential.

Samuel Antek, who played under Toscanini, had a very telling story about going to visit him in Riverdale and asking questions that required reference to the score. When we are students we always think this is what counts: Should there be a trill there, or is that a misprint? In other words, our process of learning comes out very heavily dependent on pedantic things. Only gradually does one discovers this has nothing to do with how the performance communicates itself. Most of these details could go either way and it won't make much difference to the listener's perception of the piece. There are so many other decisive issues. Higher priorities. The composer's higher priorities.

This is very hard to learn. It is difficult to evolve through a pattern of responses that have almost become reflexes, leaving your brain free to concentrate on more important and subtle things.

RCM: When I was writing a lot about Haydn recordings I received a great deal of heat from musicologists insisting that a performance could not be worth hearing if it began with a bad edition—and there were quite a few of them in use. I replied that I would much rather hear a vigorous, communicative performance from a faulty text than a lifeless one from correct material.

JL: I couldn't possibly agree more. Of course, ideally you shouldn't have to make such a choice.

RCM: But Beecham's idea of doing musicology was to settle with the score on the beach at Cannes with a box of Alfred Dunhill cigars, and if something looked odd in the music he fixed it with one of his perpetually dull blue pencils. And it was fixed with the imagination and musical resources of a remarkable man who would never dream of going to some musty old library to find a manuscript score.

Today one can hope for energetic performances from good texts, since they are easily found. Haydn was a genius, and that is apparent even from the worst of the old texts. The new editions only make that fact clearer.

JL: He always communicates, but he does it more clearly when you hear what he really wrote.

RCM: One of the things we have to realize about Toscanini is that he grew up in an Italian musical culture in which many of the musicians he faced were mediocre and indifferent, and he had to develop a rehearsal technique in which he literally beat the performance he wanted out of them. Even when he had superb orchestras—the vintage New York Philharmonic, the BBC, the NBC, the Vienna Philharmonic—it is unlikely that it ever occurred to him that he could fully share with them the performance he had in his mind. Besides, with those groups the language barrier would never have permitted such a thing.

JL: True.

RCM: That performance had to be achieved by force of leadership.

JL: That was the mentality.

RCM: But players could go to Toscanini and ask, "Maestro, which do you prefer—this?"—and play—"or this?"—and play—and he would make a choice. Sometimes it was something quite different from what he had done previously.

You hear all about the temper tantrums, but you could always approach him and get his attention with what he considered an intelligent musical question. When you see the kind of talent that surrounded him in the first chairs of the NBC Symphony, you knew he quickly realized he was dealing there with an entirely different type of musician than he knew in his youth. His awareness of this was reflected in rehearsals toward the end of his career in which he said very little. He might ask for a little more accent in a phrase, or make an adjustment in dynamics, but he might also go on for a considerable time and never speak.

I went to his rehearsals, anticipating not tantrums, but concentrated, inspired music-making.

JL: In the films of the television broadcasts you see him departing from a conventional rhythmic pattern to shape phrases with beautiful flowing gestures no truly professional musician could possibly misunderstand. In that way he is getting closer to them. He is saying, I know you will keep the rhythm without my marking it strictly, so follow me in a broad, singing phrase. This is the security I was speaking of earlier.

RCM: We can see a continuing progress over the years even in fine performances. These days we can usually begin with the assurance that the notes are all played accurately with a good tone and the performance is in something like the true spirit of the score, and, unfortunately, a great many listeners will settle for that. That may be as far as their ears can take them.

Koussevitzky once stopped the Boston Symphony in a tough passage and said it was wrong. "What are the wrong notes?" he was asked.

"No," he said, "between the notes."

This was partly his faulty English, but it illuminates the fact that in a performance the silences are as important, just as much a part of the piece, as the sounds.

JL: Szell always used to insist, "Rests are not for resting," referring to the tension in silence. And it is not simply the notes you play; it is the way you link them together, the shape of the phrase and the subtle alternation of shades of tone color and degrees of accent within the moving melodic line. When you start going into every phrase and searching for the maximum content that can be conveyed without distortion and gratuitous underlining, you are probing further and further into the heart of the music and touching the composer himself.

RCM: We both agree that Szell's Cleveland was a wonderful orchestra, but when you came to the Met you did not develop a Szell orchestra but a Toscanini orchestra. Both of us know the wonderful precision of Szell's orchestra, but Toscanini's orchestra had so many things that set it apart, such as (to choose one example at random) decisive, sharp attacks at the opening of phrases that pulled your ear into the line of the music.

JL: Certain aspects of Toscanini's genius grow stronger for me as I grow older. He was paradoxically more visceral, more physical, and at the same time more vocal. I don't feel he had either to be vocal, with no sharp attack, or to have sharp attacks at the expense of the lyric line. If you listen to performance after performance, he seems to have understood the pieces in more specific terms than any other conductor of his day. There was real insight. Listen to Toscanini performances of the Brahms Double Concerto, the Third Symphony, the *German Requiem,* and the *Liebeslieder* Waltzes. This music has more variety inside it than people expect from this composer. But it is all organic; it's all there as a unified whole. This is an unsubstantiated opinion because there are so many performances I have never heard, but on the basis of my experience, his performances of the Brahms Third are the only ones I know that really communicate what is unique about that score.

When something fails to work out the way we artists hoped it would, some people look at us as if we had done something inferior on purpose, but when you are trying to make something better it does not always happen in a straight line. And it's not always the conductor either—it involves the players and the hall and the chemistry of the situation. A good audience makes a good performance better, too, and a bad audience can make a bad performance a true disaster. When I am conducting and I have an assistant listening in the hall, I ask him to tell me about anything he thinks needs attention. I promise I'm a big enough boy that if I don't agree with him, it's no problem. I'll do what I think is right. I would die without feedback. It is absolutely essential.

RCM: When Toscanini was tense he could have memory slips. (So can I after forty years.) But I believe it was his son, Walter, who told me that in one of those 1952 London concerts he forgot the order of the program, so the downbeat for the Second Symphony became the downbeat for the *Tragic* Overture.

JL: Wow! And they beat it out for him and got it right! I once witnessed this with Szell, who had two tour programs going. Barber's *School for Scandal* Overture began one and the *Lohengrin* Prelude began the other. The last thing he said to the musicians as we left Cleveland was, "Just begin with the bow on the string at the beginning of *Lohengrin*. It can't be too soft. It can't be too soft." And there we were on tour and the programs alternated except in one city. The first night was *Lohengrin* and the next night was also *Lohengrin*. The second night he came out onstage, bowed to the audience, and without looking at the orchestra gave this huge upbeat and downbeat and they started playing *Lohengrin*. His eyes were staring, he was in shock, and all evening he was muttering, "They must think I am completely crazy, a piece *so* different. . . ."

RCM: All he did was prove that he was human like the rest of us.

JL: As you grow older you have the experience of performing works a number of times with different orchestras that, whether they intend to or not, show you different things in the music. You realize that to be honest with yourself you cannot settle for a merely smooth, professional performance. Take the Brahms symphonies I performed and recorded in Chicago. At the time—the mid-seventies—the orchestra and I were not unhappy with them. But I wanted to do them again in Vienna twenty years later, and we both hear a difference.

RCM: The Chicago performances are still wonderful, beautiful. I learned the Brahms Third and Fourth from Koussevitzky in ripe, romantic performances that probably were "just right" for me in my early twenties, when I was just starting a systematic exploration of that music, but I could not accept them today. I note they have been reissued on CD and have received enthusiastic reviews, so they have not lost their power to please.

You are now going very deep into this music and showing us the classical side of Brahms with great clarity. I have been studying the Brahms Third for fifty years; for me that Vienna performance is as complete a revelation of the work as I am ever likely to hear.

JL: In the early seventies, when I started to guest conduct the Chicago Symphony, the Boston Symphony, and the Philadelphia Orchestra in the United States, and then the Berlin Philharmonic and Vienna Philharmonic in Europe, all these orchestras had reached a peak in terms of their respective styles and had clear identities. You did not have to talk at any length because it really wasn't necessary. You were dealing with a basic canon of repertory which they knew very well. Over the years, as the season grew further into the summer and American orchestras went on fifty-two-week contracts, rehearsal time became shorter and new players came into the ensemble who, while very good, were also very inexperienced with the repertory.

I remember when Carlos Kleiber came here in 1988, to conduct *Bohème,* he went straight to description of mood, atmosphere, details of plot, etc., during the orchestra rehearsals. I asked him about that later and he said, "Don't you find it's much more necessary now than it was a few years ago?"

It's like any other aesthetic. I'm sure that since I was twenty I have changed, but certain of my most fundamental convictions have not changed at all so far as I can tell. And yet, now I am seen by some people as a more conservative musician, while I think I am only maintaining aspects I have always believed in.

RCM: But you are breaking new ground with fresh repertory. Your Ravinia performance of the Prokofiev Fifth in 1992 was extraordinary and yielded a record that is mighty impressive. This is not music people associate with you. After all, in twenty-three summers at Ravinia you only played four Prokofiev pieces.

JL: We made that Prokofiev recording because Chicago was going through a phase where some of the music we had performed so well in the past was beginning to make me anxious. We no longer had Frank Miller [principal cello] or Arnie Jacobs [principal tuba], and Ray Still [principal oboe] was nearing retirement. Ed Gordon asked what I wanted to do. I said, "You know, in 1978 they played a great Prokofiev Fifth for me, but they have never recorded it. They could really carry that off." Ed agreed, and we scheduled it.

Interestingly enough, one of the great musicians in the orchestra came to me and asked, "What are we recording next year?" and I said, "The Prokofiev Fifth." He just flipped. "That is one of our most unsung pieces," he said, "something we know we can do spectacularly well."

Reiner's broadcast performance from the fifties is so remarkable! This is a piece that was once a vogue; every conductor did it. Koussevitzky introduced it, Szell did it, Karajan did it in Europe. Everybody was playing it for a time. It never was a warhorse piece for me; I rarely ever did it. But I made my "Salzburg debut" in 1967 playing the piano part in it under Karajan, who was guest conducting the Cleveland Orchestra on a tour with Szell.

RCM: I think I heard the third or fourth performance in the United States. Right after the Boston premiere, Koussevitzky brought it to

Chicago. His was a very beautiful performance, but it did not dig very deeply into the music. The only early performance I can recall that was as powerful as yours was Artur Rodzinski's.

There is a lovely story here. Koussevitzky wanted to do something for Russian composers during the war and was told that there was an acute shortage of music paper there. So he instructed G. Schirmer in New York to make up a big box of all kinds of music paper every month and ship it to the composers' union in Moscow. At least some would get through.

When the score of the Prokofiev Fifth came to him, in the corner of the page it read G. Schirmer, New York.

JL: That's wonderful! There was a period where these big new pieces made the same rounds. Look at the Bartók Concerto for Orchestra. Koussevitzky commissioned it, and then Szell got it, and Reiner, and within a short time it was heard from all the major orchestras. It was virtuoso stuff. Nothing like that is happening today. If one orchestra has done the premiere, then another wants something it can offer as a premiere—even if it's not as fine a work. This means a certain amount of second- and third-rate music is played while first-rate scores are denied the wider audience they deserve.

RCM: It's hype values coming before artistic values.

JL: I never "play down" to audiences, assuming that somehow they can't "get" the greatest music. When I was in Cleveland, Robert Shaw programmed the Mozart G Minor for a children's concert. I asked him why.

"They're ready for it," he said. "They're open to it. Believe me, their brains don't get stronger as they grow up. Their brains right now have all the capacity to understand this work."

At the concert he turned and said to the kids, "They say you have to be mature to understand this piece, but you can never start too soon with this kind of music." And it worked. They paid attention. It was very successful.

All through my work with Szell there were moments when he would laugh demonically and say, "You shouldn't do that piece until you're forty, but get your hands on it now. You'll change your perspective after you're forty, but that's what I expect you to do."

RCM: Sir Thomas used to observe laconically, "If a conductor always plays a piece the same way he's only proving he has no musical imagination." Some of Beecham's imaginative flights were wild, but you respected him for them, nonetheless.

JL: Of course. That's the truth. It's revelatory for people who always expect the same performance, who play the same Toscanini record over and over and reject the work in any other performance, only to discover eventually that Toscanini performances changed all the time. An artist must have freedom, which includes experimenting and making mistakes.

RCM: One of the great things about having access to Toscanini's archive at his Riverdale house was the ability to document this. There might be ten different versions of a standard score on the shelf—no two alike. Walter Toscanini was interested for a time in a German machine that permitted him to change the tempo of a taped performance without changing the pitch. There were things his father would approve for release if minor corrections could be made, but it was not always possible to insert material from tapes of other broadcasts, since they were a little slower or faster. Nothing came of this, since you could not splice from Carnegie Hall to Studio 8-H and back, but it is illuminating to know of the problem.

There are Toscanini recordings available of the Beethoven *Coriolan* Overture, but they were only grudgingly approved for release. The Old Man was never really satisfied with any of his performances of that piece, broadcasts or studio work. Apparently there was one dreadful afternoon with Guido Cantelli when he brought a new *Coriolan* recording of his own that he played for Toscanini, and the Old Man didn't like it either. Cantelli begged. "*Caro* maestro, show me how it ought to go." So then they turned to the Toscanini versions, played them all, and Toscanini liked them even less. So the session ended in an absolutely black mood of frustration and despair.

JL: When we finally could hear not just one NBC performance but a wide range of things with a number of orchestras over some thirty years, they amplified incredibly our understanding of his approach. We saw how searching and diverse these performances were, and he kept on searching for ways to get closer to the essence of the work. Sometimes it was only small details, but sometimes it was really significant things.

Studying a score is, to a point, gradually forming an informed opinion of how it ought to sound. Then you reach a certain point when you start to free yourself of the printed music, and you start thinking of the reality of working with human musicians in real acoustical spaces, and you realize that the path to an honest performance is paradoxically circuitous. The more you try to be as objective as you can be, the more you run the risk that everything will be "correct" and the personality will be flushed out. But the more you let yourself go, the more you risk that serious details will get lost or misrepresented and that you will obstruct or even replace the composer's personality with your own. If you keep at it long enough, and consistently, you can once in a while transcend that problem. You can get to a point where you are playing the music with the vitality of your own personality, used to realize as much of the composer's detail as can be perceptively communicated.

RCM: The symphony that Toscanini played more than any other was the Beethoven *Eroica,* and in the rehearsals for his last performance in 1954—I heard them—there were hardly any pauses. In the first movement he stopped once to correct a balance, but it was all very smooth sailing. But before the funeral march he turned to Frank Miller [principal cellist] and asked, "I don't remember. Do we put the grace notes before the beat or on the beat?"

"On the beat" was the reply.

"Oh, *stupido* Toscanini," he said. "They go before the beat." Now this created a problem, a tricky attack while the baton was descending. But he had first-class players and after a couple of times it was going well. You hear that change in the 1954 recording.

JL: And surely it is correct! Rather like a funeral tread on a muffled drum. Didn't he say after that rehearsal that he felt he had got as close as he could get to the performance he imagined in his mind?

RCM: Yes. He said, "I can't get any closer." But here was a significant detail, and in that one performance it was different from any of his others we have.

JL: Apropos of Frank, we were rehearsing the Mahler Fourth at Ravinia in 1974. At the beginning of the last movement, when the clarinet starts the main theme, the celli have these little glissandi. Frank just played the notes straight, deh-dum, deh-dum. At the break I said to him, "What happened to the glissandi?"

And he said, "They sound so silly."

I said, "What we need is a style you guys don't use anymore, but which you are always ready to apply in Bach arias, or if you play Verdi à la Toscanini. You have all kinds of possibilities for subtle and gentle glissandi that have become theoretical no-nos in this half of the twentieth century. This is one of those things."

The next day before the next rehearsal started he said, "How's this?" and he played those few bars in such a stylish and nostalgic manner I was delighted.

"That's it," I told him. "That's what it's supposed to be, that's what the notation means."

RCM: Frank was a wonder, one of the finest men I shall ever know.

JL: I feel the same way. He was a phenomenal artist, and I learned an incredible amount from him over the twenty years I had the good fortune to work with him.

I am now at a stage of life in which I am starting to feel that there are certain pieces I really don't ever need to hear again, and this, of course, reminds me of the things that I am confident I could hear forever and still find exciting. The things I don't need to hear again are not necessarily bad pieces, but they are things which I feel offer no opportunity for further discovery. I am quite sure I know everything that is there. (Not many pieces admittedly.) Then there are things, like *Don Giovanni,* for instance, where you can never feel that way, simply because every time you go back to them you find everything new.

I am now rehearsing *Così fan tutte* in a new production here, and it just gets more and more exciting as you get to know it better. It is one of my all-time favorite pieces. It is so subtle, the musical and dramatic nuances are perfect. A miraculous score. And I already "knew" it when I worked on it at Marlboro in 1956.

RCM: Artur Schnabel used to say that he concentrated on "music better than it ever can be performed."

JL: I'm sure. That's the way we really feel.

RCM: We agree that there is far more musical content in *Don Giovanni* than can ever be put into any one performance. I'm not talking about textual variations, but interpretive viewpoints that are consistent with the spirit of the score. There are pages that can be played a number of different ways and have something distinctive to say in each of these different versions.

Then there are pieces, the Liszt *Hungarian* Rhapsody No. 2 is a good example, where you feel it is possible to find a single performance that will reveal all the content that is there.

JL: And that doesn't mean that some of these things aren't damned good pieces. The number of things we encounter in life that are inexhaustibly rich may seem to be many, but they are relatively few. But those are the things we never tire of hearing, of studying, so long as the process of discovery continues. I suspect even the Mozart G Minor might get you down if you had to play it again and again in routine performances. Routine can destroy, because it stifles the imagination.

RCM: Some people think critics set artistic standards, but I have always insisted that standards are set by artists. It is the critic's responsibility to recognize the best that has been achieved and make that the benchmark for others.

JL: For me Szell's Cleveland, Chicago as I encountered it in 1971, the legacy of Reiner and the leadership of Solti, Toscanini's New York Phil-harmonic and his NBC Symphony in its last years—these for me are some of the American orchestral high-water marks.

RCM: These are the great orchestras in the classical tradition. I have to add, in the romantic tradition, Koussevitzky's Boston and Stokowski's Philadelphia.

JL: Surely. And on that note let us not forget the history of Berlin under Nikisch, Furtwängler, and Karajan, not to forget the remarkable achievements of the Vienna Philharmonic. I think we can say of several of these conductors that they were making their main impact in a certain type of repertory but they were not playing the wide range of scores that Szell, for example, programmed. Few, for a start, played a great deal of eighteenth-century music.

RCM: The irony is that if you can play Mozart well, really well, you can play anything. Schnabel used to orient a new pupil by playing a dou-ble-octave passage from something by Liszt and then saying, "This is easy."

He would then play the opening phrase of a Mozart slow movement and say, "*This* is difficult."

JL: To play the Mozart well you *must* be a true musician. What we can learn from the past, and this is something I talk about with orchestras all the time these days, is that the orchestra used to be like a treasure chest. The sounds an orchestra could make, the way the members of the orchestra could interact with one another, were extraordinary. An organ-ism like an orchestra is like nothing else in art. Nowadays many conduc-tors may work hard enough to get what they are after, but when they get it, the organism is denatured. You sit there and hear playing that is accu-rate but without vitality, imagination, commitment. You ask, When is it going to happen, when is the music going to take on the breath of life, and eventually you realize it isn't going to happen. The premises on which the performance is based are wrong. There is only black and white where the full spectrum is crucial.

February 2, 1996. Dialogue at the Met.

JL: It is impossible to live more than fifty years without seeing certain fundamental things change in the world around me while other things stay fixed. If the heart of your point of view is based on those fundamen-tals, it will be regarded differently than it was in the past because the world is no longer the same.

RCM: I have been attending opera for fifty-eight years—fifty of them with regular visits to the Met. It is easy for me to look back to productions that were highly praised that would be completely unacceptable today. Working on a history of opera in Chicago, I am growing more and more suspicious about the supposed golden ages of the past. Let them have a nostalgic glow, especially since we know the remarkable qualities of some of the voices, but it is probably wonderful that we cannot jump into a time machine and attend some of those performances. I am convinced that most of them would be gravely disappointing. I suspect that, never having attended a performance of *Aida* with Caruso, I give it greater reverence than I would if I knew it firsthand.

JL: Absolutely. As a historian you have to say that. Those performances were of their time, and inevitably we would find much of it dated, starting with an acting style that is not of our time. Look at the difference between the films of today and those of the 1930s. We can certainly enjoy old movies, as I do incessantly, but a new film made in the style of that day would most likely not be taken seriously.

RCM: When Mary Garden was to sing *Pelléas et Mélisande* in Chicago in 1910, one of the things the company did to make clear that nothing had been spared to achieve a notable production was to announce that a stage director had been imported from Paris. This suggests that in the normal order of things, operas were, perhaps, directed to some degree by the conductor—Tommy Beecham's early London seasons are a good example—but it appears that by and large the singers were free to do pretty much what they liked. The idea of a stage filled with singers doing exactly as they please scares me silly.

The Met of the early century run by Giulio Gatti-Casazza had some incredible voices, but you have to infer from the evidence that the performances as a whole, as opposed to the singing, were not what we would regard as superior today. The voices exploited the dramatic potential of the music, but the staging did not.

JL: Well, the performances are often less than superior today, God knows, but you're right. The emphasis was on the voices. You went to theater for drama and to the opera for singing.

RCM: One of the significant things that has happened in the twenty-five years you have been at the Met is that it has finally become a part of the theater of the twentieth century. We may surmise that in the beginning of this century the theatrical practices of the great opera houses were not greatly different from those of the major dramatic theaters. But the theater of the spoken word continued a steady development, with figures such as Max Reinhardt in Europe and Arthur Hopkins on Broadway showing the way.

In the 1940s what you saw at the Met and what you saw in a major Broadway house were two different things. Operatic staging and operatic acting were conventionalized, old-fashioned, a time warp back to the previous century. Rudolf Bing tried to deal with that by bringing people, Alfred Lunt for example, in from Broadway. But when the Met moved to this new house in 1966, it was a move in time as well as space. With the facilities of this modern theater, it could enter freely into the present century, and over the years it has.

Looking back, I conclude that of all the cultural centers built in this country in the sixties, Lincoln Center is by far the most successful in its long-term impact on the metropolitan area it serves. And architecturally it has aged well and has assumed a proper monumental status. The facade of the Met with the arches, the fountain—the shot used on TV—still is a thrilling sight.

More important, the Met, because of the length of its season, the scope of the repertory it offers each year, and the character and quality of the productions it stages, has become the finest opera-producing organization in the world. There are, of course, important things being done in Europe, but anything London, Vienna, or Milan can do, the Met can do equally well if not better. We both remember the years of reverse chauvinism. If you wanted to hear real opera you had to go abroad, although I reviewed a lot of real opera in Chicago. Real opera is the only kind of opera the Met has to offer these days.

JL: The challenge of Europe had to be faced. Once it became clear what was happening after the war, with the state-subsidized experimentation even in minor theaters, no leading American theater could stay with its old ways.

RCM: To overgeneralize, viewing its jaded history, the Met in the fifties was really two opera companies, a first-class one that was capable of exceptional things and a third-class one that offered mediocrity and routine. Both were functioning in the same house, sometimes on alternating nights. And when the Met came to Chicago, the provinces, we were not supposed to be able to tell the two apart. Mr. Bing became very indignant when we professed to do so.

JL: But that variation in quality is very hard to avoid when you are faced with a schedule that requires seven performances a week.

RCM: Of course. But the range of the swing in quality can be controlled. Forty years ago it was quite wide. Today, from what I have seen, it is quite narrow. One basic element is the size and character of the company. The Met today has far more artists who view it as a priority than it did in the past, and it has much less dead wood. There are very few internationally acclaimed singers who do not appear in its roster. That was not always the case. Elisabeth Schwarzkopf was a big star in both Chicago and San Francisco before she made her Met debut in the mid-sixties. The jokers said, "Oh, she's not ready for the Met; she still has a voice."

One of the mysteries of the Bing regime was that he, with great hullabaloo, fired Maria Callas. It seemed to many of us, who, of course, were not party to the inner workings of the company, that her complaints were justified—that power politics rather than music won. She found her roles and her schedule an unreasonably difficult combination. After a few Met visits to Chicago in that period I felt I could have given Bing a much better list of people to fire.

JL: You're defining what I had to face in 1973.

RCM: And we know what you did. To use your own words, you "turned the bloody thing around."

But let's change the subject completely and look at some very basic stuff. You lead with a stick. Where do you get your batons?

JL: They are made by Dick Horowitz. He makes batons for at least two dozen Met conductors. It's his hobby. He's principal timpanist and has been in the Met Orchestra fifty years. He's a brilliant player and is still the most enthusiastic and dedicated guy to work with that any conductor could want.

RCM: Before the war there was a man with the remarkable name of Richard Wagner who worked in the basement of the Vienna Opera. He made batons for all the major conductors associated with the theater. Furtwängler and Toscanini might have different aesthetic ideas, but they both used Wagner batons. Toscanini was shattered when the supply was cut off, so to lessen the trauma his doctor, who did woodworking, started making batons for him. In some of those early NBC seasons, he had to make quite a few. The rate of attrition was high.

JL: The new Horowitz model I've been using for about ten years has a big grip, tapered with a cork sphere at the end. It would be hard to lose, but I always have a spare on the stand in any case. It weighs practically nothing.

If we are doing a piece for a small group of players I may conduct it without a baton, and even with the full orchestra there are moments when, if I can put it down easily and get it back quickly, I feel the gestural language will be more appropriate or expressive if I just use my hands. But generally I feel I need the stick to reach the stage and to make the pulse clear to people who can't hear each other, say, from the far left of the pit to the far right.

RCM: What about working clothes? Checking the TV tapes over the years I see an alternation of black tie and white tie. Now it seems to be all white tie.

JL: For continuous evening work, I'm more comfortable in white tie because the tailcoat isn't confining. Even though I have a tuxedo jacket that I sometimes use, made with open vents, tails give me greater freedom. I now wear them 75 percent of the time. They are easier for all the TV tapings, matinees or otherwise, since they will look right when the show is aired in the evening.

RCM: Let's consider some questions of repertory. As a classicist, you have done seven Mozart operas, all the "great works."

JL: The fourteen others are set aside because they must compete for attention with the string of miracles that begins with *Idomeneo,* some of the most sublime musical achievements of our civilization. But, I grant you, they deserve to be heard more frequently.

RCM: We must not forget the little one-acter, *Der Schauspieldirektor,* which has never bonded with another opera to form a stable double bill.

JL: Well, what would you choose to precede it or follow it? One-act operas are always a problem to assemble into good bills. This is very sad because there are many very great one-acters. I've done some of them at schools and festivals. But they can be murder in a big theater.

RCM: Erich Leinsdorf told me there was a period in Met history when contracts demanded an intermission in every performance so the bar and restaurant could do business. He was once asked, "What opera do you want to precede *Das Rheingold?*" He replied, "*Nothing* precedes *Das Rheingold.*" So an intermission was inserted, over Leinsdorf's protests, while Wotan and Loge were descending to Nibelheim.

JL: That made it a longer journey than usual.

RCM: Let's talk about Richard Strauss.

JL: I love Strauss lieder and do a lot of it. I love some of the orchestra pieces, particularly *Don Quixote,* my favorite of the tone poems, and I have a real soft spot for *Death and Transfiguration.*

RCM: Especially, I would guess, what Solti calls "the big ascent into C major heaven. . . ."

JL: Exactly. As obvious as it is, as the work of a twenty-four-year-old, I find, it is filled with real brilliance. As for the other short tone poems, *Don Juan* and *Till,* I love them if I don't have to do them incessantly, and I did them so often in my youth. Reiner did remarkable things with *Ein Heldenleben,* but I cannot identify with the music the way he did. I have never conducted *Also sprach Zarathustra,* and I think I would have a hard time doing it with conviction. It wasn't a Szell piece either, you will recall.

RCM: There are plenty of other people performing this music. I suspect you might also like to stay away from the *Sinfonia domestica.*

JL: Actually, that piece intrigues me. Szell began to play it more frequently later in his life. It is something that someday I might like to do. One of the most marvelous experiences of my life was in Cleveland in 1964 while Szell was preparing this music, and, of course, we have his subsequent recording. The one other big tone poem that I might like to do is the *Alpine* Symphony. But not tomorrow.

There is another Strauss work like this. If you had told me thirty years ago that I would come to have my present love for *Metamorphosen,* I would have said, "Oh, please, I'm never going to be able to get into that." But, by God, now I really love it. The Philharmonic in Berlin was closed for renovation and the management asked us to put our programs into other venues in the city. So in 1991, I made a program which contained this score for the neighboring chamber hall. By then I was fascinated with the piece and most anxious to do it. I had the most marvelous time preparing it for the public, as two years before I had enjoyed performing the Oboe Concerto, another remarkable Strauss work that is not really "standard" repertory. I had always loved the late songs, and these few things really made me a passionate advocate of the late Strauss as much as *Ariadne* or *Rosenkavalier.*

But, you know, I don't like *Salome* very much. I have to take it in small doses. I did it only one season, 1973–74, and never went back to it. In that piece the heavy atmosphere and the style of the play itself wear on me very fast. And once it does, I have to put it away again, despite many strong things. If I hear one good performance of that work every few years, it's plenty for me. It is curious for me that some people think of *Elektra* and *Salome* as essentially the same.

For me, as usual, it's the specifics, the individuality of the work that reaches me most deeply. And, in those terms, *Elektra* is an opera I can never get enough of. The great dramatic score and the incredible libretto as well as the Greek source make *Elektra* a much more classic work. I would travel great distances to hear *Elektra* any time I had the chance.

RCM: There is nothing more classic than Greek tragedy, and I think in *Elektra* Strauss has caught the mood of the Greek theater even though he uses a musical idiom that is nothing if not of the early twentieth century. Real music from ancient Greece would probably sound very odd to us.

JL: Ravel showed us in *Daphnis et Chloé* his way of dealing with the same problem in another inspired way.

RCM: Indeed, he did.

JL: Every time we do *Ariadne auf Naxos,* I want to do it again. These pieces contain all the best elements of Strauss, so clever, fluent, so talented, so irresistibly subtle at times. But there is another element which wears well in some pieces and not as well in others. I have to call it a tendency to overwriting in the *Papiermusik* sense. There are many passages of this type in *Arabella,* the big tone poems, and even *Rosenkavalier.* I'm entranced by *Der Rosenkavalier* if the cast is just perfect. Anything less and it loses much of its appeal.

RCM: And Strauss called this his Mozart opera. Your loyalties are thoroughly consistent.

JL: I have also studied *Capriccio.* I have thought of *Arabella, Die Frau ohne Schatten,* but the truth is, for myself as a conductor they are not a high priority. The singers I loved in *Frau* were—are—always urging me to do it, but each time there was something I considered more pressing.

RCM: *Capriccio* becomes possible in a big house when the audience can follow the words. The Lyric in Chicago did it with great success that way. Now that you have the wonderful asset of Met Titles, where the language barrier has been broken, audience participation is even more intense. Some years ago you said the Met would have supertitles "over your dead body," but these are different.

JL: I meant projected titles, which are, and always will be, completely inappropriate in this house with its high proscenium. In fact, there are many seats from which they could not possibly be seen. What we have installed is a completely different kind of system, one that is unobtrusive and private. The text is right there facing you on the back of the seat in front of you, if you want it. My objection to projections is still valid, and it gave us the years we needed to conceptualize, design, and install this system, which is really miraculous.

RCM: One opera you have done only once, in concert in Cleveland, and never again, to my surprise, is *Fidelio.*

JL: I think I am finally going to do it onstage at the Met in 2000–2001.

RCM: It's difficult to cast.

JL: They are *all* difficult to cast—if you want the right person for every role. I suppose my problem with Beethoven, and with this opera in particular, is that I believe so strongly how it should go, which was strongly influenced by Toscanini. As a guest I didn't have time to recast the orchestra's ideas about Beethoven. The *Fidelio* performances we heard after Toscanini's death usually have had a slack, swimming quality. I don't see *Fidelio* that way at all. The Met has a very good production, but we need a new one now, and with my rapport here, and everything else we have done together, I am no longer concerned how difficult it would be to solve the problem if you can go at it with a certain specific style in mind and make it work in the more generous rehearsal time we have for a new production.

In recent years I have had some good Beethoven experiences. Salzburg called to ask, "Would you conduct a memorial concert for Karajan?" I said, How about the *Missa Solemnis*? "Fine. With what soloists?" I named four soloists. They got them. "With what chorus? The Vienna Chorus won't be free." I said I had had a great experience with the Leipzig and the Swedish Radio Choruses. How about combining them? Historically, when you put something together in Salzburg you get an argument on every point and you wind up going through such a struggle to arrive at what for you are pretty basic principles. But this project happened as if a magic wand had been passed over it. It was one of my most pleasurable experiences with such a difficult work.

Other great experiences were a cycle of the cello sonatas with Lynn Harrell, the piano concertos with Alfred Brendel, and the Gellert Lieder with Jesse Norman—all high-water marks for those involved.

RCM: You have had considerable success with what many would regard as extremely esoteric repertory, operas by Schoenberg.

JL: They are great, great pieces, and they must be put in front of audiences as frequently as possible.

RCM: You did *Moses und Aron* at Salzburg but never here.

JL: It's scheduled for 1998–99, about twenty years later than I wanted. We're ready now! And not only with *Moses und Aron* but also with the other masterpieces of twentieth-century opera, *Wozzeck, Lulu,* and so on. We are a couple of generations removed from the time of anguish the original productions produced. Now we can really give extraordinarily beautiful and well-realized performances of music that sometimes started life in ugly if well-intended presentations.

RCM: I have insisted for years that much of the protest against new works arose from the fact that they were badly played. If a Beethoven symphony were performed that way the public would recognize the fact, but a new score is totally vulnerable. It can be butchered in a premiere and so many will say, "Oh, that's modern music for you!"

JL: These works are extremely beautiful. As soon as you confront them in that form, your opinions have to change. Schoenberg knew *Moses und Aron* was filled with beautiful things. He was afraid that generations of people accustomed to older music would not see it for what it was. There was, after all, so little encouragement of his work in his lifetime.

Stravinsky had the same difficulty. A performance of *Le Sacre du Prin-*

temps that is all together and perfectly neat solves only half the problem. Stravinsky said, in effect, Don't forget, this is a Russian orchestra piece, and if the conductor makes it a technical exercise, or a lesson in arithmetic, it is not a true representation of the score. There has to be passion. It must be precise, but with the great big, lusty physical sound of a Russian orchestra.

RCM: You have conducted three early Stravinsky operas but, so far, never *The Rake's Progress*.

JL: I've wanted to do it for years, and a new production is scheduled for 1997–98. It's funny about the *Rake*. It's hard to do well. It became dated while it sat there all but unplayed for years after a difficult premiere "birth." But it's still such a lively, inspired, and moving work. And now it is played all over the world and people are beginning to really appreciate its originality and its many unique qualities.

RCM: Let's stay with the Russians for a moment. I'm surprised you have never done an opera by Prokofiev.

JL: As you pointed out before, I haven't done much Prokofiev at all—the ballet suites, two symphonies, a piano concerto, the Sinfonia Concertante and cello sonata with Lynn Harrell, and *Lieutnant Kijé.* That is one of my favorite Reiner recordings. I don't know the Prokofiev operas as thoroughly as I would like and I think what will probably happen is we will do *War and Peace* and *The Gambler* with Valery Gergiev and maybe follow it with *The Fiery Angel* or something like that. But every time I got near these pieces, something else was a priority. I'd like to get to know the material better. But as a conductor I have other priorities.

RCM: Is the situation with the Shostakovich operas similar?

JL: Very. We all know the works starting with *The Nose* and leading to the scandal of *Lady Macbeth of Mtsensk.* But all this lies outside my immediate experience, and that immediacy is something I have to secure. *Lady Macbeth* was in the Met repertory for the first time last season, led by James Conlon, and will return soon.

RCM: I have seen both works staged in this country, and they are exciting theater. I'm surprised you have never done an opera by Hindemith.

JL: Which one? What would you have me do?

RCM: The best is the one they were offering across the plaza at the State Theater last autumn, *Mathis der Maler.* It's a truly powerful work.

JL: I flirted with that years ago and, as you know, didn't do it then. I flirted with *Cardillac* also and talked with Jean-Pierre Ponnelle about doing it. There were things about it that I found fascinating. But perhaps those two incidents simply produced in the end a negative attitude. What I ought to do with *Mathis* is to study it, more thoroughly; then I can make some intelligent decisions about what to do in my sixties. But I already have a long wish list.

RCM: There is always a shortage of comic operas. One that might deserve a revival is Weinberger's *Schwanda the Bagpiper.* It had seven performances at the Met in 1931 in a production that apparently was not funny enough to make it a success. But the music is lively and attractive, although a little repetitious. I wonder what could be done with it today.

Two American operas that I think are eminently stageworthy are Carlisle Floyd's *Of Mice and Men* and his *Susannah.*

JL: We are going to do *Susannah* in 1998–99, sharing the Chicago production. At one time when I was looking at American works, new things, or things we had done before, I became familiar with *Of Mice and Men,* and I agree it's a first-rate piece. I wouldn't be surprised if we offered it in the near future. It, like *Susannah, Vanessa,* etc., will gradually become part of the repertory and played regularly.

RCM: Surely, then, it is time to take a second look at the first opera heard in the new house, Barber's *Antony and Cleopatra,* but the revised version. It was done in Chicago and played well. We all know the story of the opening night fiasco, but it leaves the impression that Barber wrote a weak opera, which is not the case.

JL: I know the revised score. It's better than the original version—much better balanced. Our next world premiere opera production will be 1999–2000, *The Great Gatsby* by John Harbison—the third world premiere in eight years.

RCM: Basic rule: You can't expect the public to know music it never hears. The scores exist, but they have not been given a chance to establish themselves.

JL: I think the opera world is changing for the better in that respect. High on the list of the operas I haven't done—and want to do—are pieces like Berlioz's *Benvenuto Cellini.* I have been trying to get tenors with the right kind of voice to take the time, look at the music, and consider if it may not be for them. But, oh, it can be so difficult to cast a work of this type. You say, "I want to do it," and then you have to face reality. Who is going to sing it?

I am finally going to do *La Cenerentola.* It's a piece I have always wanted to do, and now it's on the schedule for 1997–98. The Met National Company did it in 1965, but it has never been produced in the main house. Someday I want to do *William Tell.* It won't happen soon—another project for my sixties—but someday I want to see what that piece feels like on the stage. This list of pieces I would like to do someday is really endless.

RCM: What about Poulenc? *Carmélites* and *Les Mamelles de Tirésias* were added to the repertory during your seasons, but with other conductors.

JL: There have been more than a few times here at the Met when there was something I would have liked to do myself but could not because of other priorities, scheduling, etc. We revive that *Carmélites* production quite often, and each time I nearly do it. But then some other pressing thing comes up and I have to give it away again.

RCM: Another opera that I would consider great for this house is Ravel's *L'Heure espagnole*.

JL: I adore Ravel's theater pieces. We have a brilliant production of *L'Enfant*. That, for me, is a real masterpiece. Someday I must do a fully staged *Daphnis et Chloé*. We have not had *L'Heure* in seventy years. Perhaps, instead of reviving our old French triple bill, we can put the two Ravel one-acters together. That could be really tempting. Perhaps we'll put some early Stravinsky (say, *Renard*) together with *Mamelles* or *L'Enfant*.

RCM: While we are discussing things French, totally missing from your repertory is the work of Jules Massenet. For me, he lacks universality. He belongs to *la belle époque*. But he represents it so well.

JL: You don't like Massenet? Well, I love it. But like the bel canto repertory, you need the right voices. Sing it or forget it! You could say that about all opera, but let's face it, Mozart or Strauss or Stravinsky have many strengths that will be felt even with less than ideal singers here or there. But in many of these nineteenth-century Italian and French scores, 95 percent of the work depends on how successfully the singers express the music and drama in the singing itself.

I love some of those pieces, and I think you will see some of them come back. More and more of the next generation are learning to sing in this style. For example, the recent *Faust* revival at the Met had all the right people—Renée Fleming, Richard Leech, Sam Ramey, and Dwayne Croft. This is repertory I know very well, but what I have tended to do is *Les Troyens, Pelléas et Mélisande, Carmen,* and *Les Contes d'Hoffmann*.

Years ago I said to Maria Ewing and Neil Shicoff that if we ever found the right little place to do it—the Met is too large—I would like to do *Werther.* But the theater has to be small enough that you can see every nuance, every eye blink. Massenet and a lot of other people were writing for European theaters. It is intimate opera, but we know certain scores that became staples of the repertory in big houses in the United States. Give *Manon* a strong cast and it will hold up in a large house. But the reason I have not given priority to Massenet is not because I dislike the music. It's because I want to do it justice, and it requires artful attention to its specific needs.

RCM: *Louise* is another opera that really deserves revival.

JL: Don't worry. Renée Fleming will do it one day.

RCM: I don't need any explanation why you have not done an opera by Michael Tippett.

JL: In my view, they are strictly for home consumption. Like certain pleasant wines you find in Europe, they don't travel well. Britten, of course, is a completely different story. It's not my imagination, is it, but you can always spot a British critic. If you read an article about music and someone clips off the byline so you can't tell who wrote it, the content can tell you where it came from. There will be a glowing reference to Bax, or Delius, or Tippett, or Brian and you know the author has to be British. You have to respect British pride in their artistic achievements; I often wish American composers got the same support, but it is often mixed with this naive chauvinism and a lack of perspective. British critics would like you to believe that the London Symphony has a recognizable timbre of the type of the Berlin Philharmonic and the Vienna Philharmonic. While it has other virtues this is not one of them.

RCM: Britten's *Billy Budd* is in the Met repertory for next season and *Peter Grimes* the following year.

JL: *Grimes* is the only Britten opera I flirted with conducting at the Met. Jon Vickers has now been succeeded by younger singers who can deal forcefully with the role. Neil Shicoff is coming back, and we have people like Ben Heppner and Philip Langridge, so it will come up often in the next seasons. But I bet when the time comes there will be something else I have to do instead. And I say in advance, I'm sorry. But one must always make the right choice. It's part of my responsibility.

RCM: The Met public demands variety in repertory and gets it. In other cities where the annual offerings are perhaps a third of the number of works you can stage, diversification is not pursued so vigorously. A quarter of the repertory of the Lyric Opera of Chicago for 1996–97 and 1997–98 is Puccini. Apparently they feel suburban subscribers demand this. The Met clearly feels no such pressure.

JL: But, Robert, don't forget that a season is not a "whole." It flows from one week into the next one. It's not a preordered unit. The Met schedule contains works of art, but *it* is never intended to be one.

We do our share of Puccini, God knows, but the pieces Met audiences traditionally find appealing are also those of Mozart, Verdi, Wagner, and Richard Strauss. This is where I have concentrated my attention, as well as the many great operas by less prolific composers.

RCM: If you were to give a quarter of your repertory to Puccini you would practically be doing his complete works annually, which would be absurd.

JL: And unnecessary.

RCM: Verdi plays an enormous role in your work at the Met. Of his twenty-six operas you have conducted seventeen. Of the nine missing ones *I due Foscari* and *Nabucco* are surely of interest, but if you never do *Alzira* it will be no loss, I think.

JL: You know, I was once asked to do it in concert performance, and I turned it down after working my way through it carefully. I feared it would be the *only* Verdi score I couldn't find a relationship to, so I didn't want to do it.

RCM: Opera America has issued figures for the 1993–94 season and informs us that half of the six most frequently produced operas in the United States are by Puccini.

JL: *Bohème, Tosca, Butterfly.*

RCM: Right.

JL: And the other three are probably *Carmen, Traviata,* and *Aida.*

RCM: There are years when you would have been right. In this case it's *The Magic Flute* rather than *Aida,* which I am sure you will regard as encouraging.

JL: But only relatively! I still love *Aida!*

RCM: You have only done one production of *Butterfly* in your career, and that wasn't at the Met. To avoid a grotesquely overplayed work like that is an achievement of some kind.

JL: True, but it's not because I don't like it. I love it! It's because it was never that high a priority for me. I was able to do works I considered more important—that is, more important for *me.*

Whether or not you can do this repertory well depends a lot on whom you've got onstage. My better verismo work has always involved strong casting—Domingo, Pavarotti, Stratas, Scotto, etc. You know, *Manon Lescaut* may not have the fine balance of elements of *La Bohème,* but for someone writing his first full-length opera at the same time that Verdi's *Falstaff* was receiving its premiere, that's an incredibly thrilling score. I come back to Puccini because these are such great theater pieces. All of them. I haven't done *Fanciulla* yet, in a sense his most remarkable opera, and I haven't done a *Butterfly* in twenty-five years, but I've performed some of the other things quite often. The *Trittico* is also, like *Bohème,* a masterpiece.

RCM: Puccini's stature was not obvious from the start. I have here a review from the *Kansas City Star* of December 10, 1900, of a Met tour production. The new piece, the critic writes, is "altogether too scholarly to ever rival *Faust.* It does not stream with melody; there is nothing to whistle unless it is the theme of the duet in the third act. Maybe the masses will grow to love it, however, though it is doubtful."

What do you think that dreary academic exercise might be?

JL: I've got to know. I can see it coming. . . .

RCM: That tuneless horror was our old friend *La Bohème,* and with Melba, no less, as Mimi. To be just to critics, the following April in Boston the redoubtable Philip Hale called *Bohème* a triumph, although adding "it might shock the purists." I am not sure whether he is referring to Puccini's harmony or the morals of his characters. But I suspect he is talking about harmony. Reading these things you realize that a century ago the model opera was probably *Faust,* a big, expansive melodic work. Puccini had not the slightest intention of writing operas of that type. He seduced the public with something new, and it went along with him. But reading this review you understand how a critic, possibly raised on Rossini and Donizetti, who has gone through the adjustment to Verdi, now encounters Puccini and really goes into culture shock.

JL: Absolutely. That must have been an amazing period. Do you know what piece is really fun to do once in a while? *Turandot.*

RCM: I can well understand why.

JL: It has a fantastic first act, everything's there and builds from this. OK, it has some problems at the end. But the conception of it is amazing.

RCM: There is a certain irony that your Met career began with *Tosca,* but it has played a relatively minor role in your repertory since then.

JL: It is on the schedule for the tour to Japan in 1997. It just wasn't one of those pieces I had to keep doing. A lot of other pieces are. But *Tosca* is lots of fun, like conducting a great old Hitchcock movie. It needs the most stylish singers.

RCM: But many feel your Italian repertory does not draw heavily on the verismo period.

JL: But I did *Francesca da Rimini,* an unfamiliar work, and I do *Chénier* and *Cav* and *Pag,* and I recorded *Adriana Lecouvreur.* I love *Gioconda* and would gladly do it if I had the right singers. Who does all these things, *Wozzeck, Pelléas, Italiani, Barbiere, The Pearl Fishers,* and the *Ring*?

RCM: Well, going to the other end of the nineteenth century, there is very little opera from the bel canto school. The revival begun by singers like Maria Callas and Joan Sutherland appears to have slowed down since they left the stage.

JL: The problem, of course, is casting—finding singers who are gifted for and trained in this style. A great Verdi singer can be a lousy "bel canto" singer, and vice versa. It's a significantly different thing. Possibly if we produced a lot more of this repertory, we would discover more voices, but I'm not so sure. And in the meantime?

There are big differences. In terms of the opera theater of that time, the bel canto operas were never intended to be long-lived. They were like Broadway theater. Do you really think people will want to hear *Cats* in 2090? Verdi and Wagner were relatively posterity-oriented. Even if you could suddenly find enough singers to do all the bel canto repertory around the world, my guess is that you would still not do all of it. It would seem that there was too much of it that just isn't first-class, or even second-class, music.

RCM: The reason we accept certain vicissitudes in late Verdi and Mozart, Wagner, and Strauss is because of the content of the piece. The more you present Mozart, the more we find there are good new Mozart voices, and it could happen with late nineteenth-century German works.

JL: In Wagner there is a tremendous amount on which to concentrate other than ideal vocalization! There is text and philosophy and orchestration . . . and . . . and. . . . In bel canto there is no other way except to sing the hell out of it, and much as you might love those pieces, if the singer hasn't got the voice and the technique and the imagination, forget it. It won't go. In Wagner, if you have a less than ideal cast, you still have an opera. In bel canto, if you haven't the singers, you haven't anything.

RCM: And this does not mean that opera must always be big and beefy. What I was hearing in *Così* this week was chamber music. Not chamber music for a drawing room. It has to be modified to carry in a big theater, but the spirit of chamber music is there, the essence of the writing.

JL: Right.

RCM: The interaction between the orchestra and that ensemble was simply amazing.

JL: Apart from doing it because I love it, there is the attendant pleasure that people who know the work intimately, and can hear what is happening, have the kind of experience you know will stay with them. That doesn't happen regularly. One wishes it happened more often. It comes from going way past the point where everyone is still concentrating on fundamentals to a point where they are free to express themselves fully in the nuances and details. As Nabokov wrote, "There is no delight without the detail."

RCM: If you go to Rembrandt's house in Amsterdam you find it's full of drawings. He was a master draftsman. He could take a rough piece of paper and a bit of charcoal and with a few strokes put down all the important elements of a picture. Then, if he wished, he could elaborate it on paper, or with etching tools on a copper plate, or with paint on canvas. But under it all was the purity, the strength, the integrity of those first lines.

One can sit in amazement in *Così* listening to how you control the musical line. One reason, Jim, that you are a splendid conductor is that you know how to draw. The line is never allowed to go slack. It is always in motion. The rhythm is always precisely defined.

JL: Even in soft articulation, I hope. We are trying very hard.

RCM: You draw in sound, of course, extracting the most from a simple phrase. And if the line is correct, that is the foundation on which you add color, dynamics, nuance, and the rest. If you are trained in the classical tradition, you can go on to anything else.

JL: You have to ask, what is the source? Where does it come from? And for me, and for instrumental composers for hundreds of years, the source is the voice. If you understand that aspect of classicism, the singing voice projecting the expressive content of a text and the sheer individuality of the voice itself, you are at the root of it all.

RCM: Charles Munch in rehearsal was always after two things, light playing and breathing. Of course, breathing was something the winds did automatically, but he wanted the strings to play the same way—a light, lyric tone punctuated as if the violinist was truly singing on the instrument and had to take a breath.

JL: Exactly. I notice how excellent players with a symphonic background come into the Met Orchestra and in the course of the first season their point of view changes—they start to follow the voices. *Everybody* is singing. They should have been playing that way always, but it has become a lost art for many maddening reasons.

RCM: The public sees you functioning as a conductor, but out of the public eye you also head the artistic department that is really the heart of the Met's operations. Can we talk now about some administrative matters? How far in advance do you plan these days?

JL: In this season, 1995–96, we are now discussing new productions for the season 2000–2001. That's four years from our next opening night. The first thing we discuss is what we feel the new productions should and can be. That dictates several things. It tells you what singers are going to be available to you in those periods. It tells you the styles of the new works, so you have some way of knowing how they must be rehearsed. You can see the interaction of the revivals and the new works. Then you decide what you want to carry over from the previous season in order to be able to play seven times a week. This explanation is very compressed—shorthand—but I think it's clear.

You have to anticipate bringing something back before the gap gets too big between revivals. When you rehearse the *Ring,* one of your major things to think about is "When will we do it next?" so we can plan what rehearsals it will need to get it ready then, too. If a work has been carefully prepared, it can easily be picked up and further developed after a season or two. But beyond a certain point, and it's different for every piece and in every different set of circumstances, you cannot count on the earlier preparation following through to the next revival.

In the 1999–2000 season we have already agreed on repertory and the major offers for leading roles are out. Leading singers usually are booked about three to four years in advance, but it's sometimes advantageous to get them even longer ahead. The casting will be finished over the balance of the spring and summer of 1996. Of course, it never fails that there are some things that never get resolved until six months before they happen. But most things are in the pipeline four years ahead.

RCM: What do you do in the case of someone who is singing well now but, as the contract draws near, suffers some kind of catastrophic event and no longer is singing to your anticipated standard?

JL: You do everything under the sun. It depends on what the problem is. You have to use your best and most carefully considered judgment. It helps that there are five of us involved in the process. If it is a situation of real decline that you don't think will turn around, you then have to go through a very often painful process of assessing what it is he can still do and whether you can find someone free and appropriate at this moment to replace him in that cast.

You have to face the fact that when each project arrives at the point when you are finally doing it, when you actually go into rehearsal, years after you thought it up, some things are going to be different from what you planned. Some things are worse; some things are better. You try to be right as often as you can be, but it is the unexpected problems that are hardest to deal with.

When someone is going through a terrible period, you may have no way of knowing if it is going to right itself or not. Did her mother just die? Is he going through a health crisis? Is her marriage breaking up? Is the fact that he has been singing too heavily for years finally catching up with him? Et cetera. This list can be hair-raisingly long. Body aging is, after all, a natural process, and thus much easier to deal with. The problem is the singer who is fading quickly, and then it may be difficult to estimate where he is going to be in five years—maybe much further downhill than you think, maybe not.

We only contract singers far in advance so we are sure we have them if the gods are smiling and everything goes successfully in the interim.

That's the only way you can do it. Since everyone in the profession does it, everyone has to do it essentially the same way. Otherwise you have to feel confident that, on shorter notice, you will find a singer you know is ready, or nearly so, and free and healthy and willing, and who can do the role. But that way is hazardous because the singer may have a higher or different priority of what or where she wants to sing, and certain big roles cannot be learned by a new singer on that kind of notice. So just as you are ready to engage her, you lose her to another project somewhere else. All casting is difficult.

RCM: One other factor is *your* availability. During these twenty-five years at the Met you have been blessed with abundant good health, so if you wished to devote an enormous amount of physical and psychic energy to the company, these resources were available to you; and your workload could be sustained without any undue cost to your well-being.

JL: It is still that way, and I am very grateful for that! There is an occasional week when I may be overtired, but I snap back. After all, is there anything worth doing that isn't tiring in some way? And this work is so exhilarating! I am trying to learn that when you are fifty-five you don't do everything you used to do when you were twenty-five, but I believe passionately in continuity. I am trying to work out for any given future season how to redevelop and rework operas in the right balance and proximity in various styles, but in a way that also increases the breathing space a little.

In the beginning I did more because it was essential to keep developing the chorus, the orchestra, the ensemble, the whole spirit of the way we were working here. In the eighties you will find seasons when I was conducting as many as a hundred performances—110 for two years. We had a labor dispute and part of my job was to pick up the pieces afterwards. It was the constant presence of a music director, and longer periods of close work with him, that made Szell's Cleveland Orchestra what it was. You might say these were the days in which the Met assumed its current distinctive character. After the progress was well along, I did not have to be around for quite the same amount of time.

RCM: You have been with the Met for twenty-five seasons; your heavy Met performance schedule was concentrated in seventeen.

JL: Maybe someone could do it with less density but not with less continuity. Now the orchestra plays concerts, which it didn't do before. The orchestra records much more than it did before. I tour with the orchestra alone, and with the company as a whole entity. At the heaviest time I often conducted between eighty and a hundred performances, depending on my tour participation. Now my season is based on fifty to sixty opera performances, plus whatever touring and recording we do.

RCM: During that period of intensive concentration you were often criticized by some for not inviting more conductors of international reputation to work at the Met. In Europe, where every big city has an opera house and an orchestra, one might almost simultaneously be doing opera in one city and concerts in another. In the United States, if you come to do an opera, that's pretty much it.

JL: It's a mistake to think I wanted to create some sort of monopoly. I've invited everybody all the time. But if they want to do a new production, they have to allow for a month or even more of rehearsal, depending on the nature of the work. Then, after it opens, you can't do most operas more than twice a week between Monday and Saturday. Some you can, but with three performances of one work in one week there are not enough rest days in succession for the singers, and the other operas that are playing in repertory with it would get short shrift by default.

The problem for a guest conductor is that he has to want to give that kind of time, and he must accept two other facts of life. He can't do anything else substantial while he's doing this. There is no time to fly around and do symphonic engagements in the middle of the run. Therefore the only income he will make is a per diem for the rehearsal period and then his performance fees, which are in no way comparable here to those at many European theaters, even many relatively small ones. A singer or conductor can earn an incredibly larger fee at the government-subsidized Vienna Staatsoper than is possible here. You wouldn't believe it. I mean 100 percent, even more than that on occasion. Not to mention the provinces—Bari!—huge fees. And though New York is loved by many, some artists cannot deal with it.

The conductors who have come have been an interesting group, though many come here and then cannot come back after they become more involved with their own home bases. Haitink did *Fidelio,* but then he became music director of Covent Garden. Claudio Abbado did *Don Carlo,* but then he went to La Scala, Vienna, Berlin, et cetera.

They could no more leave their home base for a long period in the season than I can leave mine. Carlos Kleiber was not interested in new productions per se because he wanted to work on the opera and not on the problems of costumes and scenery. He conducted with singular success works in the current repertory that he particularly felt like doing. We are in constant touch. Now he calls himself a "semi-retired" conductor, which is unfortunate for all of us who love him and his work.

I always was sorry that, try as I might, I never could get Szell back to opera. By the time I knew him, there was just no talking him into it. He wasn't going to Bayreuth, he wasn't going to Salzburg even though they were still inviting him. One day I suggested, "Let's put together a Mozart cast and do a Mozart opera in concert form with the Cleveland Orchestra. I'll even find covers for you for all the roles." He said, "It will never work. Just watch. We will be this close and then the Susannas will both be sick, and we will have to bring in someone we don't know." He had become completely negative. Even though he originally loved opera, and conducted it for years in Europe and eventually here, he had seen how complex it was to hold together, and he was at a stage of life where the orchestra was an extension of him but singers no longer were. He could not deal with them on a pragmatic basis, which was a pity.

RCM: He was the conductor of my first encounter with *Rosenkavalier* on a stage. I'll never forget it. Apparently sometime in the early sixties Kurt Adler in San Francisco invited him to do *Don Giovanni* and offered him such a perfect cast that he accepted. Then a few weeks later there was a letter saying that a cast change was necessary, and soon thereafter another letter of the same sort.

Szell said, "I wrote him and said, 'Dear Kurt, While we are still friends, find another conductor.' And he did. It was most amicable."

JL: He wanted singers whom he knew were thoroughly seasoned in this music. For me the fascination of new singers is in introducing them to the repertory. Szell could not abide the kind of ad hoc preparation that you would find in most American opera companies then.

RCM: In the sixties I was giving a lot of time to reviewing Mahler symphony performances and, as a result, giving them a lot of study. Szell invited my wife, Kathleen, and me to dinner one night, one of those superlative domestic productions that proved he could have made a career as a chef had he wished, and we got to talking over the cognac. I said I was surprised he had never performed the Mahler Sixth, and he replied that in the Vienna of his youth you were expected to respect Mahler the conductor and scorn Mahler the composer.

I objected. This is a marvelous work, I insisted. Szell was the only musician I knew who had two grand pianos in his house, one up, one down, so he could get to the keyboard quickly without bothering with stairs. But on this rare occasion we did not move to the piano because the

Sixth Mahler was not something he was prepared to play from memory. We went over the score together.

When we returned to the hotel, my wife was upset that I had gone after him too severely, so the next morning when I met him in his dressing room I apologized.

"Oh, no," he said. "That was an extremely interesting discussion." And, of course, you and I both know. He learned it. He played it. We even have a CD of it!

JL: Robert, we conductors are tremendously susceptible to that kind of suggestion. If I know a person who knows music well, who has an active mind, and who spends a lot of time listening to my work, when that person tells me something, even if I resist it at the moment, I process it in some way. I'm sure that that Mahler Sixth performance came at least in part from that conversation. You got him to concentrate on it the way that kind of discussion can do. A staff member or a musician in the orchestra could not penetrate his accustomed manner of self-assurance, but you could because you had a completely fresh perspective. I was there when he did the piece, but I did not know why he had suddenly become interested in the score right then.

RCM: A great many conductors learn a lot of music when they are young not just because they want to but because they have to, but as they grow older they become busy, or artistically calcified, or sometimes even lazy, and the steady inward flow of new things stops.

JL: They get locked in themselves and the music they know best.

RCM: There is no more appalling example than Toscanini with the New York Philharmonic. This was a period in which his repertory should have expanded. He flirted with things, Bruckner, for example, stimulated by his work with the Vienna Philharmonic at Salzburg, but his repertory did not grow significantly beyond a certain point.

Since we are talking about Toscanini, before we close, let me say that I truly believe that you have succeeded in creating at the Met the kind of opera house Toscanini wanted it to be.

JL: This was always the idea uppermost in my mind. I wanted to realize the standards associated with his work at La Scala in his happiest years there.

RCM: Obviously you have not succeeded to the degree that you can throttle back and say the job is done. For one thing, having achieved a certain level, there is the constant fight to preserve and develop it.

JL: I just keep trying harder, for the company's artistic development and my own. If the gods are smiling, I can see a light often!

March 19, 1996. Dialogue in Philadelphia.

RCM: That first run-through of the opening movement of the Mahler Third was good enough to satisfy many people, who would probably say, If it sounds that good, why do they need to rehearse any further?

JL: The "why" was evident as soon as we went back to do it again. You return to the first page of the score and start to work! I played the first movement practically without stopping because if I don't do it that way I can't get an accurate image of the place we are starting again after sixteen years' absence from here. My questions are "Where are they? What's their relationship to this piece? Have the acoustics on the stage changed any? What has changed inside the orchestra since we worked together last?"

What I felt very strongly was they haven't played the piece much at all—the last performance must have been sometime in the seventies, about twenty years ago. But they were quiet and concentrated, interested to work with me again and to work on this music. If I had tried to do in the first half of that rehearsal what I did during the second half, I could not have worked with any certainty. I had to get my bearings first. In the second half I turned to the last movement because we are never going to be able to play that movement straight through the morning of the concert and have it be any good in the evening. I've been doing this piece with regularity for the same twenty years, so I know. It is much better that they feel the enormous arc of the finale today, so they can get to know it again, and understand what has to be sustained when they come to it in the context of the five preceding movements.

RCM: Stokowski insisted he never would rehearse on the day of a concert. "You can ask them to give it to you once," he told me. "If you get everything you want in the rehearsal, the public will be cheated."

JL: He had a point, but I don't have that luxury. If I don't rehearse Thursday morning there will be no concert, since we are starting Tuesday. It was very interesting to me that there are a lot of new people in the orchestra, new principals, both the first trombone and the first trumpet starting with very major assignments, but both big, big talents.

What you said a moment ago, this thing about what people hear and what they call upon to form a judgment for themselves, how they would express the experience they have, is very mysterious indeed. What comes from knowledge, what comes from misunderstanding? When you, Robert, listen to a performance, after years of doing so on an almost daily basis, you know afterwards what has taken place. But many of the audience do not.

Going back to the Ravinia years, I was fully aware that many performances were unfinished, underrehearsed standard repertory, but they were perfectly satisfactory to thousands of listeners. Obviously we did not share the same definition of success.

RCM: I have a nightmare about a day in American music when you have a really well-trained orchestra that can play the standard works with minimal or no preparation, and symphonic music survives because you can, with modest investment in rehearsal time, offer a performance "good enough" that the majority of the public will accept it. In a way, this is a description of the London orchestra scene as I knew it forty years ago. Of course it will be a sham. Conductors like yourself will turn to drink, or concentrate on opera, or leave for central Europe, or retire to a farm, because you can't function that way. But mediocrities are always ready to take over, and they will not be frustrated in the slightest because the superlative performance is beyond them anyway. Something like this happened in central Europe under the Nazis when Jewish musicians were unable to work and it was more important to be racially or ideologically pure than talented.

I first heard the Chicago Symphony live in 1938, and in time I thought I knew it well. In 1946 Bruno Walter came to Orchestra Hall as guest conductor, and the orchestra was transformed. I had never heard it working on that level before. He had the genius, and he had the necessary rehearsals. Ideally, everyone who followed him on that stage should be judged by that standard, and the following autumn Artur Rodzinski tried to make that standard the norm for playing from week to week. So the politicians on the front stands who did not want to work that hard started a slander campaign and had him fired in 1948. The standards went back to the previous level, but there was no great hue and cry from the public. I had to wonder how many heard what Rodzinski was accomplishing.

JL: You're wondering if much of the work I do between the first run-through and the final performance is on a level that many members of the audience won't hear, and hence won't get much satisfaction from it.

RCM: Alas, yes.

JL: But if the orchestra knows the difference between the way we began and the way we finished, they will play in a completely different manner, taking collective pride in what they have achieved! That difference can be sensed. It can be like night and day to an audience. The main issue for me, and probably for every player in an ensemble as fine as the Philadelphia Orchestra, is that we don't think of producing an acceptable product for a potential consumer. It's not like making soap. If it's not good enough for us, that's what matters. The public, after all, are music lovers, but they are busy with other tasks. They cannot know the piece the way we do.

RCM: The public, I have learned, has a very vague, fanciful idea of what happens in symphony orchestra rehearsals and what a conductor really does, based in part on what experience they may have had with student and community orchestras. They may think, for a start, that a lot of time is spent correcting wrong notes, whereas in fact that is almost never done.

JL: Absolutely right. The members of the Philadelphia Orchestra don't play wrong notes unless there is clearly an error in their part or they have an accident reading it. Anyone can blink and lose his place for a moment. Do you ever notice that someone almost never coughs or sneezes on stage? They are concentrating too hard.

RCM: My conclusion is that, to use Erich Leinsdorf's terminology, you give the public a 100 percent performance, even though they may not be able to tell you why that performance is so exciting.

JL: They feel it. Right.

RCM: Many Chicago Symphony subscribers probably agree that the most exciting events of the season are those led by Solti and Boulez. But ask the guy on the aisle across from you for detail to support this conclusion and, except in the rare case, you won't get it.

Koussevitzky used to wail in rehearsals, "It is not togezzer, it is no good if it is not togezzer." Hearing Solti and Boulez we hear that it is "togezzer." Well, that's a nice start. But, in fact, one can offer 80 percent performances for quite an extended time and there may not be much protest. Leinsdorf in a wonderful talk to the American Academy of Arts and Sciences suggested that if a baseball team went on a losing streak and dropped quite a few games, everyone knew it. But if the local orchestra "dropped" an equal number of concerts, very few people might realize it—starting, unfortunately, with some august critics.

JL: That is absolutely right. Moreover, you can be sitting at a performance that is virtually flawless and, somehow, still have the feeling that the content is utterly missing. Somehow or other they are playing it all, but it is as if they haven't digested it or aren't communicating it. It's empty, vacant, processed cheese slices all exactly alike. And then, at another performance which is far from flawless, you can have the impression of the full commitment of the performers, which generates real communication.

RCM: Virgil Thomson complained that in some works the playing of Koussevitzky's Boston Symphony didn't seem to be about anything except how beautifully the Boston Symphony could play.

JL: There is a danger there. One of the things that helps when you conduct your own orchestra a lot is not to polish everything. You polish things in different ways and for different purposes. You can avoid the possibility of repetition deadening their awareness of the content. Here in Philadelphia they have not seen enough of me to be routined, especially in a piece like the Mahler Third, where every movement has radically different difficulties.

The 100 percent performance is necessary. You don't work to the standard of the patrons in boxes, you work to the standard of distinguished musicians, the vision of composers. If you permit the gradual erosion of standards, you will someday face the time when there no longer are any standards. It is essential to give an audience more than everyone is going to understand, better that than to retreat from your standard. It's your standard, after all, that the audience is paying to hear.

RCM: Right. So long as there are things to be discovered, discovery will take place. You have to provide room for growth for those with the capacity for growth.

JL: One thing is for sure. If you go and guest conduct an orchestra whose music director really rehearses, even if what he rehearses is not to your taste, you will get better results there than you will from an orchestra that is not working hard regularly. If somehow it is all in a general disarray, you will never get anywhere. In a general disarray you haven't enough time for people to learn or listen where to go and what to do.

RCM: Beginning on some foundation of order, even the wrong one, is completely different from beginning with no order at all.

JL: Right. This is fascinating stuff. One of the last summers at Ravinia, I discovered that Daniel [Barenboim] had rehearsed and conducted quite frequently in the season a Strauss tone poem I was doing. This was unknown to me, since I always made my programs independently of what they were doing downtown, but I wound up with something he had done a lot. You could tell from the expressions on the faces of the musicians that they could have just played it without working on it at all. Instead we rehearsed it, and I asked them for a lot of different things and, boy, did they play the hell out of it! My thanks to him and the synergism of it all!

It was like that when I started guest conducting Karajan's Berlin Philharmonic. If you wanted to change it, you could change it, but at least the performance they were prepared to give you had a concept. It was a performance that had been fully realized.

RCM: Leinsdorf insisted that if you demand of an orchestra that it play 100 percent, it can get into that swing and hold it. If the musicians are always working to that level, then you just arrive and it's there.

JL: You get a higher level with less pressure right from the start.

RCM: If you come in as a guest and they have been playing at 80 percent most of the season, and you are not going to stand for that, the whole rehearsal situation is different.

JL: That's right. It was great to talk to Leinsdorf when he was in that demanding mood, he said such interesting things. There was absolutely no conning him.

One of the reasons orchestras decline is that standards can slip and there is no protest from the audience. I don't mean from the press. If it's just the critics, management will try to pooh-pooh it to the board and discount it backstage. I mean a protest in which the musicians and management and subscribers all take part. If there were a protest there would be a higher standard. One reason protests don't happen is that people don't hear; moreover, there is a tendency in this country to minimize the effect of a problem until eventually it bites you in the butt.

RCM: In any city, if you refuse to face the issues until the orchestra becomes really lousy, you no longer need repairs, you need a major restoration.

JL: And that may not be easy. Since the best conductors can choose only to work with orchestras that have maintained quality, few will consider a job where they have a lot of rebuilding to do. They will say to the management and trustees, This should never have happened, but don't expect me to fix it for you! I gave that up forty years ago! That creates the paradox that the only people who will take the job are the ones who can't do it properly.

RCM: Part of the problem lies in fantasies spread on behalf of musicians' unions that everyone is always out there giving his best. James C. Petrillo used to say of his Chicago boys, "Every fiddler in Local 10 is as good as Heifetz." Of course it was nonsense. We are told that all musicians want conductors like Szell or Reiner who keep them on the edge of their chairs. The truth is there are some very capable musicians who will not work any harder than they think is necessary. The conductor has to get them to change their minds.

JL: If you're afraid of hard work, there go the standards.

RCM: But hard work doesn't destroy you. It sustains you.

JL: That's right. It gives tremendous exhilaration and energy. In music you get back what you put into it.

RCM: Solti did two concert performances of *Meistersinger*—Acts 1 and 2 one night and Act 3 the night following. As the evening ended, he didn't even look tired. The music was sustaining him.

JL: Absolutely.

RCM: When it was over and he went to his dressing room, fatigue dropped over him like a cloak. Then he was tired. After all, he was about to celebrate his eighty-third birthday. He deserved to be tired. But while those hands were moving and music was flowing, you could read in his face that he was sailing. Everything was as perfectly in place in the last four pages as in the first four pages.

JL: That piece is heaven-sent in that way. It makes you feel as if you were in the most marvelous, positive, human, hopeful festive endeavor. Robert, you were educated at a time when making musical distinctions was a major, interesting, fascinating subject. But nowadays, many serious professional musicians, in lieu of real issues, are worried about incredible superficialities, theoretical issues, instead of penetrating the content of the work. These questions of performance practices were always there, but as an appropriately sized piece of the big picture. Now, for some, it's the whole picture. That's so much easier, but it's also completely phony.

I ask, What has to happen in the music for its meaning to be fully understood, for its specific character to emerge? For you, for me, for the conductors we admire, this is the vital source of the performance.

RCM: As you know, some years ago I was involved in a Rockefeller Foundation project at USC to train young music critics. One thing I tried, which was a total disaster, was issuing them miniature scores of the Brahms Fourth, telling them to study the piece, and then playing them the first movement in a distracting and nonessential recording.

What I wanted them to do was tell me what was happening in the performance. Don't use evaluative terms, I said. Don't use descriptive terms. Don't tell me what your feelings are. Make factual statements, statements that we can determine are either true or false by replaying the record. They couldn't do it.

JL: There you have your finger on what I was just trying to explain. You were trying to teach them to listen the right way.

RCM: It can be taught. I know perfectly well how I learned it. It began with the Boston Symphony rehearsing under Koussevitzky and continued in Cleveland. Szell ran the best imaginable school for music critics. Every time he stopped the orchestra I tried to anticipate what he was going to say, and, in time, I got good at it.

But in Chicago I could not train an apprentice that way. The musicians' union kept the majority of rehearsals closed. If the defense against criticism is going to be the charge of incompetence, you can create incompetence by denying young critics the experiences they need to grow professionally. I had learned the basics of my craft before returning to Chicago in 1956. Hermann Scherchen once placed me right in the middle of the London Symphony to learn what things sounded like there. But my apprentices never had such opportunities. The union or management, or both, were creating poor working conditions in revenge for something or other I had written that they didn't like.

JL: How you listen is absolutely central, and it can indeed be taught.

RCM: What I was after was the principle that you can't be a critic unless you begin with facts. What bloody well happened in the performance? You have to know. And don't describe a visceral reaction instead.

JL: You are right. They wanted to begin, "It transported me to . . . ," which is not really a communication about the music. But I fear the objective attitude has gone out of fashion with a vengeance. The reason may be that criticism of much of today's popular music is by default totally subjective, since there is nothing objective on which to base it. So that may be carried over to classical repertory. I am unhappy when I am offered metaphysics instead of musical reality. But what did you do?

RCM: Until the protests got too strong, I made my students at USC read G. E. Moore. The theoretical basis of my critical work is all in the *Principia Ethica*. And yet no one would suggest that subjective factors in performance are not important.

JL: I discovered something conducting opera that I had never seen quite this way before. If I do ten performances of *Così fan tutte* and in the following year someone comes in to sing Fiordiligi whose conception of, say, her second-act aria is in some way noticeably different from her predecessor's—it may be a good deal slower, or a good deal faster, or less introspective, or whatever—the Met Orchestra's instinct is now to sit forward and listen hard and go with the singer but without losing the character they had before. So all of a sudden you have the possibility to hear something played four notches faster without anything else about it changing. They *love* the challenge of doing it both ways!

That is something I have been fascinated by since I was in school, this business of "good" slow and "bad" slow, "good" fast and "bad" fast. Why is it that some performances may be faster or slower than you think they should be, but that's not a problem? The problem is when the rhythmic character of the tempo is directly at odds with the expression.

I find there is a lot of room in the literal question of "What tempo?" but there is not a lot of room in what tempo *range* will allow all the elements to work at the same time. And, of course, occasionally we hear a very thoughtful, brilliant musician, whom we understand perfectly nine times out of ten, do something utterly incomprehensible to us based on nothing but some strange idiosyncrasy we do not share.

For example, the metronome markings of the Beethoven Fifth indicate that the scherzo should be faster than the finale, but Szell always played the finale faster. When he came to the crisis moment in the middle of the finale when the scherzo returns, he had to make a ritardando there instead of the indicated accelerando because he had taken the last movement faster. Not a big deal, but an interesting one. This not only did not bother him, but he insisted it was correct—I asked him, of course. He couldn't agree with Beethoven's tempo indications.

RCM: That's tradition working on him. I suspect it goes back at least to Arthur Nikisch.

JL: There were only two moments I can think of in all those years that were for me like discontinuities in which I had to process something that was completely different from the rest of our work together. Very early on when I was there he conducted the big E-flat Mozart Symphony [No. 39]. Szell rehearsed the first movement and was working away, and then came the slow movement. My jaw dropped down to the floor as for once I watched him in utter incomprehension. My problem was that, big as life in the score, it says two/four, andante con moto. He was beating it so slowly, in eighth notes—that is, in four—and, every rubato—huge—it was like a performance from a completely different kind of conductor. I waited and I listened. I was thinking, He must know something I don't know. He has forgotten more about this music than I'll ever know. Finally, after a certain number of performances of it, I worked up the nerve to knock on his door and say, "I've got to ask you something."

So I did my little speech about the andante con moto and the two/four indication. Mozart slow movements are either some form of adagio, larghetto in character, or andante, and this is andante with a con moto and two/four for good measure. After all, andante con moto two/four was the fastest slow movement marking used at that time. And I have heard it sound wonderfully right played that way by Toscanini. The notes are all there. It's not hasty, but it has a totally different character.

He said to me, "It is something Viennese that is very hard to explain, strangely nonliteral." You cannot imagine how it struck me hearing that from *him*. I thought, So you're susceptible to that too, so there are things that got under your skin when you were a kid, and you can't shake them because any alternative is missing something that you need.

He said, "If you had been trained and brought up in Vienna, you . . ."

I thought, Szell never gives you an answer about geography when you ask a question about music. But in this case he was under the spell of a feeling that went deep to his roots. I couldn't agree with him, but I considered it pointless to argue with something as subjective as this. Many years later I had an experience that was similar and stuck to me the same way.

I was rehearsing *The Magic Flute* in Salzburg in 1978 and we came to this chorus of priests, a short number, a prayer they have toward the middle of Act 2. And I started to conduct and they started to sing, and they had some kind of *misterioso* quality in the sound they made that was incredible, so lacking in pulse, so mystical and Jean-Pierre [Ponnelle] and I looked at each other and both shrugged, as if to say, "There is the Vienna thing that you can't get anywhere else. Perhaps you don't want it. But if you want it, here is where you have to come."

We played that opera more than fifty times, and no matter how the chorus rotation worked—it's never precisely the same people two times in a row—whether it was Sunday, Wednesday, or Tuesday noon, when we arrived at that number, they sang it like that. It had an incredible effect on your nerves, your sensitivity, and was absolutely unexplainable in literal terms. If another chorus master had listened to it and tried to teach his chorus to do it, at best he might come up with a good imitation.

RCM: *Wiener Blut.*

JL: Exactly. Something in the sounds and the sensibility. That is something we Americans, and foreign students from anywhere, get when we are able for a time to concentrate on Italian musicians playing Italian music and Viennese musicians playing Viennese music. Certain things happen that relate somehow to the way the composer heard those people sing and play, and the way the language is spoken by natives; this affected what he was writing. That is incredibly fascinating.

RCM: A similar thing that may be Viennese is to omit the double expositions in the first three Brahms symphonies. I learned the Third from a recording Bruno Walter made in Vienna, and later I heard a recording by Mengelberg that took the repeat and it knocked me silly. But Szell omits that repeat in his Brahms Third Symphony recording, and, for me, it weakens the value of the set.

JL: You know I always respect that double bar. It's a very specific case.

RCM: On one of his last visits to Chicago, I became very brave and went to Walter. In those days a critic could go to a distinguished conductor and be treated with professional courtesy. Now, for so many, we are malicious, incompetent sons of bitches to be turned over to the PR director.

I gave my little lecture to Walter, showing that the repeats in those three symphonies were all essential parts of the form, and he looked at me and smiled.

"I am sure you are right, my young friend," he said. "But you must understand that when I reach that double bar I cannot go back."

It was that simple.

JL: The heart over the mind. I feel that way about the First Symphony, as a matter of fact. I can't go back; it seems an absolute redundancy. And we know that Brahms himself stopped making the repeat in the Second, feeling the music was already overfamiliar even in the late 1800s! And, of course, the Fourth doesn't have a double exposition. But the Third is another matter.

RCM: Many young conductors set themselves the task of learning and, at the first opportunity, playing what they regarded as the standard works. You have done nothing of the sort, even though the opportunities were there. I gather your repertory has grown over the years based on your performing situations rather than any calculated plan.

JL: I have never been able to give a completely rational answer to that, but it is interesting to look at how one comes upon the repertory that one does. You can like a piece, but whether you have a relationship to it that might be regarded as a "conducting relationship" is another matter. To choose one striking example, when, say, I hear a performance of *Boris Godunov,* or when I look at the score, I know this is a great masterpiece. Yet I do not have any relationship to this piece that makes me want to conduct it.

When you learn a piece, when you study a piece, when you are in the process of taking a score from out here [the room] and putting it in here [his head] you either get very excited about it passing through, as a performer to the listener, or you somehow don't see yourself as a vessel for the transmission of this particular music.

Again, take Janáček. He chose marvelous dramatic subjects and set them brilliantly, and yet so far in my life I haven't felt the slightest interest in conducting a Janáček opera. That could change. But I *lust* to conduct the Berg operas, the Schoenberg operas, the Stravinsky operas. It is a funny thing that may be partly analyzable, but it is also the way it affects one's artistic imagination.

You see, and this is fundamental, I'm not interested in *conducting.* I'm interested in *music.* This is a major difference, of course. And therefore whether or not I conduct something is based on the feeling that somehow or other I can get at it as a conductor to produce the kind of result the composer's inspiration and efforts merit. The most conspicuous lacuna in my repertory as we speak is that I have never conducted a Bruckner symphony.

Zarin Mehta [current manager of Ravinia] says to me, you conduct all the Mahler symphonies, one hundred *Parsifals*, why not Bruckner? Somehow or other I cannot get a conducting relationship to those pieces. He suggested I do the Ninth my last full summer at Ravinia. I restudied the score, but I still couldn't do it. Please realize I do not dislike the work. I can sit through other people's performances with pleasure without identifying myself with the music in a way needed to play it myself.

RCM: Someone asked Klemperer who was the greater composer, Bruckner or Mahler? And he said, "Bruckner, of course." Then, he was asked, "Why do you play all this Mahler?" "Mahler got me jobs," he replied.

JL: Oh, that is great! The eternal musician thinking of the next gig. You just know he didn't really mean it!

RCM: But Mahler has got you jobs, too. People know you are such a terrific Mahler conductor, and if they want Mahler they go to you for it.

JL: I hope so. I love doing it. *All* of it. There have been some wonderful changes of viewpoint. I grew up with a certain ignorance and slight prejudice about Sibelius.

RCM: I remember one early Ravinia summer when you expressed surprise that Szell liked and had even recorded the Second Symphony.

JL: I actually heard him do a great performance of that piece. And after I had been conducting for some time I had to make a Philadelphia Orchestra program that was to come to Carnegie Hall as a New York run-out. After about eight attempts to get approval from the orchestra management for a piece to end the program (all my suggestions were already scheduled that season), I said to myself, Instead of telling them what you want to conduct, ask yourself what would the orchestra sound marvelous playing. Into my head popped "the Second Sibelius." I did not know how effectively I could do it, but I said, Let's just see. On the radio I had heard a performance that had me just entranced, and it turned out to be Toscanini's old NBC broadcast. So I did the Second Sibelius and everyone said, "This was the greatest blah, blah, blah."

I was still having difficulty, even with music that, while so original, was not crafted better. I would think, in the finale, if I hear that damn tune one more time I'll scream. So I left it for a while. Then later we were looking for something to program in Berlin, and I decided on three Sibelius symphonies—Two, Four, and Five. For me working on Four was a *profoundly* satisfying experience. I think it's the real masterpiece. Sometimes a piece changes on you in the act of working on it. You study the score, but when you start turning that score into sound, it takes on whole new aspects.

Szell wanted me to do *Pictures at an Exhibition,* and I resisted because I felt it was kind of a, well, cheap piece. I was quite skeptical of it as orchestra music as opposed to the undeniably brilliant piano original. But years later when I finally turned to it, I really enjoyed it. The Bartók Concerto for Orchestra, which I had always adored, came unglued for me the first time I rehearsed it carefully with a student orchestra. I said, "So many problems, and it turns out sounding so empty." Years later, after letting it rest, I picked it up again and the old original fascination had returned for me. I knew that now I was ready to get through the problems without letting them take all the fun out of it for me.

Sometimes your best work is done after years of playing a piece. But other times your best comes when you are your freshest with it. When we did the Brahms symphonies in Chicago in the mid-seventies, that was the first time I had dared to rehearse and perform the Third Symphony. And yet of the recorded cycle, that is the one I like the best.

RCM: It challenged you.

JL: It was a real grapple. It was not something I had done so often already that I thought I knew how to do it. I had always kept away from it—too great and too difficult. You don't always have control. In the period when I listened to a lot of Toscanini performances, I found some of them were perfunctory. And I would ask, Did he know that as it was happening? And if he did, was he powerless to change it? When I played the Brahms it was the opposite case, terrifically exciting; at the time I just knew it was good.

You are the only one ever to note that in all the Ravinia summers I never played the Beethoven Fourth.

RCM: You couldn't risk that slow movement.

JL: Of course. My inclination was always to go straight for the Seventh, which I played twice as much as any other because I knew they could play a good performance right off the stick if necessary, which it sometimes was when we needed our rehearsal time for music that was less familiar to them.

RCM: What the public heard then was a performance that had, in effect, been rehearsed throughout your entire association with the CSO.

JL: I believe so passionately in that concept.

March 20, 1996. Dialogue in Philadelphia.

RCM: Four music directors of the Chicago Symphony made their reputation at Ravinia—Rodzinski, Reiner, Martinon, and Solti. When Solti announced his retirement from the CSO, many concluded there were really only two candidates for the job: you, as the firmly established man at Ravinia; and the former principal guest conductor, Claudio Abbado. As it turned out, neither of you got the appointment because both of you were deeply involved elsewhere.

But it is interesting to see how the selection process worked. The task was given to a committee of seven made up of Solti, Henry Fogel the manager, and five members of the board. It was obvious that the five were socially prominent innocents, unqualified for the job, and that they expected Solti and Fogel to make them look good by making a wise choice.

Solti, who in more than twenty years had done almost nothing for American music, clearly wanted his successor to be a European. Fogel, who was aware that there were some qualified American conductors—Bernstein for a start—was nonetheless prepared to go along. The three American candidates had to be eliminated as quickly as possible. You had recorded with the orchestra, and Solti might have heard some of your records, but here were three Americans under consideration, and Solti had never heard any of them in a live performance with his orchestra. First to go was Michael Tilson Thomas. The old ladies in the boxes, whose approval was essential, apparently found him incompatible. Now, of course, I am delighted to see he is enjoying wonderful success in San Francisco.

The next candidate was Leonard Slatkin, who had really worked with the symphony and, earlier, with the Grant Park Symphony Concerts, to make a reputation in the city. He had many supporters. But apparently some of the older, and I suspect European-born, members of the orchestra insisted he was a dull conductor, and Solti appears to have been delighted to cross him off the list. I shall always believe that Leonard got a really dirty deal. Of course, I am overjoyed that the National Symphony in Washington, D.C., knew his potential and that we have an American conductor of this stature in the nation's capital serving as a marvelous advocate for American music.

Your name probably carried the greatest weight, since the orchestra and the public both knew you well. The answer was that you were far too busy at the Met. You didn't have the time. Since Solti had on occasion given the orchestra as little as six weeks, it seemed odd to some that you could not find three two-week slots in a season. But that is not your style. You would never accept the job anticipating only six weeks of residence. If you could not give the orchestra the time you felt was needed to do things right, you would not accept.

JL: Right in spades! That's a nice residency for a guest conductor. Rosbaud came to Chicago for periods about that length. But it's not being a music director.

RCM: Residence in Chicago for, say, ten weeks would have meant cutting back on your work at the Met, which in 1991–92 you were not prepared to do.

JL: I couldn't have done it at that time. Not a chance. I think if I live a long time, there will be a period when I could imagine finding a symphony orchestra situation I would enjoy. It would have to allow me to offer a more rapid turnover than the "usual" basic symphonic repertory, so that I could get to a lot of new music that I cannot otherwise play. I do not want a symphony connection so that I can begin the systematic repetition of the standard repertory; that doesn't interest me at all. Whoever convinces me to take a symphony job has to be ready to accept a lot of new pieces.

This involvement in the Met has been so challenging, fascinating, satisfying, that I am sure I must not leave it arbitrarily, the way I feel Lenny [Bernstein] left the New York Philharmonic. I think that was a mistake, not because he did not conduct beautifully in Vienna—he did—but because his rapport with the New York situation was so strong that nothing else could replace that combination for him, for them, for everyone! It was a great loss for the city.

When Berlin was looking for a successor to Karajan, I said to the committee, I am not one of these conduct-two-things-at-once guys, especially if one of them is the Met. Everything about it—its location, its schedule, its role in American music—requires an unqualified commitment. Between now and 2001, when my current contract ends, provided Joe Volpe continues strongly, maybe I can find a way that the artistic staff I lead does not carry such a large administrative burden that I cannot gradually work into some other permanent post. At the time Solti left Chicago, I never could have done it. The management has invited me repeatedly to return as a guest, and I simply haven't had the time. I hope to return in March 1999. That will give me a better sense of what the orchestra is like today, and on that basis I can determine what my future with it might be. As you know, I have been recording with them in recent years for a new Disney film, *Fantasia 2000*.

RCM: The gossipmongers are always predicting you have some big change in mind.

JL: That's possibly because they never have time to get all the facts. In an interview in the media today, television bites you with time and newspapers bite you with space, which is really the same thing. And the next thing you know people are seduced into thinking that they have been given the whole story, that they know all there is to the subject. That is a disaster. Reporters come to me with the same old questions, and I ask, Do you want yet another page of copy from that angle? Or shall we look at something new? Sometimes that gets them. They don't seem to grasp all the other things that might be discussed, all the other questions that might be asked. I say to them, Before you give that to your editor, sit down with me and I promise we can make it better.

It is impossible for the average reporter, a perfect stranger, to interview an artist and come up with anything but a mess of platitudes. Some feel that unless they can say something negative, they have not found anything to say.

I find it is difficult enough to get people to understand something that you actually take the trouble to explain to them. Your friends and colleagues understand, but the world in general is projecting the way it thinks things would be in your situation. And that projection is not based on experience—reality—but what has been picked up from television, tabloids, hearsay, and other unreliable sources. If you know a human being has real integrity, the general public doesn't believe it, because integrity is not something they encounter very often. What they want reinforced is that everybody is one or another sort of corrupt jerk.

RCM: And even a jerk doesn't want to think of himself in those terms.

JL: Robert, we can deal with real things. We have known each other more than thirty years. We can talk together and arrive at some genuine understanding even when we disagree!

Can you imagine Wagner and Mathilde Wesendonck, or Wagner and Cosima, when she was married to Hans von Bülow, in this day and age? It would be a twenty-four-hour distraction for the tabloids, something sleazy beyond belief. But a century ago the world "put up with it," somehow. It allowed people to get a lot more done. Today so many people want to do their thinking with buzzwords, or have it done for them by pundits or experts.

RCM: Consider that purple page in Met history, Toscanini and Geraldine Farrar. A seven-year affair of that type would be impossible in any major theater today.

JL: You're right. Toscanini probably was in deep conflict with himself about Farrar. That was no little thing. The woman was so beautiful, so passionate, and artistically so plugged in that she must have pushed Toscanini almost to the edge deciding how he was going to resolve this issue. It was a different time, a different world of opera.

RCM: Toscanini booked himself to flee to Europe on the *Lusitania* in May 1915. Fortunately, he was persuaded to take a nice Italian liner.

August 4, 1996. Dialogue in Munich.

RCM: I notice that some critics are constantly sniping at you for your tempos in *Parsifal*, and the impression they apparently want to convey is that your performance of the opera drags. Now we know there is considerable variation in the speeds at which that opera can be played. There's a fine old story of Richard Strauss dashing out the stage door of the Vienna Opera shouting to the attendant after a *Parsifal* of his, "See, twenty minutes ahead of Bruno Walter!"

JL: But I'm sure you know that no one at Bayreuth has ever played the opera slower than Toscanini. My slowest performance at Bayreuth is still faster than his by several minutes—more like Karl Muck's timings.

RCM: The bogus impression that the opera does not move firmly in your performances simply cannot stand up if one plays any of your three recordings, two of which were done live. They all move very decisively with a firm and flowing thrust in even the slowest passages.

JL: Not only are there those recordings, but also radio broadcasts from every other Bayreuth summer and a dozen or so from the Met. I'm not lacking in documentation of *Parsifal*, God knows. After a rehearsal one day, I was talking with Gerd Seifert, the great principal horn player of the Berlin Philharmonic, who also plays at Bayreuth. He is one of those people, like Frank Miller, who in the process of performing on an instrument expresses everything the composer could have wished and produces something far more eloquent than anything they could put in words.

He said, "I love playing your *Parsifal* because you are not afraid of the expression and the *tension* of slow tempo."

And then, Manfred Klier, the second horn, said, "Yeah, but Jim's speed is even slower than Knappertsbusch's," which was of course the slowest in the postwar period. And Gerd said to me, "The conductor you most resemble in this music is Muck."

I said, "How do you know that? That's the 1920s, way before your time." He said, "Now you can get it on records."

RCM: Large pieces of *Parsifal* were recorded on 78s in 1927. I had them on old blue-label Columbias.

JL: It's all now on CDs. The strongest thing about that approach to the piece is that Muck finds the tension in a slow pulse. But it means that when he wants to make an event really telling, a vocal event, a verbal event, a harmonic event—whatever it is—it is so powerful because it goes outside the pulse pattern for a moment and comes right back in. It would not have anything like that effect if it had been digested, so to speak, in an unbroken rhythmic line.

It's the same with the orchestra. A musician will say, "You're doing that faster now."

And I say, If so, it's because the tone I am getting now is deep enough in timbre for me that I don't feel I have to make up for a thin tone with a slower pace. You have to think of the expression, the feeling you want in a phrase, and realize that there is more than one way to get it. There is likely to be a way you prefer, and if you stick to it, you may get it in time, but until then you have to devise acceptable substitutes.

RCM: Muck used to insist that he could conduct any Wagner opera without changing his shirt. Those of us who have trouble exercising and staying dry might envy him that. Karl Boehm told me a story of his early days. Muck had engaged him to do a *Lohengrin* in Hamburg, where he was Generalmusikdirektor. At the close of the first act Boehm is in his dressing room peeling off his wet tailcoat. The door opens, and in comes Muck, who walks up to him, grabs his shirt collar, and squeezes out a stream of sweat. "Beginner!" he says.

JL: That's cute. But Muck had a very small beat. [Laughter.]

RCM: Arthur Fiedler played under him in the Boston Symphony, and I asked Arthur one day what Muck's beat really looked like.

"It was smaller than Reiner's and more precise," he replied.

"You mean it was invisible," I said. He conducted telepathically!

JL: Muck is renowned for his freshness and strength and vitality. But he was nonetheless one of the slow *Parsifal* guys. But you must keep phenomenal tension in details or the line will go slack.

RCM: He represents an aspect of the old Bayreuth tradition, performance sustained by a firm metrical foundation. Toscanini in his two Bayreuth summers, 1930 and 1931, introduced his own approach from La Scala in which Wagner was played with the same passionate lyric line as Italian opera.

JL: Muck was as horrified by the desecration of the temple by the first non-German and having "his" *Parsifal* taken from him after twenty-six years as he was by anything he actually heard. He resigned in 1930 when Toscanini was reengaged for the following summer and never appeared at Bayreuth in the final decade of his life. It was a pity since, actually, the two men had so much in common. I wish I had been there at that moment because it is clear that people did not see Toscanini's work as a conscious interpretive departure. They thought it was just better, not because it was faster—it wasn't—or slower, but because it communicated to them more intensely, it had internal involvement and vitality. Toscanini's changes were not limited to *Parsifal*. Toscanini's is still the longest *Tristan* in Bayreuth annals.

RCM: When Toscanini left, Wilhelm Furtwängler became "music director." Many people see him as the symbol of the Bayreuth tradition, but that is not the case. Furtwängler had made his debut in 1931 with *Tristan*. In later summers he conducted a few performances each of *Lohengrin*, *Parsifal*, the *Ring*, and *Die Meistersinger*. Heinz Tietjen was the real artistic director, and a far more important figure in Bayreuth during the Nazi period. Because of the war, the theater closed after the 1944 festival.

JL: One Wagner opera in which Furtwängler was positively phenomenal was *Tristan*. You hear all these comparisons of Furtwängler and Toscanini, as if they represented opposite poles. They really do diverge in classical repertory—Mozart, Beethoven—where their ways of getting what they want are totally different and Furtwängler's idea of rhythmic character is often the opposite of Toscanini's. But the sense of sustained tension in Furtwängler's *Tristan* is fundamentally not so far from Toscanini's idea of that same music.

RCM: In contrast, Furtwängler's *Ring* has some powerful moments but often seems rhetorical rather than dramatic for me. I am fortunate that I knew him as a live musician rather than just a name on records. On the stage he had real magnetism, but the beat was wild. He went ahead and the orchestra sometimes followed by half a bar or so.

Szell used to refer with disdain to the chef who had only one sauce in his kitchen and applied it to everything. But Furtwängler was long criticized for having a set of mannerisms which he applied to the works he played, sometimes with interesting results, sometimes disastrously.

JL: Probably because it all filtered down through his aesthetic preconceptions. I don't ask that every person who studies a score agrees with me, for God's sake. But the fundamental thing is whether you can approach it with a really open mind.

RCM: He made a recording of the Mozart G Minor which I found of some interest. but you could not possibly conceive that Mozart ever thought of that piece sounding that way.

JL: When Wieland and Wolfgang Wagner reopened Bayreuth in 1951 on the program were *Ring* cycles to be conducted by two different people, with the same rehearsal period and essentially the same singers. The two conductors who agreed to this were Knappertsbusch and Karajan. I once asked Wolfgang Wagner who was better, and he said with a twinkle, "Knappertsbusch performing and Karajan rehearsing!" I can well believe that. Karajan was very meticulous in rehearsal. Knappertsbusch, if offered the opportunity, would take advantage of someone else's meticulous rehearsing and go with it. He felt a lot of rehearsing made him repetitive and stale. The old paradox again!

RCM: How much rehearsal do you do at Bayreuth when you return for an opera you have done the summer before?

JL: It varies according to the style of the production, and whether the singers are the same, but there is a standard approach, a schedule of how it works with the orchestra, and I can do my coaching with the singers in tandem with that quite easily. It's a very intelligent system. In the *Ring,* the casts have been remarkably stable, but the work is always dicey because at no given moment can you cast all those roles uniformly. You always have to be vigilant about who's growing, who's declining, and what will hold.

RCM: Our old friend Leinsdorf was saying toward the end of his career that it might be possible to cast a satisfactory *Ring* in terms of a house as small as Bayreuth, but—thinking of the Wagnerian singers he knew in his youth—it would be impossible today to find an ideal cast for a 4,000-seat house.

JL: Right. His point is historically very well taken. And he was tired of the extent to which opera managements compromised just to be able to offer this repertory. But it is better today. We may not be able to duplicate the greatest casts of the past, but we have singers who can do justice to these roles.

The decision to go on conducting the *Ring* rather than, say, bel canto opera is this matter of degree. There are things insanely difficult to cast today in the *Ring,* but there is so much dramatic intensity and philosophical content on which to concentrate. And you must realize that if you keep the piece away from the public, you will find even *fewer* singers who want to respond to its challenges. If you are casting and you make it known to the world, I need a Siegfried, a Siegfried may appear. If Bayreuth had not continued to do the pieces during lean years, there would not have been a way for the young, up-and-coming talents to know what those pieces are. Now, for example, a tenor like Ben Heppner arrives, and it was important for him to have a way to see what those operas are. Ironically, he just missed hearing live performances by his great Canadian predecessor, Jon Vickers.

RCM: What do you see as your future in Bayreuth now that you have done the *Ring?*

JL: There are two more series of *Ring* cycles in 1997 and 1998. Wolfgang Wagner has talked with me about doing a new *Lohengrin* in 1999, but I will have a new *Lohengrin* at the Met next season. I don't know how many *Lohengrin*s I want to have on my mind at once. So I will do the one at the Met and probably leave it like that.

I went to Bayreuth for *Parsifal,* and I did it ten years. I will have done five summers of the *Ring*. These are the things I most wanted to do in the Festspielhaus. Of course there is other Wagner I have not done there, and I love the work in Bayreuth and would be happy to do other pieces. Maybe in a later phase. And in the meantime we do all of it at the Met.

RCM: We think of Toscanini as a great Wagnerian—and he was. But your repertory is larger than his and you may have a *Rienzi* somewhere in your future.

JL: It is a fairly modern notion—I don't know when it appeared, but it may have been in your lifetime—that the idea of conscious interpretation was closely tied to the music of certain composers and was especially telling in Wagner.

Wagner wrote the operas. Then he built the Bayreuth theater. Then the Bayreuth theater started to do them. And then he died. And his widow lived until 1930.

RCM: Preserving a specious tradition.

JL: That's the point. It was not consciously thought that these works were being interpreted. Everyone thought that they were doing essentially the same thing. Go back to the old programs and you will find that the conductors were not even named until 1930 and we know they were not seen at the final curtain call until 1951!

Looking back, we see a very well-defined interpretive viewpoint, what you call the old Bayreuth tradition, exemplified by men as different as Richter, Levi, and Muck, challenged by some new standards of execution when Toscanini arrived.

We knew when we grew up with, say, *Aida,* interpretively the gamut was not from *A* to *Z*. If you heard Antonietta Stella or Renata Tebaldi or Zinka Milanov sing the role, sure they had different personalities and different voices, but they were not trying to do radically different things musically. They all basically agreed about what the piece was. There was a widely accepted idea of how you do *Aida,* and all these other staple pieces, and it permitted the easy interchange of artists. Toscanini at the Met early in the century could jump in on no notice for a sick colleague without a minute of rehearsal because it was *Rigoletto,* a standard work, and everyone was on safe ground. In today's world, with its approach to production, staging, and, most of all, the music, that would be very difficult because the safe ground isn't there anymore. Go into a record store and buy three recordings of the same opera and they are likely to be very different—even ridiculously so.

We both grew up in a period in which mise-en-scène was just regarded as stage decoration. It was never thought, or expected, to be more than a frame for singing, something quite simple. As a young pianist who had a very vivid imagination and learned operas from the score, if I had the music, and played them on the piano, as well as hearing them on records and the radio, in my mind I saw staging. And when I went to the opera, with very rare exceptions, I saw pretty much what I had imagined.

This has changed so much in recent years. We now have a basic debate, even a crisis, over what the visual elements ought to be and how important they are in the totality of the performance. My operatic life centers on how the music is sung and played, notwithstanding what I may like or dislike in the production. I'm not indifferent to the staging. On the contrary, I care about it a lot. I am striving for performances as close as humanly possible to communicating what the composer's priorities were. I want to show an audience what it can have if it gets a complete performance.

RCM: Opera in concert form is nearly always a diminution of the work.

JL: Of course, by definition! Some *have* to be staged to work, like *Rosenkavalier*. But my interaction with the staging in an opera is very complex. If there is a lot happening at a certain artistic level in the music and text, this can hold your attention sufficiently. You heard Solti's concert *Meistersinger* in Chicago. How did that go?

RCM: Musically it was wonderful, but it lacked dramatic confrontations. At times it turned into a cantata.

JL: He was trying to do two things at once, make a recording and give a public performance. For recording you might sometimes prefer a much more intimate delivery than is possible if you must project the work in a hall. *Meistersinger* is a naturally staged opera. It takes real effort to produce a lousy staged *Meistersinger*. It's been done but they have to really work at it! You know, I have had some excellent concert opera experiences at Ravinia and elsewhere.

RCM: Now that you have been conducting about half the total Bayreuth performances for three summers, I feel the Bayreuth Orchestra on those nights has become a Levine orchestra; and through you, sixty-five years after his departure, Toscanini again is the dominant influence in that pit, at least for these five *Ring* summers.

JL: But the musicians come from so many different orchestras. Many good German players have chamber work and other festival work, and they don't want to give the whole summer to one job. Orchestra building at Bayreuth is very difficult because every year the schedule has to be set before we know how many new players there will be. You have to remember these are musicians who give up most of their summer vacation to play the festival. No one is going there for the money! But being at Bayreuth, playing there, has a very special meaning for them, as, indeed, it also has for the singers and conductors. So it is like working somewhere where half of what you are doing is a performance and half is an act of worship. It is an extraordinary place.

This year it happens I had to rehearse a good number of new principal players. But they quickly fit in. Everyone there already knew these pieces from their regular season work. In fact, one of the problems can be that they are *too* familiar by now. Whatever problems you may have in a festival situation like Ravinia, this is a problem you don't have. If there are some new players in Chicago they can be absorbed slowly into the orchestra during the winter concerts.

At Bayreuth you have four weeks of rehearsal and you have to be ready to go. Also don't forget the unique problem of casting—the challenge posed by a festival that does thirty performances of *only* Wagner opera. No regular opera house has to schedule dramatic sopranos and tenors like that! This summer I felt by the third night of the first *Ring* cycle [of three] that we were starting to get somewhere.

RCM: Even though Bayreuth has changed enormously in the more than a century it has been in existence, the change has taken place within an evolving tradition.

JL: Of course, no two cycles are the same, and one hopes the third will be an advance on the first.

RCM: Georg Solti insisted that I come to Bayreuth for his third cycle. One of the frustrations of being a critic is that editors demand you attend first nights and base your judgments on them. Very often I would return to a theater for a later performance and hear something far more interesting, but most of those reviews went unwritten.

JL: Ideally in opera one generation educates another. I learned from the great artists of my youth, many of whom I worked with in Cleveland in the late sixties and who were still singing when I came to the Met in 1971. In later years I was able to pass some of what I had learned from them along to younger artists who had joined the company in the interim. I have been privileged to work with great singers of the past, great singers of the present, and I am trying to develop the great singers of the future, who are a remarkably promising and exciting group.

As you grow older you appreciate that each period in life has it own special qualities. Youth is wonderful, but age brings a deeper awareness of life and the world. You go back to things you feel you know well and discover new things that increase and renew your understanding. When

I was a teenager I felt quite confident that I knew *Don Giovanni*. Ha! And your love for the work deepens even when you thought that love was already 100 percent.

RCM: In that debut year of 1971 Renata Tebaldi was still singing at the Met.

JL: I conducted what turned out to be her final Met performances, three *Otellos* in January 1973.

RCM: Richard Tucker was there until 1974.

JL: We worked together in Cleveland. The man was a living legend then. We did *Luisa Miller* in New York and several things on tour. I was delighted to know him. And from those early years, I cannot forget Cornell MacNeil, Jon Vickers, and Franco Corelli, just for a start.

Actually, I have had the pleasure of working with a phenomenal number of wonderful artists. Just a list of the sopranos—to mention one voice type—I've been blessed with illustrates the point. Astrid Varnay was with the Met until 1980, and Birgit Nilsson sang with us until 1984. Leonie Rysanek made her debut in 1959 and has just retired. Leontyne Price was very much a part of the company when I arrived, of course, and was indispensable until her self-imposed retirement in 1985. Renata Scotto had made her debut in 1965, and we had a long and very productive association, as you know. Teresa Stratas, who made her debut in 1959, was a unique partner for many years, as were Mirella Freni, Kiri Te Kanawa, Pilar Lorengar, Hildegard Behrens, etc. I can't name them all.

All these people contributed enormously to the realization of my goals for the theater. In fact, I'm surrounded with people who are literally indispensable to my artistic life and vision. Jessye Norman arrived in 1983. How could I live without her today? I'd have to hand you an exceedingly long list to name all the people I feel I must have for the realization of the projects I have in mind.

You know I am interested in far more than someone who can sing the music. I want the right person in the right role.

RCM: One of the great pleasures of operagoing after you have done it a while is to look back at all the extraordinary artists you have heard. It must be even more intense when you have worked closely to bring a production to the stage.

JL: Between my first *Parsifal* in 1979 and my most recent ones in 1995 there have been nine or ten singers in the role of Kundry at the Met. Christa Ludwig was the first, then Tatiana Troyanos, and later Leonie Rysanek and Waltraud Meier, to name just four. They were each quite different, as you would expect, since they were extraordinary artists with a firm grasp of the role, which all performed splendidly. My job was not to impose my ideas on their characterizations but rather to get the best from them so they could put these amazing resources to use for the success of the composer's whole artistic conception.

Look at the range of talent we have had in the title role: Jon Vickers and Jess Thomas early on, and more recently Siegfried Jerusalem and Plácido Domingo. Every one of them defines the character in different terms, but each brings us a performance of such integrity that I am happy to work with all of them.

Singers are sensitive, intelligent human beings, and every one of them has certain strengths and certain weaknesses—like conductors! As you work with them, you learn what these things are, and this places you in a position to give whatever support and suggestions, musical or otherwise, you can to help them give their best performances. It is absurd to seek perfection—what a stupid word!—in opera or anything else. We are always developing and improving our insight and our capacity to absorb and communicate what we find in the music. It's unending. If you say it's perfect, you say growth has ended. Nonsense!

The conductor and director must have clear objectives. They must be able to draw on the many things they have learned in their previous experience. Young singers, however talented, have often limited experience on which to draw. But if they look within themselves, they can often find what they need for a role.

RCM: Toscanini was auditioning the very young Robert Merrill for his 1946 broadcast performance of *La Traviata*. They went through "Di Provenza," and the Old Man asked, "Are you a father?"

"No," Merrill replied. "I'm not even married."

Toscanini said, "Oh, *Dio!*" or something equally encouraging, and then added, "We will work." And, of course, Merrill sang it beautifully. Anyone can go to the record and hear for himself.

JL: Singers must base interpretations to some extent on their own character. They must learn to look within themselves and find that character there. The character can be someone quite different from the singer as encountered on a daily basis. Nilsson was not Brünnhilde offstage, but she knew, really knew, what was going on in Brünnhilde's or Isolde's guts, and that made her performances what they were.

This is why I find it very difficult to make quick judgments about singers, judgments that I feel I can trust. After I have known them for a time, seen their highs and lows, I am more confident in forming an opinion. If you jump to a conclusion, you can be terribly wrong. You won't find me on a competition jury.

RCM: You look within the singer, but you must also look within the opera. In the majority of cases, there is a lot more there than first meets the eye or ear.

JL: Any really complex masterpiece has more content than can be revealed in any single approach. When singers are performing standard works season after season with different conductors and directors, they have to learn that this change can be good.

Take the singers who did the concert operas with Toscanini. They studied them with him, and this was complicated because some of them were doing them for the first time, some for the hundredth time. They did so much work together that when they sang the performance it was done his way; they had his point of view. A year later they would be singing the piece with someone else and learning that conductor's point of view, to the extent that he had one.

When you compare these NBC broadcast performances, you find what they have in common—the main line, the main stream, is always an absolute respect for the black-and-white issues as they are set down in the score. But the gray issues change.

Let's take, for a good example, opera staging. Little by little much of it gets more and more nonsensical from my point of view. Now a lot of people, you understand, will say it's me being pedantic, with a childish, stubborn insistence that an opera should always look the way I have seen it before. But that is not the case at all. It comes from composers, from their letters, essays, stage directions, everything we have to go on to show us what a composer's priorities were.

There is a well-known story about Toscanini's indignation at Salzburg in 1936 when he saw the borrowed Viennese *Falstaff* scenery was not in a Tudor style. And he would not do the rehearsals until they put a Tudor-style house on the stage. He also took the first scene of Act 3 out of Falstaff's bedroom and put it back outside the Garter Inn. He was confident he knew what Verdi imagined, and he demanded that Verdi's express intentions be respected. This is the direct opposite of many directors and designers today.

RCM: I think we can call them the revisionist school.

JL: Exactly. They feel the original stage directions can safely be ignored. A work that is more than a hundred years old can—must—be completely reinterpreted "because the original meanings have all changed." Of course, in the case of truly great works, the original meanings are just as strong today as when the work was first heard, or maybe more so.

RCM: Erich Leinsdorf quit the Bayreuth Festival in a fury in 1972 because an antireligious Marxist director of *Tannhäuser* insisted in the final scene that the pope's staff not bloom. But if the miracle does not take place, said Leinsdorf, the climax of the opera is destroyed. The entire message of redemption is gone. The reply appears to have been that religious messages of this type are meaningless today. But are they?

JL: And if so, why direct *this* opera? The tenet that an opera must be presented in a manner faithful to the composer and the librettist must not be taken to mean there is only one correct way to produce a work. On the contrary. Fidelity to the composer may be achieved in a number of very different approaches to a score.

You just saw a *Ring* I conducted at Bayreuth that in no way resembles the one I do at the Met, but in all essentials is just as faithful a vision of the work. The contrast and variety of these different viewpoints may give us even deeper and more profound understanding of the piece, in fact.

RCM: But you are saying a really great opera is a unity, and the text and the music cannot be taken separately.

JL: Absolutely. There can be no question of that if we are talking of successful operas. At the Met we employ a great many talented people, and it would be inappropriate, stifling, and counterproductive for me to force my aesthetic ideas upon them. If you want people of vital theatrical imagination working with you, you have to give them freedom to develop their ideas. But I do have a responsibility. I have to make a distinction between what the Met produces and what I conduct. If work is of high quality, we offer it proudly, even if it is not to my taste. But if my long-range goal is to have productions that reflect my ideas of fidelity to the composer and the librettist, then I have to create an atmosphere in which productions of that type can also be realized. The new *Così fan tutte* this season was carefully planned to yield what I was after, and the whole team—everybody—worked together to achieve that. This was really something that encouraged and allowed everyone to give his or her best performance, not something being provocative in all the wrong ways.

Ponnelle's *Moses und Aron* in Salzburg was exceptionally good, thrilling in the way the elements were unified while still respecting their tremendous diversity. The curse on that piece from day one—even though we had to wait until 1954 to hear it—was that the world premiere was a concert performance. It took a while to learn how to deal with a chorus that was not stationary but part of the drama. Everyone learned how difficult it is for the chorus to move like a conventional opera chorus and still sing the piece properly.

We will have the work at the Met, finally, in 1999. It's time now. Now perhaps we can do it justice. We have been giving a lot of discussion to whether the Met production should be in the original German or in English. Schoenberg wrote the text himself, and believed in opera in the vernacular, but since it is his own libretto, it is even more closely married to the music than if he had set someone else's text. Now we can have a translation in Met Titles, so the cast doesn't have to sing in English for the audience to follow the text. The question comes down to this: How good can the staging be? I don't want many places where, in order to project the words, the music will be screwed up to make the text clear, and for that clarity German may be essential. And appropriate for the opera's first Met performance.

We did *Carmélites* in English at first. We were right. We did *Mahagonny* in English, even though the German is more incisive. Lotte Lenya said the English could be incisive enough and she was right. We did *Lulu* in German because the translation was terrible and I had a cast that knew it backwards in German. The Met premiere of *Moses und Aron* will stick with the original. It would be great to be able to motivate the chorus in their own language. But we may find ways to do that anyway. A whole lot of meetings and thoughts and second thoughts go into these discussions. After the success we have had with *Wozzeck* and *Lulu, Moses und Aron* can now become part of our standard repertory.

RCM: I note an *Opera News* piece in which a few people say it is the opera they most dislike.

JL: But they don't know it. There's an excellent reason for that. It is an opera most people know from recordings rather than staged productions, and recordings simply cannot do it justice.

RCM: I agree completely with that. I saw the American staged premiere from Sarah Caldwell in Boston some thirty years ago. It can be a powerful stage piece. We all know what Solti achieved with it at Covent Garden and, to a lesser degree, in Paris. His concert version in Chicago was splendid musically but I really missed the impact the stage provides.

JL: The bottom line on the subject of staging opera is clearly that the director's function has many things in common with the conductor's function, and if the director has ideas that are not going to complement the conductor's and they cannot agree on what an opera is about, there is always going to be a disaster. This process is difficult to achieve because often you cannot get a director who has done the work before, which means you don't have a lot of information as to what you are going to get. Of course, if a director is very sensitive to what the music is communicating, you can get great results.

RCM: I feel one of the real sticky elements of fidelity to the libretto is when animals are specified.

JL: You cannot *always* follow the text. When Wagner was staging the *Ring* at Bayreuth in 1876, he came to the place in *Walküre*, Act 2, where, to open the annunciation of the death scene, "Brünnhilde comes down the rocks leading her horse." Then Wagner faced something he had not anticipated. What his poetic imagination had pictured was not necessarily something he could put on a stage. The horse had to stand there through a twenty-minute scene. It moved its weight from one side to another, and then it flicked its tail, and then it neighed, and basically became a distraction. The music was going on, but one's eye kept going to the horse. So Wagner decided that the horse should *not* come onstage. Through this process he learned how some secondary thing can destroy the effect you want.

RCM: We rarely see Fricka's chariot drawn by rams. Solti had them in 1983, but plastic rams, and there were a couple of plastic horses. You saw them as part of the scenic design, but they never made a false move. I thought it an interesting experiment. I shall always yearn for an immolation scene in which a real Grane comes onstage and Brünnhilde leaps on his back and plunges into the flames. You have to admit it's a marvelous effect, even if it is impossible to stage. Odds are I shall see it in computer simulation in the Steven Spielberg film of *Götterdämmerung*—whenever that arrives.

JL: Is Spielberg ready for *Götterdämmerung*?

RCM: Let us close with a soupçon of metaphysics. There is a question we have been talking around for quite a while, and this seems as good a time as any to confront it.

What is a work of art? The naive answer is that it is a simple, identifiable thing—a picture, a score, a poem—but we quickly sense this is an illusion. These are beginnings, but a work of art is a plurality of things. Suppose you start with what looks like a simple example, the "To be or not to be" soliloquy in *Hamlet*. It's one thing as a printed text, still another when read by John Gielgud, and something completely different if read, say, by Marlon Brando.

So what is the "real" thing, the *Ding an sich* [thing in itself] of Kant's philosophy? This is especially difficult in music since it is a re-creative art. Surely no professional musician would say that the Beethoven Fifth is the symphonic score. Music is thought of as sound, though a conductor may look at that score and hear a performance in his imagination. If you know it well enough, you can hear a performance without the score. If you go to the record catalog you may find nearly fifty recorded versions, no two alike, and every one of them is the Beethoven Fifth—but not to the exclusion of any of the others.

Understanding this issue means coming to terms with perpetual flux. And this flux can be generated by something seemingly as easily definable as a statue. One of the most celebrated works of art in the ancient world was the Aphrodite of Praxiteles at Cnidus. The original is long gone, but there is a pretty good Roman copy in the Chicago Art Institute, and I can spend long periods of time simply slowly walking around it and seeing how, with a very slight change in light or angle of view, it becomes something different from what it was the moment before.

JL: And you can look at it for years and still feel the possibility of discovery and the increase of excitement that experience and increasing knowledge make possible. Operas unfold over a time span that can be several hours long. You cannot possibly experience the entire work at once. It is a series of events.

RCM: And so is looking at a statue. We may look at Aphrodite, and move on to the next thing in the gallery, and think that you have seen her.

JL: But you haven't.

RCM: You have seen one of a zillion different possible images.

JL: And you have heard the opera in one of a zillion possible performances.

RCM: But if you look at the statue for years . . .

JL: And listen to the opera just as long . . .

RCM: You may finally have some sense of finding the essence of the work, the vital source that, by interacting with the artistic imagination, produces this multiplicity of experiences.

JL: And discoveries of that sort are some of the greatest things in life.

PART THREE

Man at Work

One of the most conspicuous phenomena in music since the mid-eighteenth century has been the rise of the conductor. At first merely a member of the orchestra entrusted with keeping things together, the maestro is now the person who governs every detail of the performance and tries to make it a realization in sound of a personal artistic vision.

The greatest conductors may appear, in the popular mind, to supplant composers. We hear of Toscanini's *Great* C Major opposed to Furtwängler's (or Schubert's), of Karajan's Bruckner, Boehm's Mozart, Beecham's Haydn, Szell's Brahms, and Koussevitzky's Debussy and Ravel. There is just cause for this. These men brought us performances that revitalized our conception of supreme works of music—their visions illuminated the lives of millions of listeners and, through recording, have the potential to continue to do so.

James Levine stands firmly in the mainstream of the development of orchestral conducting. He is the direct heir to Haydn and Wagner. His goal of a unified performance comes from Lully. Let us gain the perspective that comes from a survey of this important historical background.

The services of a conductor become necessary when a performing group reaches the size where its members cannot stay together simply by listening to one another. In the world of chamber music, the accepted judgment is that the decisive figure is eight or nine players. But if the musicians are of high quality and adequately rehearsed, a chamber orchestra of greater size can perform without a conductor. The contemporary world of music contains several examples of this type. Most of the major symphony orchestras could play a standard work without a conductor, if necessary, but the performance might lack flexibility. Toscanini's NBC Symphony Orchestra played a concert and made a recording without the maestro with thoroughly professional results.

In the seventeenth century, staying together was narrowly defined as playing at the same tempo. The conductor served the function later assigned to the metronome; he provided a steady rhythmic pulse. Listeners today would find the steady beat of a long cane on the floor an aesthetically unpleasing distraction, but at the court of Louis XIV, the steady tap of a pointed staff ensured orchestral precision. Jean-Baptiste Lully (1632–87), the truly innovative member of the select group of royal musicians, must be viewed historically as the first great conductor. The sixteen musicians of his personal ensemble offered an example of precision and collective virtuosity that excited all Europe and made plain the coarse, inexact playing that had been accepted previously. But precise instrumental playing was only part of a fine performance as Lully saw it. All the elements of the work—singers, chorus, dancers, music—must be harmoniously synchronized with one another to create an artistic unity.

Lully paid for precision with his life. In what one surmises to be a moment of intensity and abandon during a performance of his *Te Deum*, he stabbed himself in the foot with the point of his staff. Gangrene set in, and he died a lingering and agonizing death. His conducting technique now appears primitive, but Lully defined the basic principles of the modern musical theater, although it was left to others to realize their full significance.

The first general music director in the contemporary sense was Franz Joseph Haydn in the nearly thirty years, 1761–90, in which he served Prince Nikolaus Esterházy. With a dedicated patron of enormous wealth, Haydn was able to recruit and train what was probably the finest orchestra in either Austria or Hungary, direct productions in an opera house, and prepare a volume of chamber music, symphonies, concertos, and operas for performance. After the death of Prince Nikolaus, Haydn went to London, where in 1791–92 and again in 1794–95 he dazzled the public with a dozen new symphonies stamped with genius and played by an orchestra that set new standards for performance.

Haydn apparently preferred to conduct from the keyboard of a harpsichord. The lid was removed from the instrument, which faced the orchestra in center stage between the first and second violins. The concertmaster, seated at Haydn's left, shared some responsibility for maintaining ensemble unity. In the earlier symphonies Haydn was a performer as well as a leader. In the manner of the day he played continuo—that is, he supplemented the small orchestral forces by playing a bass line and, when appropriate, filled out harmonies and textures with an improvised keyboard part. In the London symphonies, which employ a large orchestra, this was no longer necessary, although Haydn wrote charming solos for the concertmaster and himself in the finale of the Symphony No. 98.

Evidence suggests that Haydn marked decisive moments in the music with his hands or a roll of music paper, but in passages in which the musicians were playing at a well-established tempo they probably looked to the concertmaster for direction. Theater conductors, it should be noted, also sat at a harpsichord in the center of the pit so they might accompany singers in recitatives. Bruno Walter, conducting at the Met in the mid-twentieth century, continued this practice, although he used a small grand piano because of its larger sound. Conductors today often prefer to have a keyboard player in the orchestra pit so they can concentrate on the instrumental ensemble.

In the final decades of the eighteenth century, it was assumed that the ideal person to conduct a new work was its composer. Haydn, judging from abundant evidence, was well qualified. Mozart supervised the rehearsals for his final operas and directed the first three performances from the keyboard before turning the production over to another conductor. His skill in this role was widely admired.

Haydn's influence on orchestral performance in England remained strong until about 1830. The conductor sat center stage at a piano keyboard, but did nothing to control the performance, which was, literally, led by what the British still call the leader—that is, the concertmaster. The practice was challenged in 1820 by Louis Spohr, who wrote to a friend, "The way of conducting here, both at the opera house and at concerts, is the most topsy-turvy one imaginable. They have two conductors, but neither really functions. The 'conductor,' as he is styled on the bills, sits at the piano and plays from the full score, but gives neither the beat nor the tempo. This is supposed to be done by the 'leader' or first violin; but as he has only the first violin part in front of him, he can't be of any help to the orchestra, so he contents himself with emphasizing his own part and letting the orchestra keep with him as best it can."

Spohr decided the British were slaves to tradition and while rehearsing a concert in May 1820 took the score from the pianist, placed it before him, drew a slender white baton from his inner coat pocket, and gave the downbeat. He was now able to establish ensemble unity, cue the brass and wind, and (as he later reported) produce in the concert "a result . . . more brilliant than I could have hoped for." Those who feel this demonstration may have changed performance practices overnight underestimate the British character. It was a dozen years before these reforms were fully established.

As time passed, it soon became apparent that some composers were excellent conductors (Spohr, Carl Maria von Weber, and Felix Mendelssohn are prime examples) and some were very bad conductors. Ludwig van Beethoven, an eminent pianist, had no practical experience in orchestral direction, and coupled with his growing deafness, this made him a liability rather than a leader. His metronome markings frequently suggest tempi he may have heard in his mind but that orchestras of his day could not possibly manage, and any attempt to achieve these speeds, plus his efforts to control dynamics with exaggerated mime shows, probably added up to general confusion. One may safely assume that most performances said to be conducted by Beethoven were really led by a concertmaster striving mightily to avert disaster.

By the early nineteenth century it was appreciated that genius in composition was something quite different from the skills required to direct an orchestral performance. Franz Schubert was at his best making music with his friends. Robert Schumann appeared as a conductor, but had no real flair for the job. Meanwhile other musicians, with no particular gift for composition, proved themselves to be admirable directors of orchestras and offered convincing performances of other men's music.

Richard Wagner, in his treatise *On Conducting,* recalls, "In the days of my youth [the 1820s] orchestral pieces at the celebrated Leipzig Gewandhaus concerts were not conducted at all; they were simply played through under the leadership of concertmaster Matthai."

Matthai probably gave decisive beats with his violin bow and played along with the ensemble the rest of the time. In established music of the classical period, it was possible to proceed in this manner and produce results that Wagner found "smooth and precise."

It would be incorrect to assume that performances conducted de facto from the concertmaster's chair are a thing of the past. In my years reviewing the Chicago Symphony, I observed innumerable examples of this procedure when a staff conductor or some unfortunate guest lost control of the ensemble.

Problems arose in new music in the romantic style, which not only called for larger instrumental forces, but for a more flexible and expressive manner of performance as well. The violin-bow conductor in center stage has remained a delightful feature of Viennese waltz orchestras to the present day, but only the foolhardy would attempt to play one of Gustav Mahler's symphonies in this fashion. In France the orchestra was usually led by a violin-bow conductor, but it was soon realized that only with the greatest difficulty could he control the stage in the opera house. Here a continuous audible time-beat with a staff similar to Lully's was used. When the intrusion of this sound became offensive, the successor to Lully's staff, a slender white baton, came into use. Since Hector Berlioz was not a violinist, he chose to direct an orchestra with a baton, opening the way for baton conducting outside the theater.

The French baton was different from those appearing about this time in Germany. In its early form the German baton was a heavy stick, grasped firmly in the middle, and used to indicate a tempo in much the same manner that a drum major leads a band today. And, like a drum major, the conductor turned his back on his musicians and faced the audience. Weber directed his opera *Oberon* at Covent Garden in London in 1826 in the old style, with a roll of paper, but it is unclear whether he faced the singers or the audience. I find it unlikely that he preferred the view of the audience to that of the stage. In Vienna his conducting was felt to be minimal. He would beat out a few measures to set a tempo and then let the orchestra play without further direction until a tempo change or some other important event required his intervention.

Future practice was being defined in the Mendelssohn household in Berlin where, in about 1825, young Felix had adopted the French baton and was conducting the family orchestra facing the players. In 1835, performing the Beethoven Second Symphony at the Gewandhaus, he had baton in hand and eye contact with his forces. Such music, he wrote, "requires conducting throughout, and by one who is not, himself, required to play." The value of this innovation was immediately recognized, and the local critic observed that "seldom has he heard [this symphony] so excellently played."

In *The Orchestra from Beethoven to Berlioz,* Adam Carse concludes: "In the year 1800 it would have been difficult, or even impossible, to find an orchestra in which the playing was controlled by a musician who did nothing but beat time and indicate by his gestures how the music should be interpreted. By 1850 it would have been difficult to find anything but small orchestras in which the playing was controlled by any other means than by a time-beating conductor."

What twentieth-century musicians would regard as modern conducting was defined midway in the century by Wagner. The decisive season may have been 1855–56, when he directed the programs of the London Philharmonic Society. He had then been conducting for twenty years. Like Lully in the distant past and Weber in his lifetime, he felt an operatic performance must be a unity. Voices, instruments, dance, direction, and decor must all fuse to produce an intensified artistic effect none of these elements of the performance might achieve by itself.

His predecessors in London had been diplomats. English society loved Mendelssohn, whose death in 1847 was deeply mourned, and delighted in the vivacity of Berlioz. Wagner, who was handicapped by knowing very little English, was a revolutionary rather than a courtier. For a start, conductors in London traditionally performed their duties wearing white kid gloves. He would have none of that. The bare-knuckle school of conducting begins with him. So does the bare-knuckle approach to dealing with musicians and their shortcomings. He knew how he wanted things to go, and he would not stop short of the desired result. It was more than the London orchestra, or the patronizing London critics, could take. He departed, not to return for twenty-two years, with one critic observing, "Another such set of concerts would go far to annihilate the Philharmonic Society."

The Germans saw him in a very different light. Even Eduard Hanslick, arch foe of Wagner the composer, agreed, "He is an excellent conductor, full of spirit and fire . . ." and his innovations "all combined to make a wonderful effect."

Wagner's baton was not used to beat time. It shaped a musical line, revealed the ebb and flow of its rhythmic pulse, and demanded of the performers that they play not from bar line to bar line, but from phrase to phrase. "Jog trot" performances, as Hanslick described them, were replaced by those that sang.

This was essential both for Wagner's own music and all the major works of the period. The romantic composer does not call for a uniform tempo. Quite the contrary, the music speeds up and slows down, rhythm yields to the melodic line [rubato], notes will be accented and held, and dramatic silences will become part of the work. All this calls for someone to have secure control over the ensemble.

We are living in a time in which a large portion of the musical public is alienated from the most characteristic works of the composers of this century, and the repertory is dominated by works a hundred or more years old. In contrast, concert programs of the mid-nineteenth century were filled with new music. The majority of the Haydn and Mozart symphonies were unknown, and those that were known were viewed as old-fashioned, quite at odds with the triumphant romantic spirit that touched every aspect of European life.

Beethoven defined what the symphony should be, but it may safely be assumed that all performances of Beethoven's symphonic works in his lifetime were dreadful. When Otto Nicolai, a baton conductor, founded the Vienna Philharmonic Orchestra in 1842 the city probably began to hear these scores in acceptable performances for the first time. The Viennese conductors were keyboard players, while French conductors were drawn primarily from the ranks of string players—a situation that continued into the present century with men like Pierre Monteux, Charles Munch, and Jean Martinon.

Erich Leinsdorf once observed to me that "Germans have difficulty taking music seriously if it is not contrapuntal," and George Szell once insisted in conversation that "a conductor really must play an instrument on which well-developed counterpoint is possible." For Szell that meant he must be a keyboard player. Toscanini studied piano at the conservatory and played it all his life, although he began his career as an orchestra cellist.

James Levine, in his ideas of operatic performance, his technique, and his concept of the conductor and his work, is a direct artistic heir to Wagner. It is the most logical thing in the world that he should be functioning at the master's Festival Theater in Bayreuth, because if we can't have

Wagner in the orchestra pit, of the conductors at work today, Levine, as I see it, appears to be the next best choice.

Wagner may be regarded as Levine's artistic great-grandfather. Wagner was there, and he was important; but Levine in his youth was more aware of his artistic grandfather, Arturo Toscanini. Toscanini was a dedicated Wagnerian to the core. In two summers, 1930–31, he revolutionized Bayreuth, and he would have done more had he remained, for example, to do a *Ring* cycle. This never happened because, despite personal pleas from Adolf Hitler, Toscanini rejected the festival once it was infected by the thoughts and presence of the Führer.

We may, indeed, generalize that the dominant twentieth-century view of the artistic function of the conductor comes from Toscanini's work. As we confront the twenty-first century, there are still, essentially, two traditions—the romantic, nineteenth-century approach in which the conductor was an interpreter, free to follow his own creative impulses and depart from the letter of the score; and the classical point of view in which the conductor must discover, respect, and, to the best of his ability, realize the artistic intentions of the composer. The great romantics—Furtwängler, Koussevitzky, and Stokowski—are long dead. There is no one of their stature to continue in their path.

In contrast, although Toscanini has been dead for forty years, his tradition lives on in good health. The Toscanini recordings remain and, indeed, are more plentiful than they ever were in his lifetime. Moreover, they have been refurbished by the most advanced engineering techniques to provide the highest-quality sound the source can yield.

But Toscanini's last public appearances were in 1954. A few individuals in their forties may remember him as a live performer, but the majority of those for whom Toscanini became a personal force through radio concerts and television are now in their sixties and seventies, or older. In that age group are individuals such as myself, once members of what we called "the Toscanini Mafia."

We who were welcome at the maestro's home, Villa Pauline, just north of Manhattan in Riverdale, are growing fewer every year. For us he was always the Old Man. We drank the red wine to which he attributed his vitality, ate the incredible risotto from the fine hand of his cook, Isolina, and had him, and his music library, open to us.

We now listen to the records and, more importantly, turn back to the nine television concerts. Realizing what they contain, we ask, "Who can make this kind of music today?"

James Levine can.

Leopold Stokowski observed a quarter century ago that there are now more fine orchestras in the world than there are fine conductors, and he wondered how long such a situation could continue. It has grown progressively worse, in part because gifted young American instrumentalists can find work, but equally gifted young American conductors have great difficulty securing the opportunities needed for professional growth. As Leinsdorf put it, about the same time Stokowski was expressing his concerns, "what American symphonic music needs is the equivalent of baseball's Texas League"—a place to gain the experience essential for a transition to the big time. Levine saw this problem and overcame it, but not everyone has been so skillful, or fortunate.

With the death of Sir Georg Solti, the number of senior conductors active in the international world of music has reached an all-time low. Carlo Maria Guilini, now the great octogenarian, appears only rarely. Carlos Kleiber calls himself retired. Pierre Boulez, now in his early seventies, devotes much of his time to composing.

There are four men consistently active on the international circuit who are equally celebrated for their work in the theater and the concert hall—Claudio Abbado, Bernard Haitink, Riccardo Muti, and Levine. Levine is the youngest and for this and other reasons the one most likely to have a lasting impact on the new century. He is the only one of the group to represent the Toscanini tradition of musicianship. He heard the broadcasts as a child and has explored the maestro's recorded legacy throughout his life. Toscanini's guiding spirit is in his blood.

Their mutual regard for the maestro provided a harmonious basis for study with George Szell, who, although Viennese-trained, was deeply influenced by Toscanini, respected his work fully, and encouraged Levine in his desire to follow the path marked clearly by the Old Man.

Levine did not have much contact with Bruno Walter, but I recall conversations in which Walter acknowledged Toscanini's influence on his work, especially after guest conducting Toscanini's New York Philharmonic in 1932. This influence can easily be documented from Walter's recordings.

Even conductors who remained in Germany in the 1940s, when Toscanini played no part in German musical life, were by no means immune to his influence. Herbert von Karajan first encountered Toscanini on recordings and then in Berlin in 1926 when he heard him conduct the visiting La Scala Opera. Five years later, Karajan sat in the pit at Bayreuth for the maestro's rehearsals. After the war, more of Toscanini's recordings were made available to him by Walter Legge.

One problem the American conductor has always faced is reverse chauvinism, the irrational idea that European musicians always have

Ten-year-old James Levine with
his brother, Tom, and his sister,
Janet, Cincinnati, summer 1953.

Studying the piano-vocal score of
Gounod's *Faust* at age nine.

The six-year-old prodigy practices at home.

Five years later, 1954, rehearsing the Beethoven Piano Concerto No. 3 at the Brevard Music Festival in North Carolina.

Eleven-year-old James shows his parents his model set for *Barber of Seville,* Cincinnati, 1954. *(Cincinnati Enquirer)*

The future maestro of the Met,
Cincinnati, 1954.

Levine (*right*) with George Szell, the great conductor of the Cleveland Orchestra (*second from left*), 1966. *(Peter Hastings/Cleveland Orchestra Archives)*

Levine (*on stairs*) with another mentor, conductor Fausto Cleva (*center*) of the Metropolitan Opera.

At Aspen, where he was conducting Benjamin Britten's *Albert Herring,*
Levine is introduced to the composer, 1964.

Levine conducting the University Circle Orchestra,
Cleveland Institute of Music, 1968.

(Peter Hastings/Cleveland Orchestra Archives)

Rehearsing with Luciano Pavarotti. *(Martha Swope)*

Rehearsing with Cecilia Bartoli. *(Vivianne Purdom)*

At the Salzburg Festival, early 1980s. Levine often collaborated with director Jean-Pierre Ponnelle (*right*). Their production of *Die Zauberflöte* was the longest-running in Salzburg Fesitival history. *(Photo Schaffler)*

Below he confers with another conducting giant at Salzburg, Herbert von Karajan. *(Robert Messick)*

Levine with Leonard Bernstein, colleague, friend, and neighbor. *(Henry Grossman)*

The two conductors appeared together at the first Concert for Life at Carnegie Hall, where they closed the concert with a moving account of the slow movement of Mozart's Sonata for Two Pianos in D major. *(Steve J. Sherman)*

Levine with Marilyn Horne, composer John Corigliano, and librettist William M. Hoffman at the world premiere of *The Ghosts of Versailles. (Below)* Former Metropolitan Opera general manager Sir Rudolf Bing visits with soprano Teresa Stratas and Levine backstage after the performance. *(Winnie Klotz)*

Levine first conducted at the Wagner shrine, Bayreuth, in 1982 (the centennial production of *Parsifal*). Here he is in the famous covered orchestra pit. *(Tom Levine)*

In 1980 Swedish soprano Birgit Nilsson sang a triumphant series of Met *Elektras* with Levine. *(Winnie Klotz)*

Levine takes a bow with the Metropolitan Orchestra after their debut concert at the Musikverein in Vienna. *(Theresia Linke)*

In October 1997, Levine received the National Medal of Arts from President Clinton at the White House. *(Official White House Photo)*

At the Met, Levine, as principal conductor and artistic director, shares responsibilities with general manager Joseph Volpe.
(Suzanne De Shillo/NYT Pictures)

The Twenty-Fifth Anniversary Gala at the Metropolitan Opera House.
Among the artists who honored Levine were Plácido Domingo, Birgit Nilsson,
Kiri Te Kanawa, and Alfredo Kraus. *(AP/Osamu Honda)*

Parsifal rehearsal at Bayreuth, 1993. Deborah Polaski as Kundry, Plácido Domingo in the title role, director Wolfgang Wagner, and conductor James Levine.

(Photo Rau: Bayreuth Festival)

With soprano Jessye Norman at Salzburg. *(Christian Steiner)*

Birgit Nilsson and Elizabeth Taylor congratulate Franco Zeffirelli, James Levine,
Eva Marton, and Plácido Domingo after a triumphant 1987 *Turandot* at the Metropolitan.

(Ruby Washington/NYT Pictures)

some advantage over someone born in the United States. One hopes it was largely destroyed by Europe's enthusiastic reception of Leonard Bernstein. Levine has proved himself to be as fine a musician in every way as the best Europe has produced in his lifetime. He has thrived there, and a number of fine American conductors now hold important European posts. But none of the Big Five American symphony orchestras (New York, Boston, Philadelphia, Cleveland, and Chicago) is presently led by an American.

Levine can equal Toscanini in performance skills. A performance worthy of the Toscanini tradition requires firm ensemble control from a person dedicated to the composer. The conductor must hear the work as a whole, as a synthesis of both its larger outlines and its detail, and carefully place all of its elements in the proper relationship to one another. He must project the score with a firm rhythmic pulse, singing line, and open texture so the ear can reach into the ensemble and savor everything that is happening. This is conducting in the modern sense of the word.

One thing we must not do is undervalue our great contemporaries in favor of musicians from past years who may be outside our experience. I am convinced that Plácido Domingo is a finer tenor and a more complete artist than Caruso, great though Caruso was. In the same light, Levine is a finer, more complete conductor than Toscanini. The historical influence of the Old Man is, of course, nothing anyone can challenge. But Levine has a vastly larger repertory than Toscanini ever offered, and a more complete mastery of musical styles.

I call Levine the well-tempered conductor, for two different reasons. As Bach demonstrated in his famed collection of forty-eight preludes and fugues, a keyboard instrument tuned to equal temperament appears to be in tune in every key. Well-tempered for Levine is not a matter of pitch but style. Eminent conductors of the past have excelled in music in the style closest to their basic artistic impulses and had difficulties of varying degree with music in a very different idiom.

Toscanini was at his best in works growing out of Italian classicism. If he played a Viennese waltz or something as intensely nationalistic as Smetana's *Má Vlast,* he lacked true feeling for the composer's native speech. The music was heard with a strong Italian accent and, although it might have some admirable qualities, was missing the ring of authenticity. It may well be that it was Toscanini's difficulties with Mahler's very Austrian manner of expression, as much as his personal aversion to the man as a professional rival, that caused him to reject his music. Mahler's symphonies, he once told his son, should only be used as toilet paper, an opinion few listeners or conductors would share today.

The opposite problem can be seen in the career of Toscanini's great contemporary Leopold Stokowski. In a discography of nearly fifty pages, there is one authentic Haydn work, the Symphony No. 53, and a celebrated Haydn fake in a Stokowski arrangement. The Mozart listings are more generous but even stranger, not a single symphony in its entirety (the Minuet of K. 550), two piano concertos, two examples of entertainment music for winds, and three shorter works. This is really not surprising. Stokowski's Mozart performances were not well played or well received. Critics found them fussy, perfumed, romanticized. The conductor's gift was for giving a phrase expressive shape in a romantic style—music that primarily requires clarity and purity of line was uncongenial.

One may plausibly argue that Toscanini and Stokowski as young men were so thoroughly immersed in an approach to music-making that came to dominate their work that these basic influences became the major factors in defining their repertory. Levine and his mentor, Szell, were deeply bound to the classical tradition, but they had flexibility. They knew when the classical approach should not be rigidly applied. Their classical roots gave them a measure of reserve.

A Levine performance of a Tchaikovsky symphony is more subdued than the characteristic Stokowski statement of this music, but it has romantic qualities. Passion and ecstasy are not to be overdone, but neither are they to be suppressed. Levine is not afraid of them, even though he would never introduce these elements into music where they do not belong.

It is this awareness of the right thing to do at the right time that produces well-tempered musicianship, but Levine is well tempered in another way. Toscanini's approach to the preparation of music was shaped by Italian orchestra players of the late nineteenth century, many of whom had limited technique, possibly even more limited musicianship, and whose objective may well have been to get the job done with minimal effort. Toscanini had in his mind a performance that demanded a maximum commitment by everyone, and if the musicians would not give it to him voluntarily, he would get it from them by abrasive and coercive means.

His celebrated rehearsal tantrums were the result, but it must be recalled that there were many occasions when nothing of the sort occurred, largely because nothing of the sort was necessary. For example, in the autumn of 1952 when he paid farewell to London audiences with two Brahms programs with the Philharmonia Orchestra, he sensed immediately he had before him a cooperative group of excellent players, and the rehearsals were pleasant experiences in which things went efficiently and well.

His son, Walter, once played him the album Bruno Walter called "The Ambush," in which the Mozart *Linz* Symphony was recorded together with all the rehearsals. It is Bruno Walter revealing his most civilized manner.

The elder Toscanini, to his son's surprise, was unimpressed.

"Why, Father?" he was asked.

"The orchestra is so good. You say diminuendo, you *get* diminuendo. You say pianissimo, you *get* pianissimo." A shrug. The Old Man liked challenging situations.

Levine, like Szell, will not tolerate indifferent work. If a musician is not prepared to function at a high level, he does not belong in a major symphony orchestra or the pit of an important opera house today. Levine had the advantage of beginning after the level of the profession had risen enormously internationally, and problems Toscanini faced routinely a century ago no longer were significant. Walter, in the mid-century, liked to come before an orchestra and say, "Good morning, my friends, let us make music together." If a fiddler on the back stands took that to mean that he could sit back in his chair and play with half a bow, in other words, coast through the rehearsal, he quickly discovered he was wrong. Walter could be as tough as Toscanini, but by firmly insisting on what he wanted, not erupting into rage. For Levine such confrontations are a waste of time and energy. Music-making should be dominated by reason and professionalism, a shared commitment to the art, and all parties must be prepared to work together harmoniously because that is the way professionals express their dedication and mutual regard. It is a matter of courtesy—to one another and to the music that is to be expressed.

One day, going over a complex passage in the score of Alban Berg's *Lulu* with the Met Orchestra, Levine had to resort to a few sharp words to get the strict attention needed for complete accuracy. So seldom used, this approach received an immediate response. "See," he observed. "We got it right. Why did you make me get nasty in order to do it?" Clearly even this minor reprimand was distasteful to him. "It wastes energy unnecessarily," he explains.

Sir Georg Solti has insisted that in more than twenty years with the Chicago Symphony he almost never had to raise his voice to secure the attention and performance he was seeking. His rehearsals, for an onlooker, were actually rather dull, the meticulous working out of detail with conductor and players communicating with one another quietly in exchanges that were short and to the point.

Levine's success as music director of the Ravinia Festival was certainly based in part on working in the same spirit. In the opening years his

English was more idiomatic and precise than Solti's (Solti's English steadily improved with residence in London), but the musicians experienced no great change in their manner of working between the winter and summer concerts, and the performances reflected this stability.

Levine is a complete musician. Many eminent conductors begin as instrumental players, but frequently, as their careers advance, they fear to have their work as an instrumentalist compared with their achievements in directing orchestral performance. Levine has no such inhibitions. In the course of his work he is at the piano practically every day of his life. It is as much a part of him as his conducting, and he moves effortlessly from making music with his own hands to shaping the work of a hundred colleagues. He can perform as a pianist of high achievement or pick up the baton and turn to the most complex vocal and instrumental ensemble, making use of its skills as if the orchestra were another sort of instrument lying under his fingers.

In terms of repertory, he is a performer of impressive range, fully equal to the complexities of the most intricate twentieth-century scores but just as content and secure with a small baroque ensemble. Talking with him, one becomes aware that there is a great deal of music he would like to perform but, for one or another reason, cannot play at this time. Similarly, one realizes that the regular traversal in a three-year cycle of a body of standard scores does not excite him. Eugene Ormandy could methodically produce Beethoven and Brahms symphonies the way a sausage-maker supplies bratwurst. (And Ormandy made good bratwurst.) But Levine has no wish to return to a standard score unless he has some new thoughts about it.

James Levine has three repertories. As a pianist he plays concertos, chamber music, and song literature. As a symphonic conductor he directs orchestral scores and large works for vocal forces and orchestra. As a theater conductor he directs operas and, on one occasion, ballet (*Le Sacre du Printemps*).

Many insist he is the finest accompanist of vocal music since Gerald Moore, and here his repertory is easily described. For all practical purposes, he plays everything. Similarly, he has performed a substantial amount of the important chamber music involving piano and, given time and opportunity, probably will play the rest. As a soloist, he prefers the concertos of Bach and Mozart. He does not have, or wish to expend, the time necessary to prepare the big romantic scores for piano and orchestra.

In twenty-three summers with the Chicago Symphony he directed nearly all of what Virgil Thomson called "The Fifty Famous Pieces," plus quantities of other music. His work as a guest conductor in recent years has emphasized Mahler and the Second Viennese School, composers for whom he feels a basic affinity. He has also directed much of the choral and orchestral repertory from Haydn onward.

In the thirty-seven years between his first performance at the Aspen Festival in 1961 and the end of the Met season in 1998, James Levine conducted eighty-one operas in their entirety and two (*Faust* and *Die Fledermaus*) in part. By the standards of today, this is an enormous repertory, particularly when one is dealing with a man in his mid-fifties who is certain to be learning new music as his career extends through another quarter century or more.

The list is cosmopolitan. There is music from Germany, Austria, and Hungary, Russian operas, a Czech opera, and, of course, French and Italian operas. Both British and American composers are represented. The styles range from the baroque to the distinctively twentieth-century voice of Arnold Schoenberg. It is characteristically the repertory of an American conductor. European conductors work out of a base provided by their national traditions, but Americans seem to have the freedom to see the world of music in the broadest terms.

The crucial test for Levine is the ability of a score to capture his artistic imagination. This is a man with exceptional artistic insight, refined taste, and extraordinary musical intelligence. It is obvious to him that there is more fine music than any one musician might possibly play. Rachmaninoff said, "Music is enough for one life, but one life is not enough for music," and Levine's decisions indicate that he agrees. He cannot possibly do everything, but there will be gifted people to do the things he chooses to pass by. He wishes to do the things he feels he will do best.

As a matter of routine, Levine insists it is destructive to direct operas with which one has no real involvement. If the work is a repertory staple, the public should not be denied the right to hear it, but he will engage someone else to bring it to the stage.

The Met is truly Levine's artistic home. Sixty-nine scores, 85 percent of the eighty-three operas in his repertory, have been presented there under his direction. Seven of the twelve operas he has directed, but never prepared at the Met, were things he did before he became principal conductor of the theater in 1973. Two are works he has recorded but has never produced for the stage. The only work he has led in a fully staged production in another theater is Schoenberg's *Moses und Aron,* which will come to the Met in the 1998–99 season. Gluck's *Orfeo ed Euridice* and Saint-Saëns's *Samson et Dalila* have been offered elsewhere in concert performances during his Met years.

Cosmopolitan though he is, performance statistics remind us that the heart of Levine's repertory is Austro-German opera. Admittedly, at the Met the score he has performed most frequently is Verdi's *Otello,* which he has directed sixty-nine times. But internationally the opera he has conducted more than any other is Wagner's *Parsifal*—101 performances, 48 at the Met and 53 at the Bayreuth Festival. Similarly, his twenty-five performances of *Die Zauberflöte* at the Met must be considered, along with fifty-one performances at Salzburg, the longest-running opera production in the history of the festival.

In terms of frequency of performance, four of the first five operas in Levine's repertory are Austro-German works. *Parsifal,* as just noted, is first, followed by *Die Zauberflöte. Otello* follows in third place. *Le Nozze di Figaro* and *La Forza del Destino* follow in fourth and fifth place with sixty-one and fifty-seven performances, respectively. Then come *Die Walküre, La Bohème, Don Carlo,* and *Don Giovanni.*

Levine has conducted all of the ten canonical operas of Wagner (half of them at Bayreuth), seven operas by Mozart, and four operas by Richard Strauss. Twenty-seven percent of his Met repertory is drawn from these three composers.

Yet the composer who has contributed the most works—seventeen—to Levine's repertory is not a German but the most distinctively Italian of musicians, Verdi. Twenty-one percent of the Levine repertory is made up of Verdi's work, sixteen operas produced for the stage and one produced only for records. Verdi is also far and away the leader in terms of the number of performances—464—essentially 30 percent of all Levine's work at the Met. The nine Verdi operas he has not performed are all early works. Two of them, *Nabucco* and *I due Foscari,* are of some importance.

Since Verdi's *Otello* is the score many associate most closely with Levine at the Met, it is not surprising that he chose it to open his twenty-fifth season. Second and third places on the Met list also belong to Verdi, *La Forza del Destino* and *Don Carlo* (which Levine meticulously presents in the original version). And, just to prove that statistics can be misleading, the work in fourth place on the Met roster is Puccini's *La Bohème,* which, however, has received only one Levine performance since 1987.

It should be noted that Levine conducted verismo opera when he was getting started because it is a major element of the repertory and produced engagements. When he was better established and could be more selective, he focused his attention on Verdi rather than his successors.

The Levine repertory stands on three legs—Mozart, Wagner, and Verdi—with a total of 988 Met performances, 63 percent of the work Levine has done at the theater. Seven Mozart operas provide a total of

236 performances in that group, and the ten Wagner operas contribute 288. This follows from the simple fact that Levine excels in the works of these three composers. He is possibly the greatest Verdi conductor who is not of Italian ancestry. His Mozart is in the grand Viennese tradition. And he is a great Wagnerian, a fact that has long been recognized and honored at the composer's Bayreuth shrine.

Levine delights in addressing himself to the widest variety of assignments and doing them superlatively well. He never appears to superimpose his own ego or interpretive ideas upon a work, but rather conveys with consistency and great conviction the impression that the composer is speaking through him in his own distinctive voice. No distinguished conductor of our day is more transparent—that is, more consistently the projection of the composer rather than himself.

Because of his secure outlook as a classicist, Levine excels in music like the early Mozart symphonies in which the content of the work grows entirely from purity of form. The unfolding line of the music need not be reshaped or emphasized for expressive purposes. Like an old master drawing, the expressive content is all there in the simplicity and purity of the line itself.

A Levine performance rests on a secure rhythmic pulse. There is always a beat, and although it can be treated with great dramatic effect, or reduced to a whisper, its integrity is always preserved. On that secure foundation he builds the inner voices, the harmony and counterpoint, that give substance to the work, and soaring above, in perfect unity with the rest, is the primary thematic line eloquently shaped and set forth.

Levine links one strong phrase with another. The music always moves confidently forward. Fussing and fiddling with the music in the manner of some romantic conductors is alien to him. Occasionally, for his own edification, he will experiment with romantic effects. In 1975 at the Chicago recording session for the Brahms First Symphony, on the first run-through of the finale, he inserted a big, rhetorical pause of the type beloved by the romantics. It is my long-established practice never to talk to conductors about their interpretive ideas under conditions like this, but as Levine was leaving the control room he caught my glance.

"Stop," he told me. "You don't have to say a word. You are the voice of George Szell. I just wanted to hear how it would sound, and I'm not going to do it again."

Levine is not afraid to shape a phrase expressively with changes in color and dynamics when he feels it is called for. For him it is the question of genuine versus bogus emotion. If the feeling is authentic, as a key to the musical content, then it must be expressed.

Finally, there are the matters of color and texture. Levine wants your ear to penetrate deeply within the music. He hates lazy ears that reach only to the surface of the score. He wants you to listen into the music, to be aware of everything that is happening, and his music is carefully balanced to make that possible. Changing orchestra colors must have a maximum effect. Levine has the ear to match the eye of a Monet or a Cézanne. Invariably it is the right color, at the right intensity. It is no surprise that he loves the music of Berlioz and plays it with the mastery one might expect of a French musician.

Although Levine is brutally self-critical, those who have followed his career from the earliest years search with great difficulty to find a memory of a truly bad performance. He has a way of turning his disappointments into lessons for the future. Clearly some performances are more successful than others. That is the nature of things. He can be vulnerable to fatigue, although it does not happen often. No musician is always at the absolute peak of his form. Toscanini used to philosophize, "No one is a genius twenty-four hours a day." It is a human impossibility. But the day-to-day norm Levine establishes and sustains is extraordinary.

In a period of music history in which there are excellent technicians who, unfortunately, lack the ability to probe the depths of a score, and fine musicians who have deep musical feelings but lack the technical resources to develop them fully, Levine has consistently displayed a superlative balance between heart and mind. Szell liked to emphasize a word which, he felt, was insufficiently employed in contemporary criticism: *taste*. Levine's taste is impeccable.

Virgil Thomson did not feel that music criticism should be "opinion mongering" but must be based on factual statements about what was happening in a performance. The truth of my statements about Levine is found in watching him at work under a variety of circumstances. Let us encounter the man in action.

II

April 24, 1995. Medinah Temple, Chicago.

James Levine and the Chicago Symphony are to record the second segment of music for the Disney Studio's *Fantasia 2000,* the sequel to *Fantasia,* its historic film of 1940. The original, with a soundtrack by Leopold Stokowski and the Philadelphia Orchestra, has long been established as a classic. A synthesis of symphonic music and often inspired animation, it has attracted millions to the works of Bach, Beethoven, Tchaikovsky—even Stravinsky. With its seventeen-track sound, Fantasound, it was some twenty years ahead of its time. This new version, with a forty-eight-track master tape, represents the present state of the art.

The original plan was to combine music from the original film with new material, but as work on the picture progresses, it becomes clear that this is an unreasonable goal. Taken by itself, the original *Fantasia* sound-track remains impressive, but directly juxtaposed with contemporary work it is clearly a historic document. The new sound and the old sound cannot be reconciled.

The new *Fantasia,* therefore, will be all new, not a mixture of Stokowski and the Philadelphia Orchestra with Levine and the Chicago Symphony, but all Levine/Chicago. He and the CSO must carry the musical side of the picture. In April 1995 this conclusion had yet to be reached. The great Stokowski was still very much part of the grand design, and Levine was content to share the honors with him.

Since animation is done to the edited music, production begins with recording. A year before, Levine and the Chicago orchestra had started the process, recording Respighi's *The Pines of Rome,* a highly compressed version of the first movement of the Beethoven Fifth Symphony, music from Saint-Saëns's *Carnival of the Animals,* and the first, and best-known, of Elgar's *Pomp and Circumstance* marches. This session calls for a remake of a short section of the Elgar and a recording of the first movement of the Second Shostakovich Piano Concerto, with Yefim Bronfman as soloist.

Medinah, a classic example of the cultural monuments constructed by the Shriners early in the century, is one of the largest halls in Chicago, with a huge stage that annually houses a circus. Levine has been making records there since 1974. It is a place to challenge engineers. Properly used, it provides a rich and spacious sound. Indifferently utilized, it yields a product that sounds as if it were recorded inside a barrel.

The orchestra, dressed in the casual, functional garb musicians invariably adopt for rehearsals and recording, is fanned out across the large stage to provide maximum stereo spread. Levine wears his usual working clothes—a white polo shirt, black trousers, and soft, tan shoes, with his trademark rolled-up towel (a dark green one this time) across his left shoulder. Later a Disney artist will present him with a drawing of Donald Duck holding a baton and wearing the same outfit.

At the stroke of one, while the orchestra completes its tuning ritual and engineers have a last look at microphone placement, Levine is in the corridor next to the control room in a brief conference with Roy Disney

Jr., nephew of the great Walt and chief of animation at the studio, and the record producer, Jay David Saks, who has been working closely with Levine since 1977. Since Disney rarely records classical music, for this project the studio has hired well-established people from BMG/RCA and CBS/Sony.

"Are you going to rehearse?" Levine is asked.

"I think we should simply start and play," he replies. "It will give us all a feel for the piece and the hall, and after we go through it a little, we can start to pick up the tempo and shape a real performance." Turning to Saks, he adds, "You tell me when you think we have begun to get it." He grins, a big face completely flooded with a smile, "I assure you, the beginning tempo will not be right!"

"We should have got that on film," Disney observes as he heads for the control room. It is immediately clear that this is a recording session for a motion picture rather than one for discs. The union rules are different. (You need give the orchestra only one ten-minute break per hour, Levine is advised.) So is the atmosphere. There is far less stress. The crew has come from New York and radiates the relaxed competence of experienced hands.

Everything goes into the forty-eight-channel data recorders, and it will all be remixed in Burbank to achieve precise balance in the final product. For the session the engineers listen to five microphones that provide the main perspective, three in a T formation at center stage and two at the extreme right and left. There are two presence mikes on the piano. The sound in the room is produced by two big monitor speakers, which no one likes very well; Saks prefers electrostatic headphones.

Although Levine has not conducted the Chicago Symphony for a year, they know each other and within five minutes orchestra and conductor are working together as if he had been directing them the previous week. They know exactly what he wants, concentration, accuracy—their best—and their respect for him is shown in the fact that he gets these things immediately. The respect, of course, is mutual. As it turns out, Levine gets through the entire session without a moment's friction—precisely the kind of working situation he prefers.

One reason for this is that, from the player's standpoint, he is an ideal conductor. From his great role model, Toscanini, and his great mentor, Szell—plus years of experience—he has acquired a baton technique that is fluid, graceful, and yet completely transparent and unambiguous. (Unlike Toscanini, whose arm muscles were tense, Levine is unlikely to suffer from bursitis.) No professional musician should have the least trouble following him. The performance is solidly focused in the stick.

This proves especially important at Medinah. In Orchestra Hall, its home for rehearsals, concerts, and most recordings these days, the musicians of the Chicago Symphony are accustomed to listening to one another and following their ears as well as the baton. In the vast space of Medinah, if the back stands of the violins try to stay with the double basses on the other side of the stage by listening to them, they will inevitably be late by that small fraction of a second that makes the difference between clarity and haze. Here they must play on the stick, stay with the beat, and recognize that the aural cues are misleading. This takes a few moments of adjustment.

Seated behind Saks in the control room are a group of people from Disney, led by Don Ernst, producer of the film. Relaxed, he listens to a few short takes and comments, "They're great when they're together." Getting them together is Levine's job, and he goes about it methodically. Invariably a few moments must be spent correcting errors in one or another musician's part. There is a discussion about a section marked pizzicato in the strings, and agreement is reached. This out of the way, a real start is possible.

Levine is meticulous in his preparation of music. He hears details that call for correction, and he picks them up promptly. On a wind chord the harmonic balance is off. "We are getting too much C," he concludes. The adjustment is made. A horn accent is intensified. These repairs produce quite a bit of stopping and starting, and Saks gets from take one to take fifteen fairly quickly.

"This music should be crisp, light, brilliant, and rhythmic with lots of energy," Levine tells his musicians. It soon takes on that character. The chain reaction has started. Conductor, soloist, and orchestra are interacting with one another, with one fine moment stimulating the achievement of the next.

About a half hour into the session Levine decides he wants to hear what is going on tape and gives the orchestra a twenty-minute break. He moves from the auditorium across the corridor into the control room, takes a seat next to Saks, and listens to the playbacks, conducting the tape with a tiny, precise beat a predecessor in Chicago, the formidable Fritz Reiner, would have admired. The sound on the tape is much tighter than that in the hall, the result of microphone placement that suppresses some of the reverberation. Years of working at Medinah have prepared Levine for this, but he finds it nice to have his expectations confirmed.

"Can I have the fiddles a little louder in relation to the basses?" he asks. "Can you do that here, or shall we do it out there?" The engineer can change the balance, and Levine is pleased. It is better this way.

Is the piano receiving flattering treatment? Levine feels the middle range seems a little duller than the top and bottom. The instrument, an American-made Steinway from Orchestra Hall, is actually quite bright in the middle. This calls for another slight adjustment.

By two o'clock the preliminaries are over and Levine and Bronfman are down to the business of shaping a finished performance. The opening bars of the movement, with the piano playing against a small wind band, are tricky if you insist on both precision and spirit. Bronfman, who must plunge into the music, is a little tense.

"Your first note is good but the second note is tentative," Levine comments. "Be stronger. Make the leap." Bronfman shrugs. It's only a recording. If I blow it, we can do it over. Gaining confidence, he plunges in, and instantly the phrase becomes firmer, more propulsive. Everyone now seems caught up in the spirit of the work, and Levine has little to say. They play together, and as they play the details fall beautifully in place. The orchestra now has the score confidently in its fingers (it has not been played in the subscription concerts for more than fifteen years), and the session seems to have become less of a job than a welcome opportunity to make music together.

"Let's see if we cannot increase the tempo," Levine suggests, "without losing this control." It works. Levine is ready to do the movement straight through, hopefully without errors. There is a false start, and on the next try it takes off, yielding something Disney can use. Ernst and his staff in the control room know it. The place is illuminated by smiles. This is what they came to Chicago to hear, and they are hearing it, probably finer than they imagined it might be.

It is a reminder that the Chicago Symphony has played superlatively well for a number of conductors in recent decades. It gave its best to Reiner, of course, but also to Stokowski, Sir Georg Solti, Erich Leinsdorf, Claudio Abbado, and, more recently, Pierre Boulez. But it doesn't play for anyone better than it plays for Levine. The musicians know he deserves all they have to give, and, for the honor of their profession, they give it to him.

With a complete performance of the piece on tape, Levine and Bronfman know their work is nearly finished, but they want to cover themselves. After a pause for a brief consultation, they decide to do it again. Levine sets the notes spinning, and the second try is quick, bright, and precise. They've got it.

While the piano is wheeled offstage, Levine considers his next task. Elgar wrote five marches with the title "Pomp and Circumstance," but the work most people know by that name is the one in D major, the first.

With the words "Land of hope and glory," it probably entered our lives as the music to which we graduated from high school. Disney is using it in a very different context, as the story of Noah's Ark with Donald Duck as Noah's assistant. (If Mickey Mouse had a major role in the original *Fantasia,* it is only artistic justice that Donald, who is practically eligible for Social Security, should have his moment in the second.)

The projected animation for the middle section would work best if the tempo were a little slower than that which Levine first adopted, so the recording is being remade. Adolph Herseth, celebrated first trumpet of the symphony, is now onstage. He arrived with his horn as the Shostakovich was being completed. "Shostakovich knew better than to put a trumpet in that piece," he observes wryly.

Levine listens to his earlier version of the Elgar and consults with Ernst. Slower is fine, but how much? They'll know when they hear it. Returning to the orchestra, he plays the final bars of the first section to ease the musicians into the second part. It is slower this time, but the Disney forces are not convinced it is the exact tempo they have in mind. The word is relayed to Levine, and he tries again.

This time he hits it—a broad, flowing pulse that sustains the melodic line beautifully and lets the orchestra sing. That's right, he's told. "Now," Ernst asks, "can we do it again with one more thing? Toward the close there is a timpani note that fits nothing in the animation and will only have a jarring effect. Can it be cut?"

Sure it can.

There is one more suggestion. In a bar where Elgar has a single timpani note, can the value of the written note be cut in half and the note a third above added at the same length, to change a duh into a da-da?

Why not?

This time the Disney people are on their feet as the performance comes through on the monitors. The tempo is perfect. The minor changes in the timpani part will match the music perfectly to the pictures, and they are hearing exactly what they wanted to get. Grins mix with cheers as the last note fades away.

After nearly fifty takes, the job is done.

"That's it for today," Ernst calls out. "We'll be back in April next year." (As it turned out, they weren't. There was a conflict with the Levine anniversary gala at the Met, and the session was in September.)

Saks picks up the intercom phone and tells Levine he can dismiss the orchestra. His smile lights up the two TV monitors covering the stage as he tells the musicians. They vanish instantly. Few things on earth move faster than a musician who has been released early from a job.

Levine returns to the control room about 4:30, glowing with the contentment of a task well done. "We got two complete performances of the Shostakovich," he notes. But he doesn't need to hear them. "I think I prefer the first, but both are good and you can intersplice if necessary. And we had a half hour to spare. I can't take all this strain," he jokes. And he begins to philosophize. "The easiest sessions are the ones when you have been playing a work and you record it right on the same stage. There are always problems if you move to a place like this where the acoustics are completely changed.

"But recording opera is always more difficult than recording orchestral music. The worst are the aria sessions. Few singers come to them without a vague feeling that they really are not in good enough voice to record the music on which their reputation rests. So there are many, many retakes, and playbacks, and a lot of agonizing. On the other hand, you will have a session with principals, chorus, and lots of contrapuntal music. You fear it is going to be heavy going and, surprise, you do a few takes and look at your watch and find you've got it done in half the time.

"The really bad sessions are those when you go to the studio after a few stage performances, and you realize from the first it is not going to fly. Everything may be precise and note-perfect, but the music just isn't there. And it don't mean a thing if it ain't got that you know what. So you have to look over the sessions ahead of you and see if you can find some way to slip these things into the schedule and do the session over with some vitality.

"Nothing destroys an operatic conductor faster than a grind of repeating standard works, *Carmen*s and *Traviata*s and *Barber*s. A long run of them will just kill you. Look what I did when I came back to the Met this spring: *Idomeneo, Simon Boccanegra, The Ghosts of Versailles, Pelléas et Mélisande.* With that you can have a *Nozze di Figaro, Der Rosenkavalier,* and *Parsifal;* they don't wear you down. To deal with all that music in a period of a few weeks kept me constantly alert and in good form. Not to mention ecstatically happy."

Only those unaccustomed to life in the jet set might imagine that because Levine had an afternoon recording session in Chicago he would spend the night there. After all, he had flown in from New York in mid-morning, only thirty-six hours after the final performance of the Met season. In the early evening he will fly on to Florida for a week's vacation.

"It will be at least an hour to the airport now," his driver advises him.

"Fine," he says. "I'm in no hurry. Let me talk to the Disney people."

The crew takes over the now-deserted control room and begins to pack up the recording equipment. It, too, flew in from New York and will probably be back there by midnight. In a few hours nothing will remain to suggest that something has happened on the Medinah stage that will be as timeless as film can make it. But a half century from now, some child may be laughing with music that came to life this day and lives on.

May 10, 1995. Orchestra Hall, Chicago.

It is only natural to think of it as a family affair. The Levine family is there: Jim, his brother, Tom, and their mother, Helen, who came up from Cincinnati for the occasion and will have a glorious exchange with her sons in Jim's dressing room after the performance.

But there is also the orchestra family, not the family of the orchestra that is playing, the Met Orchestra, but the orchestra that calls this hall home, the Chicago Symphony. For a veteran orchestra player to buy a ticket and go to a concert on a night off is even more extreme than a letter carrier going for a walk on a free day. But about a third of the CSO (lots of front stands and first chairs) are here, scattered about the main floor and the balcony, obviously excited at the prospect of hearing Levine from the unusual perspective of the audience.

After being seated in front of him for more than twenty years, when he was their music director twenty-five miles north of here at Ravinia, in Highland Park, it is now great to be behind him, relaxed and listening.

The Ravinia Festival family is there, too. On the whole, nothing is more difficult than persuading an affluent suburbanite to stay downtown on a weeknight. But this is special. Jim is back.

No one acts as if this were an examination, but it will be a test, a proof, a demonstration of Levine's powers as an orchestra builder. At Ravinia he made full use of the resources of the Chicago Symphony, but the great orchestra he led was the creation of Fritz Reiner and polished and sustained by Sir Georg Solti. Levine was trained on the superlative symphonic instrument George Szell created in Cleveland. The Met Orchestra that Levine acquired as principal conductor in 1973 was a dispirited group that rarely played one bit better than it had to and seemed resigned to mediocrity.

Reiner's Chicago orchestra of the fifties had a violinist who played brilliantly for auditions and backstage, but froze up at the sight of an audience. Life with Reiner was impossible, so he applied for an opening in the Cleveland Orchestra, and Reiner gave him a glowing recommendation.

Some years later, Szell completed the tale. "He played a wonderful audition, and I hired him at once thinking, How good of Reiner to send me such a fine musician. Of course, in a couple weeks I knew the truth and told the man he would have to leave at the close of the season. But he has found a job in the ideal place."

"Where?" I asked.

"The Metropolitan Opera Orchestra."

It was, perhaps, only poetic justice that Szell's prize student should be sent to clean out this Augean stable. Mediocrity is Levine's mortal enemy. He quickly made clear that his continued tenure at the Met depended in part on his having the necessary opportunity to lift the orchestra to higher levels. In the past, with a major conductor in the pit, it played well, but its standards were uneven. By 1980 it was playing Mahler on the Met stage. Levine chose to work slowly and methodically, and by 1991 it was doing concerts at Carnegie Hall. This Chicago concert will open a short American tour that will take them as far as California. (In 1996 the orchestra toured Europe and in 1997 the Far East.)

Jaded music critics might sigh that touring orchestras rarely play fresh programs. If they don't begin with Strauss's *Don Juan* it will be the Beethoven Fifth. Levine did choose to start with a familiar score, the Schubert *Unfinished* Symphony, possibly because the group had recently recorded this music. But the next score, *Of Reminiscences and Reflections* by Gunther Schuller, the Chicago premiere of the Pulitzer Prize–winning composition of 1994, is precisely the sort of work most tour managers consider box-office poison. And the big work after intermission, Strauss's *Don Quixote,* is less of a draw than his *Also sprach Zarathustra* or *Ein Heldenleben* (music Levine doesn't play).

The Chicago Symphony has a long and distinguished Strauss tradition (several of his most celebrated works—among them *Don Quixote*— received their American premiere at its concerts), so it was natural Levine would welcome the challenge of playing Strauss in Chicago as he delighted in playing Wagner at Bayreuth and Mozart in Vienna.

For many who do not regularly attend CSO concerts, this is a last chance to hear Orchestra Hall as it had been in the Solti period. Summer is to bring the first of three phases of physical and acoustical renovation with the hope that in 1997 the rebuilt auditorium will rival the great halls of Europe. The Solti sound and the Levine sound are made up of many of the same elements—clarity, precision, and firm registration of the orchestral voices. It is a good way to say farewell.

Levine sees the Schubert as lyric drama, a work to be played with the same classical principles as Mozart, but music that must be infused with the warmth and color appropriate to the early romantic period. The essence of the work is a bold, singing line, and this must not be weakened by sentimental incursions, nor pushed too hard, but allowed to flow in phrases that breathe like a human voice.

Apparently there are only two movements because Schubert really never did get around to finishing the score. He began a scherzo but abandoned it. Romantics who feel his passion was spent, that he could not possibly go on to write a finale, are, I fear, seriously misguided. He later wrote an extraordinary finale for the *Great* C Major Symphony, and he probably would have written a wonder of a finale for the *Unfinished* if he ever had had the chance. Both the existing movements share a time signature of three/four but their character is very different. The conductor must see the things that make them different rather than stress a common pulse.

The performance is a confirmation of the story told in Levine's recording. This is, beyond any doubt, an orchestra of the highest achievement, and it plays Schubert in a manner that would have brought cheers in Vienna.

The true poetic justice in the performance of the Schuller score is that as a young man he played horn in the Met Orchestra, from 1945 to 1959. At sixty-nine, he is one of the giants of American music, a composer of great range and artistic force, a respected figure in music education, and a candid, accurate, and outspoken commentator on the musical life.

Of Reminiscences and Reflections is another in the long series of impressive works commissioned and performed by the Louisville Symphony. Written in seventeen days in September 1993, following the death of his wife, it was first heard the following December, with the composer conducting. It calls for, and makes effective use of, an unusually large orchestra, including a very generous percussion band. The scoring is consistently bold, with changing colors and textures that strengthen the impact of strong musical ideas. Schuller saw it as a variant on the symphony, five movements played without pause but reflecting the contrasts associated with traditional symphonic form.

Levine's greatest frustration at Ravinia was that he could not play any quantity of contemporary music—first because the rehearsal time was not there, and second because of the variable weather. Therefore, it is true to form that coming to Chicago with his own well-rehearsed orchestra, he will prove his loyalties by blazing away with a powerful modern piece.

He proves something else, that a truly strong score in a fine performance can win over all but the most conservative element of the public. Far from considering the Schuller box-office poison, many ticket buyers,

I surmise, found its presence on the program a strong inducement to attend. Judging from the applause and the comments after the concert, the audience is overwhelmingly supportive.

In the innocent world of 1898, trumpets imitating sheep in Strauss's *Don Quixote* could cause a scandal. Strauss found them an excellent joke, and critics and the public have long agreed with him. *Don Quixote* is Levine's favorite of the longer Strauss scores, largely, I suspect, because it is the most classical, a theme and variations, a type of work beloved of Mozart and Beethoven, and hence far more unified than the more free-wheeling and rhapsodic of the tone poems. It is also a sort of duo concerto with a solo cello and viola, played in this case by two principals from the orchestra (Jerry Grossman and Michael Ouzounian) as the errant knight and his squire. Both are experienced soloists, and confronted with the demand that they use their instruments to define two very different characters, they respond with imagination and skill.

Levine's objective is to make us aware of the beauty, subtlety, and musical invention that permeate the score, a result that is best achieved by adroit understatement rather than striving for great effect. *Don Quixote* is filled with delightful, ingratiating things. One's attention is quickly caught up in the unfolding of character and development of events as graphically portrayed in Strauss's writing. It is the composer, obviously well served by all parties, who triumphs at the close.

When a touring ensemble plays Orchestra Hall for the first time, its reception is a fairly accurate reflection of the thoughts and feeling of the audience. You may cheer for the Boston Symphony or the Vienna Philharmonic because, you suspect, it is expected of you, but the Met Orchestra is on its own. It is going to get what it earns.

And it earns an ovation. Rarely in the half century I have been attending concerts in that hall have I seen a new orchestra received with such warmth and approval. It is not just the volume of the applause. It is the spirit of welcome, of delight, of joy in discovery.

Backstage I greeted the maestro. "Few New Yorkers would have ever dreamed the day would come when the Met Orchestra was better than the Philharmonic. And where did they get that concentration?"

"Isn't it wonderful? They are right there, fully involved, every second. To get that, you create a situation in which a musician delights in being a musician, wants to play, wants to excel, wants to be right in the middle of what's happening."

October 2, 1995. Metropolitan Opera House, New York City.

The Metropolitan Opera opened its 111th season with its 197th performance of Verdi's *Otello*. Levine, who has conducted this opera at the Met more frequently than any other, was in the pit. This was to be his sixty-third Met performance of the opera.

You can still hear music (more likely *The Phantom of the Opera* than opera itself) in the theater in which the first Met performance of *Otello* took place. It is some 800 miles west, in Chicago. The Auditorium, at Congress and Michigan, was then known as "The Met West" and long runs by the company, in this case five weeks prior to the opening of the New York season, were not unusual. Chicago felt it could not produce its own opera, and until 1911 the Met really served both cities.

The date was November 23, 1891, four and a half years after the Milan premiere of the score, and Jean de Reszke sang the title role. The Valisi Mandolin Orchestra provided the serenade to Desdemona in Act 2. Whether there was also a bagpipe, as Verdi intended, or an oboe instead (an option the composer allows us) we shall never know. De Reszke repeated the role in New York on January 11, with the Ricca Mandolin Club replacing the Valisi band.

Opera companies of the 1890s were generous in their production of new works, but might be reluctant to build a production specifically for an opera unless they were sure of a demand for its return. Stock scenery, which could be found in every house, might be used for premieres. *Otello* returned in 1894–95 in a real production for thirteen performances, four in New York, nine on the road, including two in Chicago. Francesco Tamagno, who created the role in Milan, was the Otello.

Otello is a role for supertenors, *tenore robusto* as the Italians put it. Caruso let it alone. Luciano Pavarotti learned it and sang it in concert for a live recording, but told the press it was "not my cup of tea." On the other hand, Plácido Domingo, who sang the seven performances of this run, first sang the role in 1975 and recorded it with Levine as early as 1978. He also starred in a controversial Zeffirelli film of the opera. (The 1995–96 Met production was telecast and will probably return as a laserdisc.) Since the retirement of Jon Vickers, Domingo has had no serious rival for preeminence as the tragic Moor.

Levine has conducted *Otello* in eight Met seasons and presented nearly all the celebrated interpreters of this music. Domingo has sung the title role for him twenty-five times, just behind Vickers's record of twenty-seven. McCracken sang ten performances. Milnes, with twenty-seven

Iagos, holds the record for that role. A dozen sopranos have appeared as Desdemona—including Freni, Stratas, Margaret Price, Tebaldi, Te Kanawa, Scotto, Ricciarelli, and Gilda Cruz-Romo, who appeared the most frequently, thirteen times.

The Met rarely opens with a new production, but tickets sell for as much as a thousand dollars. This is a finely tuned sales strategy based on the realization that the house will be packed simply because it is the opening, and the lure of a new show can be reserved for another night.

Operatic opening nights once were fashion shows, festivals to display the capacity for conspicuous consumption, and parades for the socially prominent (who may not always be musically the most involved or sophisticated of individuals). After thirty-five opera openings in Chicago, I now report the presence of fewer rich butterflies and more serious, affluent music lovers. New York, traditionally a more cultivated place, produces a public that enjoys a gala night at the theater for the right reasons, and Levine makes a point of giving them a full measure of what they are after.

The *New York Times* found this "a powerful evening, one in which the Met proclaimed its virtues and sins with equal virtuosity." Among the virtues, "much of the opera resides in the orchestra and chorus parts. James Levine has organized these elements into music making of great clarity and force." Among the sins, the inability to deal with "the huge scale of the stage," which "looms so large over the opera's private moments that personal pain, played before backdrops of immense oil paintings, tends to be dulled in the onlooker's sensibilities." Ideally, for the final scene, the stage should shrink to proportions appropriate to a bedchamber.

But the scale of this opening night, and the fact that this opera was later to go to the world on television, illustrated a central force in the artistic life of the nation. Opera is replacing the symphony concert as the primary vehicle for serious (or, if you prefer, classical) music.

Between the opening of the century and World War II the dominant phenomenon in American serious music was the rise of symphony orchestras. This came to an end for the same reason the once-flourishing recital business is in difficulties, a diminishing group of outstanding performers and a restricted repertory with far too little music from the present century. But while the audience for symphonic music is shrinking, the demand for opera is on the increase. A growing public finds opera essential.

Of particular significance is that while symphony concerts and recitals appeal primarily to older listeners, opera has an immediate attraction for young people. A study by the National Endowment for the Arts shows that although the eighteen- to twenty-four-year-old population group shrank 16 percent from 1982 to 1992, attendance at operatic performances increased 18 percent. Since patterns of participation in the live performing arts are generally well established by age thirty, this suggests opera will be able to recruit an audience in the new century.

Why? Opera is ultimate theater—theater in which the intensity of the words, supported and magnified by the intensity of the music, lifts you to levels unmatched anywhere else in the world of the performing arts. And well-staged opera can produce some of the grandest experiences the theater can provide. Moreover, these experiences can be duplicated in the home with the large number of operas available on video cassettes and laserdiscs. Once you learn what opera can bring you, you're hooked for life. It happened to Levine as a child, as it has happened to many others.

If a full range of operatic thrills and chills are desired, all you have to do is pair Domingo with Levine. Midway in the final act of *Otello,* as the tragic climax approached, the woman seated next to me turned to her husband and asked, rhetorically I presume, "Could anything be more dramatic?" Domingo was doing the thing he does best, play a great role in the grand manner. He is two years older than his colleague, but they have worked together since 1970 in such a wide range of projects that artistic communication between them is often close to telepathic.

They know each other with the confidence that time brings. There may be unexpected delights, but there are never complete surprises in what the other person does. It is a combination (one of the few) that can be compared to that of Toscanini and Caruso. But Caruso never was a conductor. Domingo is—a good one. In the 1996–97 Met season he is on the roster as both a singer and a conductor, a remarkable dual role. This permits him to work with another maestro with a degree of understanding that produces extraordinary things. The fact that in his mid-fifties Domingo's voice is different from that of his thirties should be taken for granted. Voices change with age like fine wine, and the freshness of youth can be replaced by the richness of maturity. This is one of the most remarkable vocal instruments in the world, a suitable resource for one of the elite group of completely rounded and fully developed operatic singers in this century.

Long experience with this score has given Levine the ability to pace it with extraordinary skill. He sees the dramatic profile of the work as a whole. Tension is created with the first notes and sustained to the last.

Within that whole, he grasps the dynamics of every scene. Each climax is carefully built with a surge of music and singing that creates a sense of dramatic inevitability.

The current Met *Otello,* designed by Michael Yeargan and produced by Elijah Moshinsky, was first seen in the 1993–94 season. It replaced a celebrated Zeffirelli version of 1972 which many still admired but management felt ready for retirement. The clear intent is to keep the action moving following current European practice. The first two acts are played without pause and the final two are similarly paired to sweep us to the crest of the closing scene. The opera lasts three hours. This is possible because the Met has a thoroughly modern theater with the stage equipment to get sets, even big ones, out of the way fast. Midway in the first act, a wall drops out of sight to open up the stage, a wonderful effect no other American opera company can duplicate.

Verdi in his later years realized that his genius deserved nothing less than a first-class libretto with which to work. He had set enough third-rate material to music for any one lifetime. He was blessed with the collaboration of Arrigo Boito, himself a gifted composer. Verdi contemplated three operas to Shakespearean texts—*Othello, The Merry Wives of Windsor,* and *King Lear,* which was never written. The text, like *Hamlet,* defies compression; Verdi was uncertain what the music should be. But *Falstaff* (which is based on the *Merry Wives*) and *Otello* are the triumphs of his old age. Boito gave him two of the finest texts ever provided a composer. They have the authentic ring of Shakespeare but the tight structure needed for opera. Singing words takes twice as long as speaking them.

This production brought us what many would call a paradigm. Levine cast singers closely associated with him for several seasons. The longest bond was with Domingo, but if this was a casting everyone might expect, a few were surprised to find James Morris singing Iago for the first time in his twenty-fifth Met season. Morris was central to Levine's first presentation of Wagner's *Ring* operas in the late 1980s. Few Wotans are also Iagos, and few Iagos would even attempt Wotan. George London was a famous exception. Tito Gobbi, the most celebrated Iago of his day, would never have made it through the second act of *Die Walküre.* But Morris's contribution to the role was not vocal stamina (important as that is) but depth and power of tone and a commanding presence. One can easily see him as the architect of this tragedy.

No one running an opera house can have a favorite prima donna, but Levine's Desdemona was Renée Fleming, one of the outstanding sopranos of the day. She first won attention by winning the National Council Auditions in 1988. Levine recognized her potential, and she made her debut at the Met in a leading role (the countess in *Le Nozze di Figaro*) three years later. She has been heard triumphantly with the leading American opera companies and is now conquering Europe.

A daughter was born while this *Otello* was being prepared. She went from the rehearsal room to the delivery room and back. The first-act duet with Otello, the serene moment of love that makes the final act all the more poignant, was wonderfully achieved.

Bernard Shaw observed that *Otello* works well as an opera because, even if Shakespeare didn't know it, the original play is an opera in the thinnest of disguises. The Verdi/Boito first act is all exposition, and with the first moments of Act 2 the drama begins to roll and build. The glory of the work is that that process never slows down, never falters, but proceeds with a sense of deadly inevitability to the final bars of the score.

If you went to the New Century Theater a few blocks from the old Met in the late 1940s to see another Shakespearean show, Cole Porter's *Kiss Me Kate* with Alfred Drake and Patricia Morison, you encountered a very different type of musical theater than you were likely to view in any opera house in America. A Cole Porter show revealed the cutting edge of stagecraft. The Met was stuck in a time warp early in the century. Its idea of how scenery, costumes, lighting, and singers should look, its standards of acting, such as they were, all belonged to the world of *Naughty Marietta*.

Credit for realizing that the world of opera and the world of Broadway had to belong to the same decade of the same century must go to Rudolf Bing, who, starting in 1950, made steady, commendable, and frequently successful efforts to bring operatic productions up to date.

Since the Met moved to Lincoln Center thirty years ago the gap between upper and lower Broadway has been closed. Indeed, with backstage equipment more sophisticated and complex than customary in the commercial theater, the Met can now stage a technically more advanced production than Broadway producers can offer. Things really have turned around. This *Otello* was as fine an example as any. The opera performances I attended as a teenager in the 1930s were often silly, old-fashioned theater. Opera is gaining new listeners today because it can rival the best the legitimate theater can stage.

Another reason, no less important, is that, as in the commercial theater, there is no longer any doubt about what is happening. You can laugh in comedy, cry in tragedy, and join fully in the show. For most opera houses the answer has been supertitles. This opening night introduced Met Titles, an ingenious system that lets you read the words being sung from a neat little screen on the back of the seat in front of you. Levine felt supertitles were wrong for the Met, and this inconspicuous and sophisticated system was developed as an alternative.

The use of titles appears to have settled once and for all the argument for operas to be sung in English translation. The unrealistic assumption was that English-speaking singers could project the text clearly enough to be understood throughout a big theater. The New York City Opera, wisely, uses supertitles even with American works set to an English text.

Met Titles have the advantage that nothing happens unless you activate the system. They are completely unobtrusive and private. But for those who want, or need, them, they are there, nicely synchronized with what is actually being sung. (In comedy the laughs come at the right place.) They are probably the most expensive solution to this problem in use today, but they are also the best.

The new titles drew some attention from the first-night audience; so did the completion of the O.J. Simpson murder trial in Los Angeles, but what was happening on the stage overcame all distractions. The *New York Times*'s Bernard Holland put it nicely: "Verdi, I am happy to report, reduced his competitors to mere footnotes."

October 15, 1995. Carnegie Hall, New York City.

The New York Philharmonic plays several times a week in a season from autumn to spring. Fine as it is, there is a temptation to take it for granted. The Met Orchestra plays three Sunday afternoon Carnegie Hall concerts in the same period and each one is an event—and rightly so. The situation is analogous to the Vienna Philharmonic, which spends most of its working time in the pit at the Vienna State Opera but emerges to play ten pairs of Saturday afternoon/Sunday morning concerts a season. (The city's week-to-week demand for concert music is met by the Vienna Symphony and others.)

The number of concerts the Met Orchestra can play is limited by the orchestra's opera rehearsal and performance schedule. "I could do ten different programs a year gladly if the schedule permitted," says Levine.

For more than sixty years the New York Philharmonic has had to compete in its home city with visiting orchestras that challenge its eminence. In the 1930s the rivalry was with Serge Koussevitzky's Boston Symphony and the Philadelphia Orchestra under Leopold Stokowski. Both ensembles played subscription series in the Philharmonic's home, Carnegie Hall.

Under Toscanini (until 1936) the Philharmonic could compete, and after 1943, under Artur Rodzinski, it could start to compete again. But for seven years it was badly eclipsed. The war limited touring, but in the 1940s, Boston, still under Koussevitzky, and Philadelphia, now in the hands of Eugene Ormandy, were potent rivals and remained so when Charles Munch succeeded Koussevitzky in 1950. The surprise came from the West when the Cleveland Orchestra under George Szell began touring in the 1950s. In 1947 Rodzinski had made his exit from New York and, in 1948, from the American scene. He died after a triumphant return to Chicago in 1958.

In the fifties, a potential rival of great force, the Chicago Symphony under Fritz Reiner, rarely toured, although Boston continued to be a challenger, especially after Erich Leinsdorf became music director in 1962. Still, for the greater part of two decades, sophisticated New York-ers turned for prime symphonic fare to Szell and the Clevelanders, a situation that ended with Szell's death in 1970 and the rapid ascendancy of the Chicago Symphony under its new music director, Solti, who dominated the picture until his retirement in 1991.

This time the challenge to the Philharmonic came from within the city. Levine's idea was that if the Vienna Philharmonic could live a double life, so could his orchestra at the Met. Indeed, it was a necessity for artistic vitality and growth. He therefore took his orchestra to Carnegie Hall at the end of the 1990–91 season.

On the basis of the early success of the Carnegie concerts, the orchestra began to play concerts in Europe and tour the United States in 1995. It is obviously advantageous to the Met to be able to show the flag abroad without having to put an entire opera company on the road. Therefore, on the 1996 European tour three operas were given in concert form in Frankfurt.

The Met Orchestra, after a quarter century with Levine, has been lifted to heights never before imagined. It is finer than the Philharmonic, which has had no such long-term association with a conductor of Levine's particular talents. Zubin Mehta, who led it from 1978–1991 was the longest-tenured conductor in Philharmonic recent history, but orchestra building is not one of his primary skills.

The emergence of the Met Orchestra as an ensemble that can play and record the symphonic repertory broadens Levine's horizons considerably. As long as I have known him, he has talked of possibly becoming music director of a major American orchestra, and his Chicago years pointed to a possible affiliation of that type. But Levine would not take an assignment of that nature unless he was prepared to do it justice in his exacting definition of the term and without disturbing the continuity of artistic growth at the Met.

At age fifty-five, he wants to play and record symphonic works, keep his hand in the repertory, but not at the cost of a severe cut in his activities in the theater. The present arrangement—three New York concerts, a tour, and a few weeks of guest conducting in Berlin and/or Vienna, Boston, or Philadelphia—seems ideal.

Although Levine is best known as a theater man and a passionate devotee of the human voice—whether opera, oratorio, or Lieder—his interests have always ranged over the entire musical spectrum. Throughout his professional life he has championed new and contemporary music. Indeed, he has often conducted new works with such composers as Cage, Milhaud, Babbitt, Carter, or Schuller present.

He intends, in the future, to explore this area further, and recent events seem to indicate that he will have more opportunity to do so. Tradition is on his side. As he points out, Toscanini conducted 80 percent of his symphonic concerts after the age of sixty.

In September 1997, the Metropolitan Opera announced that a new post, principal guest conductor, had been created at the Met for Valery Gergiev, the director of the Mariinsky Theater in St. Petersburg. The Russian conductor will conduct eight productions over five seasons. Coinciding with the announcement was the news that Levine had accepted an invitation to become chief conductor of the Munich Philharmonic, beginning in September 1999.

But now it is mid-October, the Met season is well under way, and Levine takes the Met Orchestra to Carnegie Hall for an all-Mahler program. The hall, since it opened in 1891, has been refurbished several times, most notably in 1960 when Isaac Stern and his allies saved it from destruction. New York needed Carnegie Hall, especially after 1962, when the new Philharmonic Hall in Lincoln Center proved an acoustical disaster. That was eventually corrected, but in the meantime only Carnegie gave the city a large music room worthy of the finest performers. A broad, horseshoe-shaped auditorium with shallow tiers of boxes, a third level with a shallow balcony, and a large balcony on top, it is similar to a nineteenth-century European opera house. In my lean years I heard a lot of concerts from the top, and as a critic I heard many more from the main floor. Both locations have their distinct advantage. This time I was downstairs a few rows from the stage and enveloped in Mahler.

Levine's soloist was bass-baritone Bryn Terfel. Levine does not claim to have discovered Terfel (that happened in his native Wales), but he made his American debut at Ravinia with Levine and the Chicago Symphony in the Mahler Eighth Symphony in June 1992, the year of his first London appearances at Covent Garden. He also sang a small role in a concert performance of *Samson et Dalila* and a recital with Levine that month—a typical Levine-era Ravinia coup. He made his Met debut in 1994.

Terfel is the typical Levine singer. Point one, he has a marvelous voice, a big, rich, noble instrument with a wonderful range of color and nuance. Point two, he is a sensitive, perceptive, highly trained musician. Point three, he has a natural gift for the stage (he's a Celt, after all) and moves with a fine combination of energy and grace. The night before this concert I heard him with Levine as Leporello in *Don Giovanni,* and he could hardly have been better in the role.

Mahler's *Kindertotenlieder* (Songs on the Death of Children) are some of the most profoundly heart-wrenching works in the vocal literature. The poems are by Friedrich Rückert, whose poems supplied the texts for some of Mahler's finest songs, and are based on his own experience of losing a son and daughter to scarlet fever in 1833 and 1834. Mahler's eldest daughter died in 1907, and many assume this event caused him to turn to Rückert's poems, but, in fact, the cycle had been composed in 1901–04, as if his morbid soul had foreseen the tragedy to come.

Since the poems were written by a grieving father, I have always been surprised by those who view this as a woman's song cycle. Terfel eliminated any doubt on that score, projecting the sense of mourning with the intensity and pathos one would expect from a Welsh bard. The impressive resources of the voice were fully used, and the clear, strong diction made the words carry with their full impact. Mahler selected these five texts from a vastly larger collection on the same theme, and in both the words and the music they progress from exposition to probing the depths of suffering, feeling the cutting stroke of irrevocable loss in a variety of contexts. Terfel was aware of that development in the cycle and carried the final song to a strong sense of dramatic climax and resolution.

For me the most poignant lines are those that open the second song, "I often think they've only gone out! Soon they will be back home again." When I hear them, I think of Walter Toscanini saying some months after his father's death, "I sometimes think he's just away on tour. When the concerts are over, he'll return."

Psychologically, the songs, followed by a short intermission, were a paradigm of preparation for the composer's Sixth Symphony. Many think of Mahler's friend and colleague Bruno Walter as the conductor primarily responsible for introducing his music to American listeners, but, in fact,

Walter played only five of the nine completed scores (he rejected the Tenth as unfinished) in his American years. In New York, and internationally, Dimitri Mitropoulos was a strong advocate of the rest of Mahler's work, the Third, the Seventh, the Eighth, and, in this case, the Sixth, which was first heard in the United States, in Carnegie Hall, under his direction in 1947, forty-one years after its first performance in Europe. It is interesting that Levine, although having the highest regard for Walter as a Mahler interpreter, has played the scores associated with Mitropoulos more frequently than those in Walter's repertory.

One reason Mahler's music was slow in gaining repertory status was that he was an incorrigible reviser, reworking published works and creating a confusion of texts that was not put to order until long after his death. To perform the Fifth Symphony in New York, Mitropoulos had to prepare a set of orchestral parts that agreed with the final revision of the full score. Other conductors had abandoned the work when they realized at the first rehearsal that frequently they and the orchestra were looking at different music.

Levine, working from the Mahler critical edition, was presenting the Sixth Symphony in its final form. Although the work is three or four times longer than the typical Haydn or Mozart symphony and twice as long as the longest of Beethoven's purely instrumental symphonies (the *Eroica*), Mahler here was giving unusual respect to classical forms. The opening is a sonata-allegro composition with a double exposition that should be respected, and the subsequent movements follow a pattern associated with Bruckner—scherzo, andante, finale.

The work was begun in 1903, and calling it the "Alma Symphony" in recognition of his marriage to Alma Schindler the previous year makes some sense. (The soaring lyric motif in the first movement is often labeled "the Alma theme.") But the inescapable fact is that the symphony is not filled with a bridegroom's joy but a pessimist's anticipation of doom, and the identification "Tragic Symphony" actually makes better sense.

Mahler felt that three hammer strokes would bring the tragic hero down, and the final movement builds to three climactic sections that close with the hammer falling. In the final revision of the score, Mahler, in the grip of morbid apprehension, deleted the third hammer blow as a percussive effect, although it is still there in the harmony and orchestral texture. Levine honored his wishes. Here my respect for purism is deflected by my appreciation of Mahler's increasingly neurotic behavior. Three hammer blows make better artistic sense, and the third should be restored.

It is, incidentally, one of the most difficult sounds to produce. A note in the score tells us it should be wooden rather than metallic, and it must be loud enough to carry through the instrumentation. William Steinberg once told me he had found a perfect solution for a London concert. A wooden table was placed at the rear of the stage and a percussionist climbed a stepladder and jumped on it. There were no such acrobatics at the Levine concert. The only movement onstage was the opening and closing of doors for the effect of offstage cowbells. The hammer blows, produced by a secret method, were everything Mahler might have wished them to be.

One of the delights of listening to repertory of this type from the Met Orchestra is that everything is so fresh. There is no sense of jaded feelings or routine. "Everything they do, they are doing for the first time," Levine commented after the concert. "If they can play *Salome* or *Elektra*, they can play a Mahler symphony. In fact, they should because an understanding of one will contribute to a greater understanding of the other."

This recalled Erich Leinsdorf's insistence that music cannot be played out of context, that one will never perform the Beethoven symphonies with authority unless one is familiar with Beethoven's chamber music. Mahler and Strauss were friends. Both were distinguished conductors. Both were doing their finest work in the same period. There is nothing in Mahler comparable to Strauss's operas and nothing in Strauss comparable to Mahler's symphonies. A secure understanding of either man requires some awareness of the other.

Mahler died with Mozart's name on his lips, and one can argue that the Mozart symphonies and the Mahler symphonies are the two primary elements in Levine's orchestral repertory. He does both extraordinarily well because of his comprehensive grasp of how this music is written and how it works artistically. A successful Mozart performance and a successful Mahler performance both call for the same things. The form of the work must be clearly projected for the listener. The drama must be fully developed without overstatement. And the work must move, one page following another on a firm rhythmic foundation with clarity of line in the leading voices and transparency of texture so the inner voices and their counterpoint can be appreciated.

Levine learned the Mahler symphonies starting around the age of twelve. In 1955 the most influential Mahler interpreter in the United States was still Bruno Walter, and Levine acknowledges the influence of his recordings. He was later attracted to performances by Mitropoulos and Szell. Although Levine gladly acknowledges Leonard Bernstein's important role in establishing Mahler in the American symphonic repertory, Bernstein's influence on Levine was minimal.

I did not hear Mitropoulos's 1947 performance of the Sixth, so I am unprepared to say whether this Levine account of the score was better or not. But I would predict that it will be some time before Carnegie Hall reverberates with another Mahler Sixth to equal this one.

November 21, 1995. C Level. Metropolitan Opera House, New York City.

The Met performs opera in an elegant auditorium finished in dark red and gold, but it prepares it in surroundings that are plain and functional to a fault. You enter the stage door, one level down on the north side of the house at Lincoln Center, and descend to the depths of what was once a huge, water-filled hole (commonly called Lake Bing) that sidewalk superintendents of the 1960s recall as the beginnings of the theater. Here, in a world of concrete and gray paint, are the large rehearsal rooms where the ballet and the orchestra are readied for their roles in shows to come.

The late Herbert Zipper, known to America as a conductor and music educator, was in his youth a dedicated anti-fascist who, in consequence, had the unique experience of doing time in both German and Japanese concentration camps. He used to look at the type of block construction found in the Met corridor walls and remark with Viennese irony, "Ah yes, just like Dachau."

The rehearsal room is much larger than the Met pit, large enough that the musicians can be comfortably spread out and even Wagner can be played at full volume without lacerating eardrums. There is a mirror across the north wall, behind the conductor, so that the place can accommodate ballet and staging rehearsals, but most of the time all it does is reflect the image of the players to a phantom audience consisting of themselves.

In contrast to the elegant podium and music stand at which Levine presides upstairs in the theater, this one is bleakly functional. You wonder if dedication to frugality has gone so far as to deny it a new, and badly needed, coat of paint. The conductor's music stand, a solid assembly of wooden slabs, is bolted down and reinforced on four sides—earthquake-proof construction. There is a lower shelf for the liquids Levine consumes constantly in rehearsal, in this case a large mug of iced tea *with* caffeine, which he prefers, although he has never tried a cup of coffee, and the omnipresent Evian bottle. A high stool with a low back, the type bass players like, is nearby if required. Two batons lie on the top of the stand next to the score.

The Met Orchestra plays its performances in formal dress, but it rehearses them in the marvelous array of costumes musicians select for this purpose. One player's idea of fully functional attire is rivaled only by another's imaginative concept of clothes that don't get in the way of the music. And no one is more dedicated to this cause then Levine. Toscanini appeared at rehearsals in highly polished black shoes, striped trousers, and a black jacket with a high-standing collar. Levine quietly slips into the room with the familiar folded towel over his left shoulder, looking much like everybody else. But his casual clothes do not come from Wal-Mart. He wears a new pair of $300 Mephisto running shoes, the inevitable dark blue trousers are from Knize in Vienna, and the white polo shirt has a London label. The towel may be from Hermès.

Visually, he is not set apart as the maestro. He could be the triangle player. But he is the maestro. His authority comes from his skills, not his dress. As he takes his place the room falls into dead silence. I recall the ritual of the 1940s in Studio 8-H at Radio City. The musicians of the NBC Symphony busily scraped and tooted away until the announcement from the control room, "Maestro coming down." The orchestra immediately fell into the awesome hush that greeted Toscanini as he came onstage. Here, as then, the maestro nods, the oboe gives the musicians an A, and the final rites of tuning are accomplished.

A new production of *Die Meistersinger* under Levine entered the Met repertory in January 1993. It is a classic example of the work of the Met's Wagner team, producer Otto Schenk and designer Günther Schneider-Siemssen, who, for my admittedly conservative taste, are the finest talents in their respective sectors of Wagnerian staging.

Levine is now preparing the score for five performances in December 1995. The singers are upstairs onstage with sets, costumes, and a piano in the pit, working on the staging with director Peter McClintock. Here in Nibelheim the orchestra is being readied. When the two come together next week the opera can be viewed as a totality and, it is assumed, the orchestra will be performing on a level that requires little further attention. Some might find the session dull. On Levine's part it is quiet, serious, concentrated work.

Levine used to do piano rehearsals in the theater playing the piano himself. "I realized," he recalled, "that I just couldn't put it all together that way. The pianist had to be in the pit, and I had to be in the house with a full view of the stage." Levine prepares his singers working closely one-on-one in his studio. There he is often at the keyboard, and in private they work out the details of the singer's role, phrase to phrase, until they reach a mutual understanding.

This is a technique possible with the new generation of singers but alien to artists of an older generation. One reads with amazement a letter from Rudolf Bing to Jussi Bjoerling in 1950 chiding him for not attending rehearsals. "The Italian artists are here for every rehearsal on the dot and have to rehearse ensembles, duos and everything without a tenor." Bjoerling (I speak from experience) belonged to the stand-up-and-sing school. He knew his roles, and he wanted simply to walk onstage for the performance, take a convenient place near the edge of the stage, and do his number. The fact that he was involved in a complex musical and dramatic production totally eluded him, although occasionally the performance of another artist would bring real involvement—for example, the American debut of Anna Moffo in a 1957 Chicago production of *La Bohème*.

From the start the Met Orchestra is playing a performance of *Die Meistersinger* that would have been perfectly acceptable in any opera house in the world. Traditionally, this is a rather beefy, robust, Germanic opera, but conductors are seeing it in a new light.

Some years ago the late Ferdinand Leitner, who did more for Wagner than any other conductor with the Lyric Opera of Chicago, led me through a study of the *Meistersinger* score. "See," he would exclaim repeatedly, "it is really chamber music." This is the new approach to *Meistersinger,* and it could be heard in Chicago early in the 1995–96 season when Sir Georg Solti offered the opera in concert form (for recording) and impressed his listeners with how light, how open, how delicately scored the work could be. "If they want a heavy meat and potatoes performance," he insisted, "I recorded one for them twenty years ago!"

Levine was working in precisely the same spirit. Ben Heppner and Karita Mattila of Solti's cast were singing the same roles for him. The lessons being taught in these rehearsals were that music does not have to be heavily underlined to be expressive and that light, rhythmic playing projects the work more forcefully than measured phrases. Levine feels this approach goes back to Toscanini's Salzburg performances of 1937, one of which is available for study.

The situation this morning is that Levine has worked through the first two acts of the opera in previous sessions and is now ready for the monumental third act. He lifts the stick and launches the orchestra into the Prelude. Levine's stick work is exceptionally easy for a professional to follow. The downbeat is straight and firm and the baton follows the flow of the notes in a graceful pattern. He doesn't throw you any curveballs. You sit at your stand with one eye on the maestro and one on the music and play. Everything falls neatly into place.

A seasoned member of the percussion section, one of those musicians who, in T. S. Eliot's phrase, "has known it all, already known it all," smiles at me.

"You cannot get lost with Levine. It's all in his hands. You can relax and just enjoy what you're doing. He is always right there."

Nowhere was the process more clearly defined than in the third-act Prelude. Levine played it through, and it was noble, lyric, and note-perfect. But immediately he went to work on it. What was wrong with the first playing? Levine felt it could be made more deeply expressive not by adding weight of tone, but by slightly darkening the tone color and offering more sensitive shaping of the phrases and subtle dynamic changes. He did it again, working toward these goals, and the music was transformed. Always quick to praise, he put down the stick, smiled, and nodded to the musicians, "Excellent."

In rehearsal Levine never raises his voice or yells at anybody. If he wants to make a correction he steps down off the podium and goes over and talks to the musician privately. He does not want to do anything that might embarrass one of his musicians or cause him pain. As Levine says, "Solving musical problems is difficult enough without kicking up dust and phony nonmusical agitation." Toscanini, in contrast, would shout *porco* or *pagliaccio,* regret it, and apologize afterward.

The Prelude behind them, Levine turned to the first scene. Hearing a familiar opera without voices is a new experience. In this case it makes clear the symphonic character of Wagner's writing. The orchestral part of *Lucia di Lammermoor* would not sustain your attention very long. *Meistersinger* sans singers is still remarkably attractive music.

Levine has his work cut out for him. Keep it light, keep it singing, keep it firmly rhythmic and steadily in motion. Be ever mindful of changes in tone color, particularly places where an imbalance can bring up a tonal mix unsuited to the words or the dramatic situation. When the sun is shining in the opera, it must radiate from the pit as forcefully as the stage.

Toscanini used to sing through rehearsals of this type, and the Toscanini tenor can be heard at times in his recorded operatic performances. Levine sings too, occasionally, when he feels the relationship of the vocal line to the orchestra must be made clear. Later, preparing the entrance of the guilds in the final scene, he rings out with a loud "Baaah, Baaah, Baaah" as the tailors make their exit. But generally he avoids singing in order to hear the orchestra more clearly.

There are a few listeners at the back of the room. They are armed with scores and attentively pursue whatever objective brought them there. There are people from the music staff, people from inside the house, as well. The rehearsals are otherwise closed.

For the majority of operagoers and concertgoers, what happens in a session like this is a complete mystery. Those who have played in amateur or community orchestras may think that a rehearsal with the pros is about the same as the ones in which they participated. Not so.

Speaking from experience, working with students and amateurs and working with professionals are two different worlds. You can demand of a professional musician that the notes be played with the correct pitch, rhythm, and duration. You may have to work on dynamics and accents. But you begin with accurate notes. With students and amateurs you can begin almost anywhere, and often you must finally settle for no more than the note accuracy that is the minimum requirement of professionalism. With professionals there is an opportunity for innovation and personal artistic growth. Students and amateurs are often happiest with time beaters. If you try to conduct more freely, defining the shape of the phrase, they may become confused.

Levine served a valuable apprenticeship in Cleveland and at Aspen working with student musicians (*good* student musicians, I add) in ensembles of various size. Josef Krips, thinking of how young conductors were trained in Austro-German provincial theaters, observed, "at the start the musicians teach you and, after a few years, you teach them."

But the greatest conducting talent in the world will not develop unless given an opportunity to learn by doing, by regularly conducting a group of professionals. One of the sad tales of the 1970s was the saga of Antonia Brico, who was represented in a film to be the great woman conductor who was denied a career because of her sex. She had given many years to student and community orchestras in Colorado.

On the strength of this publicity she secured a concert with the Chicago Symphony, and I attended the rehearsal. She had absolutely no idea of what to do with this orchestra that from the first downbeat gave her all the right notes in beautiful sound without a single problem. That was as far as she was able to go. Together they offered the Brahms First Symphony in what the critics used to call "a standard reading"—that is, the performance an orchestra of this stature could probably play with no conductor at all. Whether, given the opportunity, she might ever have learned to conduct an orchestra of the quality of the Chicago ensemble is forever a moot point.

George Szell used to say, "The Cleveland Orchestra *begins* rehearsing at the point when others stop." Szell's first rehearsal of the four that usually preceded a series of subscription concerts would be acceptable by many listeners as a concert. It was not acceptable to Szell, who was rarely at a loss to find things that might be improved.

Do audiences hear these things? Sir Thomas Beecham, not entirely seriously I assume, once observed, "It is absolutely necessary that an orchestra begin together and end together. What happens in between doesn't really matter." It mattered to Toscanini and Szell, and you can be certain it matters to Levine.

In one of his visits to Chicago with the Boston Symphony, Serge Koussevitzky played Debussy's *La Mer.* After the concert I went back-stage to congratulate him on an unusually beautiful effect in the first movement.

He looked at me with wise old Russian eyes. "You like dot?" he asked.

"Yes, Dr. Koussevitzky, it was marvelous."

"On dot effect I work seventeen years."

Koussevitzky's musical imagination was incredible, surpassing Tosca-nini's and seriously challenged only by Stokowski. His sense of color and texture was phenomenal. But to transform what he heard in his mind into something you might hear in a concert hall required skilled con-ducting technique, and here many a maestro of very ordinary ability sur-passed him. It took seventeen years to achieve that effect in *La Mer* because it was not defined in the stick. It came into being as a result of repetition after repetition in which the conductor exhorted his musi-cians in a mixture of French, Russian, and shattered English to play what he wanted to hear. Eventually they did.

Levine probably could achieve a similar result in less than three rehearsals. Levine had Szell in his past. Koussevitzky emerged from the bass section of the Bolshoi Theater. One must wonder what he might have done if instruction similar to what Szell offered had been available to him as a young man. Today, with the demand for technical proficiency so high, one must wonder what kind of conducting career he would have had.

Some of the romantics cultivated the strange idea that technique and refined musicianship were at odds with one another. Levine disproves that once and for all. The lesson of the *Meistersinger* orchestra rehearsals is that the man who is probably the most skillful baton technician of the day is unsurpassed in his pursuit of the most refined, expressive, and imaginative statement of the music. And because of this technique he permits you to hear things that lesser conductors may hear only in their minds.

February 8, 1996. The Metropolitan Opera House, New York City.

Così fan tutte is Mozart's most problematic opera, the third (and last) of his collaborations with Lorenzo da Ponte, who (in an exemplification of the spirit of the piece) intended the leading role to be sung by his mistress. It was first performed January 26, 1790, at the Burgtheater, Vienna. Haydn was in the audience, and, one suspects, enjoyed the work thoroughly. Amorous games were not new to him. The public liked it. A Weimar critic wrote, "That the music is by Mozart says, I believe, everything."

The work had a successful run, cut prematurely short by the death of the emperor, Joseph II, and the resulting period of official mourning. Although never a success to rival *Don Giovanni,* it was heard with the original text the following year in Prague, Leipzig, and Dresden, all cities, one assumes, in which the citizens behaved as scandalously as they did in Vienna.

Alfred Loewenberg, in his *Annals of Opera,* observes, "No other opera, has been subjected to so many different versions and attempts to 'improve' the libretto." He lists some three dozen translations and adaptations, starting in 1791. Edward J. Dent in his classic study, *Mozart's Operas,* observes, "The libretto was denounced throughout the nineteenth century as being intolerably stupid if not positively disgusting. . . ." In England the work was considered immoral. It did not reach London until 1811 and the original text was neglected for nearly a century until revived by Sir Thomas Beecham (a wicked man) in 1911.

For Beecham, "When we listen to perfect beauty, such as that of Mozart, it is impossible not to regret that with him there passed out of music a mood of golden serenity which has never returned. In *Così fan tutte* the dying eighteenth century casts a backward glance over a period outstanding in European life for grace and charm and, averting its eyes from the new age suckled in a creed of iconoclasm, sings a swan song in praise of a civilization that has passed away forever."

The special distinction of the new Met production is that it presents the opera in the light of Beecham's remarks, and this makes up, in part, for the way in which American operatic theaters ignored the work for more than 130 years. The first performance in the United States was by the Met in New York (a suitably corrupt city) in 1922. It was a success, but *Così* dropped out of the repertory until 1951, when it was revived by Rudolf Bing in a Rolf Gérard production the company was to use for more then two decades. The opera was sung in English by an English-speaking cast and skillfully directed by Alfred Lunt.

Virgil Thomson, admiring his results, implored, "Not ever again, let us hope, will conduct on the operatic stage be left to the improvisation of the singers." The opera was then firmly established in the repertory and returned the following two seasons. But the further the work was removed from the original Lunt production, the more pronounced its substitution of farce comedy for sophistication. Chicago did not hear *Così* until 1959, but it encountered it in a version considerably more elegant and authentically Viennese than the one seen at the Met in 1951.

There is nothing more characteristic of Mozart's Vienna than the idea that romantic dalliance is fun, that it is perfectly natural that men and women are attracted to one another, and there is nothing wrong in cultivating this attraction if it is mutually agreeable. Adultery is a sin, but it is the most human of failings and, in a Roman Catholic country, one of the most compelling justifications for the confessional. Mozart himself lived this way, as did his librettist, and, one assumes, the majority of the singers on the stage, the musicians in the orchestra, and the audience in the theater. Puritanical north Germans would be offended, but they had a bad opinion of Vienna to begin with.

If we are to follow Levine's precept that the opera producer is obliged to recognize and respect the intentions of the composer and the librettist, the proper way to produce *Così fan tutte* is to return to the spirit of the time and place in which it was written. That was the guiding principle behind the new staging of the work in the 1995–96 Met season.

Anticipating the opening night, Kenneth Furie in the *New York Times* proclaimed "good riddance" to the 1982 production. "Good-bye Albanian floppy shoes!" He hoped for "a production that comes to grips with the substance of one of Mozart's supreme masterpieces." And that is precisely what the Met gave its public opening night. The *New York Times* found it "handsome and respectful." Apparently some members of the public, described by the paper as "one of the most receptive and happy Met audiences in recent memory," wrote the *Times* suggesting that the production deserved a superlative or two.

The *Los Angeles Times,* one of the two or three newspapers in the United States that would send a critic across the continent to review a major debut, had Martin Bernheimer in the audience. His primary interest was the New York operatic debut of Cecilia Bartoli ("terrific, irresistible"), but he noted that the producer, Lesley Koenig, "motivated the complex action cannily, created affecting stage pictures, and never contradicted either the letter of the libretto or the spirit of the score.... The drama on stage perfectly reflected the drama in the pit. If only *Così fan tutte* were always like this," he wrote, "if only opera were always like this."

Martin Mayer in the British journal *Opera* noted, "This must be a tough opera for a female producer whose glory is that she seeks to illustrate the relations between the characters." Koenig was "too smart, too musical" to do anything less than face the problems head-on and resolve them. "Musically the performance on February 13 left criticism gasping behind. The World's Best Mozart Orchestra was on top of its form."

Levine has come to the conclusion that if he wants operas staged in a manner consistent with his aesthetic principles, he has to create production teams that will work with him to realize this common goal. You don't go out and hire a director and hope that he or she will prove congenial. But you can train a director in the house who you know shares your values. Koenig is such a person. She joined the Met staff in the 1980–81 season, and in the *Così* was in charge of a new production for the first time. Koenig's brilliance as a director mirrors Levine's brilliance as a conductor. She is invisible. Your attention is not caught by cute tricks and bright ideas but by the compelling force with which the spirit and substance of the work is projected in the most authentic and persuasive terms. It is a pleasure to watch her at work.

Sets and costumes were by Michael Yeargan, and Duane Schuler did the lighting. The visual result was a handsome production filled with ingenious things. Two trapdoors in the wooden forestage near the prompter's box served as storage lockers for props that needed to appear quickly. The prompter's box itself was a bench on which a character might rest momentarily. Bathed in the sunlight of Naples, one scene flowed effortlessly into another, producing the highly desirable effect of an unbroken musical line. (A long opera of this type, with many short scenes, suffers when there are significant pauses in the action.)

In selecting singers the idea was to produce an all-star cast that would not behave like an all-star cast but work closely together, in the old Viennese manner, as a true ensemble. *Così* is really written for a vocal sextet, three women, three men, with three short choral sections onstage and one off. It was hoped (in vain) the cast could be kept together throughout the run. Jerry Hadley and Dwayne Croft were the young men, Carol Vaness and Susanne Mentzer their sweethearts. Don Alfonso, a somewhat world-weary older gentleman, was sung by Thomas Allen, and Despina, the ladies' servant, provided Cecilia Bartoli with a debut that proved an ideal outlet for her vocal and comic gifts.

Don Alfonso questions the reality of commitment. It is nice to think it exists, but it is really an illusion. The young officers, Ferrando and Guglielmo, protest. Their betrothed, Fiordiligi and Dorabella, are models of consistency and virtue. A wager is made. The officers will pretend to leave to join their regiment, but return, in disguise, and woo the sisters. Don Alfonso plays a trick on them. Once they are in disguise, he makes it more of a test by having each man woo his friend's betrothed. If they succeed, he is the winner. If they fail, he must admit the purity of these women's love.

Alfonso recruits Despina, who shares his skeptical view of fidelity, as his ally. The officers bid their beloveds an anguished farewell, and in their place two exotic foreigners appear. The women reject them at first, but facing the fact that they are alone, and fearing boredom, agree that a flirtation might be fun. When the romantic play has reached the point that a marriage contract is about to be signed, the music signals the return of the original lovers, the foreign suitors vanish, the officers reappear, pretend to discover the truth, and the matter must be resolved. I have never seen the interplay of music, words, and action in this opera more carefully defined or more subtly achieved. After the performance Levine and I discussed where others go wrong:

RCM: The big, common mistake about *Così* is to transform it from a highly sophisticated eighteenth-century Viennese comedy into a nineteenth-century French farce. It is not a farce, and you destroy it if you try to cast it in this form.

JL: Right.

RCM: The second common mistake of recent times is that it is an exercise in misogyny, a woman-hater's tract.

JL: On the contrary. It is so sensitive, compassionate, and understanding about women, especially when you consider that at the end, in Mozart's society, the only way the women could resolve the situation was to offer the apologies they make. The fact that Mozart understood and loved them so is seen in the music he gave them at this moment. And, of course, the dramaturgy is marvelous.

The end of the apology text is a closure for the men, including Don Alfonso, but the entire finale is about what effect the outcome of this drama will have on the women—including Despina, of course. The women have experienced such a tremendous advance in self-knowledge that they could never go back to the persons they were when the opera began. And the opera is really open-ended. We know the men and women will get together again, but in which pairing? In some ways the second one put together the more compatible personalities.

RCM: We must remember that Mozart was at heart deeply religious, and nothing is more distinctive of Christianity than the idea of reconciliation. Of course, its roots are deep in Judaism. The prodigal son is a Jewish parable told by Christ. But *Così,* like *Le Nozze di Figaro,* is a great opera of reconciliation.

JL: That's right. The "disguise episodes" have encouraged growth in character and understanding in all four people, and at the end they come back together in joy. Moments like this renew my belief in classical masterpieces. Nothing surpasses them in the depth of understanding of humanity. We realize that the highest function of the opera house or the theater is not to entertain us but to enlighten us about ourselves.

The libretto is wonderful, but what Mozart did is place that drama in a musical frame of awesome dimensions. When you consider that composers like Berlioz, Wagner, and Schoenberg wrote their own librettos and understood what was wanted for their musical needs, you understand the problems of people like Mozart and Verdi, who worked to librettos by others and achieved success by making the audience feel that it participates in the emotional response of the characters.

Of course, not everyone wants to participate. The great opera of enlightenment is, of course, *The Magic Flute.* We have Tamino, who seeks enlightenment, and Papageno, who is content to live on a low level of self-awareness. Even if the Papagenos are a majority, it does not alter the fact that in any civilization worthy of the name, those who seek enlightenment must be offered the opportunity to find it. To label them elitists and deny them the opportunities for the growth they require is simply to return to barbarism. The things that Mozart understood and felt are unbelievable.

RCM: The third big mistake is that when the men come back in disguise they are clowns, sometimes refugees from a Three Stooges short. They are really exotics, gentlemen from a different culture, but individuals with dignity to whom respect is due. Dressing them up in silly costumes and turning their actions into the broadest sort of farce instantly destroys the dramatic credibility of the work. These have to be men two young, inexperienced, but elegant women might find attractive.

JL: But the soldier getup, the uniform, standardizes the men in a military framework and apparently suppresses to some degree their passion and spontaneity as lovers. They have to be more successful in the exotic costumes because they can be freer and more individual. This freedom must be conveyed fully without reducing the work to farce.

RCM: The body can rhapsodize.

JL: Right!

RCM: My first *Così* was, in fact, the first ever heard in Chicago: Elisabeth Schwarzkopf, Christa Ludwig, Leopold Simoneau, and Walter Berry, with Josef Krips conducting.

JL: How's that for a cast!

RCM: It came out of the Viennese tradition, and, of course, it was right. It defined standards. Krips really worked on it and then observed sadly, "We finally get it right and then it ends." But later, in Chicago and elsewhere, I saw productions that caused me to fear that *Così* was to become Mozart's reply to *The Barber of Seville,* productions in which the work became the crudest kind of caricature of itself. And I had to wonder what someone who encountered it for the first time in that kind of staging would think of it, for surely it has been a much misunderstood piece.

JL: Beethoven thought it was immoral.

RCM: That's Bonn, the north German legacy, showing itself despite years in Vienna.

My first encounter with the new Met production, which I came to regard as the finest *Così fan tutte* I had ever beheld in a theater, was at an 11 a.m. piano dress rehearsal. Levine conducted the singers and the pianist, Koenig was at the far left side of the stage, poised to react whenever necessary. "Stop," she would call, and instantly everything stopped as she moved in resolutely to put things right. Actually, most of what she was doing was fine-tuning what in the majority of theaters would be regarded as perfectly acceptable. But if she saw a way to improve something, tighten a composition of figures, make a gesture more significant, she was right there to do it.

In the old days at the Met, leading singers were not always required to wear costumes at dress rehearsals, but this cast had been wearing its costumes for some time.

"The clothes are part of the character," Koenig explained. "If you don't feel comfortable in them, it shows in the way you move. I want these people to be just as relaxed in eighteenth-century costumes as they would be in sweaters and jeans."

A striking *coup de théâtre* is that Despina appears to pull the sisters' house onstage. (Actually it is propelled by stagehands in concealed spaces.) On a second try it refused to move, much to the concern of Bartoli. "I thought for a moment there," she recalled at the next break, "that I might really have to pull it out by myself." Bartoli's natural aptitude for comedy and complete ease in the language and style were a delight to Koenig, who worked with her to polish her character and build on her gifts rather than simply to devise business for her to perform.

The piano dress is the final occasion when conductor and director have a really firm hands-on relationship to the production. They can still change things. Minor things can also be adjusted in the orchestra dress, but by then the show is pretty well fixed in form. What was impressive here was how smoothly everything fit together. Even so, after the pianist and the singers had gone, Levine rallied his music staff and production people around him in the front row of the theater and for a half hour they reviewed what they had just seen and heard, looking for ways to make it even better.

The opera got off to a great start. Don Alfonso's opening scene with the young officers built adroitly to the climax of the wager. Our first encounter with the ladies (contemplating portrait miniatures of their lovers) reveals them to be as chaste and loyal as the gentlemen believe them to be. Dent considers this something of a fraud, and "they are both of them at least as ready for an adventure as Rossini's Rosina."

Considering this careful exposition of the dramatic themes, I wondered how Koenig approached her work, how much was planned, and how much was improvised.

LK: When I begin to direct a scene, I have in mind a quite detailed sequence of things I would like to see happen. I have a probable solution for every thorny musical or dramatic moment. But this doesn't mean I always stick to my plans. Rehearsal is about flexibility, about seeing new things and listening to the singers' input about finding alternatives to my plans that I may like even better. Sometimes, how a singer interprets what I ask for may be quite different from, and preferable to, what I had in mind.

RCM: And how are these finely tuned nuances preserved if someone gets sick and must be replaced?

LK: Cast changes needn't be a problem if the first and second casts are both very well rehearsed. In addition to their own offstage rehearsals, the second cast, the covers, watch the first cast's stage rehearsals like hawks. The covers rarely have any stage rehearsal and yet they may be required to step in and perform at any moment. At the least, very often three or four singers are assigned to a role in a run of performances. That adds up to a lot of rehearsal, but the fact is, to create and preserve an ensemble, everyone must be thoroughly prepared.

RCM: And thorough preparation is the basic consideration at the Met today.

LK: Jim won't settle for anything less. He is always trying to improve the level of coaching for young and inexperienced singers.

I decided to be an opera director when I was pretty young, long before college, and I didn't want to study at college what I knew I could better learn later on the job. [Koenig was born in San Francisco and studied at Harvard.] Directing didn't seem to me to be a profession best taught by professors. My degree is in fine arts, master drawings. Why waste the last four years of your life when you are responsible only to yourself, training for a job like mine at a place like Harvard, where there is everything else to learn?

RCM: That, of course, runs counter to the dominant undergraduate preferences today, when humanistic education is rejected by many students, who are only interested in a job, in establishing a certain level of earning power. Apparently they have no idea of what it is like to pursue ideas for the sheer joy of doing so. How did you get from master drawings to the Met?

LK: For a couple of summers while I was at college, the San Francisco Opera hired me to be a stage manager for the Merola training program for young singers. I work now with graduates of that program all the time. Kurt Herbert Adler was running the San Francisco Opera. He was a wonderful man and a great teacher who gave me invaluable advice about becoming a director and avoiding common pitfalls of the profession.

After I graduated from Harvard, I needed money and a job, and ended up running the control room of the options trading floor of the Pacific Stock Exchange for several months. That experience made me want to get back into the opera house as quickly as possible.

I ultimately won a National Opera Institute grant to work as an assistant director with the Opera Company of Philadelphia. About six months into the one-year grant, I started looking for the next job. The New York City Opera offered me a position as an assistant director, but it didn't seem to be the right place for me at that time, so although I had no other offers, I turned them down, telling myself I was crazy. But two weeks later the Met called, and, after a lot of interviews—the last was with Joe Volpe—I joined the staging staff in the last few days of 1980. A stage director at the Met directs revivals, assists guest producers on new productions, and occasionally assists other stage directors. I was on the staff from 1980–81 through the 1993–94 season.

During those years, in the summers mostly, I traveled around and worked in other opera houses, directing my own productions or assisting Jean-Pierre Ponnelle in Germany, Austria, France, Israel, and the United States. I worked for five summers at the Salzburg Festival, three of them staging Ponnelle's *Figaro*. Jimmy conducted. Those were great summers, and they broadened my artistic horizon enormously. Sadly, in the last year, 1988, Ponnelle was very sick.

I have to say, though, that my best training has been with Jimmy at the Met. He is the perfect collaborator. He creates the most comfortable and intelligent atmosphere in which to work. Nothing is rigid or fixed. I feel free to try anything. I have often thought that if I were to ask him for a five-minute fermata, he wouldn't say no. He'd probably say, "Show me what you want to do with it," and if he were convinced by what I did, he'd go right along with my idea.

He was a great partner for me during *Così*. This was my first completely new production at the Met. I had directed a number of new stagings for the house, among them *Jenůfa, Hoffmann,* and *Peter Grimes.* But this was new territory. It isn't easy to make a debut in a house in which you have been directing for fifteen years. Jimmy has always been a great teacher, but what I learned from him this time was how to realize after years of preparation that the production was ready, that it was good, and that it was mine also to enjoy. Of course, I did enjoy it. I didn't see every performance, but it held up, even with some cast changes, right through the last night, when singers often lose a little concentration and start thinking about when the car will arrive to take them to the next job.

Some weeks after this conversation I remarked to Levine in Munich that it was ironic that in 1980 apparently he had no role in hiring Koenig.

"That was John Dexter's department, although he was about to depart, so apparently he never talked to her either. But, believe me, she was not in the house more than a few days before I became aware of her, and after that we were working together regularly. This *Così* was the logical outcome of that process."

The 1995–96 staging has been televised and should be issued on laserdiscs as a model for other companies. *Così* returned in November 1996 with a different cast and was hailed by Anthony Tommasini in the *New York Times* as "a striking achievement."

Koenig reports, "Since the cast was different, it was really like starting again from the beginning, and I changed a number of details in the staging. I feel these are improvements, which means that when some members of the first cast return in 1997, to rehearse for the Japan tour, they will have to learn the new things. But many were delighted that instead of simply repeating a success, I showed its potential for further growth."

The production has staying power. It should be an ornament and delight of the theater for many years to come.

March 17, 1996. Alice Tully Hall, Lincoln Center, New York City.

There have always been conductors who were admirable keyboard players, with George Szell a conspicuous example, but we are presently living in a period in which a number of celebrated conductors are also actively performing pianists. What sets James Levine apart in that group is that he almost never appears alone and rarely performs concerto repertory, but instead concentrates on chamber music and, especially, song recitals. New York hears him in this literature a couple of times a season, and Ravinia used to hear him in such programs nearly every summer. This repertory is also documented in his recordings.

On this Sunday evening Levine is joining Paul Groves, in his recital debut at Alice Tully Hall, one of the glories of the Lincoln Center complex. In the 1960s, when cultural centers were being built in many parts of the country, it was commonly forgotten that there is much important music that was never intended for large halls and cannot be played advantageously in rooms of that type. Alice Tully Hall is for chamber music (including chamber orchestras), duos of piano and a singer or instrumentalist, and solo instruments. It is modern, thoroughly attractive to the eye, with clean, bright sound that projects well from a simple stage.

I had been prepared for this evening a month earlier, when I attended the Saturday matinee of *Falstaff*. Groves was cast in the role of Fenton, which he played and sang exceptionally well. I am not ordinarily an eavesdropper, but Groves's father was seated right behind me, and he was not talking, he was broadcasting. His pride in his son was overflowing, but, he insisted, apart from having a gorgeous voice, the greatest thing that had ever happened to Paul Groves was getting the attention of Jimmy Levine. Levine had done everything for him—coached him in roles, guided him in the selection of repertory, advised him in selecting engagements, and, most of all, put him on the stage of the Metropolitan Opera. A gifted young singer could not hope for more comprehensive and professional support in launching a career.

Born in Louisiana, Groves is an alumnus of the Met's Young Artist Development Program and winner of the 1995 Richard Tucker Foundation Award. He won the National Council Auditions in 1991, made his Met debut the following year, and has returned regularly. His career is now taking off internationally. He has sung at the Salzburg Festival, and in the 1995–96 season he had engagements in Paris, at the Vienna State Opera, and at La Scala (Milan).

Levine needs the sort of artists that Groves represents—his interest is not completely altruistic—and he believes in finding them in America, developing them in our theaters, and making them truly part of international musical life. The Met National Council pioneered in finding and encouraging exceptional American talent. The major American singers the Met has employed over the years often had a staying power that surpassed the European imports. It makes basic good sense for an American opera company to look for artists at home.

Groves has three things going for him apart from a wonderful voice: He is intelligent. He has the sense of empathy needed to create a character or project a poetic text. And he is an excellent musician—not a singing machine, but a sensitive, perceptive performer whose voice is his instrument.

"That young man is so talented," Levine commented a few weeks later. "We really worked on that program. He actually has almost no recital experience, but he handled it beautifully—especially since he is one of those guys who in opera is very strong dramatically.

"I gave him a lot of tough stuff in that recital. It was very demanding. And we rehearsed it very carefully. He was to sing in three languages—Italian, French, and German—and the three composers—Bellini, Debussy, and Schumann—each had a very personal and distinctive style which had to be defined and respected. He dealt with the problems very well. We worked very closely together, and I was happy.

"If he goes on the road and sings conventional recitals he will choose music that goes more frequently into a higher register. But for a first recital in New York, you don't just show off high notes. I wanted him to show how much imagination he has. And that he was using his voice to show the music and not the music to show his voice!"

An event of this type is one at which the Lincoln Center Large Type program, which aging members of the audience like myself can read with their distance glasses, is a particular blessing. In the true art song the music of the poet and the music of the composer achieve a synthesis, complementing and reinforcing each other, so the song is not words set to music but a union of the two.

What Levine and Groves demonstrated on this occasion was that Bellini, Debussy, and Schumann were all masters of lyric forms, but each had his own, very individual way of going about it. Bellini, one of the masters of bel canto, is the classicist, stressing purity of line. If you really know how to sing, and Groves assuredly does, there are opportunities to produce phrases of rare lyric beauty. However, the liquid flow of Italian vowels must not be a seductive trap to sing beautiful sounds rather than words. Every pop singer knows that to put a song across, you put the words across as forcefully as possible. Too many young artists, especially when singing in a foreign language, appear to say, "They're not going to understand it anyway, what the hell."

Putting the words across is a basic element in the Levine approach to vocal literature. Groves's projection of the Italian texts was clean and strong without taking anything from the melodic beauty.

The program contrasted three styles—classicism in the Bellini, the sensuous beginnings of twentieth-century music in the Debussy (the very strongly *Parsifal*-influenced Baudelaire songs), and ripe romanticism in the Schumann. In Debussy's songs to texts by Baudelaire, one was first impressed by Groves's excellent French. Coming from Louisiana probably helps, but in a day when many listeners are resigned to hearing French texts sung with alien accents, it is pleasant to hear something that sounds genuine, especially so when the singer is an American. For subtlety in nuance and phrase, for refined exploration of the sensual and exotic, these five songs were the most distinctive part of the program.

Schumann composed his *Dichterliebe* in seven days of lyric inspiration and romantic fervor. The texts are from Heine's *Lyriches Intermezzo*, but Schumann used only a fourth of the collection, and he arranged the verses to build to a suitable grand finale. Since he was always, first and forever, a composer for the piano, the collaboration between the singer and the pianist is especially close, with many phrases in which the pianist is the dominant element in the duo.

Without in any way detracting from their musical achievement, it seemed to me in the Schumann cycle that both Levine and Groves were having a wonderful time. They loved the music. They loved what Schumann had given them to do. And they were delighted to be playing and singing these wonderful pages with a robust, romantic fervor. Music is a re-creative art, and a distinctive aspect of music-making with Levine, which we encounter regularly, is the sense of joy, the fun, the sheer delight in a creative act that he brings to his work and transmits to those who are working with him. "Could we possibly be doing anything more marvelous than what we are doing now?" appears to be the question. The answer, of course, is no.

The cycle closes with the bad songs, the bad dreams, the past sorrows and lost loves being placed in a coffin and sunk deep in the sea. So cleansed of the past, there is hope for new love, new life. On this note of shining optimism, the formal program ended.

March 19–21, 1996. The Academy of Music, Philadelphia.

The Academy of Music in Philadelphia is a sacred place, the oldest concert hall in the United States that is still in use, and, for many, the finest opera house in the nation. There are two ornate stage boxes, and between them is a pit large enough for opera orchestras of the mid-nineteenth century, but woefully small for Wagner or Strauss. On concert nights it is filled with seats. Built in 1857 with Milan's Teatro alla Scala as a model, the Academy is a horseshoe-shaped auditorium with a cubic volume of some 500,000 feet, about 300,000 feet less than Carnegie Hall in New York. This gives the Academy a sense of intimacy, but also a sense of crowding since it has 2,980 seats, 220 more than the New York hall.

It is the survivor of three opera houses with the same name that figured in nineteenth-century American musical life. The Academy of Music on Fourteenth Street in New York was the city's primary opera house until the Metropolitan opened in 1883. The Academy of Music in Chicago played an important role in that city, although it was always overshadowed by other halls. The Academy in Philadelphia remains, although the city is still in the midst of a debate whether to continue refurbishing the old hall (it is now blessed with elevators) or build a new one.

All empty theaters are haunted by the ghosts of past performers. Here is a hall in which, on December 20, 1910, less than two weeks after its world premiere in New York, Caruso sang Puccini's *La Fanciulla del West* under Toscanini's baton. Chicago's Auditorium is the other existing hall in which Caruso and Toscanini appeared together. Their primary base, the old Met in New York, has been gone for thirty years.

Go to the back row in the top circle of seats and give yourself to the vibrations of the old house. With an audience seated the acoustics are a little dry, a characteristic of Italian-style opera houses where the intention was to preserve clarity in diction. Empty, the hall resonates a little more, and the sound is as rich and full on top as it is downstairs. You ask what these walls have heard, and the mind is dazzled with thoughts of 140 years of music.

The principal ghost of the Academy is Leopold Stokowski. He came here in 1912 to head the twelve-year-old Philadelphia Orchestra. "It was a German orchestra," he once explained to me. "I liked having a German orchestra." With it he introduced Mahler's Eighth Symphony, Stravinsky's *Oedipus Rex,* Berg's *Wozzeck,* and Schoenberg's *Gurrelieder* (Levine specialties today) to the United States. It is inconceivable that Toscanini would have played any of these works. All four composers were fundamentally uncongenial to him.

Stokowski was dedicated to innovation—in orchestral seating, in recording, in repertory, and in the role of the orchestra in the community. When he played Schoenberg's Five Orchestral Pieces, he told a rustling audience, "You have a right to make noise, we on our part have a right to play the things we believe in." Amazingly, considering the conservatism of his board and his flair for controversy, Stokowski lasted twenty-four years. Eugene Ormandy came to Philadelphia in 1936, and Stokowski continued there in a role of diminishing importance until 1941.

But this was the hall in which, in experiments with the Bell Telephone Labs, stereophonic recording was born, the hall in which the original *Fantasia* soundtrack was recorded in 1939 in seventeen channels of sound-on-film. Most of all, for those of us collecting records in the thirties and forties, it was the hall in which the incredible series of Victor Red Label discs by Leopold Stokowski and the Philadelphia Orchestra was made.

No one was more aware of these things than Levine. The Philadelphia Orchestra was one of the first American symphonic ensembles to recognize his promise and invite him as a guest conductor. He recorded the Mahler Fifth Symphony with them in 1977 and went on to more Mahler and an edition of the Schumann symphonies. He had not been back to the Academy since he did a pension fund concert there with Leontyne Price in the early eighties.

To return to the Philadelphia was therefore substantially different from returning to the Chicago, Berlin, and Vienna orchestras, which he conducts regularly and with which he can quickly reestablish a firm working relationship. In this case, he was facing a considerable amount of new personnel, beginning with someone as vital as the first trumpet.

In Philadelphia the conductor may invite guests to rehearsals, unlike Chicago, where union paranoia and vengeance ban visitors until the day of the concert. I was not only admitted, I was welcomed! Everyone was friendly and cooperative. It was a happy reminder that civilization is not dead.

Levine had chosen Mahler's Third Symphony for this program. He was to prepare it on Tuesday, Wednesday, and Thursday morning and play it Thursday, Friday, and Saturday nights. For him it was practically a week off—no twelve-hour days and only one piece of music to play.

At 10:20 Tuesday morning the musicians are leisurely taking their places on the stage. Since the hall is still used regularly for opera (an *Aida* was due soon) the concert shell must be light enough that it can be moved on and off the stage without a huge crew of stagehands. From the house it looks acceptable. Close up it is somewhat shabby and worn, and, for my taste, too thin at the bottom to retain all the bass produced by the players. Backstage the hall reveals its age. Amenities for the performers are minimal. But a great hall with tacky dressing rooms is preferable to an ordinary one with sumptuous backstage facilities.

A group of wind players is seated on stage warming up and, as the spirit moves them, fussing about reeds. At center stage are a simple podium, a large music stand, and a high chair if the maestro chooses to sit. Tom Levine appears with a large bottle of Evian. Brother James is fueled at work by mineral water. There is no appropriate place to put it within easy grabbing distance, so he departs and returns with a small table that goes at the maestro's right. The cap is loosened. No plastic cups are provided. Levine takes his Evian straight from the bottle.

At 10:30 the orchestra is seated and tuned up. One of the players who is also a union representative makes an announcement, and Levine enters quickly and silently, a green towel over his shoulder. He is all business with no lost motion. He takes his place, lifts the baton, and gets to work. For the first six-and-a-half bars you hear an Austrian marching tune played in unison by eight horns. They immediately split up and by bar ten are going separate ways (in pairs), as they will do for most of the remainder of the score. But Levine keeps them together through the song with a beat that is remarkably economic and precise.

Within a matter of minutes you can sense a sort of bonding taking place. Orchestral musicians can be thoroughly skeptical about an unfamiliar guest conductor. Forty years ago he might be tested with wrong notes. If he didn't stop and correct them, he was fair game for sloppy playing. But the conductor of today does not make corrections of this type because the player of today is supposed to hear his errors and fix them himself. Once Szell, dumbfounded in a rehearsal by someone who had just made the same mistake for the fourth time, stopped and asked, "Is there an error in your part?"

One of Levine's greatest assets is that, like Toscanini, he is unsurpassed as a leader. You look at the music and look at the baton and wonder how any professional could go wrong. The performance is right there in the stick, and since for all practical purposes this is a new orchestra, Levine is taking no chances. The beat is strong, basic, and clear.

Mahler's Third Symphony is closely associated with Levine, who played (and recorded) it with Chicago in 1975 and many times since has directed it in New York, Berlin, Vienna, Israel, and London. It is one of the last Mahler scores to become familiar to American audiences, first because of its length (with six movements it is an entire evening of music) and second because of the large performing force required: an oversized orchestra, a mezzo-soprano soloist (who, however, appears only briefly), and both adult (women) and children's choruses. In spirit and in musical substance, it has much in common with one of the Mahler symphonies first assimilated in the American repertory, the Fourth. With these works Mahler's attention shifts from a romantic view of nature touched with Austrian folklore to more abstract and dramatic themes.

The normal assumption would be that Levine would prepare the work straight through from the beginning, but he had to deal with the fact that his vocal forces would not be available until the last day. Thus the first rehearsal was given to the first and last movements, both instrumental, and the second concentrated on the second and third movements—contrasting instrumental works. The Thursday night concert audience was the first to hear the work in its correct sequence. Because of the length of the first movement, one of the longest and most unconventional Mahler ever wrote (104 pages of a 230-page score), Levine, following Mahler's practice, inserted an intermission in the program.

A few moments into the rehearsal, Levine pauses to correct a ragged phrase and takes a swig of Evian before going on. Indeed, as it turns out, every pause in the music becomes an occasion to replenish the liquid balance. Levine works hard and perspires freely. His need for liquids is a practical measure to combat dehydration.

Actually the first thirty-five minutes of the rehearsal pass with relatively few pauses. Levine's first objective is to read through the score, find out what the orchestra brings to the work, and then begin the process of refinement. The improvements he will make will be heard by him, the orchestra, and experienced concertgoers. They represent the type of playing that separates excellence from the routine.

The process begins with the final pages of the first run-through. "Release all the sound," he asks the musicians in the climactic pages. The instruments should sing out freely without any suppression of tone. But at the beginning, the movement is lighter and more open, what Donald Francis Tovey called "a big orchestra pretending to be a small one." Small details are exposed and, thus, must be right.

"Contrast!" Levine requests when the music starts to become monochromatic. "Keep the triplets even," he cautions the string players when the pulse falters. A moment later he reminds the first violins that "every note really has an accent." He is demanding, but he is quick to praise. "That was wonderful," he says when a desired effect is produced exactly to his liking. And the practical outcome of all this is that the music is more richly expressive, more subtly and imaginatively stated.

As the symphony builds to its first monumental outburst, Levine is after a sense of abandon. "Start wild and end wild!" he tells them. "Make it fiery." He works carefully to find the best means for the dramatic intensification of these pages. It is not just a matter of playing loud (although clearly that is part of it), it is the careful ascent to the climax, pacing the work so that the rhythmic and harmonic peak of the music stands out.

And after this there is contrast again. "This should be light and smoothly flowing," he says, "it should be well focused and slightly crisp." A following passage calls for a different approach. "Keep it lyric and flowing," he asks, "don't shorten the notes, sing all the way through the phrase." And to show them what he wants, he sings the phrase to them. They play it. He likes the results, has a hefty swig of Evian, and shouts, "Excellent." After an hour of concentrated work, everyone is ready for a twenty-minute break at 11:30.

Levine wants to turn to the finale. "You can go from working on the first movement to working on the finale," he tells me later, "but you can't work intensively on music in the style of the choral pages and ask them to switch instantly to something as different as that final movement. On the other hand, if you've already prepared it, the transition isn't so bad."

Unlike the first two Mahler symphonies that close with everything going flat out, the finale of the Third is quiet and slow, a sort of mystical vision of nature filled with the distinctive emotional qualities of late central European romanticism. Levine finds the orchestra highly responsive. He works on precision ("more even") and refinement in dynamics, particularly in transitional phrases ("let it fade away"), but the hour goes quickly in pleasant and productive work, and Levine is clearly delighted with what he is hearing. It is also clear that the old members of the orchestra, who know him from the past, have returned to a happy collaboration, while the new people, who have encountered him for the first time, have decided he is a good guy, deserving of their best.

The second movement of the symphony, to which Levine first turns on Wednesday, is a ten-minute piece marked tempo di minuetto. It is as good an example as any of why Toscanini probably found the Mahler symphonies incomprehensible. It has nothing whatever to do with the classical minuet movements of Haydn or Mozart but is completely Austrian in the spirit of the countryside rather than the city. It is clearly intended to provide dramatic contrast. After the tremendous finale of the first movement, the intensity drops, and Mahler here begins to build the work into another big arch with the climax in the final pages. But the minuet is tricky. To play it well you must acquire with repetition a natural feeling for the rhythm, the way the phrases move and the themes flow. The Philadelphia Orchestra has played enough Mahler that these things are not new to the musicians.

Levine (he is wearing a purple towel today) quietly slips onstage at 10:30, pauses to open his bottle of Evian, and gives the downbeat. A wind player has a problem on one of the opening pages. Levine pauses, and the musician raises his point.

"That is a very good question," Levine replies.

Musicians who came to Fritz Reiner with queries of this type often were permitted to state their case only to hear, "We will do it my way." Levine, in contrast, is quite open. He welcomes the idea of solving the problem together, and, with a little further discussion, they reach a tentative solution. They play it. It works. The matter is closed. Five minutes into the rehearsal everything is going smoothly, the orchestra is playing lightly and accurately with a secure grasp of the style. Levine carries the music to a close at once brilliant and graceful, and has a big drink of Evian.

The third movement is twice as long as the second and quite different in character. This is the most highly developed folklorish piece in any Mahler symphony. About halfway through the movement we hear the first of several long solos for posthorn, evocative of the post rider playing his horn as he rides through mountain valleys. The posthorn is a circular brass instrument without valves, first cousin to the bugle, and beloved of Austrian composers. Mozart included it in what is (not surprisingly) known as the "Posthorn Serenade." In the Mahler Third it appears at times to be playing themes from Richard Strauss's *Der Rosenkavalier,* a remarkable thing since the symphony was composed between 1893 and 1898 and *Rosenkavalier* had its premiere in 1911.

It is possible in Austria there were posthorn players capable of playing this music on that instrument, but brass players in American orchestras invariably choose something with valves to ensure more accurate intonation. In this case the first trumpet of the Philadelphia selected one of his regular instruments. The difference in timbre is unlikely to be noticed. What you will notice is the refined tone, the seamless phrasing, and the accuracy of David Bilger's playing.

At reference number 23 in the movement, for dramatic contrast Mahler is seeking a rough, rowdy passage from trumpets, horns, bassoons, and lower strings, and marks the music *Grob* ("rough" or "coarse"). It is not *grob* enough for Levine. "No," he says, "Mahler wants that to be coarse." That is the opposite of the Philadelphia sound, but this time they must give him what he asks for.

The musicians are now into the spirit and style of the piece, and it goes well with a secure grasp of the idiom, light playing, and good accents. No conductor I have heard in rehearsal since Charles Munch is more consistent than Levine in his demands for a light touch. "Lightly, lightly, breathe"—play the phrase with the breaks a singer would have to make. Levine knows that just because you can reverse a bow flawlessly does not mean that it is always the right thing to do. Le Maître and Levine make the same demands.

"Those notes should be lighter and longer," he says, but elsewhere he can want more tone. "Celli, bassoons, let me have a lot of resonance," and a moment later others are told, "No, that should be mezzo-forte, not pianissimo." The definition of harmony is important. "If you have an E or an E-flat," he advises, "let's have it nice and clear. It's needed here." And the cumulative effect of this is that the orchestra is really rolling as musicians pick up the significance of what has been said to others, apply it to their music, and make further comment unnecessary.

At reference number 30, Levine reminds them the music is now two beats to the bar and they are building a crescendo even if, at the start, the strings have mutes. It is a typical extended Mahler close, growing more complex as it progresses. Under Levine's firm beat, it flows and builds splendidly, reaches its peak, and sounds great.

"Want a break?" he asks.

At 10:30 Thursday morning, Levine is about to violate one of Leopold Stokowski's basic rules, no rehearsal on a day when there is to be a concert. No one broke that rule more frequently, and tragically, than Szell, whose Thursday rehearsals (fortunately often heard by students) often had a freshness lost in the Thursday evening concert. As the sportswriters used to say of a boxer who overtrained, "He left the fight in the gym."

Waltraud Meier, soloist in the fourth movement, appears. One of the great beauties of today's world of opera, she is simply dressed in the great rehearsal tradition and takes her place center stage awaiting the maestro. Protocol demands that he is the last to come onstage; the artists wait for him.

Actually no one waits very long. Levine appears promptly and immediately gets to work, paying virtually no attention to the audience. This time he must balance a voice, a voice singing pianissimo at that, with orchestra. The text is "Zarathustras Mitternachtlied" (Zarathustra's Midnight Song) from Nietzsche's *Also sprach Zarathustra,* the philosophical work that also inspired Strauss to compose his tone poem of that title.

Concertgoers, who rarely, if ever, attend symphony rehearsals, often have strange ideas about what happens in them. Forty years after his death, Toscanini's tantrums are remembered and create completely inappropriate expectations. Levine conducted Meier's Bayreuth debut in *Parsifal* in 1983, and they have worked together innumerable times since, including Mahler's Third in Vienna in 1990. It is good to see two complete professionals, bound by mutual respect, apply themselves to the music at hand. But those who feel that the confrontation of a great diva with a great maestro must inevitably produce some fireworks would have found this situation disappointing, even dull. It is all business, conducted in moderate tones.

Although Meier has lots of voice, she still wants to be at her best for the evening, so the quicker the job can be done, the better. Levine is completely sympathetic. The accompaniment is very open and light, and he keeps it that way. Meier is singing softly and beautifully, but she projects firmly and is fully audible. The first six lines of the text are followed by a brief, contrasting section for a larger group of instruments, but with the return of the voice the lighter texture returns. Joy will overcome grief, Zarathustra prophesies, and reach into eternity. As these words are spoken the music expands joyously, fades away, and leaves us hanging on a bass pedal point for the entry of angelic voices. Both Levine and Meier know what must be done, and with minimal verbal exchanges, do it. They smile at one another, and she sits down.

The angels are children, of course, the American Boy Choir, joined in the fifth movement by women of the Philadelphia Singers Chorale. The children imitate bells, singing "bimbam," a German equivalent of "dingdong." The text that follows from the women is from *Das Knaben Wunderhorn,* a collection of folk literature that deeply influenced Mahler in this period of his life.

The poem is about forgiveness of sin, and Meier returns briefly to sing a half dozen lines representing a penitent, accompanied most of the way by the angel children's bell sounds. The chorus affirms that heavenly joy has been granted to all who seek redemption, and the bells lead us into that mystical final movement. It all goes smoothly and well. The visitors may well regret that they did not hear the entire work, but they were given something to cherish.

Thursday night the hall is filled with the kind of well-dressed, well-mannered, attentive audience that has been attending Philadelphia Orchestra concerts for more than eighty years. The orchestra has replaced its casual rehearsal clothes with concert dress. Levine appears in a tailcoat, sans towel. One of three things can happen: The orchestra can more or less reproduce what happened in rehearsal. It can take off from the rehearsals and play an even better performance than it has so far. Or, disaster, it can go through the notes without duplicating the best things it did in the rehearsal period. This happens occasionally, but not with a conductor of Levine's experience. Everyone seemed to feel, this is the real thing, we have an audience out there, show them what we can do.

It was a phenomenally successful concert, a powerful and convincing statement of one of Mahler's most complex and still lesser-known works. It was also an eloquent reminder that to hear the Philadelphia Orchestra in the Academy with a distinguished conductor is one of the finest musical experiences in the nation. At the close Levine is tired but smiling, and delighted to congratulate the musicians who come to greet him for *their* achievement. As the last departs, he glances down at a soggy shirt, announces, "I have got to get out of these wet clothes," and vanishes into his dressing room.

For audiences such triumphal nights end with a ride home filled with the glow of the event or, possibly, a retrospective conversation at a friendly bar. For performers, the close may be peeling off a salty tee shirt and wringing out your socks.

In an interview with the BBC *Music Magazine* in October 1994, Levine said, "With opera, you do six, eight, ten performances spread over a period of time, often with different singers during the run. This is completely different from conducting a symphonic program. For me, a guest conducting engagement to perform, say, Mahler's Third Symphony four days in a row, I find nearly impossible."

But Thursday night Levine's thoughts were focused on the first performance of the Mahler and what it meant. His Philadelphia connection, valued in his youth, had been reestablished.

April 27, 1996. Metropolitan Opera House, New York City.

Officially it was a gala, the silver anniversary of James Levine's debut conducting at the Metropolitan Opera. At moments in the rehearsals it was more like a party. And, as it ended, you realized it was a feast of love, an outpouring of thanks, respect, admiration, but, most of all, affection for the man whose baton had led six hours of song. To eliminate the slightest doubt about this, the audience (few members of which, I suspect, had been in the Met auditorium at two in the morning) refused to leave. The applause went on and on, without the usual polite gestures to bring it to a halt, and did not die away until the message was clear beyond the slightest doubt:

"Maestro, we are filled with pride in the Met as it is today, and we know that you are architect of this grand design. Accept our gratitude for what you have brought to our lives."

Acclamations had begun at the Waldorf-Astoria Hotel ten days before, at the sixteenth annual membership luncheon of the Metropolitan Opera Guild. Bruce Crawford, president of the Metropolitan Opera Association, wrote in the program book: "When James Levine first raised his baton at the Metropolitan Opera twenty-five years ago few could have known that a turning point in Met history had arrived. Of course no sooner had Jim made his debut than the critical encomiums announced the advent of a major new talent. But how completely and thoroughly he would fulfill that initial promise could never have been guessed.

"I served four seasons as the Met's General Manager with James Levine as Artistic Director. Those years left me with an unforgettable, first-hand appreciation of his boundless energy and musical genius."

There were spoken tributes by Joseph Volpe, the present general manager of the company, and soprano Teresa Stratas, who made her Met debut in 1959 and is one of the few singers to be with the company through Levine's quarter century. Vocal tribute was offered by two of the Three Tenors, Plácido Domingo and Luciano Pavarotti.

"It is impossible to believe," Volpe said, "that a quarter of a century has gone by since James Levine and I first started working together. We have had what might be considered parallel lives at the Met, so that when I became General Manager six years ago, it was not a beginning but rather a continuation and deepening of what is an ideal collaborative relationship, and one that I believe is unique in the opera world today.

"As multi-faceted as Jim is, two things stand out in my mind—his unflinching commitment to the highest musical standard, and his single-minded devotion to our company. No music or artistic director anywhere gives as much time or energy as Jim gives us season after season."

Stratas did not fear superlatives. "James Levine? The greatest conductor of our time? The conductor most opera singers prefer to make music with? The most loving and generous conductor around?

"No, he is much more than that. . . . He doesn't act like a genius. He is one.

"Jimmy, I would have to be a poet to describe what you really mean to me. Did you know that you are one of the three most important influences in my life. (The other two are my mom and Mother Teresa.) On the wings of your love and faith I have flown to magical places. If I were a poet I would write love sonnets about your smile and your towel. God bless you with good health so you may continue to fill our breasts with your glorious music-making. I love you, Jimmy, and celebrate you. Long may you reign."

Those who were not able to speak responded with a flood of personal tributes, a type of correspondence Szell or Reiner, for all their musical eminence, would probably never have received.

Jon Vickers was nostalgic. "There are many happy memories, not only of performances, but of the times following performances when we went out to a simple restaurant way down somewhere on the East Side and talked about your own considerations. . . . You had strong opinions about what you wanted to accomplish, and I remember saying that I felt you should not settle for less than a ten-year contract—and there you are, twenty-five years later!"

Frederica von Stade wrote. "It is with awe that one regards his talent and his knowledge. It is with awe that one regards his ability to manage so much so beautifully, as though nothing was difficult, as though nothing was costly. But it is with affection that one regards him, the man, the mentor, the teacher, the guardian angel of music and singing."

James Morris began by asserting, "It is no secret that he is my favorite conductor. Not only is Jimmy the most knowledgeable and versatile musician I know. He is a singer's conductor. His rapport with the stage is unique; when he smiles or gives a 'thumbs up,' you realize you are not only making music, but also having fun."

Dwayne Croft began, "Quite simply and without a doubt, I owe my career to James Levine. There's a reason why so many singers consider him the best. He breathes with you, he feels with you, and ultimately he sings with you and the orchestra."

Contrast those words of a young singer with those of an honored prima donna, Leontyne Price. "It was an honor to have participated in this achievement with you. Your contribution to classical music worldwide has been enormous and deserving of high praise. At our house, the Met, you have achieved and maintained the highest possible standards of excellence."

"The first time I met you in Cleveland as assistant to George Szell," Christa Ludwig recalled, "is even longer ago, and later on I had this wonderful opportunity to make music with you—not only to sing with you. No, making music is something else. There are waves of understanding each other by the music and we lived this special joy not only in opera but also in our recitals. You unfolded a musical carpet, you breathed with me, because you love the human voice."

For Ben Heppner, "my debut as Idomeneo was one of the highlights of my career. I cannot imagine a more supportive and inspiring way to begin one's relationship with this prestigious company. Each collaboration since then has increased my appreciation for your musical depth, your genuine care and sensitivity for the stage, and . . . the human voice."

Elisabeth Söderström recalled a "first rehearsal of *Rosenkavalier*. A stuffy, dusty room. Maestro with a Turkish towel over his shoulder. A Swedish soprano who has sung the "Marschallin" for twenty-five years—what a couple for a romantic story of Vienna in the eighteenth century. And yet it took only about ten minutes and we were there, in Vienna, in the bedroom, in the bed, chocolate and all. Music is a holy art!"

Neil Shicoff said, "Twenty years have passed since you conducted my debut. Your obsession, I would say, was to share your exceptional gifts. You did this almost as a brother would, leading his younger sibling in pursuit of an elusive perfection."

Renata Scotto was certain. "I've had the best years of my career working with you," she wrote.

Samuel Ramey stressed a different aspect. "For me," he wrote, "some of the most unforgettable hours with him have been the one-on-one rehearsal situations when he was at the piano, exploring with me the secrets behind the printed note on the page. That's when his genius is most revelatory."

Leonie Rysanek, who had recently celebrated her own twenty-fifth anniversary at the Met, wrote that Levine was "greatly responsible for my success in *your* house, not to mention the wonderful work we did together in the centennial *Parsifal* at Bayreuth. I never thought someone could tell me how I could lose my fear before the very delicate and difficult 'Prayer' in the third act [of *Tannhäuser*] and stay in tune. 'Take a deep breath,' you said, 'and try to smile thinking of *Erlösung* ["redemption"].' I made it, and how unbelievably it worked!"

And from the Met Chorus, not unexpectedly, came a chorus of praise: "He is articulate, aware, awesome, a bon vivant, brilliant, charismatic, a conciliator, consistent, cherubic, a consummate gentleman—and musician, detailed, divine, dynamic, ebullient, enriching, expressive, fabulous, a gifted angel, generous, a genius, heavenly, indefatigable, inspiring, intense, intuitive, judicious, kind, legendary.

"Without saying he is the greatest living conductor of Mozart and Wagner. He is the *maestrissimo,* monumental, nonpareil, nurturing, outgoing, patient, peerless, perfection and a perfectionist, questing, a rara avis, pithy, pulsing, singer-friendly, spiritual, succinct, super, supportive, tenacious, upbeat, visionary, wonderful, genial, youthful, and zestful."

The last thing in the world that Levine would tolerate was a carelessly prepared gala that exploited the fact that an audience in a celebratory mood might accept routine run-throughs of familiar music. Every singer had to be rehearsed. Six or more hours a day on Wednesday, Thursday, and Friday were given to preparation.

The only real problems in the rehearsal involved the chorus. Levine insisted that the words be heard clearly, so adjustments in placement had to be made and tested to achieve the desired effect. Since the chorus was not always rehearsing on the same set on which it was to sing this particular music, it had to maneuver not in terms of the scenery it saw now but the scenery it would encounter Saturday.

"Move them forward," Levine suggested.

"Tighten the group—less spread out," the chorus master suggested.

It was rewarding to see how quickly professionals, thoroughly familiar with the house, solved the problems in minimal time.

In a recorded interview to be broadcast during the first intermission, Garrick Utley asked Levine how he managed to conduct six hours of music. "Well," he said, "if I do it, it is because of the inspiration from the music and my colleagues, which is so enormous that I guess it is very energy-giving."

This recalls a conversation with Sir Georg Solti, who remembered an occasion while conducting a Wagner opera when he was already fatigued. "About twenty minutes from the close, I asked myself, How am I going to make it? Can I go on? But you find you must go on, the music won't let you stop. So you do another page, and the one after that, and before you know it you are at the end. It is a miracle. You had it inside you to do it. But when it is done, you really are tired."

In fact, outrageously long days are not unusual in Levine's schedule. Two days before the gala, he had offered one of his incredible iron man routines. He conducted a gala rehearsal from eleven to three, took a break, met with several gala artists for piano rehearsals, and after a short nap of sorts, dressed and returned to the pit at 8 p.m. to conduct *Andrea Chénier,* with the added stress of the understudy singing the title role with no notice to speak of.

The *Chénier* performance ran until 11:15 p.m. It had been a twelve-hour day, but the final scene of the opera was filled with passion and energy that swept the performance to its dramatic and emotional peak. If you didn't know the man, you might suspect he had spent the morning in bed, as Sir Thomas Beecham liked to do before a performance.

Toscanini and Sir Georg Solti in their fifties might have matched this stamina, but the number of conductors with this kind of psychic and physical energy will always be small. For Levine, the problem of the gala was not so much its length as the constant changes of style.

"What is incredible is to put a program together that has such an array of great artists, great music, everything in different styles, and that's very different from preparing even a very long opera that is all by the same composer, all one piece. So I am constantly shifting gears from one piece to the next, and the orchestra too, and the listener too."

The normal run of things was that an artist would appear, exchange a word or two with Levine, and go through the music to be sung. It was all very relaxed, with smiles on all sides and many a kiss blown between the pit and the stage. But it was also all business, and the time was used with close to maximum efficiency.

Characteristic of the mood of the proceedings was Samuel Ramey strolling onstage (with Plácido Domingo close behind) to rehearse their scene from the first act of *Faust*.

"Sam!" Levine called out.

"Hi, Jim," Ramey replied.

Toscanini would never have been part of such an exchange because Toscanini felt he needed authority based on fear to secure a fine performance. If you felt you could say, "Hi, Arturo," he was sure it meant you also felt you could sing like a pig and get away with it. In the case of Ramey and Domingo, full partners in Levine's community of values, informality does not stand in the way of concentrated work together.

On the other hand, they felt they could ham up the stage action of Faust signing his soul over to Mephistopheles with broad gestures reminiscent of a Marx Brothers routine. Levine joined in the joke, knowing perfectly well that they would not repeat it before an audience. They finished their number and looked at the conductor.

"Print it!" Levine called out.

Kiri Te Kanawa sang "Mi tradì quell'alma ingrata" from *Don Giovanni* and returned for the sextet of Act 2 with Renée Fleming, Hei-Kyung Hong, Jerry Hadley, Julien Robbins, and Bryn Terfel. Te Kanawa's dress was long, dark, figure hugging, and seemingly eminently sedate until you realized how high the skirt was slit, the better to reveal in black hose what well may be the longest and most sensual legs in opera.

Terfel here played Leporello disguised as his master. Te Kanawa, as if to show that Donna Elvira still lusts for Don Giovanni, embraced him from behind, wrapping one of her shapely legs around him with an ardor that should have produced instant reconciliation. Terfel grinned—he was probably enjoying this enormously—and played along with the scene.

It must be added that Te Kanawa's eminence in this department was challenged in the final moments of the gala when Frederica von Stade appeared with her colleagues in a red dress with a skirt short enough to make you regret that she sings so many trouser roles.

It was clear in the rehearsal that a great personal triumph was to come to Carlo Bergonzi, who was celebrating the fortieth year since his Met debut. In "Quando le sere al placido" from *Luisa Miller* was a master's lesson in voice placement and tone production that could be taken to heart by every younger tenor in the house. When he returned a second time, stepping in for the ailing Pavarotti in the "Qual voluttà trascorrere" trio from *I Lombardi,* it seemed fully appropriate that one distinguished artist should replace another.

On Saturday at 6 p.m. the theater was full, some four thousand elegantly dressed and attentive people, many of whom had bought their tickets months before, and some who had come a considerable distance to be present. But the true audience was beyond measure. Through the generosity of several sponsors, the event was seen in the United States via public television. It would reach an international audience. And, on a CD, tape, and laserdisc to be released later in the year, it would become a document in sight and sound to be seen and heard by who knows how many generations.

Confronting the gala in this multiplicity of formats, you realized a single series of events on the Met stage produced, in fact, two quite different performances. The audience, the four thousand, heard real opera, the unique impact of the live voices in the hall, but from the familiar theatrical perspective. This happened once and was gone forever.

The television program concentrated on close-ups, the vast stage was largely unseen and the screen framed a face, or a tightly composed group of faces. This sequence of images was frequently punctuated by the face of Levine (who looked incredibly fresh at 2 a.m.), which the audience in the hall could not see at all.

The live performances had to contain rest periods, two hours of intermissions to balance six hours of music. The television program began at 7 p.m., running tape of the first hour as the second hour was being recorded. But when the performance in the hall paused for intermission, the telecast broke for only a few minutes and the tape rolled on. By the end of the second intermission the television program and the live performance had caught up with each other, and the final third of the program was in real time—presenting events as they actually took place. It is to the credit of the Public Broadcasting producers that the final twenty-minute ovation, which could not have been anticipated, was not cut off quickly but was amply documented.

Older listeners might have been present almost exactly thirty years before, when the old Met closed on another Saturday, April 16, 1966. Those of us who attended both events are likely to debate endlessly which one was a more spectacular evening, but this can be a chancy business since the memory can play tricks over three decades. The Met of 1966 had some incredible voices, but the evening was as much involved in nostalgia as it was with singing. As a whole, I found the Levine gala more impressive. It has the advantage that a permanent document remains to which one can return.

This was a very different sort of evening, a documentation in depth of the new Met, drawing on some singers who had appeared thirty years earlier, but also serving as a showcase for the prime talent of today, some of them older singers, some members of the extraordinary group of young artists Levine has cultivated. It would be misleading to suggest that with forty-four numbers some moments were not brighter than others, although personal taste and loyalties enter into such determinations. It always held one's attention.

Considering the high degree of organization characteristic of Levine projects, the gala was remarkably fluid right up to the end. Some sixty singers participated, as well as Birgit Nilsson, an honored guest from the past, who offered a spoken tribute and then sang for only a moment. Many invitations were mailed out when the event was first announced, and to the surprise, delight, and consternation of the planners, nearly all were accepted. A few singers were already under contract to appear elsewhere that night. Inevitably illness took its toll. Five artists who had planned to appear became ill and were forced to cancel.

There were three programs—the printed program book, prepared some time in advance, and the large-type program were outdated, but a four-page program insert, apparently printed that morning, was reliable.

Bergonzi was a secure link to the old house but also a reminder of the old way of doing things. Rudolf Bing was a producer of opera but a consumer of talent. He had to buy it on the open market at going rates. Levine must do this too, but he quickly saw the wisdom of finding a talent source that gave him the services of excellent young artists at reasonable prices. This required a broader vision of the house, the Met as both a music-producing organization and a graduate school of the advanced performing arts. The result was his Young Artist Development Program in 1980. The Levine touch was made apparent by the fact that some of the brightest moments in the gala came from singers he discovered and coached—Dawn Upshaw and Dwayne Croft are prime examples.

But the doors are also open to young singers of great promise who have first made their reputations elsewhere. Here there was no better example than Angela Gheorghiu and Roberto Alagna, newly wed and prepared to bring to Mascagni's "Cherry Duet" a romantic aura that came fresh from an important moment in their lives. It was lovely in the theater, but nothing approaching the effect of the television in which all the nuances of facial expression and body language are preserved in music that evokes the consummation of young love.

Television was equally successful in projecting rage as Waltraud Meier sang Isolde's "Narrative" and "Curse." The red-headed Meier has the advantage of looking like an Irish princess, and the strength of the image, combined with the intensity of her performance, made for one of the greatest moments of the evening. With a program of this length and variety, with a succession of performances on the highest level, it is impossible to cite every great moment. Von Stade appeared twice, as Cherubino and La Périchole, and made both arias delightful studies in characterization. Renée Fleming's promise as the soprano who will restore *Louise* to the Met repertory was fully revealed in her singing of "Depuis le jour." The Met's Wotan, James Morris, brought the first portion of the evening to a powerful close with the farewell from Act 3 of *Die Walküre*.

Ruth Ann Swenson as Juliet, Dawn Upshaw as Figaro's Susanna, and Alfredo Kraus as Werther brought great moments in the second part, while Jessye Norman drew all the pathos from "D'Amour, l'ardente flamme" from *The Damnation of Faust*. Here the closing scene was Verdi's "Va pensiero" from *Nabucco,* and the ensuing aria, sung by Ramey and the Met Chorus.

In the final third of the evening Catherine Malfitano and Dwayne Croft found high drama in the concluding moments of *Eugene Onegin,* an interesting contrast to "Prenderò quel brunettino" from *Così fan tutte* sung by Carol Vaness and Susanne Mentzer. It was wonderful that Levine's first Met leading lady, Grace Bumbry, was present to sing "Mon coeur s'ouvre à ta voix" from *Samson et Dalila*. Striking contrast was found between Maria Ewing's poignant singing of "My Man's Gone Now" from *Porgy and Bess* and Jane Eaglen's impassioned traversal of the Immolation scene from *Götterdämmerung*. Music of Wagner also ended the evening: The final moments of the gala were, appropriately enough, the final pages of *Die Meistersinger.*

Before the Meistersingers were heard, Birgit Nilsson appeared with a spoken tribute. It is cut in both the compact disc and laserdisc recordings of the gala, but deserves to be preserved intact.

"Thank you very much," she began—after being greeted by a true ovation. "What an incredible evening tonight, such marvelous music, such wonderful, wonderful singers, orchestra, and chorus. I have been singing along in my heart with Maestro Levine the whole evening, and believe me, singing with Maestro is as joyful as to listen to him not only tonight but through twenty-five glorious years.

"Dear Jimmy, I am very proud and happy that you chose me for your very first Elektra in 1980. What a fabulous performance you made. And you inspired me so much that you helped me to widen my horizons in a role that I thought I already had under my skin. But, when you get a maestro like that, you learn many more wonderful things.

"When we were finished with our *Elektra* performances, you wanted to talk to me about further engagements. Even though I knew that I had my future more behind than ahead of me, I invited you for luncheon in my apartment. And you arrived on the dot, happy and with a big wonderful smile. But without your usual trademark. And I think you were missing it, because all of a sudden you went to my bathroom and picked up my biggest bath towel and put it on your shoulder. And then you felt at home and we had a very nice talk and, I think, equally nice luncheon.

"Time runs fast in your company, and soon you had to go away for more rehearsals, so with a big warm hug and many kisses you rushed out with my towel over your shoulder. I would have been glad to have given it to you, but it was a towel I had got from one of my fans, and embroidered all over the place, 'I love Birgit my Swedish songbird.' And I couldn't think of having my maestro walking down Columbus Avenue and up to the Met with this advertising billboard over his shoulder. It would be good for me but what would the other songbirds have said when you come in the house? So I ran up and grabbed the towel and got it just as you went to the elevator.

"Dear Maestro, I want to thank you for twenty-five glorious years and congratulate you. It has been a fantastic era for the Metropolitan Opera House. On an occasion like this, if it would have been in Sweden, we would all have saluted you with four hoorays. But I am a daughter of the Vikings, and I will do it my way . . ."

And she sang a resounding "Ho-jo-to ho!" to remind us that the voice that thrilled us for so many years has not lost that power.

It is especially pleasing that this speech was taped with cameras on both Levine and Nilsson, so you can read his response to her words from his eloquent face.

For many the gala demonstrated conclusively what the Met had become in the Levine years—the most phenomenal opera-producing organization in the world today—but the gala in rehearsal demonstrated with equal force why and how these results have been achieved. The Met of today is based solidly on two things: dedicated musicianship of the highest order (Levine—like Szell before him—can't be bothered with people who are unprepared to work on this level) and love.

Dedicated musicianship has been discussed frequently in these pages. But love, in the sense I intend it, may not be entirely clear. It is the love shared by the members of a happy band who are working together, under nearly ideal conditions, to achieve a common goal. Levine's Met is a happy fellowship joined together by a community of values. It involves the exchange of affection, support, coaching, and technical advice (when needed), praise (when deserved), and lasting dedication to music—real esprit de corps.

Toscanini's problem, and that of Szell in his youth, was that in days past the singer who was a dedicated, highly trained musical professional was a rarity. The artists produced today are an entirely new breed of opera singer. They make possible a type of operatic production that would have been next to impossible fifty years ago.

Josef Krips summed up the old days crisply when he said, "Singers were taught by conductors." Today, especially in the case of men like Levine, singers and conductors teach each other. And this produces a very different type of operatic performance.

That different type of performance defines Levine's new Met. And standing in the hall at 2 a.m. in that final outpouring of applause, it took no great exercise of the imagination to hear the distinctive hoarse timbre of the Toscanini tenor shouting *"Bene, Bene, Bravo!"*

July 20, 1996. Giants Stadium, East Rutherford, New Jersey.

Approaching Giants Stadium on the New Jersey plain you are reminded of the impact craters on the moon. It looks as if something very large dropped out of the sky very fast throwing up a circle of earth. It is part of the Meadowlands Sports Complex, and technically it is in East Rutherford. Actually it is nowhere, an exit marked on Route 3 on the way to the Lincoln Tunnel and the West Side of Manhattan some six miles away. If you lack wheels, it might as well be on the moon unless, like Levine, you can arrive by helicopter. When traffic permits, the trip from the city can be relatively quick and painless.

It is here that New Yorkers will hear the hottest act in classical music, the Three Tenors, in their first appearance in the eastern United States. If the full capacity of the stadium is used, it seats nearly 78,000 persons. If you build a stage on one end, you lose some seats in the stands, although you gain many seats back since the playing field becomes the main floor of your improvised theater. This evening's audience was 56,000. The normal activity at the stadium is football of both the American and European varieties, but it has been the site of fifteen sold-out pop concerts with a gross of about $38 million. In 1995 it was home to a papal mass, and if the pope will go there, how can anyone else see it as an unworthy place in which to appear?

The Three Tenors (José Carreras, Plácido Domingo, and Luciano Pavarotti) first appeared together in 1990 at the now famous concert at the Baths of Caracalla in Rome. The audience was only 8,000. Zubin Mehta conducted that concert and its 1994 Los Angeles sequel. The 1990 concert was a celebratory occasion, marking Carreras's recovery from leukemia and the World Cup soccer matches. The tenors donated their fee to charity. The concert was televised and has become a staple of fund-raising campaigns by public television channels in the United States. The official producer of the concert, Mario Dradi, an impresario based in Bologna, had the rights to the soundtrack. He sold them to the British Decca company for a flat fee. Decca thought it was too high but took the chance and found itself with the best-selling classical record of all time, a vein of pure gold. As the 1996 tour began, the Rome concert had sold 23 million copies in combined audio and video formats, and the tenors, bound to a contract that did not anticipate anything like this, had not received a single lira in royalties.

Inevitably, there was a demand for a second concert. It took place at Dodger Stadium in Los Angeles in 1994 in conjunction with the soccer world championships. An estimated 1.3 billion people in a hundred countries the world over saw the concert on television, a new record for an event featuring operatic singers and operatic music. The producer of the Los Angeles event was Tibor Rudas, who was best known for his work in Las Vegas, but had been presenting Pavarotti to large audiences in concert since 1982. This time the recording went to Warner Music with Rudas's name dominating the label.

The success of the Los Angeles concert led immediately to discussion of a possible world tour, but since artists of this stature are booked years in advance, the summer of 1996 offered the first possible dates. Mehta's schedule was already too tight, and Levine was invited to take his place. He was able to work around his schedule at Bayreuth, so he accepted.

The musical arrangements are by the same man, Lalo Schifrin. Matthias Hoffmann entered the picture as the producer who had been booking Carreras, and later Domingo, in European concerts since the mid-eighties. The deal that was finally consummated made Rudas the producer with Hoffmann presenting the concerts, staking about $100 million that the public would respond and fill his seats. In retrospect, one can say it was not much of a risk. The Three Tenors are now established as one of the greatest international box-office magnets of all time.

The tour as originally announced began June 29, 1996, in Tokyo and proceeded, on a more or less weekly basis, to London, Vienna, New York, and Munich. There was an immediate demand for additional dates. Göteborg was added between New York and Munich, and Düsseldorf was put on the calendar for the end of August. A New Year's Eve concert was given in Vancouver, followed four days later by a program in Toronto.

Five more concerts were scheduled for 1997. The tenth in the series was in Melbourne, March 1, 1997. Levine was forbidden by his doctor to take the trip because of a sinus infection. He went instead directly to Florida, where he conducted the Miami concert March 8. Marco Armiliato, the cover conductor for the tour, did the Australian date.

On June 17 the tenors were in Modena, Italy (Pavarotti's hometown) to sing a benefit for the rebuilding of La Fenice, the opera house in Venice, and on July 13 they showed up in Barcelona, Carreras's hometown, for a benefit for that city's opera house, the Liceu. The Three Tenors were scheduled to see in the New Year in Osaka, Japan, followed soon after by stops in Madrid and Mexico City, Domingo's childhood home. In July 1998 the trio and Levine would once again appear at the World Cup in Paris.

The show, officially a "megaproduction," is played on a stage 180 feet wide framed by twenty columns. It is much too large for intercontinental travel. (Sixteen trucks are needed to move everything.) The 1994 Los Angeles set is used in North America. A second set was built for Europe, and a third constructed for Asia.

Levine was able to get his own Met Orchestra in New York, but various and varied orchestras were used for the remainder of the tour. The Toronto Symphony played the Canadian concerts. The Philharmonia Orchestra of London was heard in several of the European programs and in Tokyo and Miami. The Melbourne concert used players from two local orchestras. The Turin Philharmonic played in Modena.

The Three Tenors concerts are, unabashedly, mass-market commercial entertainment. They would never take place without the expectation that lots of money would change hands. The *New York Times* estimated that each tenor would earn about $10 million from the original dates. However, since the tour has been extended, the final figure may be twice that amount. A revised estimate in September 1996 gave the three singers collectively an income of $40 million for the year, with half of that going to Pavarotti.

"My God, it's good money," he is quoted as saying, to which impresario Hoffmann replied, "If Janet Jackson can sign a deal for $80 million, the Three Tenors are totally, totally underpaid." Levine was reported to receive $500,000 a concert, about $200,000 an hour once the orchestra is prepared. This must be balanced with two months of difficult, intensive work at Bayreuth for all but nothing.

Nothing, surely, is more un-American in the traditional view than indifference to making money. Show-biz celebrities use their earning power as the ultimate status symbol. But after seeing Levine in action on the tour at close range, I conclude that he is doing this for fun as much as for the money. The impression I receive is that, for Levine, money is an abstraction to which he must, occasionally, pay attention, but that it really does not mean a great deal to him. In many respects, he may still have the attitudes formed in his Cleveland commune.

Those who cultivate the humanities, who are traditionally underpaid, may conceal their envy of a colleague who had found a source of higher fees with the charge that the person has sold out. But is there any moral stigma attached to attracting a crowd of 56,000? What we find here is the basic highbrow prejudice: If it's popular it can't be good.

The Three Tenors program (essentially the same music is heard in every city) is ingeniously constructed to appeal to a wide range of tastes. It is unlikely that anyone who attends will not hear something that he will find exceptionally thrilling and rewarding.

"There is a vast repertoire to choose from," Carreras observes. They begin with opera, opera in highly charged four-minute segments that made the old windup acoustical phonograph a cultural symbol. From there it is an easy step to Viennese operetta, movie music, Broadway show tunes, and American and European popular songs. But it is always strong material, a good example of its genre, something that has been accepted and enjoyed by a public for years. How many people have heard "Because" sung at their wedding? It does not deserve comparison to even the weakest works of Hugo Wolf, but it is part of the life and memories of millions of people. Who can say that it should not be heard in a performance of this character? Had the tenors elected to sing Elvis Presley songs a protest would be in order.

If, as writer Ann Douglas has suggested, the tenors at times "seem on the edge of satirizing themselves" they are aware that the ordinary person's idea of an opera star is itself largely a caricature and thus a legitimate target for a joke. They make no pretentious claims for these concerts.

The majority of listeners without a musical education are afraid of the unknown. They are terrified of being bored, and they return to what they know. Turn the first Tchaikovsky piano concerto into a popular song and the parent work starts to sell. Put a Mozart piano concerto into a movie soundtrack and it becomes a hot item. I suspect that a few, perhaps no more than 5 percent, but some, who hear the Three Tenors concert will take the leap and buy opera tickets, probably to an opera in which one of the three appears. I am also sure that quite a few of those present have been going to opera for some time and want to hear distinguished artists in a new setting.

But the majority probably want exactly what they are offered, a mixture of styles containing a certain number of things that cannot fail to please. And this is a product they will go on buying as long as it is offered to them.

"I love these guys and what they are doing," Levine says of the tenors. "They are communicating their love of music, and our love of making music together, which, over the years, we have done in many different circumstances. It matters a lot to artists to reach so many people who might enjoy what they are doing. Many of those in Giants Stadium are people who for one reason or another would hesitate to come to a performance at the Met. But they will enjoy the arias they hear, and if a song like 'Because' or 'Moon River' or 'O sole mio' means something to them, they will never hear a performance like this one again. It can be an experience they will remember for years.

"You can listen to records, but there is something fundamentally different about being present, even in a place that seats thousands, at the actual moment the performance is taking place. There is an intensity of communication when these guys are in action that cannot be duplicated except in another live performance."

Domingo comments, "I think the three of us are lucky to have Maestro Levine with us. He knows us very well. It is very unusual to have someone of this stature who enjoys making music the same way we do."

Levine is well aware that the last thing anyone should suggest is that the Three Tenors concerts are something new. For Levine, "This is in a time-honored tradition of reaching out to a larger public."

For a precedent one need only look back in the history of the Met to the extensive concert activities of its greatest tenor of the early century, Enrico Caruso. He made one of the first crossover records, George M. Cohan's "Over There," and did a vaudeville turn with Al Jolson. He even starred in a silent film!

Most important, he toured the country singing, without amplification (it didn't exist), in the largest hall a city might possess. He made his Mexico City debut singing in *Samson et Dalila* on an improvised stage in the Plaza de Toros. At the end of his career he was earning $2,500 an operatic performance, but the fee for a concert appearance was $7,000.

Since in the average opera he sang three arias, in concert he also sang three arias. The format of the events was inflexible: First a violinist, one Francis Xavier Cugat, appeared to play the "Meditation" from *Thaïs* or some similar piece made familiar by the windup phonograph in the parlor. Then a soprano, usually Nina Morgana, appeared and sang an aria. Finally the great man took the stage and sang his first aria. The sequence was repeated and there was an intermission. For the second half, the violinist, soprano, and tenor all made one appearance, after which Caruso might return to sing a couple of Neapolitan songs—unless he had to catch the 11:15 train for Omaha.

The Three Tenors are generous. Each of them sings four times, and then they appear together for two extended medleys. The encores are equally bountiful.

"We are very good friends," Carreras explains, "and we know the incredible joy each of us feels singing with the others onstage. We all believe in this concert."

Domingo adds, "You can see that each one is breathing for the other when he is singing. Because we know how difficult it is, and I think the success of one reflects on the general success." If the next concert is a week away, and a limo is waiting, why not have fun?

Preparation for the Three Tenors concert begins on C Level of the Metropolitan Opera House. What is billed as members of the Met Orchestra assemble in the summer version of their functional rehearsal clothes to run through the program with Levine.

It would have been absurd to import a British orchestra to New York, where Levine has one of the great ensembles of the world. As he sees it, he is doing this gig with his own band, and the smile on his face as he enters the rehearsal room makes it clear that he enjoys the opportunity.

"This is a great show," Levine announces to his players, "but very short." That means it does not last as long as the Prelude and Act 1 of *Götterdämmerung*. Levine is not especially concerned about playing through the accompaniments to the arias, music the orchestra has performed many times. But he wants to go through the new things, the arrangements. "Moon River" is not a tune the Met Orchestra does very often in the ordinary course of its activities. It quickly proves it can do it beautifully on the first try. Levine has all the new music on the stands, gives a downbeat, and the orchestra plays the material with secure feeling for the changing styles as if they had been doing it all summer.

"Excellent," Levine says as he lays down his baton. He cautions, "Be aware that when they are singing in unison they take some liberties; watch the harmony and look out for possible changes in the material on your stand. This can be very tough."

But one of the delights of this orchestra is that it is made up of such good musicians that you can count on them to adjust to what they hear. "Listen to the singer and stay with him," Levine cautions. "Watch the beat, but be able to follow your ears. If he is holding a note, you hold it with him." In several passages of the arrangements, just to give the feel of a voice, Levine sings along with the orchestra.

He is concerned about balance. "If I look to you for more sound," he cautions, "give it to me right away. The engineers will see that it is not overpowering. He gives them a test case and it works. "Wonderful," he tells them.

The program has a couple of orchestral works, Bernstein's Overture to *Candide,* to cover the seating of latecomers, and the "Bacchanale" from *Samson et Dalila,* to give the tenors a break in the second half.

"Someone ask me why we are doing this particular piece," Levine says.

"Jim," calls a voice from the trombones, "why are we doing this piece?"

"Because it is as far removed from *Siegfried* as possible," he answers. "And it is in complete contrast to the things that are sung!"

Levine spent the month of July zigzagging between rehearsals for the Bayreuth Festival and Three Tenors concerts. The schedule was so tight he did not have time to use commercial flights out of Nuremberg, forty miles away, but used charter planes that could land in the much smaller Bayreuth airport. Within a few hours of the final downbeat for the New York concert he would be on the Concorde headed back to Europe.

"You're really shifting gears these days," I say.

His face broke into the biggest smile in Manhattan. "I learned it at Ravinia!" he replies.

A second rehearsal is scheduled for early Friday evening, and the tenors will then join Levine and the orchestra so the engineers can test the sound system. But rain threatens, and most of the time is given to running through accompaniments. The final work can be completed at 5 p.m. the next day.

Friday the weather is threatening, but Saturday brings a perfect summer night. (No one even wants to think about a possible rain-out.) Arriving for the rehearsal, you find yourself in the midst of a frantic construction job. The stage has been in place twenty-four hours, but the floral arrangements along the front and sides are still being assembled. A large crew furiously lays red carpet. Status is nicely defined by the amount of carpet in your vicinity, lots in front, less in the rear.

"When are we supposed to be through with this job?" one carpet layer asks.

"Tuesday" is his weary supervisor's sarcastic reply.

While the carpet goes down, the band plays on. Levine and his forces are spread across a huge stage surrounded by transparent pillars that are lit from within. The eye may be deceived to think that they hold up the stage roof, but they do not. It hangs on steel arches that support it and a ceiling filled with lights. There is a shallow balcony at the rear of the stage for the New Amsterdam Singers, who will perform at intermission. The glitter is all facing the audience. Backstage access to the stage level is by a steep and narrow unpainted staircase.

Sitting on the field are narrow, armless, metal folding chairs that have been secured row on row. The thousand-dollar ones in front have a cushion. Those farther back offer nothing more comfortable than black steel.

The sound system at Giants Stadium appears to be a classic type of American installation, combining electronic and acoustical amplification by loading the speaker drivers into horns on high towers. If you know how the tenors sound on the stage of the Met, the stadium sound is coarse and lacking the true brilliance and sheen of these voices, although that vocal refinement is in the signal from the stage and can be heard in the TV audio.

Backstage one passes a truck from the bomb squad, quietly ready for action, and encounters improvised dressing rooms, where in the break the orchestra members will eat a modest supper from a box and, if they can find a table, play cards until the 9 p.m. concert time

Every few minutes an airplane goes by—the stadium is just a few miles from Newark Airport—but it is a minimal distraction. Levine does not appear to notice. (He is used to the train at Ravinia.) After an hour with the orchestra, he is plainly ready for the tenors to appear. There is still work to do. When they finally arrive onstage they reveal, in contrast to the tailcoats they will wear later, a variety of casual clothes to rival the least inhibited orchestra member. Pavarotti looks like a Sicilian bandit—a large Sicilian bandit.

Domingo complains to the sound engineers that he cannot hear himself, and adjustments are made. Nowhere in the stadium does one hear live sound. Even on the stage, which lacks walls and an acoustically efficient ceiling, the music is fed in from speakers. None of the tenors seems especially eager to rehearse. They are cautious about peaking too soon—before the concert. It's Levine's job to keep things together. They sing until they feel comfortably warm and ready in the throat, and turn to the new encore. One of the features of the tour has been preparing a special number for the city visited, and this time it is "New York, New York."

They know the words and, with a couple of run-throughs, get it right. Levine calls it quits and the orchestra vanishes backstage.

I cannot stay without a ticket for the concert. I had earlier been told if I want one it will be $1,000, cash on the barrel. Of course, I will be sitting within a few yards of former president George Bush, but I politely decline and elect to join the pay TV audience in Manhattan. Even in the stadium, TV is essential for the success of the concert. The stage is flanked by two enormous screens, and those at the rear, who cannot possibly see the faces of the figures on the stage, look instead to the huge close-ups that television supplies.

Once more I am aware of an event that exists simultaneously in two different forms. The music is the same, but the experience of the tenors for the stadium audience and the TV audience, which sees all close shots, proves very different. The TV gets off to a bad start with a voice intruding into the music, but that is fixed and the quality of the sound proves superior to that outdoors. (When the program resurfaces on PBS some months later, the voice is not heard.) Although 56,000 in Giants Stadium is a huge crowd, it is, in a way, a studio audience for a television concert that will reach many times that number over the years. It's a good TV show—well-paced, attractive material, delivered with zest by real artists.

Intermission brings a moment of pure Levine as he talks with an interviewer. He has a bottle of Evian in his hand and replenishes his liquids as he is speaking. Sadly, this is not in the PBS version.

And when Domingo puts his hand on Carreras's shoulder in the encore of "Moon River" and sings, "Three tenors, off to see the world . . ." you have to say, "Bon Voyage!"

July 27–August 1, 1996. The Festspielhaus, Bayreuth, Germany.

Every critic probably has a hall that he regards as the holy of holies, a place consecrated by events to stand alone as a symbol of musical culture. In Italy this is the role of La Scala, Milan. In France it is that of the Opéra, Paris. For many Germans it is the Bayreuth Festspielhaus, the festival theater Wagner built as a frame for his four operas of *Der Ring des Nibelungen.* The theater opened in 1876 with the first complete production of these works. Later (as long as the copyright held) it became the unique home of *Parsifal.* Crowned heads and all of musical Europe attended these performances.

Bayreuth was the first great international summer festival. It hit its stride, after the composer's death, under the supervision of his redoubt-able widow, Cosima, and the family runs it today. Wolfgang Wagner, the composer's grandson, is the chief executive. In recent years the theater has been restored to its appearance of a century ago, although subtle modern innovations like improved ventilation have been introduced. The back-stage areas and auxiliary buildings, which are not designated historic landmarks, are as up to date as those of any major German theater.

The Friends of Bayreuth and some sixty large corporate sponsors underwrite the budget, together with gifts from the Bavarian state and the Bavarian Radio, which has exclusive broadcast rights. The theater is small, with about 1,900 of the most Spartan seats in any opera house in the world. Wagner built his theater after Greek models. There are no aisles. One enters from the side, with the fifteenth seat of the sixteenth row almost the exact midpoint of the hall. You walk to your seat and stand until those who must pass you take their places. At the end of an act those in the middle of the hall are trapped until those at the end of the aisles stand or depart. It is unconventional, but it works. No one ever leaves early, and there is never an empty seat.

To the levelers in American society, Bayreuth would be a symbol of elitism at its most arrogant. Production costs are high. Good tickets to a *Ring* cycle are $1,000. The audience is, with rare exceptions, elegantly dressed, the men in dinner jackets, the women in fashionable gowns of various lengths. The theater stands in a well-kept park at the top of Green Hill, the high point of the city. There are delightful restaurants and kiosks for food and drink a step away, and there is time to enjoy them. Most per-formances start at four in the afternoon. Intermissions are an hour, which means that most operas end a little after ten. Many complain that there is much post-performance confusion in the parking lots, but parking is free and, by American standards, the confusion is quickly over.

I love Bayreuth as I love no other place in the world of music. I feel a sanctity there unmatched by any other place except possibly the high altar of St. Peter's in Rome. The levelers see it as an excess, government money being spent on a theater in which the affluent amuse themselves, an artificial situation in which performances that could never survive as mass commercial entertainment are sustained by artificial means. But the performances are heard by a mass audience. They are aired to every-body, and millions listen. They are recorded, and in recent years some have become available on videotapes and laserdiscs.

What sets Bayreuth apart from commercial mass entertainment is pre-cisely that sense of sanctity. In the United States today we survey an array of social and ethnic groups, each with its own agenda and values, and realize that the nation that once thought of itself as a melting pot is no longer melting very well. Instead of becoming one people, we are becoming balkanized. But in Germany the idea is widely held that the nation stands firm on a community of values, and these values are defined and supported by the masterpieces of German art and literature.

Even on Sunday (when almost every store in the city is closed) you can walk into a large bookshop in the main railway station in Munich and buy the works of Goethe, Schiller, and Thomas Mann. They are on the shelves because they sell, and they sell because they are read. Knowing them is a basic part of being an educated German.

It was natural, inevitable, that someone with Levine's deep roots in central Europe would go to Bayreuth. He was only the third American to conduct there. (The first two, Lorin Maazel and Thomas Schippers, appeared briefly more than thirty years ago.) Levine arrived in 1982 to take charge of the centennial production of *Parsifal*. The century opened by Hermann Levi led to a second century inaugurated by another Levite. Levine stayed to direct *Parsifal* fifty-three times. In 1994 he began the first of five summers given to a new Bayreuth *Ring* cycle.

He had conducted his first complete *Ring* cycle five years before in New York. He began working the tetralogy into the Metropolitan schedule in September 1986 and by April 1989 all were in place. He led three complete cycles that season to great critical and popular acclaim. Otto Schenk was the producer, with sets and designs by Günther Schneider-Siemssen. Rolf Langenfass was responsible for the costumes, and Gil Wechsler was in charge of the lighting. The cycle was telecast in 1990 and is available on laserdiscs. I regard it as one of the great recordings of all time.

Toscanini might have brought us a *Ring* of equal intensity, but he never had an opportunity to do so. If you speculate what a Toscanini *Ring* might have been like, you may well conclude that Levine's Met *Ring* is the nearest thing to it you are ever likely to hear. The very different Bayreuth cycle was produced by Alfred Kirchner, with sets and costumes by Rosalie. Gero Zimmermann was technical director, and the lighting was designed by Manfred Voss.

In the nineteenth century there was only one way to stage the *Ring*— as German romantic opera. Now there are three main approaches to the cycle. The first respects the German romantic tradition. Levine's Met *Ring* is of that type. The 1983 Bayreuth *Ring,* produced by Peter Hall with designs by William Dudley, was a romantic re-creation of the drama. It was conducted the first summer by Sir Georg Solti, who then withdrew from the project. The conductor for 1984–87 was Peter Schneider.

A second approach is a *Ring* that takes Wagner's music and text more or less at face value but departs from the romantic tradition in staging. The 1988 Bayreuth *Ring,* produced by Harry Kupfer with sets by Hans Schavernoch, and conducted by Daniel Barenboim, had this character. I found it stronger visually than musically, but it made a great impression.

The Levine/Kirchner/Rosalie *Ring* is of the same genre, although completely different in detail and execution. What you hear is more impressive than what you see, but the result is still an imaginative and stimulating presentation of the operas.

The third type of *Ring*—the deconstructionist, post-modern *Ring*— dates from the Bayreuth centennial production of 1976 produced by Patrice Chéreau with sets by Richard Peduzzi and conducted by Pierre Boulez. The basic theme of the cycle, redemption through love, is rejected, and one has the impression that two radical Frenchmen have gone to war against one of the citadels of German culture. I found this production fascinating to see and hear, but I was not sympathetic to its goals or the means it chose to reach them.

Hall, in introducing his production, said his inspiration was to "examine the text and to have faith in it." This, I believe, is the right way. The *Ring* should not be moved (as Chéreau did) from a world of fantasy, outside history, to the nineteenth century. Dressing Wotan as Wagner, as Chéreau (and others) have done, is an effective vehicle for expressing anti-Wagner feelings, but destructive of the drama. Wagner was no more Wotan than Shakespeare was Lear. I reject the idea that all truly modern stagings of the cycle must take a strong revisionist approach growing from hostility to Wagner and his ideas, although in fashionable intellectual circles many will probably defend this viewpoint.

The two productions Levine has conducted are different, indeed, but he can come to terms with both of them because neither violates what he regards as the essential spirit of the work. He is pro-, not anti-Wagner.

The Kirchner/Rosalie *Ring* is usually described as reflecting the style of pop art. If the phrase *avant-garde* means anything anymore (alas, it doesn't), it might be used. This *Ring,* as I saw it, was anti-romantic, high-tech, in a manner that might best be described as contemporary slick. Bayreuth audiences love to express themselves by booing—especially in the final curtain calls. Booing a design can mean that the work was too radical or, conversely, that it was not radical enough. It's hard to tell. During the first cycle of the summer of 1996, Kirchner and Rosalie, especially Rosalie, bravely faced many boos. People simply did not like what they saw. Levine and the singers, on the other hand, were greeted with tidal waves of applause. Everyone seemed to agree that they were hearing something remarkable.

Levine conducted the Met production of the *Ring* again at the close of the 1996–97 season. He then returned to Bayreuth for the fourth summer of that cycle. It is unusual for any conductor to do two *Ring* cycles back-to-back, especially when they are so different in approach. Does he find this a problem? He didn't in 1996.

"I am going to do the *Ring* again at the Met in the spring. And I thought. This is going to be fun because with the experience the company has had with the music, they can hold inside all they have learned from previous performances and move on from that to gain a grasp of something deeper in the score. "

Over the years I have heard these operas many times at Bayreuth and other leading operatic theaters. I am resigned to the fact that I will never encounter a production that completely realizes the work as I conceive it. But by and large, the most perfectly satisfying *Ring* I have heard so far was the Levine/Met version, which I experienced live onstage, on TV, and on audio, videotape, and laserdiscs.

The two Levine versions of the cycle raise a basic question: To what degree is our response to the musical content of an opera influenced by the visual dimension? In theory the music remains the same. There were moments at Bayreuth in 1996 when I simply closed my eyes and eliminated what I found to be a distressing stage picture. Some critics have felt that Levine's performance in Bayreuth has achieved even greater maturity and depth than that of the Met years. I agree. He is totally focused on this music. Wagner was being wonderfully well served.

Levine, one must recall, began at Bayreuth with a production of *Parsifal* that was in no sense conventional. In 1989 it was replaced with a new staging that was also unorthodox, but in different ways. The new Met *Parsifal* of 1991, another Schenk/Schneider-Siemssen collaboration, is, on the contrary, quite conservative.

"I find this Bayreuth version artistically interesting," Levine says soon after the close of the first cycle for 1996. "When it is unsuccessful, it is unsuccessful in different ways from those in which most *Ring*s fail to come up to expectations. That is very interesting. I can encompass the Met *Ring* and this one and many others, too. The *Ring* is so complex, and any idea that there is one right way to present it is ridiculous. Wagner knew that; it lies behind his statement at the end of the first cycle in 1876 that 'next time it will all be different.' Unfortunately, there never was a 'next time' in his lifetime and performance practices that should not have been forged into tradition were given an authority they did not deserve."

My problem with Rosalie's *Ring* design is that it combines brilliant strokes with odd and ordinary things. The basic set, a huge disc that was to return throughout the cycle, offered limited possibilities and even these were exploited with varying levels of success.

The opening scene of *Das Rheingold* with the amorous Alberich pursuing the Rhine maidens was done as skillfully as I have ever seen it staged, rivaled only by 1983 when Solti demanded, and got, "real [naked] vimmen in real water." Rosalie put the Rhine nymphs on a carousel that rose and fell and revolved around the gold. It was simple, striking, and wonderfully effective stagecraft.

Every director and designer must find the second scene of *Rheingold* difficult. The music is not very exciting, and there is far too much talk in relation to the action. This version was visually weak. The giants, always a problem, are these days a near-fatal invitation to cute tricks. In this production, having mortal-sized singers supporting a huge mask did not succeed. The best giants, and Levine apparently agrees, were the real giants in Chéreau's 1976 production, an effect achieved by hiring professional wrestlers to carry the singers around on their shoulders.

For vivid contrast, the third scene of *Rheingold* was one bold stroke of imagination after another, with the most subtle, telling, and inspired realization of the dragon I have encountered anywhere.

The final scene has the advantage of a lot of action both in the music and on the stage, leading to what can be a wonderful moment, the entry of the gods into Valhalla over a rainbow bridge. In too many modern productions we are denied a look at Valhalla—why I'm not sure. Here a spectacular rainbow bridge led the eye to the distant fortress.

The opening of *Die Walküre* was simplistic but effective. It played well. I found the second act less successful, largely because it made it impossible to follow Wagner's stage directions. But the third act, when the ride of the valkyries put each horseless lady in her own private flying capsule, you saw a highly ingenious solution to one of the major problems in staging the opera. The final scene, with Brünnhilde sleeping within a wall of fire, was a striking close.

I asked Levine how the valkyries' ride was staged.

"That could only be done in Bayreuth because it's not a repertory house where you have to have more than one show hanging at a time. If you tried this in a repertory house you would never have time to set it up. Because at Bayreuth the performance starts at four, you have time to do a full turnaround between shows. The special rigging for those capsules the girls are in is installed separately, so the capsules follow different paths and can't hit each other. Here they are all controlled separately by a great stage manager."

The greatest moment in the first act of this *Siegfried* was the bear scene, a moment that (when it is not cut) usually produces a man moving awkwardly in a bear suit. This time the hero arrived at the forge followed by a large teddy bear—a toy, not a wild beast—and they exchanged a bountiful bear hug on parting. This was innovative, scenic virtuosity. The forging procedure that closed the act would have reduced any metallurgist to laughter but adequately served the purpose of storytelling.

As the second act opens, the audience inevitably is wondering how the great dragon fight will be staged. Everyone waits for the dragon's entrance. Rosalie's trick is that the dragon is always there, the green lump that fills the back of the stage. This was clever, but inconsistent with the dragon as it is described in the libretto and precludes the possibility of the sort of dragon fight Wagner describes. But after the fight was over I liked the reappearance of Fafner as a giant in the agony of death.

The first half of Act 3 was effectively staged. The final scene, with Siegfried and Brünnhilde, was not. There was too much variance between what the characters were saying and what they were doing.

The Norns scene that opens *Götterdämmerung* was poorly focused and lacked a climax. Presumably Siegfried and Brünnhilde were living the lives of the homeless on the fire-rimmed rock, but you had to be moved by their farewell duet. The hall of the Gibichungs was awful; nothing you saw seemed to fit what you heard. The Brünnhilde/Waltraute scene suffered from a grievous lack of scenery, a problem that continued in the scene with Siegfried (as Gunther) that followed.

Act 2, however, had a reasonably functional set and went well. The scene by the Rhine that opens the third act was effective, but in the next scene I could not accept a half-dozen telephone poles as a forest, and I protested when the funeral march was played but no funeral procession was seen. The short scene in which Siegfried's body is returned to the Gibichung hall was a strong transition to the most difficult scene in all Wagner, Brünnhilde's immolation. Rosalie kept it in fairly simple terms, and it worked.

With a few exceptions (the Wanderer, Erda) Rosalie's costumes were consistently dreadful. Levine found many of them distracting and uninvolving. For me they were ugly, inappropriate to the character and the action, and difficult in which to move and sing.

Levine had brought this cycle (his Wotan and Brünnhilde sang these roles in the Kupfer cycle) through three summers with the original casts essentially intact. There have been a few changes in the ranks of the valkyries, but not until 1996, when there was a new Hunding (by default, Hans Sotin was ill) and a new Gutrune, were there different voices in leading roles. Carefully prepared, their first performances were sure and confident.

After three summers in which Levine conducted roughly half the total number of performances, the Bayreuth Orchestra has become another Levine orchestra on the same lines as the Met. In 1996, he felt, a large number of new players were not assimilated until midway in the first *Ring* cycle, but after that he had the unity of approach he desired. This is the Wagner sound introduced to Bayreuth by Toscanini, transparent singing lines both onstage and in the pit, with strong attacks and a long, powerful flow of legato melody. It is very different from the conducting of Siegfried Wagner that dominated the festival in the early part of the century.

Levine is thoroughly aware that in the *Ring* Wagner covers nearly the full range of human feelings in music of supreme dramatic force. There is no greater love music than that of *Die Walküre,* nothing more evil than Alberich and his gang, nothing nobler than Brünnhilde's self-sacrifice to set the moral order right once more. Levine's aim is to get to the root of all this, to study and play these scores until their secrets have been discovered, and he is well on his way to that goal.

John Tomlinson was the Wotan/Wanderer of this production with Hanna Schwarz as Fricka and Birgitta Svendén as Erda. Siegfried Jerusalem sang Loge. René Pape and Eric Halfvarson were the giants. Ekkehard Wlaschiha was Alberich and Manfred Jung was Mime. Poul Elming and Tina Kiberg were Siegmund and Sieglinde, respectively, with Matthias Hölle as Hunding. Deborah Polaski was Brünnhilde. Wolfgang Schmidt sang Siegfried. The final opera brought Falk Struckmann as Gunther, Halfvarson as Hagen, and Anne Schwanewilms as Gutrune. Schwarz appeared as Waltraute. It was a good solid cast, never less than fully competent, often brilliant.

Why, one might ask, does Bayreuth keep introducing new *Ring* productions every five years or so? Why not find a good one and stay with it? Because that would not be serving the *Ring,* it would be betraying it. There is far more content in these operas than any one production, however successful, can reveal. You keep doing them again. You keep returning to the festival. And in time the full majesty of this work, in all its many aspects, may be revealed.

August 3, 1996. Olympic Stadium, Munich.

By traveling some four thousand miles, I am finally going to hear the Three Tenors live (via amplification) as part of a vast audience. This time the concert is within the host city, at the Olympic Stadium. Built in 1972 for the 20th Summer Olympic Games, it is the largest structure in the Olympic Park, an area of 667 acres in the northern part of the city, which had previously been used as a military airport. It is now an impressive recreational area combining excellent landscaping with a number of distinctive structures in essentially the same fluid, modern style.

The stadium seats 78,000 and is unique among facilities of its type because of the tent roof that partly shields the seating area from the weather. This and the tall, slanting banks of floodlights give the place a distinctive look. The public enters from the top and comes down to the field on a monumental staircase, a wonderful sight.

Normally the stadium is dedicated to football and track and field events, but the Three Tenors, for one night, have converted it into a music hall. The playing field is filled with narrow, armless, metal folding chairs of the ubiquitous type previously encountered in Giants Stadium, and the European stage is identical to that in New York. But in Munich everything is finished and in place hours before the concert is to begin. There are no workmen in sight. *Alles in Ordnung.* All is in order.

The public has been told that if one arrives at 7 p.m. (those with the most expensive tickets may arrive at 6:30) it is possible to hear the final hour of the rehearsal. This time it is the *only* rehearsal for this event. Levine arrived from Bayreuth, where he had just completed the first of his three *Ring* cycles of the summer, the Philharmonia came up from Salzburg (where it was playing *Oberon*), and the tenors arrived from various points of the compass. Since this is the same conductor with whom they have done the show five times previously, as far as they are concerned all that is needed is an opportunity to check the sound system. Those who came early expecting to hear some real rehearsing are disappointed. There is just enough singing to get the golden voices nicely warmed up, and that is it.

The producer provided the tenors with a security net worthy of a chief of state. Since the concert is sold out, there is no need to meet the press, and journalists find them inaccessible. Even so, Carreras made the local front page the day of the concert with a six-million-mark gift to benefit Munich children with cancer. "What do the Three Tenors do when they aren't singing?" the paper asks. The answer, Carreras spends, Pavarotti cooks, and Domingo jogs. No one talks.

As in New York, the stadium is awash in red carpet. In front it is generously arrayed, and the hard metal of the seat is again tucked away beneath a cushion with the Three Tenors logo. In the most expensive seats (they fetched the Deutsche mark equivalent of their New York counterparts) a bag containing Three Tenors opera glasses hangs from the front of the cushion and a smartly packaged gift is placed on the seat, toiletries for the women and, strangely enough, a hair-growing product for the men.

The Munich sound system is placed much lower than the one in New York—in the stadium rather than above it—and appears to consist of large electroacoustic panels. Like all outdoor systems, it lacks low bass, but the voices are faithfully reproduced with their true timbre and overtones, and electronic delay gives the illusion of reflecting walls.

Less pleasant is the discovery that after a week of rehearsals and four concerts the Philharmonia is now just a pale image of the virtuoso group Walter Legge founded some fifty years ago and that was carried to great heights by Karajan, Klemperer, and Toscanini.

The musicians are attentive, cooperative, and professional in the great British spirit, but London musicians are so busy going from one job to another that many are denied the opportunity for growth that comes with extended, close work with one conductor and one group of colleagues. And you can hear it, starting with the overture to Bernstein's *Candide,* which lacks the sparkle and verve the Met musicians brought to it. Despite a demanding week in Bayreuth and a sinus infection, Levine is all business, holding nothing back.

About twenty minutes into the concert I conclude that the event really is better as a television show. In fact, my previous thoughts that even in public performance it *is* a thinly disguised television show are correct. Producer Tibor Rudas has been thoroughly aware that, however many seats are filled, the television audience will be many times greater than those physically present, and the important thing is that the concert look good on the tube. From the back of the stadium you need a telescope to see a performer's face. As in New York, this is remedied by the two huge television screens on either side of the stage. When Levine is conducting, you see a Levine twenty feet tall, and when someone is singing a giant head becomes visible to represent the diminutive figure at a microphone a few yards away.

I find myself seated between a large lady in black satin and a wiggly gentleman who gave the impression he would much rather be somewhere else. The lady is constantly lifting a hand to greet members of the orchestra. The seats had not been designed with individuals of our size in mind, but my own bulk preserves me a perch, and as the first half of the concert progresses, I am grateful that she is at least warm.

Starting about eight o'clock the clouds begin spitting rain, and as time passes it gets worse. Nothing is gained by the fact that due to traffic problems the festivities begin some fifteen minutes late, at which point a soft, steady drizzle has begun. The performers have a roof over them. Levine plunges into the overture apparently oblivious of the weather.

The public on the field is unprotected. I have a light raincoat, but I cannot put it on because I am solidly grasped in a friction fit between my neighbors. In the hope of improvising a rain shield, the man on the right begins ripping up the expensive extra-illustrated program he had purchased, but he is never pleased with the results. The large lady is deeply concerned for her hair. I assume a stoic attitude.

Hearing "Il Lamento di Federico" from Carreras with water dripping down my neck is at least a novel experience. Still, nobody leaves. For a start, all, except those on the aisles, are jammed together so tightly it is a physical impossibility, but more to the point, one senses German discipline. This is *Kultur* (it was also an expensive ticket); we shall have a good time in spite of everything.

On the stage the performers seem unaware that we are being slowly soaked. And so the program progresses into the first medley, ending with a performance of "Torna a Sorrento" that is almost hot enough to dry you out.

At intermission the large lady departs backstage never to return. The gentleman who had been seated on her left, but is not her companion, also departs with an air of resolution that suggests we will not see him again. Released from the vise, I stand up and finally put on my raincoat, and at that moment the drizzle starts to slack off. It ends before the concert closes. As the audience returns, two markedly attractive ladies about thirty, who have obviously been cruising to improve their seating, spot the two empty chairs and descend upon me.

They are a change for the better. But ten minutes or so in the second half of the program, he who had exited with resolution reappears and, squeezing his way down the row with heroic resolve, demands his seat. The displaced lady takes refuge in her companion's lap. The two represent greater cubic volume than the large lady, but since they are arranged on a vertical rather than a horizontal axis, I am more comfortable.

All three tenors look youthful onstage, but there is a considerable age spread in the group. Carreras is forty-eight, Domingo fifty-five, and Pavarotti sixty—although you'd never guess it. No two voices are alike.

Domingo sings Wagner as well as Italian repertory. Pavarotti is ideal for Verdi and Puccini staples. The special charm and beauty of the Carreras tenor is its lyric quality. Unfortunately there are moments when he lost this by forcing his tone.

The second half runs its course. When Pavarotti sings his climactic number, "Nessun dorma" from *Turandot,* there is no mystery about his ability to reach out and captivate a huge audience. This is the magic that makes these events such a success. Again the ending is a medley, this one with a Vesuvius-like outpouring of "O sole mio." With the stadium drying out, the audience is in a happier mood, and the encores could have gone on indefinitely. You can feel the mood of the crowd. The shower has been forgotten. This will be remembered as a great night.

Going to Olympic Park in the early evening was no problem. The trains were nearly empty. You strolled leisurely under the trees to the stadium. Going back to the city at midnight in the company of perhaps 70,000 other people is another matter. I have to leave by a different way than I entered, and finding the road back to the subway station is a problem. It is 2 a.m. when I open the door to my hotel room. The trip back had lasted almost as long as the concert.

September 28, 1996. Medinah Temple, Chicago.

Fantasia 2000 will begin with *The Pines of Rome,* recorded in 1995, and end with four sections from Stravinsky's *Firebird* ballet, which Levine and the Chicago Symphony are to record this morning. The music selected lasts about fifteen minutes, and a three-hour recording session plus a possible hour of overtime has been called.

At 9:50 a.m. the stage is filled with musicians deeply involved in the rites of tuning up. The engineering crew is the familiar one, commuters from New York who have been part of this project from the beginning. Levine is in the control room chatting with Don Ernst, producer of the film, and Jay David Saks, director of the session. After a few friendly exchanges he departs to see if his chair and music stand have been set at the right height. They have. The score is in place, two batons are at the side of the stand, and a fresh bottle of Evian is nearby.

There is the original *Firebird* ballet score of 1910, which many regard as the finest version of the work, and a number of *Firebird* suites. The one most frequently played was arranged by the composer in 1919, and this has been cut to fit the Disney story line and slightly reorchestrated by

Bruce Coughlin, who is there to help if needed. Ernst sits beside him in the control room.

Saks, who has given up on monitor speakers, takes his place wearing the electrostatic earphones he prefers to use these days. He and Levine have been working together for twenty years and each knows exactly how the other functions. Saks is a quiet, concentrated, utterly unflappable person whom Levine can trust with all the technical details.

There is a short burst of applause as Levine takes his place onstage. "As you know," he says, "we are finishing this job today. I have seen *The Pines of Rome* with the animation, and it is incredible, a new art form. The pictures and the music are synchronized and interacting in a manner that is simply fantastic—made me feel like the kid I was when I saw the original *Fantasia.*"

Levine is now to lead the Chicago orchestra for the third time since he ended twenty-three years of association with the Ravinia Festival in June 1993. There have been several changes in personnel, and his approach makes it clear that he feels he cannot take things for granted. The "You know me, I know you" basis no longer applies. The beat is simple, clear, and precise, and in the cavernous spaces of Medinah he is taking no chances.

Disney is using this music to tell a completely different story than that of Stravinsky's ballet. "In 1940 you could end *Fantasia* with the Schubert 'Ave Maria,' " Ernst remarks. "In this day of multiculturalism, that is no longer possible. We wanted a universal story of death and resurrection on which to close with a powerful message about the renewal of life. We see a peaceful landscape. A volcano erupts, bringing universal desolation. And then, in time, life returns. There are flowers from the ashes."

Levine and the orchestra go through the first part of this arrangement, the Round Dance of the Princesses. It sounds great. This, after all, is the Chicago Symphony playing a basic repertory score.

"How is it?" Levine asks on the intercom from the stage.

"Sounds fine," Ernst replies.

Levine goes on to the next section, the music that, as it turns out, will call for a lot of work. It is the dance of the evil magician Kastchei and his monsters. Scored for large orchestra, it is fast, rhythmic, and complex since, thematically, several things are often happening at once. Levine insists that the notes be given full value. "Bom, bom, bom," he sings to the brass, "separated but not short." With a piece like this, articulation is a matter of primary importance; and articulation, it soon proves, becomes the keyword of the session.

The Chicago Symphony was long accustomed to playing with great precision. It did so for more than twenty years with Sir Georg Solti and continued when Solti became laureate conductor, and with Pierre Boulez, its principal guest maestro. It can do it for Levine, if there is the time to let it happen. Mercifully, they do. He goes back to the opening pages.

"I need more sound at the end of the phrase," he cautions, "and keep it dolce all the way." He is now following his usual practice, going beyond the accurate realization of the printed notes to create a real performance. There is a little cello solo played with great sensitivity, and Levine smiles.

"I like this," he says.

The spirit he is evoking for me is that of the old recording that taught me this music, a product of the 1930s by Leopold Stokowski and the Philadelphia Orchestra. Languorous, sensual lyricism is filled with the atmosphere of exotic Russian legend.

In the first break I speak with Levine about that recording. "Wasn't it wonderful?" he says. "Stokowski could put more atmosphere into a scratchy old 78 rpm record than anyone else. And you know, if the atmosphere was right, he didn't care if there were mistakes. Listen carefully and you will catch quite a few of them. But if he had to remake a four- or five-minute side, hoping to get the same performance a second time, he obviously wouldn't do it. If the feeling of the performance was right, he would sacrifice note accuracy. It's something to remember."

Coughlin hears a harmonic clash in the strings and rushes onstage. There has been a cut and the familiar parts had to be changed to make a smooth transition.

"Don't play the same notes you've been playing for thirty-five years," Levine says. "Follow the part. It's an E and a C," he indicates to one section, and, turning, "for you it's a G and an E." There is some muttering from the old hands, but they make note of the change.

"We have a lot of marcato notes close together here," Levine observes a moment later. "Play short eighths or the crescendo gets muddier instead of brighter."

At 10:50 the rehearsal ends. Levine calls out, "Let's take it from the beginning." The tape begins to roll, and they play it through. The orchestra then gets a twenty-minute break and Levine appears in the control room.

"We've got a lot of great stuff," Ernst reports, obviously pleased that everything is going so quickly and so well. Levine sits down to listen, lets the music flow by him, and decides, "We need more contrast."

When he returns to the orchestra, he is upbeat. "This was excellent, but we can do more with color and dynamics. And when it gets fast, we must watch articulation; the style does not permit slurs between notes when they are not marked."

They go to work. One of the easiest mistakes to make in these early Stravinsky ballets is to deny the rests their full rhythmic value. "I want to hear eighth notes followed by a full eighth rest." Levine insists. "Don't hold the note and clip the rest. That gives a completely wrong effect."

Again he feels they are dragging a little. "Don't hold on to the note," he insists. "Set it flying." And things improve. A few moments later he is praising them. "Excellent. Beautiful."

Like most orchestras, the Chicago Symphony has been taught to listen to the ensemble and be guided by its ears. But the Medinah stage does not permit this. The reflecting surfaces are too far away. If you count on your ear for a cue, you will be late.

Levine is unhappy in the Kastchei Dance. "It has to begin with a really big attack. And we're not playing together. You have to follow me. We won't get the sound we want any other way." So for once they play glued to the stick, and it works. A few moments later Levine is beaming. "Just great!" he says.

At 12:15 the orchestra has a second break. Levine returns to the control room and tells Saks, "We are nearly there."

"I have five little things," Saks reports.

"Let's do them as inserts," Levine replies. "If we take things all the way through again it will start to go because of fatigue."

In one case the problem is not in the playing but the tempo. The Disney people are not sure the music and the animation will go together. Could it be a trifle slower? No difficulty. They will do it again.

"The last take was spectacular. The tempo is perfect," Ernst reports after another try.

At the close of the piece Coughlin has written a roll on the bass drum in place of the single thwack Stravinsky specified. They try it both ways.

"The thwack is better," Levine feels.

Coughlin agrees. Better attack. He deletes his change in the percussion part. The Kastchei Dance still has a couple of bars in which the brass is not totally together.

"If you think you can get it cleaner just playing with each other and ignoring the stick, do it that way," Levine suggests. It works. They are, in fact, perfectly in sync with his beat, but truly playing together as a section.

When records were made on analog tape, splices had to be made in moments of silence. In digital technology, editing is much more flexible, and once Saks is convinced that somewhere on some take he has an absolutely perfect version of everything, the rest can be left to what is called post-production—that is, fine-tuned editing in the lab.

The finale is written in ⅞, an unusual signature, and contains four bars for the brass that Stokowski cut for many years because he was fearful that there was no way to play them accurately. Levine is not going to give up, although nearly three hours of highly concentrated work are taking their toll on him as well as the musicians. They have another try. It is good.

"Let's do it once more for safety's sake," Levine suggests, and the passage is repeated.

"In between the two we have it all perfectly," Saks reports. After more than thirty takes, the session ends at three minutes to one. There is a brief burst of applause and many members of the orchestra come to greet the maestro. Stagehands begin to rip the set apart, and the Disney people set up a place where Saks and Levine can be interviewed for a documentary on the making of the film which is simultaneously in production.

Seventeen months before, when the second session for the film took place, there was more free time at the close and Levine was relaxed and happy. This time he is weary. The orchestra got breaks, but he has been working at maximum concentration for three hours and he is at the end of a month of grueling preseason Met rehearsals. He retires to his makeshift dressing room, dries himself off, changes his clothes, and returns to the hall to tape the interview. Since he is a pro, fatigue or no fatigue, he does it and does it well.

Roy Disney, chief of animation at the studio, who has been taking candid pictures of the participants at work, clicks off a few more frames. Levine manages a weary smile.

I offer congratulations. "The absolute precision you finally achieved is astonishing."

"You have to work for it," he replies. "But with musicians like this, it comes. It's there. They know how. Other aspects come more easily but they mustn't lose this precision that they used to take for granted."

Levine and his staff gather their things together and slowly walk down the corridor to the limousine that will whisk them to a waiting jet. They are tired, but at the same time, happy. An important job has been done well. They will be back in Manhattan by late afternoon and the Met season opens on Monday night.

In the control room the crew are disconnecting cables and stowing sound gear in the red trunks in which the equipment travels. Levine will probably be sleeping when they return to New York.

The young blonde woman engineer who has monitored forty-eight channels for the three sessions observes philosophically, "It takes eight hours to set this up and test it, and it takes six hours to take it down. And we use it three hours."

But what a three hours! The product is fifteen minutes of dazzling ensemble virtuosity that can set a standard for the world.

PART FOUR

The Recordings

No operatic conductor in history has had his repertory documented in recordings to the degree that Levine's work has been preserved for the future. In theory we can hear at least one example of every opera he has done in full at the Met, although about a third of this material (from television and radio broadcasts) awaits release.

Herbert von Karajan realized how an advancing technology could preserve operatic performances with greater impact and on a larger scale than ever before, but he died before he could make the fullest use of the new resources. Leonard Bernstein was thoroughly aware of the power of television. But neither man had a base of operations comparable to Levine's. And Levine interacts in a purposeful and effective manner with the electronic media. Toscanini had no grasp of the recording process. He viewed it with fear and hatred, as an intrusion of electronics into music. The result was that he often failed to realize the best possible results in recording sessions.

Levine turns to television and recordings as a natural extension of the live performance. He was greatly impressed by Disney's *Fantasia* as a child. His role models in forming an attitude toward music in the larger world of films, television, and discs were Stokowski and Toscanini. He was particularly impressed by Toscanini's willingness to conduct the NBC Symphony on radio for seventeen years. He reached a vast "electronic" audience far beyond the few hundred in RCA Studio 8H. It is therefore no surprise that with the exception of a few performances from the early part of his career, nearly everything operatic Levine has done has been preserved. His symphonic repertory is generously represented on compact discs, and although one might wish for more, examples of his finer achievements as an accompanist and chamber player are available.

Of the sixty-nine operas Levine conducted in full in his first twenty-seven years at the Met, forty-six are available on commercial recordings. Twenty-five have been recorded in radio or television broadcast but await release. The one major ballet, Stravinsky's *Le Sacre du Printemps,* which he has done at the Met, has also been commercially recorded. Twenty-nine of the operas, a generous 43 percent, are available on video—the nearest thing to a live performance. Fourteen of the operas on laserdiscs are available only in a video format. There are also CDs of two operas Levine has never directed in any theater.

Levine has, on occasion, conducted single acts of operas. His performance of Act 2 of *Die Fledermaus* is on a laserdisc, as are his performances of Act 3 of *Otello* and Act 3 of *Rigoletto.* Both of the Verdi operas have been recorded in their entirety for CD. His 1990 performances of Act 2 of *Faust* and Act 3 of *Madama Butterfly* were not documented. (He has conducted

Butterfly in its entirety, but not at the Met.) One opera from his Met reper-tory, *Tosca,* exists in a superb recording, but not that of a Met performance.

Eleven works Levine has not recorded in any other form have been seen on television and hence exist on edited videotape. If the demand for them is great enough, they will be released in the laserdisc format. There are also TV tapes duplicating repertory on CD. This leaves twelve works which have been broadcast in the Saturday afternoon series and taped in that form. Under existing union rules, the broadcasts may be issued as historic recordings only after twenty-five years. But this rule was waived for the Levine twenty-fifth anniversary album, and further exceptions might be made. The important thing is that they exist. These perfor-mances endure. (The documentation of Levine's Met repertory is given in full on page 311.)

Toscanini's televised concerts were a major influence on Levine as a child. We have a little more than ten hours of Toscanini's work in a visual format, technically uneven, often primitive, products from the early days of television, and yet priceless. He shows us how he did it. The stick moves. The music sounds. The eyes flash and the glance holds you. For someone like Levine, who is concerned with defining and transmitting an approach to music, this is an essential link to the past. Ironically, we have nothing like ten hours with the camera on Levine. Laserdiscs show him conducting overtures, but the minute a singer appears, he vanishes. Listening to a particularly fine effect in an ensemble, I am filled with curiosity about what the baton is doing, but it is never revealed.

Mahler, we read, set new standards of operatic production in Vienna. His earlier work in Budapest was admired by Brahms. I believe it, but it is impossible to give the statement much depth of meaning. What were the old standards? What started happening in performances under Mahler's direction that had not been happening before? One assumes, for a start, there was greater ensemble precision, a return to the authentic spirit of the score. But for a complete understanding we need details we will probably never know. In the case of the Met, the detail is there. Play a Levine per-formance of *La Forza del Destino* against one from earlier years, and the changes in the approach to the work over the years become clear. Some of the older versions contain marvelous singing, but substantial cuts.

For those of us who began collecting recorded operas when a work of average length became a big, heavy album of 78 rpm discs, the technical advance from the scratchy four-minute side to a laserdisc that plays for about an hour is phenomenal. Some thirty years ago we were captivated by stereo operatic recordings that suggested movement on an invisible stage, and later, with four-channel decoders, it was sometimes possible to create the effect that you were onstage and the opera was being played around you. Now you can see as well as hear, and it is easy to be thoroughly spoiled by the new technology.

"If laserdiscs required a compromise in sound quality," Levine comments, "you might debate whether to take them over the excellent sound on compact discs. But for those of us who want to hear good sound, the sound on the laserdiscs is so good, and now it is married to a picture, so you have opera with a fullness of experience no CD can match."

The laserdisc, moreover, provides a running translation of the words at the bottom of the screen, a system many find preferable to supertitles in the theater or even the ingenious Met Titles. Admittedly one can listen to CDs with a score or libretto at hand, but titles on the screen are much more convenient. The eye can stay focused on the action, and the facial expressions and body language that accompany a line of text can be fully appreciated.

Of course, there are historic operatic recordings to be treasured, played, and replayed, but as a general rule, if one wants to hear an opera at home and a laserdisc is available, it is preferable to a CD album. Levine is not yet ready to say that CD opera sets are facing obsolescence. But in the past, recording companies have entered into expensive projects like operatic recording with the assumption that the costs can be amortized over twenty years or more of sales. One can seriously question the demand for new CD operatic recordings in even five years' time.

The recording industry is presently in a transitional state, and laserdiscs, at the moment, are more important in some markets than others. Not surprisingly, they are widely in use in New York and environs, Chicago, and other large cities. But smaller places in mid-America are slow in becoming aware of their existence. In this part of the world, opera with sight and sound is opera on VHS tape. New recording formats arriving on the American market have been designed so older discs may still be played.

The seasoned operagoer knows that experiencing an opera is a complex series of impressions, none more basic than one's visual link to the performers. For many years that demanded one's presence in a theater. When you are here and the conductor is there, the singers are on the stage, people are all around you, and the music fills the hall, you experience a real operatic performance. Films of opera can be attractive but offer a totally different experience. Television and laserdiscs create in the home a situation that is different from attending opera in the theater but have an immediacy that produces strong effects. In my home I have my own little opera house in which I can see and hear any of my favorite scores whenever I like, and it is a wonderful resource. King Ludwig of

Bavaria, Wagner's allegedly mad patron, who liked to have operas performed for him alone, had no such repertory at his command.

The laserdisc introduces something we have long taken for granted in films, the close-up. The full expanse of the broad operatic stage is seen when appropriate, but generally we watch smaller, more tightly composed groups of figures, and we view them from several angles, even, occasionally, from one impossible in the theater—directly overhead. Facial expressions become a critical part of the interpretation. True, there are those who bring powerful binoculars to the opera and peer through them at the stage, but few can fiddle with an apparatus of this type and still concentrate on the music. The fact must be accepted that we now have two ways of viewing opera, each with certain advantages, and if we are wise we will enjoy both.

Levine's laserdisc recordings document his work in the theater, but they also give us an accurate, well-rounded portrait of the man. Many conductors (Bernstein was a good example) create a public image of themselves that is quite different from the man offstage. There is only one James Levine, the happy, warmhearted workaholic who gives himself without reserve to making music because it is the entire focus and meaning of his life. There is nothing else he would rather do.

We can begin with Levine making music at the piano. In the 1986 laserdisc recording of chamber music by Mozart and Beethoven, made with the Ensemble Wien-Berlin in the hall of the Schloss Heilbrunn in Salzburg, and directed by Ponnelle, the forty-three-old pianist is clearly the dominant member of the group. He leads, he shapes, and he inspires, but it remains chamber music, not a mini-concerto for the keyboard instrument. The five musicians are listening to each other, interacting freely, and combining their concentrated efforts to serve the different styles and ideas of the two composers. The goal is communication. This is not show business. It is art business.

Two years later Levine joined Luciano Pavarotti for a song recital on the Met Stage that yielded a telecast and a laserdisc. The two men obviously have the highest respect for each other, but Pavarotti is clearly pleased to have an accompanist who thoroughly understands the technique of singing. Many conductors create problems for singers by demanding that they produce a vocal line that realizes the conductor's musical preconceptions. Levine deals with possible, not theoretical, results. He wants to understand exactly how the singer produces a musical phrase, and he is there to assist that process and work toward the realization of a work, even a simple song, in terms of grace and beauty both will admire.

In the introduction to Plácido Domingo's disc *Homage to Seville,* we must pretend we are eavesdropping on a conversation between Domingo, Levine, and director Jean-Pierre Ponnelle at the beginning of the project. It is dramatically convincing, a delightful way to start the action. Levine is relaxed, confident, both open to suggestion and willing to improvise. This is the man I have known for thirty years.

The Roman Catholic confessional is no more private than the closed, one-on-one sessions in Levine's studio in which he is at the piano and a singer joins him to work out the details of a performance. This is not a coach teaching a singer a part. The singer knows the music thoroughly. They are refining the interpretive and technical points of a performance and can be totally honest with each other. There is no possibility of an ego being bruised before colleagues. And, as Levine sees it, this permits working closely with the music in an essential manner that provides intimacy and will build a transition to the next, more public, work on the stage.

There is an opportunity to experience a session of this type in the rehearsal sequence that follows the prologue of the laserdisc recording of *Ariadne auf Naxos.* The rehearsal becomes an opportunity for shared delight in the achievement of something of remarkable beauty. As they sing, Levine is right there with the encouraging word ("excellent timing there"), but, in the pit, with all his forces before him, he can also be demanding ("this is too heavy and not enough brilliance"). The one thing that best characterizes Levine's rehearsals is concentrated work. When there is laughter, it comes from delight in a musical success, the leap over the staff that produces something luminous and wonderful to hear.

Working at the piano with Kathleen Battle he asks at one point, "Do you have to start later?"

"I don't have to, no," she replies.

"You don't have to. Because I'm not with you there [i.e., your music is independent of mine], and I would go on unless you needed a rest."

They do it with the piano. "Sensational," he says. "Now, wait and start whenever you want. This place you can start without recourse to the upbeat. I have made the upbeat already. And then you sing, and I'll be there. The interesting thing is that for me the tempo is good as long as the very first phrase isn't heavy."

A moment later he asks, "Am I pushing you too early there? I always wonder, am I doing *what you want me to.*" [Italics added.] "Do you need time to get up to A?"

"It's like a lottery," Battle replies. And they both laugh.

"Lord," Levine says, "let me win the lottery! OK. I understand."

Since few operagoers are familiar with opera rehearsals, especially on this level, many hearing this laserdisc will not realize that Levine is giving the singer much more freedom than many other conductors can or would. The performance is a true collaboration, something they have achieved together, and this is why singers will come to the Met to work with him when they might earn considerably more in an engagement at another theater.

Later, rehearsing at arm's length with Norman, she says, "I wish we could be this close together onstage."

"We are," he replies.

"Yes?"

"We are, just like when we do Strauss recitals. I know exactly what you're doing, and the orchestra can flex, just like that, so you can linger where you want to when you want to."

She goes on magnificently, comes to the end of a phrase, and he says quietly, "Doesn't that tickle you?"

And that relaxed confidence demonstrates supreme mastery of the art of operatic conducting, the source from which miracles spring.

The credibility of this rehearsal sequence comes from the fact that Levine is working with people he knows very well. No one seems aware of the camera, and one senses this is not a show, this is how it usually goes. If you have talent, if you share Levine's commitment, it is fun. Preparing an opera becomes the most wonderful thing in the world.

Inevitably I look back to the old days, the experience of rehearsing an opera with Toscanini. Except in rare cases, he would never ask a singer what he or she wanted because he was fearful that what the singer wanted was something stupid or unmusical, an interpolated high note, for example. But for much of his life Toscanini was dealing with singers who were not trained musicians. Many could not read music, fewer still could teach themselves a part. They were singing machines who had roles drilled into them by coaches and were taught to go on the stage and obey the conductor.

The Met of today is possible because the singers who come there are the best educated in history. Juilliard, Curtis, New England, Eastman, Mannes, Indiana, and any one of a number of other good places have made them musicians, and Levine works with them as musicians. If they could not meet this standard, he would have nothing to do with them.

With this glimpse into the workshop, let us turn to the operas on laserdiscs. It should be noted that nearly all the laserdisc releases are also available in VHS tape, a somewhat less expensive and technically less satisfactory format.

Historically, there is nothing in this group more important than the first project, Strauss's *Elektra* with Birgit Nilsson from February 1980. This is one of the great documents in the history of opera in this century. Nilsson has observed ruefully, with her typical wit, that when she and Levine first worked together, "most of my future was behind me." But here is one of her supreme roles, and the vocal and dramatic skills, fine-tuned by many performances, produce high drama indeed. The cast, as a whole, is exceptionally strong. This is a landmark release that caused us to reconsider the entire idea of operatic recording.

So did another Levine video, another Strauss score, *Ariadne auf Naxos*, with Battle, Norman, and James King (just discussed). Here is one of the composer's most captivating flights of fancy, exquisitely realized.

For sheer magnitude, Levine's laserdisc edition of Wagner's *Ring of the Niebelung*, made in 1989–90, stands alone. There are many Wagner recordings of great value going back seventy years, but this union of sight and sound remains a supreme and unique achievement. Inevitably one speculates what difference might be made if several great Wagnerian voices of the recent past, starting with Nilsson, had been available. But Levine had put together as fine a cast as you would have encountered at any of the world's great opera theaters in that period.

Forty years ago many record collectors would have given anything for a first-class professional recording of *Siegfried* or *Götterdämmerung*. However, there was a myth in the industry, shortly to be exploded by the success of Solti's Vienna set on London, that a complete *Ring* cycle on records was not feasible, since there was no possible market for a recording of *Das Rheingold*. The idea of being offered the entire cycle in a unified production that could be *seen* as well as heard would have fulfilled our wildest dreams.

Elsewhere in the Wagner repertory, Levine's laserdiscs have preserved Tatiana Troyanos's Venus in *Tannhäuser*, Leonie Rysanek's Ortrud in *Lohengrin*, and Waltraud Meier's Kundry in *Parsifal*, three performances that set standards for these roles. And the ladies are surrounded by strong casting. Levine is the only conductor to record *Parsifal* three times with different casts and in two different media. Each set contains things of the highest level, but surely anyone offered the opportunity to experience both the audible and visual dimension of Meier and Siegfried Jerusalem together in the second act of *Parsifal* will take it. This gives the laserdisc edition priority over the two CD versions, fine as they are.

Levine has not directed his attention exclusively to popular operas. There is a laserdisc of Corigliano's *The Ghosts of Versailles* (a most ingenious piece), Zandonai's highly theatrical *Francesca da Rimini*, and a work of sublime genius, Berlioz's *Les Troyens*, in the remarkable 1983 staging with Troyanos, Norman, and Domingo. It is glorious to have an opera that is so important, and yet so little known, available in this form.

Levine's video recordings bring us a remarkably fine *Carmen* with Agnes Baltsa and José Carreras and a poignant *L'Elisir d'Amore* with Battle and Luciano Pavarotti. Three Puccini performances easily surpass in effect anything on CD: There is a warm, romantic *Manon Lescaut* with Renata Scotto and Domingo, a wonderfully moving *La Bohème* with Teresa Stratas and Carreras, and a sumptuous *Turandot* with Eva Marton and Domingo.

There is Mozart, but not what you might expect. Although these were televised performances, Levine would prefer not to make a laserdisc of *Don Giovanni* or *Le Nozze di Figaro* until, like the 1996 *Così fan tutte,* there is a production he finds to be right. *Così fan tutte* was telecast and a laserdisc can be expected. We have the excellent Ponnelle film of *La Clemenza di Tito,* a remarkable *Idomeneo* with Hildegard Behrens and Pavarotti (among others), and *Die Zauberflöte,* achieved with a prime Metropolitan cast. It is one thing to hear that overture, another to experience something impossible in the theater, the radiant look on Levine's face as he gives the opening downbeat. (There is also extant an Austrian television tape of the Levine/Ponnelle Salzburg production of this work which should be released.)

Not surprisingly, the laserdiscs include a lot of Verdi, nine complete operas and selections from two more. The extent of the riches can be seen in the fact that we now have two editions of *Simon Boccanegra,* from 1984 and 1995, respectively. Both performances are splendid achievements, with the newer one benefiting from engineering advances and the presence of Kiri Te Kanawa and Domingo. A real prize is the rarely heard *Stiffelio,* with Domingo boldly expanding his repertory and gaining glory from a remarkable performance.

A major historic document is the *Il Trovatore* of 1988 with Pavarotti in his vintage years. A similar gift to history is *La Forza del Destino* with Leontyne Price and the music cut in the past restored. *Don Carlo,* an opera that is often heard without its first act, was telecast in 1983 with a powerhouse cast—another gift for the ages.

I have a special regard for *Falstaff,* and Paul Plishka has made it one of his finest roles. It is also the most Mozartian of the Verdi operas, one reason, I suspect, Levine does it with such obvious affection.

Un Ballo in Maschera is another Pavarotti specialty, and we have it from 1991. Those who admire *Ernani* can be delighted it exists in a Pavarotti performance from 1983. We have a brief look at Pavarotti as the Duke in *Rigoletto* in the 1991 gala performance of Act 3. The same gala gives us the third act of *Otello* with Domingo, but we shall probably have him in the entire opera in a video of the 1979 or 1995 production. Characteristic Met casting makes the recording of *Aida* representative of the current standards at Lincoln Center.

The Met gala videos are the best kinds of souvenirs of wonderful nights in the theater. It is a pity that the final gala in the old house in 1966 and the farewell to Rudolf Bing in 1972 could not also be available in this form. The Bing gala was televised in part, but only a single recording was released, no video. The Levine 25th Anniversary Gala of April 1996 has been released in part on both CD and laserdisc.

We would have no Levine laserdiscs if they had to be the product of recording sessions. Work of that type remains prohibitively expensive in the United States. They are the most important spin-offs of the television series *The Metropolitan Opera Presents*. One unusually fine performance becomes the basis for the master tape, with material from other performances of that season inserted when some necessary and possible change can be made. Levine's wish is to do as little editing as possible, but even wonderful realizations of a score may contain something that calls for correction. In any case, the discs bring us Levine working in the pit of the theater, not the recording studio, where multiple takes are the order of the day.

Whenever possible in recent years, Levine has shown that he would like to make CDs the same way, in public performances, but the majority of his sound recordings are studio work. Their level is demonstrated by the fact that he regularly brings us performances that seem certain to be regarded among the great recordings of the century. It is a logical fallacy that any collection of more or less similar things (recordings of the Dvořák *New World* Symphony, for example) can always be arranged in a hierarchy in which one is clearly the best. The significant differences needed for such an ordering process may not exist.

Frequently there are several recorded performances which, when all the relevant factors are given appropriate weight, appear to be different but equally meritorious. If we separate recent from historic work (performances made twenty years or more in the past), Levine's *New World* has no real competition, and comparison of his two editions, made thirteen years apart, shows the attentive ear the manner in which he has grown as an artist. The 1994 sound reflects contemporary technology. A work that is often given a slick, superficial performance is here fully explored to its musical depths.

I offer the following list of Levine recordings of the present decade which will undoubtedly be regarded by future listeners as defining critical standards, recordings that will stand among the finest performances of these works ever recorded. I do not suggest that the list is exhaustive. More than ten recent Levine releases are on this level, but the merits of this group have received particularly wide recognition.

1) Berg: Violin Concerto (Anne-Sophie Mutter), Chicago Symphony, 1992
2) Brahms: The Four Symphonies, Alto Rhapsody, Tragic Overture, Vienna Philharmonic, 1992–95
3) Carter: Variations for Orchestra, Chicago Symphony, 1990
4) Dvořák: Symphony No. 8, Dresden Staatskapelle, 1990; Symphony No. 9 (*From the New World*), Dresden Staatskapelle, 1994
5) Mozart: *Le Nozze di Figaro,* Te Kanawa, Upshaw, von Otter, Troyanos, Furlanetto, Hampson, Plishka, Laciura, Met Orchestra and Chorus, 1990
6) Prokofiev: Symphony No. 5, Chicago Symphony, 1992
7) Schoenberg: *Verklärte Nacht* [1943 version], Berlin Philharmonic, 1991
8) Sibelius: Symphony No. 4, Berlin Philharmonic, 1994
9) Strauss: *Metamorphosen,* Berlin Philharmonic, 1991
10) Stravinsky: *Le Sacre du Printemps* [1947 version], Met Orchestra, 1992

Perfect is not a word that music critics use very often, first because genuine perfection is, understandably, the rarest quality to be defined or discovered in musical performance, but also because it suggests the end of growth—something no serious musician will consider desirable. A judgment of perfection has a large subjective component. It suggests an ideal realization of one's conception of a work, and different listeners will, invariably, have different ideals. Levine's *Figaro* easily surpasses the wonderful old set from the Glyndebourne Festival, which taught this music to a generation in the mid-century. The casting is spectacular, with the opportunity to hear even a lesser role like Marcellina sung by an artist of the stature of Troyanos. Furlanetto is a Figaro worthy of Pinza, and Upshaw is his ideal bride. The noble couple, Hampson and Te Kanawa at her most ravishing, offer the precise balance and contrast the work requires.

Most important of all is Levine's complete control of the orchestra, his unfailing demand for the purest classicism, and the imagination and skill with which he demonstrates that within that style one can achieve all the humor, drama, and emotional depth of romanticism. This opera, especially in a performance such as this, becomes one of the greatest artistic expressions of the humanistic spirit that, I sense, is the foundation for everything Levine does.

As Hermann Broch wrote: "The eighteenth century was the last great epoch in Europe's culture . . . outstanding is the century's significance in literature and in international spirit, embracing all Europe, reaching a potency and breadth which gives nourishment still to us, poorer descendants, as we remember their glory. A noble, generous humanism, an unconditional awe of human nature and an ideological belief in the future greatness of human culture speaks out of every document from the period, even the satirical and farcical.

"The human being has been put in the seat of the Gods, with the dignity of humanity and the crowning of the world the foundation of every creed. This new religion, born in English and French revolutions, with Kant its most profound prophet and Weimar its final flowering, this ideal humanism, was the basis of an inexplicably rich culture."

Levine's ability to validate this statement sets his performance apart, and in the absence of a Levine video edition, this is the *Figaro* recording to which one should turn. (Those who feel they must have a videodisc can view an admirable production directed by Ponnelle and conducted by Boehm.)

The ten CD's I've listed here are notable for their stylistic range and the manner in which each of these styles is precisely and consistently defined in performance. Levine's understanding of Brahms takes nothing from his comprehension of Carter. He gives a remarkable sense of structure and form to both Stravinsky's driving rhythms and Schoenberg's most flamboyant romanticism. And he can enter a very different musical world to reveal the architecture of the Sibelius Fourth Symphony. One of the most common problems of listeners, especially in music of this century, is their inability to perceive form, and one of Levine's greatest strengths is his ability to reveal form clearly in performance.

How does Levine regard his recordings once they are available to the public?

RCM: I know your admiration for Stokowski. When we were in Philadelphia in March 1996, I looked for his old townhouse. The garage had been torn down, but the house was still there. It's now an art gallery. You wander through the rooms, remembering that Stokowski once observed, "The most interesting things about my life cannot be told," and wish the walls could talk. What they might tell! In France there would be a bronze marker on the building, but unfortunately in the United States we don't do things like that very often.

One of the remarkable things about Stokowski was that he was constantly playing records, but almost never his own. He was endlessly fascinated with what other people were doing. I gather you are rather like that. To what extent do you listen to records, especially your finished recordings?

JL: After the sessions I give a *lot* of time to the mixing and post-production stuff, and after that I leave them alone. I will go back to one of my old records on one of two impulses. First, I will just happen to think of the piece or the performance, and there will be something I can't remember. That can stimulate me to check it. The second case is if I am about to prepare a piece again. Sometimes just before rehearsals I will turn to what documentation I have of my last performance just to help me clarify what I recall as being deficient. That way I can concentrate on whatever the problem was and try to get it right. But these things occupy relatively little of my time. One of the great things about CDs is that you can chapter them. If I wish to be reminded how Toscanini handled a certain page in the score, it's not that hard to find.

RCM: Are there any halls in which you particularly like to work?

JL: One problem I have always had making records is the character of the recorded sound. I do not like the resonance of the performing space to be so great that clarity and detail in the performance are lost. It is going back to Szell and the questions about what the third bassoon is doing. I think you should be able to hear that for yourself. I astonish many people when I tell them I like the records Toscanini made in Studio 8-H. They were very dry, but, boy, could you hear! The engineers won't let me make records like that because they insist the public wants resonance; clear, dry sound will not sell. But something in-between is possible—and more desirable.

The Musikverein in Vienna is probably the best concert hall in the world, and I have made countless records there. The place is a miracle! Manhattan Center, my recording venue in New York, is another fine place to work. You can get good results. I was happy most of the time with the sound of my Chicago discs. Once you learned how to place microphones in those halls, the sound was excellent. But big, booming overly resonant halls and the kinds of records that come out of them are not for me.

RCM: You like to play records by other people.

JL: Sure. I play records whenever I have time. I particularly like to become familiar with conductors I couldn't possibly have encountered in the flesh, like Karl Muck. Muck is fascinating.

RCM: Carlo Maria Giulini gave an impassioned performance of the Brahms Fourth with the Chicago Symphony in 1969 and recorded it. A few years later he was due to play the work again in Chicago and some people begged him to play the record and repeat the earlier performance.

JL: And he was horrified.

RCM: Of course. "What?" he asked me. "I am to stop growing as a musician and go back to what I was in 1969?" It recalls Ernest Hemingway's remark that when a writer starts rereading his old work it shows he is really burned out.

JL: The two cases are the same.

RCM: But some things are so good I think that even after a number of years you can be happy with them. If someone came to me and said, "I'm confiscating all your Levine CDs except one album," I'd keep the complete Mozart symphonies.

JL: I can go with that. I'm happy about that set.

RCM: Stokowski once said to me, "I don't think much about the past. I think about the future. You can still do something about that." I would gather that, especially in recording, you agree with him.

JL: I sure do.

Stokowski was so accustomed to working within the limitations of the 78 rpm disc that even when tape became the standard recording medium, he would sometimes divide a score into short sections and record it that way, staying with a segment of the work until he had it on tape to his satisfaction, and then going on to the next.

Toscanini, on the other hand, hated to stop after a 78 rpm side had been made and delighted in being able to go on for a complete movement if he wished. And Furtwängler, for all their differences, felt the same way.

Levine's recording technique is essentially Szell's. He wants to play the piece through, listen to it carefully, and then either do it again, correcting whatever was unsatisfactory in the first take, or make a few inserts to cover passing errors. Levine now feels that if he has a work prepared to his satisfaction, you can do it in concert and capture the energy of a performance before an audience without concern for correcting mistakes that may never be made. Real performances have a special quality he enjoys.

I have never attended a Levine recording session in Europe, but his working methods appear to be consistently applied wherever he is—unlike several of his celebrated predecessors. Fritz Reiner would get irritated and say nasty things to the musicians. ("That was a capital offense!") Georg Solti would get tense and upset and start tearing the hair he didn't have, if, after several tries, he failed to hear what he wanted from the tape. But Levine's CSO sessions were so bloody serious, studies in efficiency and concentration, that there was little to say except that the performance heard in public a day or two before had been reproduced for the microphone with even more refinement. In time I stopped going to his recording sessions in Chicago because they gave me so little to write about that the ordinary reader would find interesting.

In an excellent article in the *New York Times*, Anthony Tommasini addressed the complaint that Levine's conducting is "brilliant but faceless." How does a conductor acquire a face, a quality that instantly identifies his work? For Toscanini it was his personal intensity. No one else had that kind of drive, drive that (to his despair) might be excessive. No one could surpass Koussevitzky for the sheer beauty of orchestral sound. No one else could rival the sensual, exotic quality Stokowski might evoke, although he could be quite at a loss in music such as a Mozart symphony, where such an approach was out of place.

Eugene Ormandy recalled his first interview with the great Leopold after they became colleagues in Philadelphia. Stokowski insisted, "You have had such fine classical conservatory training. *You* play the Mozart and Haydn."

Put a record on the machine, and one may admire the force of the performance without noting any personal practices that cause one immediately to shout, "Levine!" For those dedicated to the romantics, or the great individuals, this is a weakness. Levine, they suggest, is a great technician but slightly unimaginative. But one is reminded of Toscanini performances of seventy years ago with the New York Philharmonic when he was not overly intense and what one heard was playing of unusual clarity and force in which the music, shaped by an incredible musical imagination, yielded its most profound secrets.

Tommasini concludes, "The notion that Mr. Levine's conducting lacks a personal stamp is absurd. Clearly anyone who can satisfy the cerebral [Milton] Babbitt, conduct revelatory performances of Sibelius, and bring down the house with the overture to *La Forza del Destino* is doing something right."

That "something" is calling upon the listener to concentrate on the music rather than the performer and giving the music the opportunity to presents its own case forcefully. Your attention is drawn into the music. It enfolds you and speaks to you in its distinctive language. And you understand.

The Levine discography contains some 450 titles. You can listen to every one of them with pleasure, for the quality level of all is very high. Toscanini made some records flawed by poor engineering or stylistically misguided performances. You play them and find little to support his reputation. Levine's have always had first-class engineering. The performances invariably have merit, although, as in all human endeavors, some are more successful than others.

The finest musicians do not replace but supplement one another; they challenge us to increase our own range of artistic awareness, to see the full range and musical content of a work. Since Levine has recorded a large number of scores already represented in the catalog by a substantial number of other editions, many of them from distinguished musicians, critics have sometimes preferred alternative versions of the music in question to his. This is only to be expected. One must always make allowances for differences in taste.

Let us consider the Levine operatic recordings on compact disc that have no laserdisc counterpart. From the Mozart operas we have a single work, *Le Nozze di Figaro,* a supreme achievement, just discussed. A favorite Levine opera that has produced one of the finest Levine operatic recordings is Stravinsky's *Oedipus Rex,* which he presented in concert form with the Chicago Symphony at the 1991 Ravinia Festival and recorded downtown in Orchestra Hall. With excellent soloists and Margaret Hillis's exceptional Chicago Symphony Chorus, the work had a tremendous effect in live performance. My regret is that the English narration, by F. Murray Abraham, which had a powerful impact, was replaced for international release by the French text and a French narrator, who is unlikely to have similar power of communication with American listeners.

Another important, short twentieth-century opera which Levine brings us in an illuminating 1989 recording is Schoenberg's *Erwartung,* a monodrama here entrusted to the remarkable skills of Jessye Norman. The piece is a masterpiece of German expressionism, saturated with Freudian psychology. My possibly perverse interpretation of the work is that it is a study in denial. Before the opera begins, the protagonist has found her lover in a tryst with another woman and has killed him. As the work opens she is wandering aimlessly, refusing to accept the reality of her act, until she returns to the scene of the crime. She finds the body not by accident, but because she knows where it is. Conductor and singer have both captured the spirit of the score with chilling skill.

Levine's career as a conductor of opera on records begins in 1973, and from 1973 to 1980 we see what might be called the Levine Italian opera company of London at work on a variety of works in a series of halls. The first year brings Verdi's *I Vespri Siciliani* and *Giovanna d'Arco*. The *Vespri* moved from this recording studio to the stage of the Met.

Giovanna is the only Verdi opera Levine has recorded but never led in a theater. Domingo and Milnes, who were to become stalwarts of the company, are in both casts. Martina Arroyo is the leading soprano in the *I Vespri* recording, having replaced Montserrat Caballé on two days' notice. Caballé, who sang *I Vespri* at the Met, is Giovanna d'Arco in that recording.

The next year Levine was back to do *Norma* with Beverly Sills in a recording of historic interest that Sills's admirers would undoubtedly like to see reissued.

One of the most interesting of the early Levine operatic recordings is *The Barber of Seville* made in London in 1975 with Sills, Nicolai Gedda, and Milnes. With his recording, Levine was saying farewell to this opera (he has not touched it since) by recording every note that legitimately belongs to the score. He brought us a performance notable for its style, taste, and zest.

On the schedule for 1976 was *Andrea Chénier* with Renata Scotto, Domingo, and Milnes and *La Forza del Destino* with Domingo and Milnes joined by Leontyne Price. The following year Scotto returned to London for *Adriana Lecouvreur,* again with Domingo and Milnes. (This is another opera which exists in a particulary great Levine recording but which he has never conducted in public.)

The 1978 productions were *Otello* with Scotto, Domingo, and Milnes and *Cavalleria Rusticana* with Scotto and Domingo. Scotto sang the title role in the 1979 recording of *Norma* with Tatiana Troyanos, Giuseppe Giacomini, and Paul Plishka. Finally in 1979 there is *La Bohème* with Scotto, Alfredo Kraus, and Milnes and, in 1980, *Tosca* with Scotto, Domingo, and Renato Bruson—the only documentation we have of the work with which Levine made his Met debut. The same year Levine recorded *The Magic Flute* in Vienna, following the Salzburg performances, and henceforth his operatic recordings were made in central Europe, Chicago, or New York. In 1989, when he did a classic Italian work, *L'Elisir d'Amore,* with Kathleen Battle and Luciano Pavarotti, the sessions were not in London but in Manhattan.

Levine quickly realized the potential of the new technology of operatic video recording, which began in 1977, and shifted his primary interest from CDs to laserdiscs. Thus his most important projects for compact discs, the Wagnerian repertory, all eventually were duplicated in the visual medium.

Levine had been appearing at the Salzburg Festival since 1976, but his summer activities changed dramatically in 1982, when he added the Bayreuth Festival to his schedule. In 1986 Levine went to Vienna to make a beguiling version of *Ariadne auf Naxos* with Anna Tomowa-Sintow, Baltsa, and Battle. The next year took him to Dresden for a recording of *Eugene Onegin,* one of his favorite operas, with an international cast. Fearing, I surmise, that the Met would not get a new production of *Così fan tutte* for some time, he recorded it on CD in Vienna in 1988 with Te Kanawa, Murray, and Hampson. Two years later this led to the miraculous *Nozze di Figaro* recording at the Met.

Evidently persuaded that there was an audience for Verdi on CD, in 1991 Levine began a series of Verdi recordings in New York. *Aida, La Traviata, Luisa Miller,* and *Il Trovatore* were made in the three years, followed by *Don Carlo,* and an as yet unfinished *Rigoletto.* In 1996 he recorded *I Lombardi.* All represent current Met casting and standards.

In the midst of the series Levine recorded *Manon Lescaut* with Freni and Pavarotti in 1992, and *Idomeneo* and *Der fliegende Holländer* in 1994.

Levine, like Solti, began his recording career as a pianist, in this case as accompanist in a 1970 recital by Jennie Tourel that retains a high degree of interest and charm. His first studio recordings of opera in 1973, discussed earlier, are fine, craftsmanlike work, and his first orchestral recordings, from the following year, reveal him to be completely at home working for the microphone. I was present at Medinah Temple in Chicago in July 1974 when he recorded the Mahler Fourth Symphony after playing it with great success at Ravinia. It is significant that the first symphony he recorded was a Mahler work. So, indeed, was his second symphony recording, the Mahler No. 1, made in London the following month.

The session was complicated by the fact that this was to be a four-channel edition, and there was considerable discussion with the producer, Thomas Z. Shepard, over the distribution of the instrumental voices in four channels in a manner that was sonically effective and still faithful to Mahler. The members of the orchestra, some of whom were as intrigued as Levine with the new technology, were welcomed into the discussion, often with highly constructive results.

At the close of the second session, Judith Blegen appeared, fresh and smiling, and sang the *Knaben Wunderhorn* song three times. Any one of the takes would have been perfectly acceptable without editing. Shepard made her do it over because it was difficult to believe she would have it perfect on the first try. Flying from New York to sing less than ten minutes of music seemed ridiculous. Since he had her there, Shepard wanted some backup tape. (She worked about forty minutes.) On release the disc was praised as an unusually effective four-channel release. We now hear it in a two-channel mix with somewhat less impact.

Considering Levine's work for CD, it is clear that certain scores closely associated with him for many years still await their first studio recording. The Ravinia archives contain tapes of WFMT broadcasts from the festival, and the extensive repertory includes the Beethoven Ninth Symphony, the Second and Eighth Mahler Symphonies, Schoenberg's *Gurrelieder,* and Stravinsky's Symphony of Psalms—another Levine specialty. In the past Levine has remarked offhandedly that eventually he hopes to do them all.

Two of Levine's greatest achievements are the editions of the Mozart symphonies and violin concertos made in Vienna in the finest concert room in the world, the Grosser Musikvereinssaal. It is small, only 1,680 seats, and almost square in profile, sixty feet high and sixty-five feet wide, with a volume of 530,000 cubic feet (320,000 cubic feet smaller than Carnegie Hall in New York). Orchestra and audience are intimately joined in resonant space. Itself inspired by the first Gewandhaus in Leipzig, it was the inspiration for the pre–World War II Philharmonie in Berlin and Symphony Hall in Boston—both much larger concert rooms. For Levine this has been a near-perfect recording environment.

There are many recordings of Mozart symphonies. The Levine edition is set apart by three factors. First, in the Levine performances you actually hear the entire work the way the composer intended. Its scale has not been altered by the gratuitous elimination of repeats. Second, these are performances in the pure classic manner by a musician who lives and breathes the classical style. Levine is a finer Mozart conductor than Toscanini, who was usually too intense, or Bruno Walter, who could be too romantic. Both men brought us beautiful things, but it is in the Levine performances that I find the stamp of authenticity. Third, the orchestra is the Vienna Philharmonic, which has this music in its blood and needs only to draw on its own inner resources with a perceptive leader to achieve miraculous things.

The qualities that make these Mozart discs outstanding return in Levine's other recordings of the composer's work—the three serenades, the oboe concerto, two masses, and the chamber music. He is a Mozartean of the purest type. I do not think he learned this from Szell. Indeed, I question if it can be learned from anyone. If you have it, you have it in your blood. But Szell showed him how to polish this skill to even greater brilliance.

The unfortunate thing about Mozart and Haydn symphonies in the era of the long-playing record is that if you omitted most of the repeats they would fit nicely on one side of a disc, leaving the other surface for another work. This attracted the marketing people who, in turn, put the pressure on the record producers, who, in turn, put pressure on the conductors. Thus in the historic Walter/New York Philharmonic recording of the Mozart G Minor (K. 550) the repeat of the exposition of the first movement is missing, something Walter would never have done in concert. Some conductors rebelled. When Erich Leinsdorf recorded the *Jupiter* Symphony in Boston, he insisted on playing all the repeats and thus carried the work over to the second side of the record. But cases of this type were few. Levine, working in a CD format with seventy minutes of playing time, can make all the indicated repeats and the music can be combined in sensible groups.

Anyone who doubts the importance of this need only compare the impact of one of the major late works—the *Prague* Symphony is a splendid example—first playing a version with few or no repeats and then playing the Levine. Levine shows you the true stature of the piece.

We think of Mozart as a pianist, but we may forget that his father, a celebrated violin teacher, insisted that Wolfgang could be the first violinist in Europe if he would practice. (He didn't. He had other things to do—playing billiards, chasing girls, and writing operas.) But the violin concertos reveal both a mastery of the instrument and the strongest affection for it. Levine and Itzhak Perlman are well matched in this music and play it with insight and love.

Looking at the Levine discography you note the relatively small number of concerto recordings. "Ideally," he says, "you record a concerto after a series of performances in which you and the soloist come to know each other and the work with a sense of true rapport. The Beethoven edition Alfred Brendel and I did in Chicago is a perfect illustration. All of my concerto recordings are related in some way to performances at Ravinia, Berlin, and Vienna. Going into a recording session with a soloist to do a concerto from scratch is much more difficult."

One of the perplexing things about the Levine discography for some is that with composers who are usually paired, Haydn and Mozart, Beethoven and Brahms, Bruckner and Mahler, Levine has selected one member of the duo and concentrated on him. He plays Haydn beautifully, but he has yet to record a Haydn symphony. He has given us, however, a powerful realization of two of the composer's later choral works. *The Creation* was inspired by Haydn's first encounter with the Handel oratorios. Levine shows us why it has always been a popular work. The

Missa in Tempore Belli/Paukenmesse, the first of the final six Haydn masses that are, in spirit, choral symphonies, has received a Levine recording that makes us eager for him to complete the series.

Beethoven is represented in the Levine discography by one symphony, the *Eroica,* recorded (in a wonderfully fresh and imaginative performance) in 1993. It is revealing that in a period in which most conductors are eager to offer a Beethoven edition, Levine has bided his time. The Levine/Brendel album of the piano concertos is another feast of mature musicianship, growing from the greatest mutual regard.

In the Bruckner/Mahler pairing we find Levine recordings of most of the major Mahler scores and not a note of Bruckner. He is attracted to Mahler by the drama, but insists he is unable to identify with Bruckner's large, slowly unfolding musical forms. It should be observed that Levine's edition of eight Mahler symphonies dates from 1974 to 1980. All this material is prime for re-recording.

George Szell rightly regarded himself as a Schumann specialist, and thus it is no surprise that the Schumann symphonies have had a significant role in Levine's repertory from the beginning of his career. The early Philadelphia edition is excellent; the later Berlin one benefits from a decade or more of advances in recording technique and a deepening knowledge of the music. Much the same can be said of the two editions of the Brahms symphonies. The first was rightly hailed in the 1970s as a superior piece of work, and the new one for me is beyond praise, the performances I have always dreamed of hearing. For many years the only recording of the Brahms First that truly swept me away was Toscanini's. The Levine, in the same spirit with infinitely better sound, now takes its place. His 1983 recording of the German Requiem, with Chicago forces, remains a major achievement despite the fact it was his first performance of the work.

Levine's success performing romantic music is easily explained. He plays romantic scores with the same integrity and discipline he brings to Mozart. The music is given expressive force by being played with a purity of form and line worthy of the eighteenth century. Levine's 1984 Chicago recording of Tchaikovsky's *Pathétique* Symphony is one of the finest realizations of that work we have. The way he builds the third movement is phenomenal. For some reason, the merits of this disc were never sufficiently recognized. Levine can take a sugarplum like the Saint-Saëns organ symphony and by the simple process of playing down the pages that invite excess make it sound much better than it really is.

In the Mendelssohn *Scotch* Symphony, the opening, so often heard in a perfunctory manner, is exquisitely shaped and colored to create a mood and make a deeply profound statement of the musical ideas. As the work progresses, there is one miraculous insight after another in pages in which often only the most superficial features of the music are heard. The *Italian* Symphony is filled with color and joy and, of course, Levine knows the first-movement repeat is indispensable.

One of the great events in Levine's early Ravinia years was his first performance of the *Great* Schubert C Major Symphony. Recorded in 1983 after its fifth Ravinia performance, it is a monument to his first decade at the festival. With Szell for a teacher it is to be expected that Levine would have the fullest sympathy for Dvořák and Smetana. His approach to their work—simple, straightforward, and dramatic—combines his gifts for creating refined orchestral color with his skill in drawing the highest degree of lyricism from a phrase.

A touchstone of Levine's taste is his skill with the music of Berlioz, who demands all the artistry called for in Dvořák with the appreciation of one of the most individual and imaginative minds in the history of music. Berlioz tempts the conductor with obvious effects, but Levine knows that Berlioz is after something far more sophisticated.

Few associate Levine with French music, although he plays it with finesse and skill. His limited recorded repertory of Debussy and Ravel suggests untapped possibilities. The young Stravinsky was deeply influenced by both French masters, and Levine is a superlative Stravinsky conductor. Far too many of his colleagues feel that once they have solved the technical problems they have a performance. Levine knows (as Szell did) that this is the point at which you begin to create a performance. An accurate statement of the notes is never enough. His disc of *Le Sacre du Printemps* with the Met Orchestra follows the 1947 text (many performances use an older edition to avoid paying royalties) and surpasses the composer's own recording in dramatic force. We have too little Stravinsky in the Levine discography; we ought to have much more. His Stravinsky disc from Ravinia calls for re-release.

Prokofiev is another composer Levine has not played with great frequency but has obvious understanding of his music. The success of what he has done suggests the justification for future work. Ironically, despite Shostakovich's debts to Mahler, Levine has played very little of the Russian, although the composer is represented in *Fantasia 2000*.

It is revealing that Levine has little identification with the big rhetorical tone poems of Richard Strauss but achieves a phenomenal success with a very late, and atypical, work, *Metamorphosen,* and the Oboe Concerto. He sees *Death and Transfiguration* as an outpouring of youthful talent, and he admires the classical variation form as developed in *Don Quixote.*

Rather than cultivate the neo-romantics, Levine has cultivated the twentieth-century Viennese School—Schoenberg, Berg, and Webern. In each case the list is relatively short, but the performances reveal the deepest understanding and sympathy. Bartók does not figure prominently in the Levine discography, but the two recorded performances we have reflect a full command of the material.

My greatest regret is that Levine has recorded very little American music, in part, I suspect, because European labels feel American music is difficult to sell in the international market. What he has done, however, is noteworthy. One of the most commercial things Levine did at Ravinia was make a Gershwin record—his own lively performance of *Rhapsody in Blue* in the original (jazz band) orchestration. It's ideal summer music.

In revenge, as the French would say, he then offered an uncompromising collection of Babbitt, Cage, Carter, and Schuller. Introduced to the festival audiences over a period of several days, the four scores distressed those suburban conservatives who hated twentieth-century music indiscriminately and hence could make no distinction between a major score like the Carter and a lesser work like the Cage. The orchestra could not have been more responsive.

It is clear, talking to Levine, that he would like to do further work of this type. His Ravinia performance of the Ives Second Symphony suggested a flair for that composer that might be cultivated. The symphony of Shulamit Ran, which won the Pulitzer Prize for Music in 1991, would appear to be a perfect Levine score, and there are many more.

There is a single Bach disc in the listings, a spin-off of the *Music from Ravinia* series. Levine admires baroque music and plays it exceptionally well. But where is he going to play it at this point in his career? The limitations of the discography sometimes reflect limited opportunities, not limited interest.

Levine's problem recording chamber music is that his colleagues, although invariably skilled, dedicated musicians, are rarely as good as he is. His best efforts come largely from the Ravinia years, especially a splendid series of cello and piano duos with Lynn Harrell. Matched in Mozart with Chicago Symphony principals in 1977, or with the LaSalle Quartet in 1980, he is in his element.

The song recitals that were an important part of the Ravinia summers became equally significant at Salzburg. His collaborations with Kathleen

Battle and, later, Jessye Norman are particularly glorious achievements, and so are his recent Debussy disc with Dawn Upshaw and the *Italian Songbook* of Cecilia Bartoli. Levine has recorded the two greatest Schubert song cycles, *Die Winterreise* with Christa Ludwig in 1987 and *Die schöne Müllerin* with Uwe Heillmann in 1992. Both are highly rewarding.

Levine's only solo piano disc, Scott Joplin rags, if taken in connection with Jelly Roll Morton's claim that a good piano player could always get a job in New Orleans, suggests that in an earlier life this white kid from Cincinnati could have been a whorehouse pianist of the first rank.

Levine's recorded repertory, at this stage of his career, is clearly openended—a work in progress. It is incomplete, but what he has done to date is of the greatest significance. It serves music and the musical public in a way that few artists can rival. Most importantly, it provides a secure foundation for years of future activity filled with remarkable promise. After all, most of the greatest conductors did most of their best work after the age of sixty.

Epilogue

RCM: Your namesake, my nine-year-old son, James, along with his public school classmates in a Wisconsin village of 1,800, has been taught to read music. He sings and can play a rather primitive plastic instrument from written notes. Music is a form of expression and communication he is learning along with verbal skills. When he hears his mother playing one of the Bach *French* Suites, he recognizes it as statements in a language he knows.

JL: That's the way to begin.

RCM: This is the kind of musical education I received in Chicago public schools sixty years ago. But when the Soviets put *Sputnik* in orbit in 1957, music and art were considered inessential and the kind of teaching I had received ended. Yet Chicago has a world-renowned art museum, symphony orchestra, and opera company. How are these to thrive if the public schools do not give young people the basic knowledge required to make good use of the opportunities they provide?

JL: The implication is that these things are inessential as well. And, of course, they couldn't be more important.

RCM: We live in Wisconsin surrounded by cows and corn. The instrument in our living room is the only large grand piano in town. If you want to visit an art gallery or hear serious music you must make a twenty-five-mile journey to Madison. Not many people in town make a trip for that purpose very often. But they want music and art in the school because they see these things as valuable for their own sake.

JL: This is a respect for traditional values which you might expect in a midwestern farming community. I heartily approve to put it mildly.

RCM: We would agree, I think, that a civilization is upheld, a society is sustained, when the public recognizes a body of shared values and honors them in its way of life. But today we must ask whether our society in its daily life acknowledges and reinforces the values that will sustain the cultural achievements of the past. Some thinkers, we know, are pessimistic about this.

JL: What we see is a conflict of value systems, different groups that respect different things. That kind of pluralism can be healthy, stimulating, provided the rights of individuals are respected. What must be rejected is the idea that to be democratic we must be the same in matters of taste or anything else. I don't go to heavy metal concerts and my neighbor may not go to the opera, but neither of us should be denied the right to go where we wish.

RCM: We were talking earlier about *The Magic Flute.* Tamino strives for excellence. He wants personal growth, spiritual enlightenment. Papageno is quite content with a pretty girl and a glass of wine.

JL: And Mozart, in the breadth of his humanity, easily understood both. Mozart, certainly, enjoyed girls and wine. There is abundant evidence for that. He, like Papageno, had his *Naturmensch* dimension as well as his Tamino side.

RCM: Papageno, as seen by José Ortega y Gasset, is an example of the mass man. The mass man, or mass woman, is not Marx's proletarian. This is the lowest-common-denominator individual the ad boys are looking for, the best potential customer for the soap you're selling. This is the person who is primarily involved in getting along, finding gratification for the fundamental human needs. He doesn't understand what Tamino has on his mind, so he is unlikely to grasp the all-encompassing humanism Mozart represents and you reflect every time you lift your baton.

JL: My performances, inevitably, reflect what I feel most deeply to be important. If I compromise, I am betraying myself. I hope the majority of the audience will get something valuable from listening to this performance and their response suggests I am right. But you know how I feel about talking down to people. It's demeaning for both parties.

RCM: Socrates' basic idea was that the unexamined life was not worth living. It is the capacity to examine life, to look within ourselves, that distinguishes us from charming and intelligent creatures like orangutans. But the process of examining life can take many forms. We see the opera house as a place where this can happen.

JL: Certainly. The remarkable thing about the greatest operas is that you can approach them on a number of different levels. Even a sublime comedy of reconciliation like *Le Nozze di Figaro* can, I suppose, be enjoyed just for the good tunes and the funny things. If you are first attracted to the opera by those moments, fine. Keep coming back. The more opera you hear, the better prepared you will be to understand it more fully. But the final ten minutes of *Figaro* can be a transcendent experience, something that lifts us out of our egos and demands of us that we take the deepest kind of look at ourselves.

In this case, the central thing is the count's willingness to see his folly and the countess's willingness to forgive him. That is reconciliation, one of the great religious ideas. She forgives him even if she doesn't think he'll really change. It's a form of unconditional love.

RCM: All this talk in the air about elitism frequently seems to be an attack on those who are looking for transcendent experiences. To know psychic events of this type, your concerns have to go beyond those basic human needs. There are many good things but few transcendent experiences on TV.

JL: In *Parsifal,* when in the final scene he steps forward and touches the wound with the spear, everything that has been played and sung up to that point comes sharply into focus and you feel the triumph of light over darkness. No matter how many times you have heard it, or conducted it, it's miraculous, extraordinary.

RCM: The reason we must have opera houses and the other elements of the cultural life is that they are temples of humanism, and are dedicated to the values on which civilization rests.

JL: I am always dismayed at the level on which many people seem content to live their lives. They have all these options, but they remain indifferent to them. One thing the schools are supposed to do is make children aware of the range of things open to them, the potential richness of their lives. Teaching them music is certainly one of the ways.

RCM: If you are lucky, at some point while it still can make a difference, you run into a Socratic character, a teacher, a friend, a religious person, and start to look inside yourself at what you value the most. I tried to play that role, with what success I cannot say.

JL: But I'm sure you are an excellent teacher! You never get enough of the same things I never get enough of, finding something of real substance about how one works in music and what goals mean in the world we live in. The whole quality of life depends on how deeply *into* life you are prepared to go. That involvement with the fullness, the infinite incredible variety of life is why opera is not elitist entertainment. It is an invitation to look deeply into ourselves. It does to us all the things— emotional, spiritual, and intellectual—that are the function of great art.

When the Met gave its first performance of *Parsifal* in December 1903, it was a matter of common knowledge in the city, front-page news. There were twelve sold-out performances. Nothing we ever do today attracts comparable attention. *Scientific American* had an article showing how the stage had been prepared for special effects like the transformation scenes. Today no such article would be possible because probably not one percent of those who read even that magazine know what *Parsifal* is.

RCM: Since for thirty years Bayreuth tried to keep *Parsifal* to itself, there was tremendous interest in the piece. One of the first performances outside Bayreuth was in Barcelona. The young Fritz Reiner conducted. The clock struck twelve, the copyright expired, and down came the stick.

JL: Don't you love things like that! And it wasn't just Reiner; it was happening in theaters all over Europe. It is a disaster that so many things that once were a part of common knowledge now are known only to those with specialized interests. You learned Greek mythology as a child, I'm sure. When you first heard *Ariadne auf Naxos,* you knew who Bacchus was.

RCM: An old pal of mine.

JL: Kids today are unlikely to know these things. It adds up to a very important loss.

RCM: In the early part of the century general culture was defined by what is taught in the schools. Today general culture is defined by the media, primarily television. TV has 100 percent social penetration, and minds are shaped by what is seen on the tube.

You have to forgive the prejudices of someone who has given years to educational broadcasting. The broadcast media, radio and later TV, offered the greatest possibilities for mass education the world had ever known. One of the decisive events in American cultural history came in the 1920s, when it was decided that broadcasting was to be developed by private industry rather than become a state monopoly as it was in Canada and many European countries. That meant the content of American broadcasting was, in the long run, to be determined by advertising agencies. The best program was the one that moved the most product. Only the level was not to be elevated but actually lowered if that was required for high ratings.

When that became the criterion, eventually the NBC Symphony concerts and the broadcast concerts of the New York Philharmonic that we both grew up with vanished from commercial broadcasting. They cost too much and drew too small a public. In retrospect, you must admire David Sarnoff of NBC and William S. Paley of CBS, with that deep-rooted respect for culture and learning, spending all they did to keep these programs on the air season after season.

JL: Hardly anyone today would dream of commercial programming of that type, or, if they did, they would put it out of their minds before they went to the office! But through all those years Texaco was right there sponsoring the Saturday Met broadcasts as it does today. How many operas did you hear for the first time on that series?

RCM: Nearly the entire basic repertory.

JL: It was very much the same for me. I can't begin to think of all the works of music I heard for the first time on the radio. What a difference it made!

RCM: My broadcasting career began on the BBC, which was for many years a secure paternalistic monopoly that offered a light program, but on the home service brought you lots of classical music because, damnation, it was good for you. And since it was there, people listened and many decided they liked it. The British audience for classical music cuts right across social and economic divisions. Sociologists have discovered that in the United States, where if the working class wanted to listen to pop music all day it was always readily available, the primary factor in determining musical interest is the educational level. Classical music for many years was the music of the college graduate. In some places I see it offered as fancy consumer goods for the affluent.

JL: That's wrong. The finest music ought to be heard by everybody because it has something to say to everybody. It is not about gender or ethnic background or social status; but about the real lowest common denominator, our shared humanity. Even including the subtleties that can only really be understood by a small group. That is why I was delighted to take part with the Chicago Symphony in *Fantasia 2000*. I remember as if it were yesterday the effect of the original *Fantasia* film I saw as a kid.

One last paradox: I find electronically reproduced music—TV, radio, recordings—bears really very little resemblance to live music heard in an opera house or concert hall. So why do I do it? Precisely because of the tremendous number of people whose only way of hearing music is through these various media. My music is for anyone who wishes to listen. I value the public's attention. There is something I have to say that I want it to understand, and the heart of that message is that the bonds that hold us together are, in the long run, vastly more important than the things that may seem to set us apart. The respect and appreciation—delight really—in difference and individuality is the predominant theme that must unite all humanists.

The Levine Discography
1970–1998

Levine recordings are issued worldwide and in the course of their life in the catalog may have a variety of identifying numbers. For the purpose of simplification, the number given here is that of the current American catalog or, if the record is out of print (OP), the number under which it was most recently available in the United States. If a recording is OP in the United States but available in another country, the number of that edition is indicated. Only LP and CD discs are listed, but Levine recordings have been issued in various cassette formats.

The symbol # indicates the work is duplicated in a video edition (laserdisc and/or tape), although possibly with a different cast and place and date of recording.

The symbol ★ indicates a laserdisc that has no CD counterpart. For details, please see the separate listing of recordings in this form.

Some recordings were scheduled but never done, such as a 1980 Tchaikovsky Symphony No. 4 with the Chicago Symphony. The CSO mistakenly lists it in its discography.

1970

Jennie Tourel (farewell recital)
Beethoven: "An die Hoffnung," "Ich liebe Dich"; Berlioz: "Absence"; Dargomijsky: "Romance"; Debussy: "Trois Chansons de Bilitis"; Glinka: "Doubt," "Vain Temptation"; Hahn: "Si mes vers"; Liszt: "Comment disaient-ils," "Mignon's Lied," "Oh quand je dors," "Über allen Gipfeln is Ruh," "Vergiftet sind meine Lieder"; Massenet: "Elegy"; Monsigny: "La Sagesse est un trésor"; Offenbach: *La Barbe bleue*/"Laughing Song"; Stradella: "Per Pietà"; Tchaikovsky: "None but the Lonely Heart"
James Levine, piano; Gary Karr, bass.
Alice Tully Hall, New York
Vox Box CDX5126
Live recording

Eleanor Steber in concert
Beethoven: "Ah, Perfido!"; Strauss: Four Last Songs
University Circle Orchestra
Severance Hall, Cleveland
VAIA 1012
Live recording

1972

Puccini: *Manon Lescaut,* "Tu, tu, amore! Tu!"
Montserrat Caballé, Plácido Domingo, Metropolitan Opera Orchestra
From the Rudolf Bing gala
DG 449 229-2
Live recording

1973

Verdi: *I Vespri Siciliani*
Martina Arroyo, Plácido Domingo, Sherrill Milnes, Ruggero Raimondi, John Alldis Choir, New Philharmonia Orchestra
Walthamstow Town Hall, London
RCA 0370-2RC

Giovanna d'Arco
Montserrat Caballé, Plácido Domingo, Sherrill Milnes, Ambrosian Opera

Chorus, London Symphony
Abbey Road Studios, London
EMI CMS 7 63226-2

1974

Bellini: *Norma*
Beverly Sills, Shirley Verrett, Enrico Di
   Giuseppe, Paul Plishka, John Alldis
   Choir, New Philharmonia Orchestra
All Saints, Tooting, London
ABC ATS 20017-3 OP

Debussy: Sonata for Cello and Piano
Lynn Harrell, James Levine, piano
RCA Studio A, New York City
RCA ARL 1-1155 OP

Dvořák: Cello Concerto
Lynn Harrell, London Symphony
Walthamstow Town Hall, London
RCA 6531-2 RG

Mahler: Symphony No. 1 in D
London Symphony
Walthamstow Town Hall, London
RCA ARL 1-0894 OP / Japan
   BVCC7307-09

Symphony No. 4 in G
Judith Blegen, Chicago Symphony
Medinah Temple, Chicago
RCA ARL1-0895 OP/ Japan BVCC
   7307-09

Mendelssohn: Sonata for Cello and
   Piano
Lynn Harrell; James Levine, piano
RCA Studio A, New York
RCA ARL 1-1568 OP

Prokofiev: Sonata for Cello and Piano
Lynn Harrell; James Levine, piano
RCA Studio A, New York
RCA ARL 1-1155 OP

Schubert: Arpeggione Sonata for Cello
   and Piano
Lynn Harrell; James Levine, piano
RCA Studio A, New York
RCA 6531-2 RG

Verdi: *I Vespri Siciliani,* Act 4
Metropolitan Opera 21

Webern: Three Little Pieces, Op. 11
Lynn Harrell; James Levine, piano
RCA Studio A, New York
RCA ARL 1-1155 OP

1975

Brahms: Symphony No. 1 in C Minor
Chicago Symphony
Medinah Temple, Chicago
RCA 09026-61715-2

Mahler: Symphony No. 3 in D Minor
Marilyn Horne, Women of the Chicago
   Symphony Chorus, Glen Ellyn Chil-
   dren's Chorus, Chicago Symphony
Medinah Temple, Chicago
RCA 1757-2 / Japan BVCC7301-03

Rossini: *The Barber of Seville*
Beverly Sills, Nicolai Gedda, Sherrill
   Milnes, Renato Capecchi, Ruggero
   Raimondi, John Alldis Choir, London
   Symphony
All Saints, Tooting, London
EMI 7243-5 66040-25

Stravinsky: *Les Noces*
Jann Jaffe, Isola Jones, Philip Creech,
   Arnold Voketaitis, Ravinia Chamber
   Soloists and Chorus
Medinah Temple, Chicago
Music from Ravinia Vol. 2
RCA ARL 1-3375 OP

L'Histoire du soldat Suite
Ravinia Chamber Soloists
Medinah Temple, Chicago
Music from Ravinia Vol. 2
RCA ARL 1-3375 OP

1976

Beethoven: Sonatas for Cello and Piano
Lynn Harrell; James Levine, piano
RCA Studio A, New York
RCA ARL 2-2241 OP

Brahms: Symphony No. 2 in D
Chicago Symphony
Medinah Temple, Chicago
RCA CRL 4-3425 OP / Japan BVCC 5012

Symphony No. 3 in F
Chicago Symphony
Medinah Temple, Chicago
RCA 09026-61849-2

Symphony No. 4 in E Minor
Chicago Symphony
Medinah Temple, Chicago
RCA CRL 4-3425 OP

Giordano: *Andrea Chénier*
Renata Scotto, Plácido Domingo, Sherrill
  Milnes, John Alldis Choir, National
  Philharmonic
Walthamstow Town Hall, London
RCA RCD2 2046

Joplin: Piano Rags: "The Cascades,"
  "The Chrysanthemum," "The Easy
  Winners," "Elite Syncopations," "The
  Entertainer," "Maple Leaf Rag," "Orig-
  inal Rags," "Paragon Rag," "Pine Apple
  Rag," "Scott Joplin's New Rag,"
  "Sugar Cane," "Weeping Willow"
RCA Studio A, New York
RCA ARL 1-2243 OP

Verdi # *La Forza del Destino*
Leontyne Price, Fiorenza Cossotto, Plá-
  cido Domingo, Sherrill Milnes, John
  Alldis Choir, London Symphony
Walthamstow Town Hall, London
RCA RCD3 1864

1977

Bach, J. S.: Cantata No. 202 (*Wedding
  Cantata*)
Kathleen Battle, Ravinia Chamber
  Soloists
Medinah Temple, Chicago
Music from Ravinia Vol. 1
RCA/BMG 09026 61365-2

Brandenburg Concerto No. 2 in F
James Levine, harpsichord; Ravinia
  Chamber Soloists
Medinah Temple, Chicago
Music from Ravinia Vol. 1
RCA/BMG 09026 61365-2

Brandenburg Concerto No. 5 in D
James Levine, harpsichord; Ravinia
  Chamber Soloists
Medinah Temple, Chicago
Music from Ravinia Vol. 1
RCA/BMG 09026 61365-2

Cilea: *Adriana Lecouvreur*
Renata Scotto, Elena Obraztsova, Plácido
  Domingo, Sherrill Milnes, Ambrosian
  Opera Chorus, Philharmonia Orches-
  tra
Abbey Road Studios, London
CBS M2K 79310

Mahler: Symphony No. 5 in C Minor
Philadelphia Orchestra
Scottish Rite Cathedral, Philadelphia
RCA ARL 2-2905 OP / Japan BVCC
  7307-09

Symphony No. 6 in A Minor
London Symphony
Walthamstow Town Hall, London
RCA ARL 2-3213 OP/ Japan BVCC
  7301-03

Mozart: Quartet in G Minor for Piano
  and Strings, K. 478
James Levine, piano; Robert Mann, vio-
  lin; Michael Ouzounian, viola; Lynn
  Harrell, cello
Medinah Temple, Chicago
Music from Ravinia Vol. 3
RCA ARL 1-3376 OP

Quintet in E-flat for Piano and Winds,
  K. 452
James Levine, piano; Ray Still, oboe;
  Clark Brody, clarinet; Willard Elliott,
  bassoon; Dale Clevenger, horn
Medinah Temple, Chicago
Music from Ravinia Vol. 3
RCA ARL 1-3376 OP

Puccini: *La Bohème,* Finale Act 1
Metropolitan Opera 21

Schumann: Symphony No. 2 in C
Philadelphia Orchestra
Scottish Rite Cathedral, Philadelphia

RCA ARL 3-3907 OP/Germany 74321 20294 2

Stravinsky: *Petrouchka* [complete 1947 version]
Chicago Symphony
Medinah Temple, Chicago
RCA ARL 1-2615 OP

1978

Mahler: Symphony No. 10 Adagio (first movement)
Philadelphia Orchestra
Scottish Rite Cathedral, Philadelphia
RCA CTC 2-3726 OP/ Japan BVCC 7304-06

Mascagni: *Cavalleria Rusticana*
Renata Scotto, Plácido Domingo, Pablo Elvira, Jean Kraft, Ambrosian Opera Chorus, National Philharmonic
Walthamstow Town Hall, London
RCA RCD1-3091

Schumann: Symphony No. 1 in B-flat
Philadelphia Orchestra
Scottish Rite Cathedral, Philadelphia
RCA 09026 61849 2 / Germany 7421 20094-2

Symphony No. 3 *(Rhenish)* in E-flat
Philadelphia Orchestra
Scottish Rite Cathedral, Philadelphia
RCA ARL 3-3907 OP / Germany 74321 20294 2

Symphony No. 4 in D Minor
Philadelphia Orchestra
Scottish Rite Cathedral, Philadelphia
RCA ARL 3-3907 OP / Germany 74321 20294 2

Smetana: *The Bartered Bride,* Overture
Metropolitan Opera 21

Verdi: # *Otello* [Act 3]
Renata Scotto, Plácido Domingo, Sherrill Milnes, Ambrosian Opera Chorus, National Philharmonic
Walthamstow Town Hall, London
RCA RCD2 2951

1979

Bellini: *Norma*
Renata Scotto, Tatiana Troyanos, Giuseppe Giacomini, Paul Plishka, Ambrosian Opera Chorus, National Philharmonic
Henry Wood Hall, London
Sony SM2K 35902

Mahler: Symphony No. 8 in E-flat *(Symphony of a Thousand)*
First movement, "Veni, creator spiritus"
Carol Neblett, Judith Blegen, Jann Jaffe, Isola Jones, Birgit Finnilä, Kenneth Riegel, Ryan Edwards, John Cheek, Glen Ellyn Children's Chorus, Chicago Symphony Orchestra and Chorus
Broadcast recording from the Ravinia Pavilion
Chicago Symphony Archive Centennial Album OP

Symphony No. 9 in D
Philadelphia Orchestra
Scottish Rite Cathedral, Philadelphia
RCA ARL 2-3461 OP / Japan BVCC 7304-06

Symphony No. 10 (movements 2–5)
Cooke version
Chicago Symphony
Medinah Temple, Chicago
RCA ATC 2-4245 OP

Puccini: # *La Bohème*
Renata Scotto, Alfredo Kraus, Sherrill Milnes, Ambrosian Opera Chorus, National Philharmonic
Walthamstow Town Hall, London
EMI CD-CFPD 4708

Strauss: *Ariadne auf Naxos,* Conclusion of Prologue
Metropolitan Opera 21

Verdi: *Luisa Miller,* Act 2, Scene 3
Metropolitan Opera 21

Wagner: *Parsifal,* Act 2, Duet
Metropolitan Opera 21

1980

Mahler: Symphony No. 7 in E Minor
Chicago Symphony
Medinah Temple, Chicago
RCA ATC 2-4245 OP / Japan
  BVCC7304-06

Mozart: # *Die Zauberflöte*
Ileana Cotrubas, Zdislawa Donat, Eric
  Tappy, Christian Boesch, Martti
  Talvela, Members of the Vienna State
  Opera Chorus, Vienna Philharmonic
Grosser Musikvereinssaal, Vienna
RCA 4586-2-RG

★ *La Clemenza di Tito* [film]

Puccini: ★ *Manon Lescaut*

Tosca
Renata Scotto, Plácido Domingo, Renato
  Bruson, Itzhak Perlman, Ambrosian
  Opera Chorus, Philharmonia Orches-
  tra
Kingsway Hall, London
CBS 7 49364

Schumann: Piano Quintet
James Levine, piano; the LaSalle Quartet
RCA Studio 10, New York
DG 453 071-2

Strauss: ★ *Elektra* [First laserdisc]

1981

Dvořák: Symphony No. 9 *(From the New
  World)*
Chicago Symphony
Medinah Temple, Chicago
RCA 09026-61716-2

Mozart: Symphony Nos. 40 in G Minor,
  K. 550 / 41 in C, K. 551 *(Jupiter)*
Chicago Symphony
Medinah Temple, Chicago
RCA 09026 61397-2

1982

Mozart: *Eine kleine Nachtmusik;* Post
  Horn Serenade
Vienna Philharmonic

Grosser Musikvereinssaal, Vienna
DG 410-085-2 OP
Reissued with Symphony No. 32 as DG
  445 555-2

★ *Idomeneo*

Violin Concertos No. 1, K. 207; No. 2,
  K. 211; No. 4, K. 218; Adagio, K. 262;
  Rondos, K. 261a and 373
Itzhak Perlman, violin; Vienna Philhar-
  monic
Grosser Musikvereinssaal, Vienna
DG 445 535-2
No. 1 and No. 5 DG 427 813-2
No. 2 and No. 4 DG 415 975-2

Puccini: ★ *La Bohème*

Wagner: ★ *Tannhäuser*

Leontyne Price and Marilyn Horne in
  Concert at the Met, March 28
Price: Mozart: *Le Nozze di Figaro,* "Dove
  sono"; Verdi: *La Forza del Destino,*
  "Pace, pace, mio Dio"; Puccini: *La
  Rondine,* "Che il bel sogno di Doretta"
Horne: Handel: *Rodelinda,* "Vivi,
  tiranno!"; Rossini: *L'Assedio di Corinto,*
  "Non temer, d'un basso affetto";
  Meyerbeer: *Les Huguenots,* "Non!—
  non, non, non, non, non! Vous n'avez
  jamais, je gage"
Duets: Mozart, *Così fan tutte,* "Ah, guarda,
  sorella"; Handel: *Rinaldo,* "Fermati!
  No, crudel"; Verdi: *Aida,* "Silenzio!
  verso noi s'avanza"; Bellini: *Norma,*
  "Mira, o Norma"; Puccini: *Madama
  Butterfly,* Flower Duet
Orchestral works: Verdi: *I Vespri Siciliani:*
  Overture; Bellini: *Norma,* Sinfonietta
Metropolitan Opera Orchestra
Metropolitan Opera House, New York
RCA CR2-4609 OP
Live recording

★ *Homage to Seville* [Domingo]

1983

Beethoven: Concerto for Piano No. 1 in
  C, Concerto for Piano No. 2 in B-flat,

Concerto for Piano No. 3 in C Minor,
Concerto for Piano No. 4 in G, Con-
certo for Piano No. 5 in E-flat
(*Emperor*)
Alfred Brendel, piano; Chicago Sym-
phony
Orchestra Hall, Chicago
Philips 456 045-2
Live recording

Berlioz: ★ *Les Troyens*

Brahms: Concerto for Piano No. 1 in
D Minor
Emanuel Ax, piano; Chicago Symphony
Orchestra Hall, Chicago
RCA ARC 1-4962 OP

A German Requiem
Kathleen Battle, Håkan Hagegård,
Chicago Symphony Orchestra and
Chorus
Orchestra Hall, Chicago
RCA 09026 61349-2

Songs: Kathleen Battle, Håkan Hagegård
Battle: "Juchhe" (Op. 4/6), "Das Mäd-
chen spricht" (Op. 107/3), "Meine
Liebe ist grün" (Op. 63/5), "Wir wan-
delten" (Op. 98/2)
Hagegård: "Wiegenlied" (Op. 49/4), "O
wüsst ich doch den Weg zurück" (Op.
63/8), "Von ewiger Liebe" (Op. 43/1),
"Nachtwandler" (Op. 86/3)
RCA Studio A, New York
RCA ARC2 5002 OP

Schubert: Symphony No. 9 in C (The
Great)
Chicago Symphony
Orchestra Hall, Chicago
DG 413 437-4GH OP
Reissued in Europe with music from
Rosamunde as DG 445 559-2

Verdi: ★ *Don Carlo;* ★ *Ernani;* ★ *La Traviata*
(film, released in the U.S. on tape)

★ Metropolitan Opera Centennial Gala

1984

Berlioz: *Les Troyens,* Act 5, Scenes 2/3
Metropolitan Opera 21

Dvořák: Symphony No. 7 in D Minor
Chicago Symphony
Orchestra Hall, Chicago
RCA ARC1-5427 OP

Mendelssohn: Incidental music to *A
Midsummer Night's Dream*
Judith Blegen, Florence Quivar, women
of the Chicago Symphony Chorus,
Chicago Symphony
Orchestra Hall, Chicago
DG 415 137-2

Mozart: Symphony Nos. 28/29/30
Vienna Philharmonic
Grosser Musikvereinssaal, Vienna
DG 435006-2 OP
Reissued as DG 435 380-2
No. 28 issued separately as DG 419
606-2 OP

Orff: *Carmina Burana*
June Anderson, Philip Creech, Bernd
Weikl, Glen Ellyn Children's Choir,
Chicago Symphony Chorus and
Orchestra
Orchestra Hall, Chicago
DG 415 136-2

Ravel: *Daphnis et Chloé* (complete)
Vienna State Opera Chorus, Vienna Phil-
harmonic
Grosser Musikvereinssaal, Vienna
DG 415 360-2 OP

Schubert: Overture and Ballet music
from *Rosamunde*
Chicago Symphony
Orchestra Hall, Chicago
DG 415 137-2

Tchaikovsky: Symphony No. 6 in B
Minor *(Pathétique)*
Chicago Symphony
Orchestra Hall, Chicago
RCA RCD1 5355 OP

Verdi: ★ *La Forza del Destino;* ★ *Simon Boccanegra*

Zandonai: ★ *Francesca da Rimini*

Kathleen Battle: Salzburg Recital, *now* Kathleen Battle in Concert
Fauré: "Mandoline," "Les roses d'Ispahan," "En Prière," "Notre amour"; Handel: "O Had I Jubal's Lyre"; Mendelssohn: "Bei der Wiege," "Neue Liebe"; Mozart: "Ridente la calma"; Purcell: "Come All Ye Songsters," "Music for a While," "Sweeter Than Roses"; Strauss: "Schlagende Herzen," "Ich wollt' ein Strausslein binden," "Sausle, liebe Myrte." Spirituals: "Honor, Honor, His Name So Sweet," "Witness," "He's Got the Whole World in His Hands"
James Levine, piano
Kleines Festspielhaus, Salzburg
DG 415 361-2

1985

Berg: *Wozzeck,* Scenes 1–5
Metropolitan Opera 21

Mozart: Violin Concertos No. 3 (K. 216); No. 5 (K. 219); and Rondo (K. 373)
Itzhak Perlman, violin; Vienna Philharmonic
Grosser Musikvereinssaal, Vienna
DG 445 535 2
Nos. 3 and 5, DG 410 020-2
Nos. 1 and 5, DG 427 813-2
(not available in U.S.)

Symphony Nos. 25/26/27/31/32/34
Vienna Philharmonic
Grosser Musikvereinssaal, Vienna
DG 435 008-2 OP
Reissued as DG 435 360-2
No. 32 now duplicated on DG 445 555-2

Schubert: "Ariette der Claudine," "Liebhaber in allen Gestalten," "An die Laute," "Geheimes," "Seligkeit," "Alinde," "Suleika," "Nacht und Träume," "Nähe des Geliebten," "Ständchen," "Lachen und Weinen," "Gott in Frühlinge," "Die Männer sind mechant," "Rastlöse Liebe," "Die junge Nonne," "Lied der Delphine," "Der Hirt auf dem Felsen."
Kathleen Battle, soprano; James Levine, piano; Karl Leister, clarinet
Kleines Festspielhaus, Salzburg
Completed Aula der Universität, Salzburg, 1987
DG 419 237-2

Wagner: # *Parsifal*
Waltraud Meier, Peter Hofmann, Hans Sotin, Simon Estes
Live recording
Festspielhaus, Bayreuth
Philips 416 842-2

1986

Beethoven: # Quintet for Piano and Winds
Ensemble Wien-Berlin
Aula der Universität, Salzburg
DG 419 785-2

Berg: Three Pieces for Orchestra
Berlin Philharmonic
Jesus-Christus-Kirche, Berlin (Dahlem)
DG 419 781-2

Dukas: *L'Apprenti sorcier*
Berlin Philharmonic
Jesus-Christus-Kirche, Berlin (Dahlem)
DG 419 617-2

Dvořák: Violin Concerto
Shlomo Mintz
Berlin Philharmonic
Jesus-Christus-Kirche, Berlin (Dahlem)
DG 419-618-2
Also issued in Europe as DG 449 091-2

Mozart: # Quintet for Piano and Winds
Ensemble Wien-Berlin
Aula der Universität, Salzburg
DG 419 785-2

Symphony Nos. 21/22/23/24/33/38/39
Vienna Philharmonic

Grosser Musikvereinssaal, Vienna
DG 435-008-2 OP
Reissued as 435 360-1
No. 33 issued separately as DG 419
606-2 OP
Nos. 38 and 39 issued separately as DG
423 086-2 OP

Saint-Saëns: Symphony No. 3
Simon Preston, organ; Berlin Philhar-
monic
Philharmonie, Berlin
DG 419 617-2

Schoenberg: Five Pieces for Orchestra
Berlin Philharmonic
Jesus-Christus-Kirche, Berlin (Dahlem)
DG 419 781-2

Sibelius: Violin Concerto
Shlomo Mintz, Berlin Philharmonic
Jesus-Christus-Kirche, Berlin (Dahlem)
DG 419 618-2

Smetana: *The Bartered Bride* Overture,
Polka, Furiant, and Skocna
Vienna Philharmonic
Grosser Musikvereinssaal, Vienna
DG 427 340-2 [with *Moldau, From
Bohemia's Meadows and Forests*]

Má Vlast
Vienna Philharmonic
Grosser Musikvereinssaal, Vienna
DG 431 652-2
Live recording

Strauss: # *Ariadne auf Naxos*
Anna Tomowa-Sintow, Agnes Baltsa,
Kathleen Battle, Gary Lakes, Hermann
Prey, Dawn Upshaw, Vienna Philhar-
monic
Grosser Musikvereinssaal, Vienna
DG 419 225-2

Verdi: *Falstaff,* Act 3, Scene 2
Metropolitan Opera 21

Wagner: *Lohengrin

Webern: Six Pieces for Orchestra
Berlin Philharmonic

Jesus-Christus-Kirche, Berlin (Dahlem)
DG 419 781-2

1987

Bizet: * *Carmen*

Haydn: *Die Schöpfung*
Kathleen Battle, Gosta Winbergh, Kurt
Moll, Rundfunk-choir, Stockholm
Kammerchoir, Berlin Philharmonic
Jesus-Christus-Kirche Berlin (Dahlem)
DG 427 629-2 OP

Mozart: Great Mass in C Minor, K. 427
Kathleen Battle, Leilla Cuberli, Peter
Seiffert, Kurt Moll, members of the
State Opera Choir, Vienna Philhar-
monic
Grosser Musikvereinssaal, Vienna
GD 423 664-2

Symphony Nos. 35/36
Vienna Philharmonic
Grosser Musikvereinssaal, Vienna
DG 435 008-2 OP 435 360-2
Also issued in Europe as DG 423 663-2

Puccini: * *Turandot*

Schubert: *Die Winterreise*
Christa Ludwig
Brahmssaal, Vienna
DG 445 521-2

Schumann: Symphony Nos. 2 and 3
(Rhenish)
Berlin Philharmonic
Jesus-Christus-Kirche, Berlin (Dahlem)
DG 423 625-2

Tchaikovsky: *Eugene Onegin*
Mirella Freni, Anne Sofie von Otter,
Neil Shicoff, Thomas Allen, Rund-
funk Choir, Leipzig, Dresden
Staatskapelle
Lukas-Kirche, Dresden
DG 423 959-2
Excerpts DG 445 467-2

Wagner: # *Die Walküre*
Hildegard Behrens, Jessye Norman,
Christa Ludwig, Gary Lakes, James

Morris, Kurt Moll, Metropolitan
Opera Orchestra
Manhattan Center, New York
DG 423 389-1/24

Music for Life: Levine conducts the overture to Bernstein's *Candide;* Bernstein
and Levine conduct Ives, *The Unanswered Question;* Verdi: *Don Carlo,* "Elle
ne m'aime pas" with Samuel Ramey;
Puccini: *Turandot,* "Nessun dorma"
with Luciano Pavarotti; *Tosca:* "Vissi
d'arte" with Leontyne Price; Bellini:
"Vaga luna che inargenti"; Tosti:
"Marechiare" with Pavarotti (Levine,
piano); Levine plays Mozart: Sonata
for Two Pianos, andante only, K. 448,
with Bernstein

Pickup orchestra, Carnegie Hall DG 427
486-2 entire concert OP; excerpts DG
429 392-2. The one CD version omits
the Ives, the Bellini and Tosti songs,
and the Tosca aria.

1988

Berlioz: *Les Nuits d'été*
Anne Sofie von Otter, Berlin Philhar-
monic
Jesus-Christus-Kirche, Berlin (Dahlem)
DG 427 665-2 OP

Les Nuits d'été and "Premiers transports
que nul n'oublie" from *Roméo et Juliette*
DG 445 823-2

Roméo et Juliette
Anne Sofie von Otter, Philip Langridge,
James Morris, RIAS Chamber Choir,
Ernst-Senff Choir, Berlin Philharmonic
Jesus-Christus-Kirche, Berlin (Dahlem)
DG 427 665-2

Bruch: *Kol Nidre*
Matt Haimovitz, cello; Chicago Sym-
phony
Orchestra Hall, Chicago
DG 427 323-2

Debussy: *Pelléas et Mélisande,* Act 2,
Scenes 2/3
Metropolitan Opera 21

Lalo: Concerto for Cello in D Minor
Matt Haimovitz, cello; Chicago Sym-
phony
Orchestra Hall, Chicago
DG 427 323-2

Mendelssohn: Symphony Nos. 3 *(Scotch)*
and 4 *(Italian)*
Berlin Philharmonic
Jesus-Christus-Kirche, Berlin (Dahlem)
DG 427 670-2

Mozart: *Così fan tutte*
Kiri Te Kanawa, Anne Murray, Marie
McLaughlin, Thomas Hampson, Hans
Peter Blochwitz, Ferruccio Furlanetto,
Vienna State Opera Chorus, Vienna
Philharmonic
Grosser Musikvereinssaal, Vienna
DG 423 987-2

Poulenc: Elégie pour cor et piano; Sextuor pour piano, flute, hautbois, clarinette, basson et cor; Sonate pour
clarinette et piano; Sonate pour flûte
et piano; Trio pour piano, hautbois
et basson
Aula der Universität, Salzburg
DG 427 639-2

Saint-Saëns: Concerto for Cello No. 1 in
A Minor
Matt Haimovitz, cello; Chicago Sym-
phony
Orchestra Hall, Chicago
DG 427 323-2

Strauss: ★ *Ariadne auf Naxos*

Verdi: ★ *Il Trovatore*

Wagner: # *Das Rheingold*
Christa Ludwig, Birgitta Svendén, James
Morris, Siegfried Jerusalem, Ekkehard
Wlaschiha, etc., Metropolitan Opera
Orchestra
Manhattan Center, New York
DG 445 295-2

Siegfried
Hildegard Behrens, Birgitta Svendén,
Reiner Goldberg, James Morris, Heinz

Zednik, etc., Metropolitan Opera
Orchestra
Manhattan Center, New York
DG 429 407-2

*Kathleen Battle and Plácido Domingo Live in
Tokyo,* 1988
Donizetti: *Don Pasquale,* "Quel guardo il
cavaliere" with Battle; *Lucia di Lammer-
moor,* "Tombe degl'avi miei" and "Fra
poco a me ricovero" with Domingo.
Duets: Verdi: *La Traviata,* "Signora!
Che t'accadde?" and "Parigi, o cara"
(with Margaret Jane Wray); Donizetti:
L'Elisir d'Amore, "Caro elisir," "Tralla-
rallara," and "Esulti pur la barbara";
Gounod: *Roméo et Juliette,* "Va, je t'ai
pardonnée" and "Nuit d'hyménée";
Mozart: *Don Giovanni,* "Là ci darem la
mano"; Lehár, *The Merry Widow,* "Lip-
pen schweigen."
Orchestral works: Rossini, *L'Italiana in
Algeri,* Overture; Verdi, *La Forza del
Destino,* Overture. Metropolitan Opera
Orchestra
Bunka Kaikan, Toyko
DG 427 686-2
Live recording
A television tape exists of this concert

★ Pavarotti recital

1989

Bartók: Concerto for Orchestra
Chicago Symphony
Orchestra Hall, Chicago
DG 429 747-2 OP

Music for Strings, Percussion, and
Celesta
Chicago Symphony
Orchestra Hall, Chicago
DG 428 747-2 OP

Bellini: Oboe Concerto
Hansjörg Schellenberger, Berlin Philhar-
monic
Jesus-Christus-Kirche, Berlin (Dahlem)
DG 429 750-2

Berlioz: Requiem
Luciano Pavarotti, Ernst-Senff-Choir,
Berlin Philharmonic
Jesus-Christus-Kirche, Berlin (Dahlem)
DG 429724-2

Donizetti: # *L'Elisir d'Amore*
Kathleen Battle, Dawn Upshaw, Luciano
Pavarotti, Leo Nucci, Metropolitan
Opera Orchestra and Chorus, Man-
hattan Center
DG 429 744-2

Holst: *The Planets*
Chicago Symphony Orchestra and
Chorus
Orchestra Hall, Chicago
DG 429 730-2

Mozart: Oboe Concerto
Hansjörg Schellenberger, Berlin Philhar-
monic
Jesus-Christus-Kirche, Berlin (Dahlem)
DG 429 750-2

Symphony K. 19a/45a/74/
84/112/114/124/128/130 and Nos. 40,
K. 550/41, K. 551
Vienna Philharmonic
Grosser Musikvereinssaal, Vienna
DG 431711-2 [early works] OP; DG 435
008-2 [40/41] OP; reissued as 435 360-
2; Nos. 40/41 DG 429 731-2

Schoenberg: *Erwartung*
Jessye Norman, Metropolitan Opera
Orchestra
Manhattan Center, New York
Philips 426 261-2

Strauss: Oboe Concerto
Hansjörg Schellenberger, Berlin Philhar-
monic
Jesus-Christus-Kirche, Berlin (Dahlem)
DG 429 750-2

Vier Letzte Lieder
Jessye Norman, Berlin Philharmonic
Philharmonie, Berlin
Philips (unreleased)

Stravinsky: Symphony of Psalms
Chicago Symphony Orchestra and
  Chorus
Broadcast recording from the Ravinia
  Pavilion
Chicago Symphony Archive Centennial
  Album OP

Verdi: * *Aida*

Wagner: * *Die Walküre,* # *Götterdäm-
merung*
Hildegard Behrens, Cheryl Studer,
  Reiner Goldberg, Bernd Weikel, Matti
  Salminen, etc., Metropolitan Opera
  Orchestra and Chorus
Manhattan Center, New York
DG 429 385-2
Excerpts available in Europe on DG 435
  489-2

The Ring of the Nibelung [originally *The
  Compact Ring,* DG 144 350 OP] con-
  tains excerpts from the four complete
  Ring operas just cited. DG 437 825-2

1990

Babbitt: *Correspondences* for Strings and
  Tape
Chicago Symphony
Orchestra Hall, Chicago
DG 431 698-2

Berlioz: *Symphonie fantastique; Les Troyens:*
  Royal Hunt and Storm RIAS Chamber
  Choir, Berlin Philharmonic
Jesus-Christus-Kirche, Berlin (Dahlem)
DG 431-624-2

Cage: *Atlas eclipticalis*
Chicago Symphony
Orchestra Hall, Chicago
DG 431 698-2

Carter: Variations for Orchestra
Chicago Symphony
Orchestra Hall, Chicago
DG 431 698-2

Dvořák: Symphony No. 8 in G
Dresden Staatskapelle
Lukas-Kirche, Dresden
DG 447 754-2

Gershwin: *An American in Paris, Catfish
  Row* Suite [from *Porgy and Bess*],
  Cuban Overture, *Rhapsody in Blue*
James Levine, piano [in the *Rhapsody*];
  Chicago Symphony
Orchestra Hall, Chicago
DG 431 625-2

Mozart: *Le Nozze di Figaro*
Kiri Te Kanawa, Dawn Upshaw, Anne
  Sofie von Otter, Tatiana Troyanos, Fer-
  ruccio Furlanetto, Thomas Hampson,
  Paul Plishka, Metropolitan Opera
  Orchestra and Chorus
Manhattan Center, New York
DG 431 619-2

Schoenberg: *Brettl-Lieder*
Jessye Norman, James Levine, piano
Manhattan Center, New York
Philips 426 261-2

Schubert: Quintet in A *(Trout),* D. 667
James Levine, piano; Gerhart Hetzel,
  violin; Wolfram Christ, viola; Georg
  Faust, cello; Alois Posch, bass
Kirche St. Konrad, Abersee
DG 431 783-2

Schuller: *Spectra*
Chicago Symphony
Orchestra Hall, Chicago
DG 431 698-2

Verdi: # *Aida*
Aprile Millo, Dolora Zajick, Plácido
  Domingo, James Morris, Samuel
  Ramey, Metropolitan Opera Orchestra
  and Chorus
Manhattan Center, New York
Sony S3K 45973

Wagner: * *Das Rheingold*

* *Siegfried*

★ *Götterdämmerung*

\# *Battle and Norman Sing Spirituals:* "In That Great Gettin' Up Morning"; "Great Day"; "Sinner, Please Please Don't Let This Harvest Pass"; "Over My Head"/"Lil' David"; "Oh, What a Beautiful City"; "Lord, How Come Me Here?"; "I Believe I'll Go Back Home"/"Lady, Won't You Help Me"; "Witness"; "Give Me Jesus"; "Swing Low, Sweet Chariot"/"Ride Up in the Chariot"; "Deep River"; "Certainly, Lord"; "Ride On, King Jesus"; "Oh, Glory"; "Scandalize My Name"; "Talk About a Child"; "Ain'-a That Good News"; "You Can Tell the World"; "Calvary"/"They Crucified My Lord"; "My God Is So High"; "There Is a Balm in Gilead"; "He's Got the Whole World in His Hands"
The CD omits "Witness," "Give Me Jesus," "Deep River," "Certainly, Lord," and "Ain'-a That Good News" but contains "Gospel Train," which is not on the laserdisc.
Kathleen Battle, Jessye Norman, pickup orchestra with assisting artists, chorus directed by Robert de Cormer
Carnegie Hall, New York
DG 429-790-2

Jessye Norman Salzburg Recital
Beethoven: *Sechs Geistliche Lieder,* Op. 48; Debussy, "Nuit d'étoiles," "Beau soir," "Romance," "Les cloches," "Mandoline"; Wolf: from the *Spanisches Liederbuch,* "Bedecke mich mit Blumen," "Tief im Herzen trag' ich Pein," "Bitt ihn, O Mütter," "In dem Schatten meiner Locken," "Alle gingen, Herz, zur Ruh," "Geh', Geliebter, geh' jetzt!"; From the *Italienisches Liederbuch,* "Heut' Nacht erhob ich mich," "Wie soll ich frolich sein," "Verschling der Abgrund meines Liebsten Hütte," "Non lass uns Friedenschliessen," "Mein Liebster hat zu Tische mich geladen," "Ich hab' in Penna einen

Liebsten wohnen"
Jessye Norman; James Levine, piano
Manhattan Center, New York
Philips 422-378-2

1991

Beethoven: *Missa Solemnis*
Cheryl Studer, Jessye Norman, Plácido Domingo, Kurt Moll, Leipzig Rundfunkchoir, Stockholm, Eric Ericson Kammerchor, Vienna Philharmonic
Grosses Festspielhaus, Salzburg
DG 435-770-2
Live recording

Berlioz: *Benvenuto Cellini* Overture; *Roman Carnival* Overture; *Corsaire* Overture
Berlin Philharmonic
Jesus-Christus-Kirche, Berlin (Dahlem)
DG 429724-2

Donizetti: ★ *L'Elisir d'Amore*
Haydn: *Paukenmesse* [Mass in Time of War]
Sylvia McNair, Dolores Ziegler, Hans Peter Blochwitz, Andreas Schmidt, RIAS Chamber Choir, Berlin Philharmonic
Kammersaal of the Philharmonie, Berlin
DG 435 853-2
Live recording

Mozart: *Idomeneo,* Act 2, Scenes 2/5
Metropolitan Opera 21

★ *Die Zauberflöte*

Kegelstatt Trio, K. 498
Manhattan Center, New York
DG 431 782-2

Krönungsmesse
Sylvia McNair, Dolores Ziegler, Hans Peter Blochwitz, Andreas Schmidt, RIAS Chamber Choir, Berlin Philharmonic
Kammersaal of the Philharmonie, Berlin
DG 435 853-2
Live recording

Schoenberg: *Verklärte Nacht* [1943 version]
Strings of the Berlin Philharmonic
Schauspielhaus, Berlin
DG 435 883-2
Live recording

Schumann: Symphony Nos. 1 (*Frühling*) and No. 4 and *Manfred* Overture
Berlin Philharmonic
Jesus-Christus-Kirche, Berlin (Dahlem)
DG 435 856-2

Sibelius: *Finlandia*
Berlin Philharmonic
Philharmonie, Berlin
DG 437 828-2

Symphony No. 2
Berlin Philharmonic
Schauspielhaus, Berlin
DG 437 828-2
Live recording

Valse triste
Berlin Philharmonic
Philharmonie, Berlin
DG 437 828-2

Strauss: *Metamorphosen*
Berlin Philharmonic
Kammersaal of the Philharmonie, Berlin
DG 435 883-2
Live recording

Stravinsky: *Oedipus Rex*
Florence Quivar, Philip Langridge, Donald Kaasch, James Morris, Jan-Hendrik Rootering, Jules Bastin, narration [in French]
Chicago Symphony Orchestra and Chorus
Orchestra Hall, Chicago
DG 435 872-2

Verdi: # *La Traviata*
Cheryl Studer, Luciano Pavarotti, Juan Pons, Metropolitan Opera Orchestra and Chorus
Manhattan Center, New York
DG 435 797-2

Luisa Miller
Aprile Millo, Wendy White, Florence Quivar, Plácido Domingo, Jan-Hendrik Rootering, Paul Plishka, Vladimir Chernov, Metropolitan Opera Orchestra and Chorus
Manhattan Center, New York
Sony S2K 48073

Il Trovatore
Aprile Millo, Dolora Zajick, Plácido Domingo, Vladimir Chernov, James Morris, Metropolitan Opera Orchestra and Chorus
Manhattan Center, New York
Sony S2K 48070

Wagner: Siegfried Idyll
Berlin Philharmonic
Jesus-Christus-Kirche, Berlin (Dahlem)
DG 435 883-2

Der fliegende Holländer: Overture
Metropolitan Opera Orchestra
Manhattan Center, New York
DG 435 874

Lohengrin: Prelude to Act 3
Metropolitan Opera Orchestra
Manhattan Center, New York
DG 435 874-2

Die Meistersinger: Prelude
Metropolitan Opera Orchestra
Manhattan Center, New York
DG 435 874-2

Rienzi: Overture
Metropolitan Opera Orchestra
Manhattan Center, New York
DG 435 874-2

Tannhäuser: Overture and Venusberg Music
Metropolitan Opera Orchestra
Manhattan Center, New York
DG 435 874-2

* Metropolitan Opera Gala: 25 Years at Lincoln Center

1992

Berg: Concerto for Violin
Anne-Sophie Mutter, violin; Chicago
  Symphony
Orchestra Hall, Chicago
DG 437 093-2

Lulu Suite/*Wozzeck* excerpts; Three
  Pieces for Orchestra
Metropolitan Opera Orchestra
Manhattan Center, New York
Sony SK 53 959

Brahms: Alto Rhapsody
Anne Sofie von Otter, mezzo; Arnold
  Schönberg Choir; Vienna Philhar-
  monic
Grosser Musikvereinssaal, Vienna
DG 439 887-2/also 449 899-2
Live recording

Symphony No. 3 in F
Vienna Philharmonic
Grosser Musikvereinssaal, Vienna
DG 439 887-2/also 449 899-2
Live recording

Tragic Overture
Vienna Philharmonic
Grosser Musikvereinssaal, Vienna
DG 439 887-2/also 449 899-2

Corigliano: ★ *The Ghosts of Versailles*

Debussy: *Images*
Berlin Philharmonic
Philharmonie, Berlin
Sony SK 53 284
Live recording

Elgar: *Enigma* Variations
Berlin Philharmonic
Philharmonie, Berlin
Sony SK 53 284
Live recording

Fauré: *Berceuse in re majeur*
Anne-Sophie Mutter, violin; Vienna
  Philharmonic
Grosser Musikvereinssaal, Vienna
DG 437 544-2

Mahler: *Das Lied von der Erde*
Jessye Norman, Siegfried Jerusalem,
  Berlin Philharmonic
Philharmonie, Berlin
DG 439 948-2
Live recording

Massenet: "Meditation"
Anne-Sophie Mutter, violin; Vienna
  Philharmonic
Grosser Musikvereinssaal, Vienna
DG 437 544-2

Mussorgsky/Ravel: *Pictures at an Exhibi-
tion*
Metropolitan Opera Orchestra
Manhattan Center, New York
DG 437 531-2

Prokofiev: Symphony No. 1 in D
  (Classical)
Chicago Symphony
Medinah Temple, Chicago
DG 439 912-2

Symphony No. 5 in B-flat
Chicago Symphony
Medinah Temple, Chicago
DG 439 912-2
Last DG sessions with Chicago Sym-
  phony

Puccini: # *Manon Lescaut*
Mirella Freni, Luciano Pavarotti,
  Giuseppe Taddei, Dwayne Croft,
  Metropolitan Opera Orchestra and
  Chorus
Manhattan Center, New York
London 440 200-2

Ravel: *Tzigane*
Anne-Sophie Mutter, violin; Vienna
  Philharmonic
Grosser Musikvereinssaal, Vienna
DG 437 544-2

Rihm: *Gesungene Zeit* (Time Chant) for
  Violin and Orchestra
Anne-Sophie Mutter, violin; Chicago
  Symphony
Orchestra Hall, Chicago
DG 37 093-2

Sarasate: *Fantasie du concert sur les motifs de l'opéra Carmen, Zigeunerweisen*
Anne-Sophie Mutter, violin; Vienna Philharmonic
Grosser Musikvereinssaal, Vienna
DG 437 544-2

Schubert: *Die schöne Müllerin*
Uwe Heilmann; Levine, piano
Margrave's Opera House, Bayreuth
Decca 440 354-2

Sibelius: Symphony No. 5
Berlin Philharmonic
Philharmonie, Berlin
DG 445 865-2

Stravinsky: *Le Sacre du Printemps* (1947 version)
Metropolitan Opera Orchestra
Manhattan Center, New York
DG 437 531-2

Tartini/Zandonai: Sonata in G Minor *(The Devil's Trill)*
Anne-Sophie Mutter, violin; Vienna Philharmonic
Grosser Musikvereinssaal, Vienna
DG 437 544-2

Tchaikovsky: Ballet suites: *Swan Lake, Sleeping Beauty,* and *The Nutcracker*
Vienna Philharmonic
Grosser Musikvereinssaal, Vienna
DG 437 806-2

Verdi: Ballet music from *Aida, Don Carlo, Macbeth, Otello,* and *Les vêpres siciliennes*
Metropolitan Opera Orchestra
Manhattan Center, New York
Sony SK 489

Don Carlo
Aprile Millo, Dolora Zajick, Michael Sylvester, Vladimir Chernov, Ferruccio Furlanetto, Samuel Ramey, Metropolitan Opera Orchestra and Chorus
Manhattan Center, New York
Sony 3K 52 500

★ *Falstaff*

Wagner: # *Parsifal* [recording begun in 1991]
Jessye Norman, Plácido Domingo, James Morris, Kurt Moll, etc., Metropolitan Opera Orchestra and Chorus
Manhattan Center, New York
DG 437 501-29

Wesendonk Lieder
Jessye Norman, Berlin Philharmonic
Philharmonie, Berlin
Philips (unreleased)

Wieniawski: *Légende en sol mineur*
Anne-Sophie Mutter, violin; Vienna Philharmonic
Grosser Musikvereinssaal, Vienna
DG 437 544-2

1993

Beethoven: Symphony No. 3 *(Eroica)*
Metropolitan Opera Orchestra
Manhattan Center, New York
DG 439 862-2

Berg: Three Fragments from *Wozzeck, Lulu* Suite, Three Orchestra Pieces, Op. 6 Renée Fleming [*Wozzeck* and *Lulu* excerpts], Metropolitan Opera Orchestra
Manhattan Center, New York
Sony SK 53 959

Brahms: Symphony No. 1
Vienna Philharmonic
Grosses Festspielhaus, Salzburg
DG Japan POCG 9595 / also 449 829-2
Live recording

Mozart: Opera Arias (13)
Kathleen Battle, Metropolitan Opera Orchestra
Abyssinian Baptist Church, New York
DG 439 949-2

Schubert: Symphony No. 8 *(Unfinished)*
Metropolitan Opera Orchestra
Manhattan Center, New York
DG 439 862-2

Verdi: # *Rigoletto*
Sheryl Studer, Denyce Graves, Vladimir

Chernov, Luciano Pavarotti, Roberto Scandiuzzi, etc., Metropolitan Opera Orchestra and Chorus
Manhattan Center, New York
DG (unreleased)

★ *Stiffelio*

1994

Brahms: Symphony No. 4
Vienna Philharmonic
Grosser Musikvereinssaal, Vienna
DG 449 829-2
Live recording

Dvořák: Symphony No. 9 *(From the New World)*
Dresden Staatskapelle
Lukas-Kirche, Dresden
DG 447-754-2

Mozart: # *Idomeneo*
Carol Vaness, Heidi Grant Murphy, Cecilia Bartoli, Plácido Domingo, Thomas Hampson, Frank Lopardo, Bryn Terfel, Metropolitan Opera Orchestra and Chorus
Manhattan Center, New York
DG 447 737-2

Sibelius: Symphony No. 4
Berlin Philharmonic
Jesus-Christus-Kirche, Berlin (Dahlem)
DG 445 865-2

Wagner: *Der fliegende Holländer*
Deborah Voigt, Brigitta Svendén, James Morris, Jan Hendrick Rootering, Ben Heppner, Paul Groves, Metropolitan Opera Orchestra and Chorus
Manhattan Center, New York
Sony S2K 66342

Bryn Terfel Arias: Mozart: *Le Nozze di Figaro:* "Non più andrai"; *Don Giovanni:* "Deh, vieni alla finestra," "Madamina! il catalogo è questo"; *Così fan tutte:* "Rivolgete a lui lo sguardo"; *Der Zauberflöte:* "Der Vogelfänger bin ich, ja"; Wagner: *Tannhäuser,* "O du mein holder Abendstern"; *Der fliegende Holländer:* "Die Freist. ist um"; Offenbach, *Les Contes d'Hoffmann:* "Scintille diamant"; Gounod: *Faust,* Mephistopheles's serenade; Borodin: Prince Igor's aria; Donizetti: *Don Pasquale:* "Bella siccome un angelo"; Rossini, *La Cenerentola:* "Miei rampolli"; Verdi: *Macbeth:* "Perfidi! All'angelo contra v'unite!"; *Falstaff:* "L'Onore? Ladri!"
Metropolitan Opera Orchestra
Manhattan Center, New York
DG D112644

1995

Brahms: Symphony No. 2
Vienna Philharmonic
Grosser Musikvereinssaal, Vienna
Live performance
DG 449-829-2

Debussy: *Vasnier Songbook/Ariettes oubliées/ Cinq poèmes de Baudelaire*
Dawn Upshaw; Levine, piano
Manhattan Center, New York
Sony SK 67190

Strauss: *Don Quixote*
Jerry Grossman, cello; Michael Ouzounian, viola; Metropolitan Opera Orchestra
Manhattan Center, New York
DG 447 762-2

Tod und Verklärung
Metropolitan Opera Orchestra
Manhattan Center, New York
DG 447 762-2

Verdi: *Hymn of the Nations*
Luciano Pavarotti, Philharmonia Orchestra and Chorus
The Colosseum, Watford, England
Decca 448 700 2

★ *Simon Boccanegra*

Wagner: *Götterdämmerung:* Siegfried's Funeral Music; *Lohengrin:* Prelude to Act 1; *Die Meistersinger:* Prelude to Act 3; *Parsifal:* Good Friday Music;

Siegfried: Forest Murmurs; *Tristan und Isolde:* Prelude and *Liebestod; Die Walküre:* Ride of the Valkyries
Metropolitan Opera Orchestra
Manhattan Center, New York
DG 447 764-2

1996

25th Anniversary Gala ★ and CD.
 Excerpts. Live recording at the Met,
 April 27. Bizet, *Les Pêcheurs de perles:*
 "Au fond du temple saint," Roberto
 Alagna, Bryn Terfel; Charpentier,
 Louise: "Depuis le jour," Renée Flem-
 ing; Gounod, *Faust:* Duet, Act 1, Plá-
 cido Domingo, Samuel Ramey; Lehár,
 Giuditta: "Meine Lippen, sie küssen so
 heiss," Ileana Cotrubas; Verdi, *Don
 Carlo:* "O don fatale!," Dolora Zajick;
 Mozart, *Don Giovanni;* Sextet, Act 2,
 Kiri Te Kanawa, Bryn Terfel, Renée
 Fleming, Jerry Hadley, Hei-Kyung
 Hong, Julien Robbins; Gounod, *Roméo
 et Juliette:* Waltz song, Ruth Ann Swen-
 son; J. Strauss, *Die Fledermaus:* Watch
 duet, Act 2, Karita Mattila, Håkan
 Hagegård; Massenet, *Werther:*
 "Pourquoi me réveiller?," Alfredo
 Kraus; Saint-Saëns, *Samson et Dalila:*
 "Mon coeur s'ouvre à ta voix," Grace
 Bumbry; Wagner, *Tannhäuser:* "Dich,
 teure Halle!," Deborah Voigt; Offen-
 bach, *La Périchole:*" Ah, quel dîner,"
 Frederica von Stade; R. Strauss, *Der
 Rosenkavalier:* Trio, Act 3, Anne Sofie
 von Otter, Heidi Grant Murphy,
 Renée Fleming; Spoken tribute
 [abridged]: Birgit Nilsson
Metropolitan Opera Orchestra and
 Chorus
DG 449 177-2

Verdi: *I Lombardi*
June Anderson, Luciano Pavarotti,
 Richard Leech, Samuel Ramey, Metro-
 politan Opera Orchestra and Chorus
Manhattan Center, New York
Decca 455 287-2

An Italian Songbook: Bellini, Donizetti,
 Rossini
Cecilia Bartoli, James Levine, piano
Margrave's Opera House, Bayreuth
Decca 455 513-2

1997

Beethoven: Piano Concertos 2 and 5
Evgeny Kissin, Philharmonia Orchestra
London SK 62926

Collections

Fantastic Levine: Orff: *Carmina Burana*
 (opening chorus), (1984); Holst: *The
 Planets,* "Jupiter" (beginning), (1989);
 Bartók: Concerto for Orchestra, First
 movement (beginning), (1989);
 Berlioz: *Symphonie fantastique,* Fifth
 movement (beginning), (1990); Saint-
 Saëns: Symphony No. 3, Second
 movement (beginning), (1986); Schumann: Symphony No. 3, Fifth movement, (1987); Wagner: *Siegfried,* Act 2,
 Forest Murmurs (1988); *Götterdämmerung,* Act 3, Siegfried's Funeral
 Music (1989); Ravel: *Daphnis et Chloé,*
 Part 3, Dance (1984); Smetana: *Má
 Vlast,* "Vltava" (beginning), (1986);
 Mozart: Symphony No. 23, First
 movement (beginning), (1986); Serenade No. 9, Fourth movement (beginning), (1982); Symphony No. 40,
 Fourth movement (1989). Special CD
 sampler for Japan, c. 1990
DG DC1 1041

James Levine Dirigent Volume 1 [JL con-
 ducts DG limited edition 427 028-2
 OP, only available in Europe]: Mozart:
 Eine kleine Nachtmusik (1982); Schu-
 bert: *Rosamunde* Overture and ballet
 pieces (1984); Smetana: *Má Vlast,*
 "Vltava" (1986);
Dukas: *The Sorcerer's Apprentice* (1986)

James Levine Dirigent Volume 2 [JL con-
 ducts DG limited edition 429 370-2
 OP, only available in Europe]: Mozart:
 Symphony No. 31 *(Paris),* (1985);

Mendelssohn: Overture, Nocturne, and Wedding March from the Incidental Music to *A Midsummer Night's Dream* (1984); Smetana: *The Bartered Bride,* Overture and three dances (1986); Verdi: *La Forza del Destino,* Overture (1988).

Maestro of the Met: James Levine and Friends: CD #1 Verdi: *La Forza del Destino,* Overture (1988); Donizetti: *L'Elisir d'Amore,* "Una furtiva lagrima" (1989); "Saria possible?" (1989); Puccini: *Manon Lescaut,* "Tu, tu, amore! Tu!" (1972), Madrigal (1992), "Sola, perduta, abbandonata" (1992); Wagner: *Die Walküre,* Ride of the Valkyries (1987), "Nicht sehre dich Sorge um mich" (1987), "Leb' wohl, du kühnes herrliches Kind" (1987); *Götterdämmerung,* Funeral March (1989), "Fliegt heim, ihr Raben" (1989). CD #2 Rossini: *L'Italiana in Algeri,* Overture (1988); Mozart: *Le Nozze di Figaro,* "Non so più" (1990), "Hai gia vinta la causa!" (1990), "Dove sono" (1990), "Deh vieni, non tardar" (1990); Donizetti: *Lucia di Lammermoor,* "Tombe degl'avi miei" (1988); Verdi: *La Traviata,* Prelude to Act 1 (1991), Brindisi (1991), "Parigi, o cara" (1991); Wagner: *Parsifal,* Good Friday Music (1992); Mussorgsky-Ravel: *Pictures at an Exhibition,* "The Great Gate of Kiev" (1992)
Metropolitan Opera Guild Historic Collection
James Levine 25th Anniversary Collection
Highlights of Metropolitan broadcasts, 1971–1996
Available from the Metropolitan Opera
Met 21 3CDs

Laserdiscs and Video Recordings

The first number given is a laserdisc. If there is an alternative tape edition, that number follows.

Berlioz: *Les Troyens*
Tatiana Troyanos, Jessye Norman, Plácido Domingo, Allan Monk, Paul Plishka, Metropolitan Opera Orchestra and Chorus
1983
Pioneer PA 85-137 / tape 9736 12509-3

Bizet: *Carmen*
Agnes Baltsa, Leona Mitchell, José Carreras, Samuel Ramey, Metropolitan Opera Orchestra and Chorus
1987
GD 072 509-1 / tape 072 509-3

Corigliano: *The Ghosts of Versailles*
Teresa Stratas, Marilyn Horne, Graham Clark, Håkan Hagegård, Metropolitan Opera Orchestra and Chorus
1992
DG 440 072 530-1 OP / tape 072 530-3 OP

Donizetti: *L'Elisir d'Amore*
Kathleen Battle, Luciano Pavarotti, Juan Pons, Enzo Dara, Metropolitan Opera Orchestra and Chorus
1991
DG 072 532-1 / tape 072 532-3

Mozart: Mozart: *La Clemenza di Tito* film soundtrack (Ponnelle)
Eric Tappy, Tatiana Troyanos, Carol Neblett, Anne Howells, Catherine Malfitano, Kurt Rydl, Vienna Philharmonic, Vienna State Opera Chorus
Musikvereinssaal, Vienna
1980
DG 072 507-1 / tape 072 507-3

Idomeneo
Ileana Cotrubas, Hildegard Behrens, Frederica von Stade, Luciano Pavarotti, John Alexander, Metropolitan Opera Orchestra and Chorus
1982
Pioneer PA 85-134 / tape 9736 02372-3

Die Zauberflöte
Kathleen Battle, Luciana Serra, Barbara

Kilduff, Francisco Araiza, Manfred Hemm, Kurt Moll, Heinz Zednik, Andreas Schmidt, Metropolitan Opera Orchestra and Chorus
1991
DG 072 524-1 / tape 072 524-3

Puccini: *La Bohème*
Teresa Stratas, Renata Scotto, José Carreras, Richard Stilwell, Allan Monk, James Morris, Metropolitan Opera Orchestra and Chorus
1982
Pioneer PA 85-135 / tape 9736 02365-3

Manon Lescaut
Renata Scotto, Plácido Domingo, Pablo Elvira, Renato Capecchi, Metropolitan Opera Orchestra and Chorus
1980
Pioneer PA 88-215 / tape 9736 12554-3

Turandot
Eva Marton, Leona Mitchell, Plácido Domingo, Paul Plishka, Metropolitan Opera Orchestra and Chorus
1987
DG 072 510-1 / tape 072 510-3

J. Strauss: *Die Fledermaus* (Act 2)
Barbara Daniels, Anne Sofie von Otter, Barbara Kilduff, Hermann Prey, Gottfried Hornik, celebrity guests, Metropolitan Opera Orchestra and Chorus
Metropolitan Opera Gala
1991
DG 072-528-1 / tape 072 528-3

R. Strauss: *Ariadne auf Naxos*
Jessye Norman, Kathleen Battle, Tatiana Troyanos, James King, Franz Ferdinand Nentwig, Metropolitan Opera Orchestra and Chorus
1988
DG 072 511-1 OP / tape 072 511-3

Elektra
Birgit Nilsson, Leonie Rysanek, Mignon Dunn, Robert Nagy, Donald McIntyre, Metropolitan Opera Orchestra and Chorus
1980
Pioneer PA 88-221 / tape 9736 12611-3

Verdi: *Aida*
Aprile Millo, Dolora Zajick, Plácido Domingo, Sherrill Milnes, Paata Burchuladze, Dimitri Kavrakos, Metropolitan Opera Orchestra and Chorus
1989
DG 072 516-1 / tape 072 516-3

Don Carlo
Mirella Freni, Grace Bumbry, Plácido Domingo, Louis Quilico, Nicolai Ghiaurov, Ferruccio Furlanetto, Metropolitan Opera Orchestra and Chorus
1983
Pioneer PA 84-075 / tape 9736 02363-3

Ernani
Leona Mitchell, Luciano Pavarotti, Sherrill Milnes, Ruggero Raimondi, Metropolitan Opera Orchestra and Chorus
1983
Pioneer PA 92-449 / tape 9736 12507-3

Falstaff
Mirella Freni, Marilyn Horne, Barbara Bonney, Paul Plishka, Bruno Pola, Frank Lopardo, Metropolitan Opera Orchestra and Chorus
1992
DG 072 534-1 / tape 072 534-3

Il Trovatore
Eva Marton, Dolora Zajick, Luciano Pavarotti, Sherrill Milnes, Metropolitan Opera Orchestra and Chorus
1988
DG 072 513-1 / tape 072 513-3

La Forza del Destino
Leontyne Price, Giuseppe Giacomini, Leo Nucci, Metropolitan Opera Orchestra and Chorus
1984
Pioneer PA 88-227 / tape 9736 12607-3

Otello (Act 3)
Mirella Freni, Plácido Domingo, Justino
Diaz, Paul Plishka, Metropolitan
Opera Orchestra and Chorus
Metropolitan Opera Gala
1991
DG 072 528-1 / tape 072 518-3

Rigoletto (Act 3)
Cheryl Studer, Brigitta Svenden, Luciano
Pavarotti, Leo Nucci, Nicolai Ghiau-
rov, Metropolitan Opera Orchestra and
Chorus
Metropolitan Opera Gala
1991
DG 072 528-1 / tape 072 528-2

Simon Boccanegra
Anna Tomowa-Sintow, Sherrill Milnes,
Vasile Moldoveneau, Paul Plishka,
Metropolitan Opera Orchestra and
Chorus
1984
Pioneer PA 88-225 / tape 9736 12609-3

Kiri Te Kanawa, Plácido Domingo,
Vladimir Chernov, Robert Lloyd, Metropolitan Opera Orchestra and Chorus
1995
DG 440 072545-1 / tape 440 0725545-3

Stiffelio
Sharon Sweet, Plácido Domingo,
Vladimir Chernov, Paul Plishka, Met-
ropolitan Opera Orchestra and Chorus
1993
DG 073 216-1 / tape 072 216-3

Un Ballo in Maschera
Aprile Millo, Florence Quivar, Harolyn
Blackwell, Luciano Pavarotti, Leo Nucci,
Metropolitan Orchestra and Chorus
1991
DG 072 525-1/ tape 072 525-3

Wagner: *Lohengrin*
Eva Marton, Leonie Rysanek, Peter Hofmann, Leif Roar, John Macurdy, Metropolitan Opera Orchestra and Chorus
1986
Pioneer PA 88-224 / tape 9736 12610-3

Parsifal
Waltraud Meier, Siegfried Jerusalem,
Kurt Moll, Bernd Weikl, Franz
Mazura, Jan-Hendrik Rootering, Met-
ropolitan Opera Orchestra and Chorus
1992
DG 072 535-1 / tape 072 535-3

Tannhäuser
Eva Marton, Tatiana Troyanos, Richard
Cassilly, Bernd Weikl, John Macurdy,
Metropolitan Opera Orchestra, Cho-
rus, and Ballet
1982
Pioneer PA 86-159 / tape 9736 12509-3

Der Ring des Nibelungen
The *Ring* as a boxed set is DG 072
522-1 / tape 072 522-3.

Das Rheingold: Christa Ludwig, Mari
Anne Haggander, James Morris,
Siegfried Jerusalem, Ekkehard
Wlaschiha, Heinz Zednik, Jan-Hen-
drik Rootering, Matti Salminen, Met-
ropolitan Opera Orchestra
1990
DG 072 518-1 / tape 072 518-3

Die Walküre: Hildegard Behrens, Jessye
Norman, Christa Ludwig, Gary Lakes,
James Morris, Kurt Moll, Metropoli-
tan Opera Orchestra
1989
DG 072 519-1 / tape 072 519-3

Siegfried: Hildegard Behrens, Brigitta
Svenden, Dawn Upshaw, Siegfried
Jerusalem, James Morris, Heinz Zednik, Ekkehard Wlaschiha, Matti Salminen, Metropolitan Opera Orchestra
1990
DG 072 520-1 / tape 072 520-3

Götterdämmerung: Hildegard Behrens,
Christa Ludwig, Hanna Lisowska,
Siegfried Jerusalem, Matti Salminen,
Anthony Raffell, Ekkehard Wlaschiha,
Metropolitan Opera Orchestra and
Chorus

1990
DG 072 521-1 / tape 072 521-3

The *Ring* at the Metropolitan Opera contains the entry of the gods into Valhalla from *Das Rheingold,* the close of Act 1, and Brünnhilde's battle cry from *Die Walküre,* the death of Fafner from *Siegfried,* and the choral scene from Act 2 and the finale of Act 3 of *Götterdämmerung.*
DG 073 217-3

Zandonai: *Francesca da Rimini*
Renata Scotto, Plácido Domingo, Cornell MacNeil, Metropolitan Opera Orchestra and Chorus
1984
Pioneer PA 87-180 / tape 9736 12553-3

Released on Tape Only

Verdi: *La Traviata* film soundtrack (Zeffirelli) 1983
Stratas, Domingo, MacNeil, Metropolitan Opera Orchestra and Chorus 1983
Elektra tape MCA 80048

Collections

Mozart/Beethoven Quintets
1986
DG 072 2184 OP
For details see the CD listing

Battle and Norman Sing Spirituals
1990
For details see the CD listing
DG 072 249-1 OP / tape 072 249-3

Plácido Domingo. *Homage to Seville:* Beethoven: *Fidelio,* "Gott! Welch Dunkel hier!"; Bizet: *Carmen,* "La fleur que tu m'avais jetée"; "C'est toi! C'est moi!"; Mozart: *Don Giovanni,* "Fin ch'han dal vino"; Penella: *El Gato Montes,* "Me llamabas, Rafaeliyo?"; Rossini, *Barbiere di Siviglia,* Almaviva-Figaro duet (Act 1); Verdi: *La Forza del Destino,* "La vita e inferno all'infelice!" and "O, tu che in seno agli angeli"

Vienna Symphony
1982
DG 072 287-1 / tape 072 287-3

Meet the Met: Scenes from laserdiscs listed here. Mozart: *Die Zauberflöte;* Puccini: *Turandot;* J. Strauss: *Die Fledermaus;* R. Strauss: *Ariadne auf Naxos;* Rossini: *Il Barbiere di Siviglia;* Verdi: *Aida; Un Ballo in Maschera, Otello; Il Trovatore;* Wagner: *Götterdämmerung*
DG 072-294-1 / tape 072 294-3

Metropolitan Centennial Gala 1983
Levine conducts Smetana: *The Bartered Bride,* Overture; Puccini: *Turandot,* "In questa reggia," Eva Marton; *Madama Butterfly,* Final duet Act 1, Leona Mitchell, Giuliano Ciannella; Mozart: *Le Nozze di Figaro,* "Dove sono," Kiri Te Kanawa; Verdi: *Otello,* "Dio! mi potevi scagliar," James McCracken; "Già nella notte densa," Mirella Freni, Plácido Domingo; *Ernani,* "Ernani, involami," Anna Tomowa-Sintow; *Un Ballo in Maschera,* Duet Act 2, Leontyne Price, Luciano Pavarotti; Donizetti: *L'Elisir d'Amore,* "Una furtiva lagrima," Nicolai Gedda; R. Strauss: *Der Rosenkavalier,* Final trio, Kathleen Battle, Elisabeth Söderström, Frederica von Stade; Giordano: *Andrea Chénier,* Final duet, Monserrat Caballé, José Carreras; Gounod: *Faust,* Final trio, Katia Ricciarelli, William Lewis, Nicolai Ghiaurov; Rossini, *L'Italiana in Algeri,* Finale Act 1, Diane Kesling, Edda Moser, Gail Dubinbaum, David Randall, John Darrenkamp, Sesto Bruscantini, Ara Berberian; Saint-Saëns: *Samson et Dalila,* "Mon coeur s'ouvre à ta voix," Marilyn Horne, "Bacchanale"; Wagner, *Tristan und Isolde,* Isolde's Narrative and Curse, Birgit Nilsson; "Happy Birthday to You." Other numbers are conducted by Richard Bonynge, David Stivender, Jeffrey Tate, Leonard Bernstein, Sir John Pritchard, and Thomas Fulton.

Metropolitan Opera Orchestra
Pioneer PA 84-049 / tape 9736 02364-3

Metropolitan Opera Gala: 25 Years at Lincoln Center 1991
J. Strauss: *Die Fledermaus* (Act 2), Barbara Daniels, Anne Sofie von Otter, Barbara Kilduff, Hermann Prey, Dwayne Croft. Verdi: *Rigoletto* (Act 3), Cheryl Studer, Brigitta Svenden, Luciano Pavarotti, Leo Nucci, Nicolai Ghiaurov; *Otello* (Act 3), Mirella Freni, Plácido Domingo, Justino Diaz, Paul Plishka, Metropolitan Opera Orchestra
DG 072 528-1 / tape 072 528-3

Pavarotti recital: Bellini: "Dolente immagine di fille mia," "Malinconia, ninfa gentile," "Vanne, o rosa fortunata," "Belle Nice, che d'amore," "Ma rendi pur contento," "Vaga luna"; Denza: "Occhi di fata"; Flotow: *Martha:* "M'appari tutt'amor"; Mascagni: "La Serenata"; Massenet: *Werther,* "Pourquoi me réveiller?"; Mozart: *Così fan tutte,* "Un'aura amorosa"; Puccini: *Tosca,* "Recondita armonia"; *Turandot,* "Nessun dorma"; Respighi: "Nevicata, Pioggia, Nebbie"; Rossini: "La Promessa," "La Danza"; Sibella: "La Girometta"; Tosti: "Marechiare"; Verdi: *I Lombardi,* "La mia letizia infondere"
1988 Decca 071 219-1

James Levine, 25th Anniversary Gala Recorded Live, April 27, 1996. The selections are in the order in which they were heard at the gala, but were usually separated by other material.
Wagner, *Rienzi:* Overture; *Tannhäuser:* "Dich, teure Halle," Deborah Voigt; Verdi, *Don Carlo:* "Restate! O signor," Thomas Hampson, Roberto Scandiuzzi; Charpentier, *Louise:* "Depuis le jour," Renée Fleming; Mascagni, *L'Amico Fritz:* Cherry duet, Angela Gheorghiu, Roberto Alagna; Lehár, *Giuditta:*

"Meine Lippen, sie küssen so heiss," Ileana Cotrubas; Verdi, *Don Carlo:* "O don fatale!," Dolora Zajick; Wagner, *Die Walküre:* "Loge hör!," James Morris [who began somewhat earlier with "Leb wohl!"]; Bizet, *Les Pêcheurs de perles:* "Au fond du temple saint," Roberto Alagna, Bryn Terfel; Gounod, *Roméo et Juliette:* Waltz song, Ruth Ann Swenson; J. Strauss, *Die Fledermaus:* Watch duet, Karita Mattila, Håkan Hagegård; Wagner, *Tristan und Isolde:* Isolde's Narrative, Waltraud Meier; Verdi, *Luisa Miller:* "Quando le sere al placido," Carlo Bergonzi; Tchaikovsky, *Eugene Onegin:* Final scene, Catherine Malfitano, Dwayne Croft; Saint-Saëns, *Samson et Dalila:* "Mon coeur s'ouvre à ta voix," Grace Bumbry; Offenbach, *La Périchole:* "Ah, quel dîner," Frederica von Stade; R. Strauss, *Der Rosenkavalier:* Trio, Act 3, Renée Fleming, Anne Sofie von Otter, Heidi Grant Murphy; Gounod, *Faust:* Duet, Act 1, Plácido Domingo, Samuel Ramey; Mozart, *Don Giovanni:* Sextet, Act 2, Kiri Te Kanawa, Bryn Terfel, Renée Fleming, Hei-Kyung Hong, Jerry Hadley, Julien Robbins; Spoken tribute: Birgit Nilsson [abridged]; Wagner, *Die Meistersinger:* Final scene [abridged]
Metropolitan Opera Orchestra and Chorus
Vol. 1 DG 440 072 551-1

An equal amount of material is theoretically available for release as Vol. 2.
Recorded but not released on laserdisc: Rossini, *Barber of Seville:* "Largo al factotum," Vladimir Chernov; Mozart, *Le Nozze di Figaro:* "Voi che sapete," Frederica von Stade; Cilea, *L'Arlesiana:* "Il Lamento di Federico," Richard Leech; Corigliano, *The Ghosts of Versailles:* Quartet, Act 1, Hei-Kyung Hong, Wendy White, Christian Goerke, Håkan Hagegård; Verdi, *Un Ballo in Maschera:* Trio, Act 2, Ghena Dimitrova,

Franco Farina, Juan Pons; Dvořák, *Rusalka:* "Song to the Moon," Gabriela Beňačková; Verdi, *Ernani:* Trio, Act 4, Deborah Voigt, Plácido Domingo, Roberto Scandiuzzi; Massenet, *Werther* aria by Alfredo Kraus is on the CD; Berlioz, *La Damnation de Faust: "D'Amour l'ardente flamme,"* Jessye Norman; Mozart, *Le Nozze di Figaro:* "Deh vieni, non tardar," Dawn Upshaw; Lehár, *The Land of Smiles:* "Dein ist mein ganzes Herz," Jerry Hadley; Offenbach, *Les Contes de Hoffmann:* Septet, Act 3, Florence Quivar, Rosalind Elias, Alfredo Kraus, Charles Anthony, James Courtney, Paul Plishka, Metropolitan Opera Chorus; Verdi, *La Forza del Destino:* "Madre, pietosa Vergine," Sharon Sweet; Puccini, *Turandot:* "In questa reggia," Gwyneth Jones; Verdi, *Nabucco:* "Va pensiero," Samuel Ramey and Metropolitan Opera Chorus; *I Lombardi:* "Qual voluttà transcorrere," June Anderson, Carlo Bergonzi, Ferruccio Furlanetto; Mozart, *Così fan tutte:* "Prenderò quel brunettino," Carol Vaness, Suzanne Mentzer; Verdi, *Un Ballo in Maschera:* "Morrò, ma prima in grazia," Aprile Millo; Gershwin, *Porgy and Bess:* "My Man's Gone Now," Maria Ewing; Wagner, *Götterdämmerung:* Immolation Scene, Jane Eaglen; Mozart, *Don Giovanni:* "Mi tradì quell'alma ingrata," Kiri Te Kanawa

The Levine Recordings by Composer

\# indicates a work available both on laserdiscs and CD.

★ indicates a work available on laserdiscs only.

The date following the slash / is that of the laserdisc.

Babbitt: *Correspondences* for Strings and Tape, 1990

Bach: *Brandenburg* Concerto Nos. 2 and 5, 1977
Cantata No. 202, 1977

Bartók: Concerto for Orchestra, 1989
Music for Strings, Percussion, and Celesta, 1989

Beethoven: "Ah, Perfido" (concert aria), 1970
"An die Hoffnung," 1970
Concertos for Piano and Orchestra (5), 1983
Concerto Nos. 2 and 5, 1997
★ *Fidelio,* "Gott! Welch Dunkel hier!" and "In des Lebens Frülingstagen," 1982
Missa Solemnis, 1991
Quintet for Piano and Winds, 1986
Sechs Geistliche Lieder, Op. 48, 1990
Sonatas for Cello and Piano (5), 1976
Symphony No. 3 *(Eroica),* 1993

Bellini: Concerto for Oboe, 1989
Norma, 1974/1979
"Mira, o Norma," 1982
Sinfonia, 1982
★ Songs (6), 1988; (9), 1996
"Vaga luna che inargenti" (separate from the above group), 1987

Berg: Concerto for Violin, 1992
Lulu Suite, 1993
Three Pieces for Orchestra, 1986/1993
Wozzeck [excerpts], 1993
Scenes 1–5, 1985

Berlioz: "Absence," 1970
Benvenuto Cellini Overture, 1991
La Damnation de Faust, "D'Amour l'ardente flamme," 1996 (unreleased)
Le Corsaire Overture, 1991
Les Nuits d'été, 1988
★ *Les Troyens,* 1983
 Royal Hunt and Storm, 1990
 Act 5, Scenes 2/3, 1984
Requiem, 1989
Roman Carnival Overture, 1991
Roméo et Juliette, 1988
Symphonie fantastique, 1990

Bernstein: *Candide* Overture, 1987

Bizet: ★ *Carmen,* 1987
★ "La fleur que tu m'avais jetée;" duet "C'est toi! C'est moi!", 1982
Les Pêcheurs de perles, "Au fond du temple saint," 1996

Borodin: Igor's aria *(Prince Igor),* 1994

Brahms: A German Requiem, 1983
Alto Rhapsody, 1992
Concerto No. 1 for Piano and Orchestra, 1983
Songs (8), 1983
Symphony No. 1, 1975/1993
Symphony No. 2, 1976/1995
Symphony No. 3, 1976/1992
Symphony No. 4, 1976/1994
Tragic Overture, 1992

Bruch: *Kol Nidre,* 1988

Cage: *Atlas eclipticalis,* 1990

Carter: Variations for Orchestra, 1990

Charpentier: # *Louise,* "Depuis le jour," 1996

Cilea: *Andrea Lecouvreur,* 1977
L'Arlesiana, "Il Lamento di Federico," 1996 (unreleased)

Corigliano: ★ *The Ghosts of Versailles,* Quartet, Act 1, 1996 (unreleased)

Dargomijsky: "Romance," 1970

Debussy: *Image pour orchestre,* 1992
Pelléas et Mélisande, Act 2, Scenes 2/3, 1988
Sonata for Cello, 1974
Songs (5), 1990/1995
"Trois Chansons de Bilitis," 1970
Vasnier Songbook, etc., 1995

Denza: ★ "Occhi di fata," 1988

Donizetti: # *L'Elisir d'Amore,* 1989/1991
"Caro elisir," "Trallarallara," and "Esulti pur la barbara," 1988
★ "Una furtiva lagrima," 1983
Lucia di Lammermoor, "Tombe degl'avi

miei" and "Fra poco a me ricovero," 1988
Don Pasquale, "Bella siccome un angelo," 1994
"Cheti, cheti, immantinente," 1996 (unreleased)
Songs (5), 1996

Dukas: *The Sorcerer's Apprentice,* 1986

Dvořák: Concerto for Cello, 1974
Concerto for Violin, 1986
Rusalka, "Song to the Moon," 1996 (unreleased)
Symphony No. 7, 1984
Symphony No. 8, 1990
Symphony No. 9 *(From the New World),* 1981/1994

Elgar: *Enigma* Variations, 1992

Eller: Bassoon Sonata
Schoenbach, bassoon
CSP AMS 642
[Listed in the *Schwann Catalog* as James Levine, piano. The James Levine with whom we are concerned here insists he is not the pianist in this performance.]

Fauré: *Berceuse,* 1992
Songs (4), 1984

Flotow: ★ *Martha,* "M'appari tutt'amor," 1988

Gershwin: *An American in Paris, Cuban* Overture, 1990
Porgy and Bess Suite, 1990
"My Man's Gone Now," 1996 (unreleased)
Rhapsody in Blue, 1990

Giordano: *Andrea Chénier,* 1976
★ Final Duet, 1983
"Nemico della patria," 1996 (unreleased)

Glinka: "Doubt," 1970
"Vain Temptation," 1970

Gounod: # *Faust,* Duet, Act 1, 1996
Mephistopheles's serenade, 1994
★ *Faust,* Final scene, 1983

Roméo et Juliette duets "Va, je t'ai pardonnée" and "Nuit d'hyménée," 1988
Juliette's Waltz Song, 1996

Hahn: "Si mes vers," 1970

Handel: *Rinaldo* duet "Fermati! No,
crudel!", 1982
Rodelinda, "Vivi, tiranno!", 1982
"O Had I Jubal's Lyre," 1984

★ "Happy Birthday to You," 1983

Haydn: *Die Schöpfung,* 1987
Paukenmesse, 1991

Holst: *The Planets,* 1989

Ives: The Unanswered Question, 1987

Joplin: Piano Rags (12), 1976

Lalo: Concerto for Cello, 1988

Lehár: # *Giuditta,* "Meine Lippen, sie
küssen so heiss," 1996
The Land of Smiles, "Dein ist mein ganzes
Herz," 1996 (unreleased)
The Merry Widow, Duet "Lippen
schweigen," 1988

Liszt: Songs (5), 1970

Mahler: *Das Lied von der Erde,* 1992
Symphony No. 1, 1974
Symphony No. 3, 1975
Symphony No. 4, 1974
Symphony No. 5, 1977
Symphony No. 6, 1977
Symphony No. 7, 1980
Symphony No. 8, 1979
Symphony No. 9, 1980
Symphony No. 10, 1978

Mascagni: *Cavalleria Rusticana,* 1978
★ "La Serenata," 1988
L'Amico Fritz: Cherry duet, 1996

Massenet: Elegy, 1970
"Meditation," 1992
Werther, "Pourquoi me réveiller?",
1996/1988

Mendelssohn: "Bei der Wiege," 1984
Incidental Music to *A Midsummer Night's*

Dream, 1984
"Neue Liebe," 1984
Sonata for Cello and Piano, 1974
Symphony No. 3 *(Scotch),* 1988
Symphony No. 4 *(Italian),* 1988

Meyerbeer: *Les Huguenots,* "Non!—non,
non, non, non, non! Vous n'avez
jamais, je gage," 1982

Monsigny: "La Sagesse est un trésor,"
1970

Mozart: Arias
Kathleen Battle, 1993
Concerto for Oboe, 1989
Concertos for Violin, K. 207, 211, 218;
Adagio, K. 262; and Rondos, K. 261a
and 373, 1982
Concertos for Violin, K. 216 and 219,
1985
Così fan tutte, 1988
Duet "Ah, guarda, sorella," 1982
★ "Un'aura amorosa," 1988
"Rivolgete a lui lo sguardo," 1994
"Prenderò quel brunettino," 1996 (unre-
leased)
Der Zauberflöte, 1980/1991
"Der Vogelfänger bin ich, ja," 1994
★ *Don Giovanni,* "Fin ch'han dal vino,"
1982
"Madamina, il catalogo è questo," 1994
"Deh, vieni alla finestra," 1994
Sextet, Act 2, 1996
"Mi tradì quell'alma ingrata," 1996
(unreleased)
Eine kleine Nachtmusik, 1982
Great Mass in C Minor, 1987
Idomeneo, 1994–95/1982
Act 2, Scenes 2/5, 1991
★ *La Clemenza di Tito,* 1980
Kegelstatt Trio, 1991
Krönungsmesse, 1991
Le Nozze di Figaro 1990; "Dove sono,"
1982, ★ 1983
"Non più andrai," 1994
"Voi che sapete," 1996 (unreleased)
"Deh vieni, non tardar," 1996 (unre-
leased)
Posthorn Serenade, 1982

Quartet for Piano and Strings, K. 478, 1977
Quintet for Piano and Winds, K. 452, 1977/1986
"Ridente la calma," 1984
Sonata for Two Pianos, K. 448, 1987
Symphonies Early, 1989
Nos. 28/29/30, 1984
Nos. 25/26/27/31/32/34, 1985
Nos. 21/22/23/24/33/38/39, 1986
Nos. 35/36 [No. 37], 1987
Nos. 40/41, 1981/1989

Mussorgsky/Ravel: *Pictures at an Exhibition,* 1992

Offenbach: *La Barbe bleue,* "Laughing Song," 1970
Les Contes d'Hoffmann, "Scintille diamant," 1994
Septet, Act 3, 1996 (unreleased)
La Périchole, "Ah, quel dîner," 1996

Orff: *Carmina Burana,* 1984

Penella: ★ *El Gato Montes* duet "Me Ilamabas, Rafaeliyo?", 1982

Poulenc: Elégie pour cor et piano, Sextuor pour piano, flute, hautbois, clarinette, basson et cor, Sonate pour clarinette et piano, Sonate pour flûte et piano, Trio pour piano, hautbois et basson, 1989

Prokofiev: Sonata for Cello and Piano, 1974
Symphony No. 1, 1992
Symphony No. 5, 1992

Puccini: # *La Bohème,* 1980/1982, Act 1, Finale 1977
La Rondine aria, 1982
Madama Butterfly, Flower Duet, 1982
★ Act 1, Final duet 1983
Manon Lescaut, 1992/1980
Sola, perduta, abbandonata 1984
Tosca, 1980
"Vissi d'arte," 1987
★ "Recondita armonia," 1988

★ *Turandot,* 1987
"Nessun dorma," 1987/★ 1988
"In questa reggia," ★ 1983, 1996 (unreleased)

Purcell: Songs (3), 1984

Ravel: *Daphnis et Chloé,* 1984

Respighi: ★ Songs (3), 1988

Rihm: *Gesundene Zeit,* 1992

Rossini: *Il Barbieri di Siviglia, 1975*
★ Almaviva/Figaro duet (Act 1), 1982
"Largo al factotum," 1996 (unreleased)
L'Assedio di Corinto, "Non temer, d'un basso affetto," 1982
La Cenerentola, "Miei rampolli," 1994
★ "La Danza," 1988
★ *L'Italiana in Algeri,* Finale Act 1, 1983
★ "La Promessa," 1988
Songs (6), 1996

Saint-Saëns: Concerto for Cello, 1988
Samson et Dalila, "Mon coeur s'ouvre à ta voix," 1996/1983/1988
★ "Bacchanale," 1983
Symphony No. 3, 1986

Sarasate: *Fantasie du concert sur les motifs de l'opéra Carmen,* 1992
Zigeunerweisen, 1992

Schoenberg: *Brettl-Lieder,* 1990
Erwartung, 1989
Five Pieces for Orchestra, 1986
Verklärte Nacht, 1991

Schubert: Arpeggione Sonata, 1974
Die schöne Müllerin, 1992
Overture and Ballet music from *Rosamunde,* 1984
Quintet for Piano and Strings *(Trout),* 1990
Songs, 1985
Symphony No. 8, 1993
Symphony No. 9, 1983
Die Winterreise, 1987

Schuller: *Spectra,* 1990

Schumann: *Manfred* Overture, 1991
Piano Quintet, 1980
Symphony No. 1 1978/1991
Symphony No. 2, 1977/1987
Symphony No. 3, 1978/1987
Symphony No. 4, 1978/1991

Sibelius: Concerto for Violin, 1986
Finlandia, 1991
Symphony No. 2, 1991
Symphony No. 4, 1994
Symphony No. 5, 1992
Valse triste, 1991

Sibella: ★ "La Girometta," 1988

Smetana: *The Bartered Bride* dances, 1986
★ Overture, 1978/1983
Má Vlast, 1986
Spirituals
1984, 1990

Stradella: "Per Pietà" 1970

J. Strauss: *Die Fledermaus* ★ (Act 2), 1991
  # Watch duet, Act 2, 1996

R. Strauss: *Ariadne auf Naxos,* 1986/1988
  Prologue, Finale, 1995
Concerto for Oboe, 1989
Death and Transfiguration, 1995
★*Der Rosenkavalier,* Final trio Act 3, 1983
  # 1996
Don Quixote, 1995
★ *Elektra,* 1980
Four Last Songs, 1970/1989/1995
Metamorphosen, 1991
Songs (3), 1984

Stravinsky: *Le Sacre du Printemps,* 1992
Les Noces, 1975
L'Histoire du soldat Suite, 1975
Oedipux Rex, 1991
Petrouchka, 1977
Symphony of Psalms, 1989

★ Swedish song: "I Remember When I
  Was Seventeen," 1983

Tartini/Zandonai: *Devil's Trill* Sonata,
  1992

Tchaikovsky: Ballet music *(Nutcracker,*
  Sleeping Beauty, Swan Lake), 1992
Eugene Onegin, 1987
  ★Final scene, 1996
"None But the Lonely Heart," 1970
Symphony No. 6 *(Pathétique),* 1984

Tosti: "Marechiare," 1987/★ 1988

Verdi: # *Aida,* 1990/1989
  "Silenzio! Aida verso noi s'avanza,"
  1982
  Ballet music, 1992
Don Carlo, 1992/1983
  "Elle ne m'aime pas," 1987
  Ballet music, 1992
  ★ "Restate! O signor," 1996
  # "O don fatale!," 1996
★ *Ernani,* 1983
  ★"Ernani, involami," 1983
  Trio, Act 4, 1996
  (unreleased)
★*Falstaff,* 1992
  "L'Onore? Ladri!", 1994
  Act 3, Scene 2, 1986
Giovanna d'Arco, 1973
Hymn of the Nations, 1995
I Lombardi, 1996
  ★ "La mia letizia infondere," 1988
  "Qual voluttà trascorrere" 1996
  (unreleased)
I Vespri Siciliani, 1973
  Overture, 1982
  Ballet music, 1992
  Act 4, 1974
Il Trovatore, 1991/1988
La Forza del Destino, 1976/1966
  1984
  ★ "La vita è inferno all'infelice!" and
  "O, tu che in seno agli angeli," 1982
  "Madre, pietosa Vergine," 1996
  (unreleased)
La Traviata, 1991/1983
Luisa Miller, 1991
  ★ "Quando le sere al placido," 1996

Act 2, Scene 3, 1979
Macbeth ballet music, 1992
"Perfidi! All'angelo contra v'unite!", 1994
Nabucco, "Va, pensiero," 1996 (unreleased)
Otello, 1978/★1991
  Act 1 Final duet, 1983
  ★"Dio! mi potevi scagliar," 1983
  Ballet music, 1992
Rigoletto, 1993 (in progress)
  ★ Act 3, 1991
★ *Simon Boccanegra,* 1984/1995
★ *Stiffelio,* 1993
★ *Un Ballo in Maschera,* 1991
  ★ Act 2 duet, 1983/1996 (unreleased)
  "Morrò, ma prima in grazia," 1996 (unreleased)

Wagner: *Der fliegende Holländer,* 1994
  Overture, 1991
"Die Frist um ist," 1994
Die Meistersinger Prelude, 1991
  ★ Finale, 1996
★ *Lohengrin,* 1986
  Prelude to Act 3, 1991
Parsifal, 1985/1992
  LD, 1992

Act 2, Duet, 1979
Rienzi # Overture, 1991/1996
Der Ring des Nibelungen
Das Rheingold, 1988/1990
Die Walküre 1987/1989
  ★ "Loge hör!", 1996
#*Siegfried,* 1988/1990
Götterdämmerung, 1989/1990
  Immolation scene, 1996 (unreleased)
  Siegfried Idyll, 1991
★ *Tannhäuser,* 1982
  Overture and Venusberg Music, 1991
  #"Dich, teure Halle," 1996
  "O du mein holder Abendstern," 1994
★ *Tristan und Isolde,* Isolde's Narrative and Curse, 1983/★ 1996
Wesendonk Songs, 1992 (unreleased)

Webern: Three Little Pieces, 1974
Six Pieces for Orchestra, 1986

Wieniawski: *Légende,* 1992

Wolf: From the *Italienisches Liederbuch,* 1990
From the *Spanisches Liederbuch,* 1990

Zandonai: ★ *Francesca da Rimini,* 1984

The Levine Met Repertory

This is a concise guide to the availability (actual or potential) of Levine's Metropolitan Opera repertory on video and sound recordings from the theater. Many of these works also exist in commercial recordings that are not necessarily based on Metropolitan Opera performances. When such duplication exists, the opera is marked CR. The list is founded on the assumption that the preferred format is video and hence omits broadcast duplication of works that exist in a video edition.

L&T = available commercially on laserdiscs and tape
TV = date of yet unreleased TV performances
B = dates of yet unreleased broadcast performances of works unavailable on TV
CR = commercial recording of TV and B items with date

Aida L&T CR 1990
Andrea Chénier TV 23 April 97 CR 1977
Ariadne auf Naxos L&T CR 1986
Il Barbiere di Siviglia B 7 April 73 CR 1975
The Bartered Bride TV 21 Nov. 78
La Bohème L&T CR 1980
Carmen L&T
Cavalleria Rusticana TV 6 April 78 CR 1978
La Cenerentola B 24 Jan. 98
La Clemenza di Tito L&T B 14 Feb. 87/20 April 94 [The laserdisc is a Ponnelle film from 1980, with the Vienna Philharmonic.]
Les Contes d'Hoffman B 13 Feb. 93
Così fan tutte TV 27 Feb. 96 CR 1988
Don Carlo L&T CR 1992
Don Giovanni TV 2 April 90
Duke Bluebeard's Castle TV 1 Feb. 89
Elektra L&T
L'Elisir d'Amore L&T CR 1989
Die Entführung aus dem Serail B 12 April 80/3 April 82/24 March 90/14 Dec. 91
Ernani L&T
Erwartung TV 1 Feb. 89 CR 1989
Eugene Onegin B 18 Feb. 78/25 March 89 CR 1987
Falstaff L&T

Die Fledermaus [Act 2] L&T
Der fliegende Holländer B 7 April 79/30 Dec. 89 CR 1994
La Forza del Destino L&T 1 CR 1976
Francesca da Rimini L&T
The Ghosts of Versailles L&T
Gianni Schicchi TV 14 Nov. 81
Götterdämmerung L&T CR 1989
Idomeneo L&T CR 1994–95
L'Italiana in Algeri TV 11 Jan. 86
Lohengrin L&T
I Lombardi B 15 Jan. 94 CR 1996
Luisa Miller TV 20 Jan. 79 CR 1991
Lulu TV 20 Dec. 80/2 April 88
Macbeth B 18 Dec. 82
Mahagonny TV 27 Nov. 79
Manon Lescaut L&T CR 1992
Die Meistersinger von Nürnberg B 11 Apr. 98
Norma B 13 Feb. 82 CR 1974/1979
Le Nozze di Figaro TV 14 Dec. 85 CR 1990
Oedipus Rex B 2 Jan. 82 CR 1991
Otello [Act 3] L&T / TV 13 Oct. 95 CR 1978
I Pagliacci TV 5 April 78
Parsifal L&T CR 1985 and 1992
Pelléas et Mélisande B 4 March 78/22 Jan. 93/30 Jan. 88/ 6 April 95
Porgy and Bess B 23 March 85/8 Feb. 86/27 Jan. 90
The Rake's Progress B 17 Jan. 98
Das Rheingold L&T CR 1988
Rigoletto [Act 3] L&T / TV 7 Nov. 77/15 Dec. 8 CR 1993
Der Rosenkavalier TV 7 Oct. 72

Le Rossignol B 2 Jan. 82
Salome B 6 Jan. 74
Siegfried L&T CR 1988
Simon Boccanegra L&T
Stiffelio L&T
Suor Angelica TV 14 Nov. 81
Il Tabarro TV 14 Nov. 81
Tannhäuser L&T
Tosca [Apparently there is no recording of a Levine Metropolitan Opera performance of this score, the work with which he made his Metropolitan Opera debut.] CR 1980

La Traviata B 28 March 81 [There is a tape of the Zeffirelli film, 1983.] CR 1991
Tristan und Isolde B 31 Jan. 81/24 Dec. 83
Il Trovatore L&T CR 1991
Les Troyens L&T
Turandot L&T
Un Ballo in Maschera L&T
I Vespri Siciliani B 9 March 74/12 April 75 CR 1973
Die Walküre L&T CR 1987
Wozzeck B 6 Mar. 80
Die Zauberflöte L&T CR 1980

Levine has conducted the following twenty-three operas at the Met, which presently exist only as documentary recordings:

The Bartered Bride
La Cenerentola
Les Contes d'Hoffmann
Don Giovanni
Duke Bluebeard's Castle
Die Entführung aus dem Serail
Gianni Schicchi
L'Italiana in Algeri
Lulu
Macbeth
Mahagonny
Die Meistersinger

I Pagliacci
Pelléas et Mélisande
Porgy and Bess
The Rake's Progress
Der Rosenkavalier
Le Rossignol
Salome
Suor Angelica
Il Tabarro
Tristan und Isolde
Wozzeck

Index

Abbado, Claudio, 79, 119, 134, 160, 172

Abraham, F. Murray, 267

Academy of Music, Philadelphia, 208

Adler, Kurt, 120, 203

Adriana Lecouvreur (Cilea), 268

Aida (Verdi), 24, 30, 31, 102, 113, 141, 209, 261, 269

Alagna, Roberto, 223

Albert Herring (Britten), 26

Alice Tully Hall, 205

Allen, Woody, 55

Alpine Symphony (Strauss), 106

Also sprach Zarathustra (Strauss), 106, 176, 214

Altenberg Lieder (Berg), 64, 79

Alto Rhapsody (Brahms), 262

Alzira (Verdi), 113

American Academy of Arts and Sciences, 124

American Boy Choir, 215

American Conductor's Project, 27

"Amour, l'ardente flamme, D'" (Berlioz), 224

Andrea Chénier (Giordano), 220, 268

Annals of Opera (Loewenberg), 196

Antek, Samuel, 92

Antony and Cleopatra (Barber), 110

Aphrodite of Praxiteles, 149–50

Arabella (Strauss), 107

Arcana (Varèse), 80

Argerich, Martha, 31

Ariadne auf Naxos (Strauss), 26, 82, 106, 107, 257, 259, 269, 280

Armiliato, Marco, 228

Arroyo, Martina, 268

art, defining of, 149–50

Aspen (Colorado) Festival and School of Music, 26–27, 63, 84, 194

Atlanta Symphony, 36

Babbitt, Milton, 186, 266, 274

Bach, Johann Sebastian, 99, 161, 169, 274
  Brandenburg Concertos, 73
  French Suites, 277
  Piano Concerto No. 1 in D Minor, 49

Ballo in Maschera, Un (Verdi), 37, 260

Baltimore Symphony, 27

Baltsa, Agnes, 260, 269

Barber, Samuel:
  Antony and Cleopatra, 110
  School for Scandal Overture, 95
  Vanessa, 110

Barber of Seville, The (Rossini), 30, 35, 36, 201, 268

Barenboim, Daniel, 54, 125, 237

Bartók, Bela, 274
  Concerto for Orchestra, 97, 133

Bartoli, Cecilia, 197, 201, 275

baton, 104–5, 156–57

Battle, Kathleen, 82, 259, 260, 268, 269, 274–75
  Levine's work with, 257–58

Baudelaire, Charles-Pierre, 207

Bavarian Radio, 235

Bax, Arnold, 112

Bayreuth Festival, 75, 138–43, 160, 176, 229, 232, 269, 279–80
  Leinsdorf at, 146–47
  Ring cycles at, 140–43, 234–36, 238
  tradition of, 138, 141

Bayreuth Orchestra, 142–43, 241

BBC Orchestra, 93

Beecham, Thomas, 64, 92, 97, 102, 153, 195, 196, 220

Beethoven, Ludwig van, 52, 53, 139, 164, 178, 201, 256, 271
  as conductor, 155
  Coriolan Overture, 98
  Fidelio, 107–8, 119
  Levine's recordings of, 272
  Mass in D Major (*Missa Solemnis*), 50, 108
  Piano Concerto No. 1, 30
  Piano Concerto No. 3 in C Minor, 21
  symphonies of, 158
  Symphony No. 2 in D, 157
  Symphony No. 3 in E-flat ("Eroica"), 72, 99, 188, 272
  Symphony No. 4 in B-flat Major, 133
  Symphony No. 5 in C Minor, 75, 81, 88, 129, 150, 169, 176
  Symphony No. 6 in F Major ("Pastoral"), 72, 86, 87–88
  Symphony No. 7 in A Major, 133
  Symphony No. 9 in D Minor ("Choral"), 73, 75, 270
  Wellington's Victory, 74
Behrens, Hildegard, 144, 260
Bellini, Vincenzo, 206, 207
  Norma, 268
Benvenuto Cellini (Berlioz), 110
Berg, Alban, 69, 131, 274
  Altenberg Lieder, 64, 79
  Lulu, 40, 75, 77, 79, 108, 148, 163
  Piano Sonata, Op. 1, 65
  Violin Concerto, 79, 262
  Wozzeck, 77, 108, 148, 208
Bergonzi, Carlo, 221–22, 223
Berlin Opera, 27
Berlin Philharmonic, 74, 89, 90, 95, 101, 106, 112, 125, 135, 137, 209
Berlioz, Hector, 56–57, 157, 168, 200, 273
  Benvenuto Cellini, 110
  as conductor, 156
  The Damnation of Faust, 224
  Requiem, 52, 79
  Les Troyens, 36, 50, 71, 111, 259–60
Bernheimer, Martin, 197

Bernstein, Leonard, 32, 59, 134, 135, 161, 189, 232, 253, 256
  Candide, 232, 243
  Trouble in Tahiti, 31
Berry, Walter, 201
Bilger, David, 213
Billy Budd (Britten), 79, 112
Bing, Rudolf, 39, 45, 48, 183, 192, 196, 223, 261
  Met tenure of, 31–33, 34, 40, 41, 42, 103, 104
Bizet, Georges:
  Carmen, 24, 31, 111, 113, 260
  The Pearl Fishers, 26
Bjoerner, Ingrid, 30
Björling, Jussi, 31, 192
Blegen, Judith, 269
Bliss, Anthony A., 38–40, 44, 47
Bliss, Cornelius N., 38
Boehm, Karl, 138, 153, 263
Bohème, La (Puccini), 35, 46, 96, 113, 166, 192, 260, 268
Boito, Arrigo, 182
Boris Godunov (Mussorgsky), 131
Boston Pops, 63
Boston Symphony, 32, 63, 90, 93, 95, 101, 124, 127, 138, 161, 178, 184–85, 195
Boulez, Pierre, 90, 124, 160, 172, 237, 247
Brahms, Johannes, 53, 80, 91, 153, 162, 164, 254, 271
  Alto Rhapsody, 262
  Double Concerto, 94
  German Requiem, 77, 94, 272
  Liebeslieder Waltzes, 94
  Piano Concerto No. 2 in B-flat, 68
  symphonies of, 130–31
  Symphony No. 1 in C Minor, 131, 167, 194, 262, 272
  Symphony No. 2 in D Major, 29, 95, 131, 262
  Symphony No. 3 in F Major, 94, 130, 133, 262

Symphony No. 4 in E Minor, 72, 127, 131, 262, 265

Tragic Overture, 95, 262

Brandenberg Concertos (Bach), 73

Brando, Marlon, 149

Brendel, Alfred, 52–53, 71, 108, 271, 272

Brian, Havergal, 112

Brico, Antonia, 194

Britten, Benjamin:

Albert Herring, 26

Billy Budd, 79, 112

Peter Grimes, 112, 204

Broch, Hermann, 263

Bronfman, Yefim, 169, 172

Bruckner, Anton, 121, 132, 153, 272

Bruson, Renato, 268

Bülow, Cosima von, 136

Bülow, Hans von, 89, 136

Bumbry, Grace, 33, 34, 37, 224

Bush, George, 234

Caballé, Montserrat, 268

Cage, John, 186, 272

Caldwell, Sarah, 148

Callas, Maria, 45, 104

Candide (Bernstein), 232, 243

Cantelli, Guido, 98

Capriccio (Strauss), 107

Cardillac (Hindemith), 109

Carmen (Bizet), 24, 31, 111, 113, 260

Carnegie Hall, 42, 176, 184, 185–86, 208, 270

described, 186

Carnival of the Animals, The (Saint-Saëns), 168

Carreras, José, 227, 228, 231, 234, 242, 244–45, 260

Carse, Adam, 157

Carter, Elliott, 183, 263, 274

Variations for Orchestra, 262

Caruso, Enrico, 38, 102, 161, 181, 208

concerts of, 230–31

Cassidy, Claudia, 67, 68

Cavalleria Rusticana (Mascagni), 268

Cenerentola, La (Rossini), 110

chamber music, 153

Chapin, Schuyler, 34, 37–38

Charpentier, Gustave:

Louise, 112, 224

Chéreau, Patrice, 237, 239

"Cherry Duet" (Mascagni), 223–24

Chicago Symphony Chorus, 267

Chicago Symphony Orchestra, 34, 38, 47–48, 50, 52, 69, 73, 76, 77, 80, 82, 83, 88, 89, 90, 95, 100–101, 123, 124, 156, 161, 164, 175, 185, 194, 209, 265, 266, 274, 281

conductor selection process of, 133–34

Fantasia 2000 score recorded by, 168–69, 170–71, 172, 245–49, 281

Levine recording with, 74

Strauss tradition of, 176

uniqueness of, 84–85

Chicago *Tribune,* 67

Cilea, Francesco:

Adriana Lecouvreur, 268

Cincinnati Symphony, 18, 21

Cincinnati Zoo Opera, 24

Clemenza di Tito, La (Mozart), 260

Cleva, Fausto, 24, 27, 41

Cleveland Concert Association, 30

Cleveland Institute of Music, 30

Cleveland Orchestra, 27, 42, 48, 86, 94, 96, 100–101, 118, 161, 175, 185, 194, 194

Levine's debut with, 28–29

Cohan, George M., 230

concertmaster, 154, 155

Concerto for Orchestra (Bartók), 97, 133

conductors, conducting:

bare-knuckles school of, 157–58

baton use in, 104–5, 156–57

in Britain, 155

composers as, 155–56

composer's intentions and, 98–99

concertmasters and, 154, 155

European vs. American styles of, 160–61

conductors, conducting *(cont.)*
  in France, 156, 158
  gestures and, 89
  guest, 89, 119, 125, 209–10
  Haydn's influence on, 154–55
  Levine's technique of, 86–87
  Lully's influence on, 153–54, 156, 157
  as maestros, 153
  Mendelssohn's influence on, 155, 157
  orchestra's relationship with, 86–88
  orchestra's traditions, character and,
    89–91, 95–96
  originality and, 65
  public image of, 256
  romantic style of, 156, 158, 159
  singers and, 256–57
  of summer musicals, 64–65
  Toscanini tradition and, 159–62
  training of, 194
  working clothes of, 105
Conlon, James, 109
Contes d'Hoffmann, Les (Offenbach), 111,
  204
Corelli, Franco, 33, 144
Corena, Fernando, 36
Corigliano, John:
  The Ghosts of Versailles, 174, 259
Coriolan Overture (Beethoven), 98
Così fan tutte (Mozart), 25, 26, 46, 100,
  115, 116, 128, 147, 196, 224, 260, 269
  Levine on, 199–201
  Met production of, 196–97, 197–99,
    200–202, 204
Coughlin, Bruce, 245–46, 247, 248
Crawford, Bruce, 44, 216–17
Creation, The (Haydn), 271
Creech, Philip, 52
criticism, *see* music criticism
Croft, Dwayne, 111, 198, 218, 223, 224
Cruz-Romo, Gilda, 180
Cugat, Francis Xavier, 231

Damnation of Faust, The (Berlioz), 224
Daphnis et Chloé (Ravel), 106, 111

da Ponte, Lorenzo, 196
Davis, Colin, 32
Death and Transfiguration (Strauss), 105, 274
Debussy, Claude, 153, 206, 207, 273, 275
  La Mer, 195
  Pelléas et Mélisande, 102, 111, 174
Delius, Frederick, 112
Del Monaco, Mario, 24
Dent, Edward J., 196, 202
"Depuis le jour," (Charpentier), 224
Dexter, John, 37, 39, 40, 204
Dialogues des Carmélites, Les (Poulenc), 79,
  111, 148
Dichter, Misha, 68
Dichterliebe (Schumann), 207
"Di Provenza" (Verdi), 145
Disney, Roy, Jr., 169–70, 249
Disney, Walt, 170
Domingo, Plácido, 30, 34, 43, 113, 145,
  161, 179, 181, 182, 217, 221, 227, 228,
  230, 231, 233, 234, 242, 244–45, 257,
  260, 261, 268
Don Carlo (Verdi), 24, 45, 46, 119, 166,
  258, 267
Don Giovanni (Mozart), 30, 100, 120,
  144, 166, 187, 196, 221, 260
Donizetti, Gaetano:
  L'Elisir d'Amore, 260, 268
Don Juan (Strauss), 29, 105, 176
Don Quixote (Strauss), 105, 176, 178, 274
Double Concerto (Brahms), 94
Douglas, Ann, 229
Dradi, Mario, 227
Drake, Alfred, 183
Dudley, William, 236
due Foscari, I (Verdi), 113, 166
Durbin, Deanna, 58
Dvořák, Antonin, 273
  Symphony No. 8 in G, 262
  Symphony No. 9 in E-flat (*New World*),
    56, 82, 261, 262

Eaglen, Jane, 224
1812 Overture (Tchaikovsky), 74

Einstein, Albert, 57
Elektra (Strauss), 106, 189, 259
Elgar, Edward, 173
  Pomp and Circumstance, 169, 172–73
Eliot, T. S., 193
Elisir d'Amore, L' (Donizetti), 260, 268
Elming, Poul, 241
Emmy Award, 35
Enfant et les sortilèges, L' (Ravel), 40, 79, 111
Englander, Gertrude, 21
Ernani (Verdi), 260
Ernst, Don, 171, 172–73, 245–46, 248
Erwartung (Schoenberg), 267
Esterházy, Nikolaus, 154
Eugene Onegin (Tchaikovsky), 224, 269
Ewing, Maria, 111, 224

Falstaff (Verdi), 34, 113, 146, 182, 204, 260
Fanciulla del West, La (Puccini), 113, 208
Fantasia (film), 168–69, 246, 253, 281
Fantasia 2000 (film), 135, 273
  Chicago Symphony recording of,
    168–69, 170–71, 172–73, 245–49, 281
Farrar, Geraldine, 138
Faust (Gounod), 23, 35, 111, 114, 165,
    221, 253
Festspielhaus, Bayreuth, 234
Fidelio (Beethoven), 107–8, 119
Fiedler, Arthur, 63, 138
Field, Marshall, IV, 66
Fiery Angel, The (Prokofiev), 109
Firebird, The (Stravinsky), 245, 248
Five Orchestral Pieces (Schoenberg), 209
Flagstad, Kirsten, 41
Fledermaus, Die (Strauss), 24, 165, 253
Fleming, Renée, 111, 112, 182–83, 221,
    224
fliegende Holländer, Der (Wagner), 269
Floyd, Carlisle:
  Of Mice and Men, 110
  Susannah, 110
Fogel, Henry, 134
Forza del Destino, La (Verdi), 45, 50, 166,
    254, 259, 266, 268

Francesca da Rimini (Zandonai), 259
Frau ohne Schatten, Die (Strauss), 107
Freischütz, Der (Weber), 86
French Suites (Bach), 277
Freni, Mirella, 144, 180, 269
Friends of Bayreuth, 235
Furie, Kenneth, 197
Furtwängler, Wilhelm, 56, 89, 101, 104,
    139, 153, 159, 265

Gambler, The (Prokofiev), 109
Garden, Mary, 102
Garfield, John, 19
Gatti-Casazza, Giulio, 44, 79–80, 102
Gedda, Nicolai, 268
Gentele, Goeran, 34–35, 37
Gérard, Rolf, 196
Gergiev, Valery, 109, 186
German Requiem (Brahms), 77, 94, 272
Gershwin, George:
  Porgy and Bess, 36, 224
  Rhapsody in Blue, 274
Gheorghiu, Angela, 223
Ghosts of Versailles, The (Corigliano), 174,
    259
Giacomini, Giuseppe, 268
Gielgud, John, 149
Giordano, Umberto:
  Andrea Chénier, 220, 268
Giovanna d'Arco (Verdi), 268
Giulini, Carlo Maria, 160, 265
Glossop, Peter, 33
Gluck, Christoph Willibald:
  Orfeo ed Euridice, 165
Gniewek, Raymond, 33–34
Gobbi, Tito, 34, 182
Goldstein, Helen, see Levine, Helen
  Goldstein
Goldstein, Morris, 18
Gordon, Edward, 49–53, 68, 71, 84, 85,
    96
  Levine on, 50–51
Götterdämmerung (Wagner), 149, 224, 231,
    240, 259

Gounod, Charles:
  Faust, 23, 35, 111, 114, 165, 221, 253
Great Gatsby, The (Harbison), 110
Greenbaum, Mr. (cellist), 91
Grosser Musikvereinssaal, 270
Grossman, Jerry, 178
Groves, Paul, 205–6
Gruppen (Stockhausen), 79
Gurrelieder (Schoenberg), 50, 63–64, 75, 79, 208, 270

Hadley, Jerry, 198, 221
Haitink, Bernard, 88, 119, 160
Halfvarson, Eric, 241
Hall, Peter, 236, 237
Hamlet (Shakespeare), 149, 182
Hampson, Thomas, 262, 269
Handel, George Frideric, 271
Hanslick, Eduard, 157–58
Harbison, John:
  The Great Gatsby, 110
Harrell, Lynn, 108, 109, 274
Having Wonderful Time (Kober), 19
Haydn, Franz Joseph, 91, 153, 158, 188, 196, 212, 266, 270–71
  conducting influenced by, 154–55
  The Creation, 271
  Mass No. 9 in C (*Missa in Tempore Belli*) (*Paukenmesse*), 272
  Symphony No. 53 in D Major ("Imperial," "Festino"), 162
  Symphony No. 98 in B-flat Major, 154
Heifetz, Jascha, 126
Heine, Heinrich, 207
Heldenleben, Ein (Strauss), 105, 176
Hemingway, Ernest, 265
Heppner, Ben, 112, 140, 192, 218
Herbert, Jocelyn, 40
Herseth, Adolph (Bud), 76, 173
Heure espagnole, L' (Ravel), 111
Hillis, Margaret, 85, 267
Hindemith, Paul:
  Cardillac, 109
  Mathis der Maler, 109

Hitler, Adolf, 159
Hoffmann, Matthias, 227, 228–29
Holland, Bernard, 184
Hölle, Matthias, 241
Hollywood Bowl, 30, 31
Homage to Seville, 257
Hong, Hei-Kyung, 221
Hopkins, Arthur, 103
Horne, Marilyn, 36, 39
Horowitz, Dick, 104
Hungarian Rhapsody No. 2 (Liszt), 100

Idomeneo (Mozart), 105, 174, 260, 269
Ingpen, Joan, 41
Ives, Charles:
  Symphony No. 2, 80, 274
  Three Places in New England, 80

Jacobs, Arnie, 96
Janácek, Leos, 131
  Jenůfa, 204
Jenůfa (Janácek), 204
Jerusalem, Siegfried, 145, 241
Johnson, Thor, 21
Joplin, Scott, 275
Juilliard School of Music, 85, 258
  Levine enrolled at, 26
  Levine evaluated by, 23–24
June Festival, 33
Jung, Manfred, 241

Kansas City Star, 113–14
Kant, Immanuel, 263
Karajan, Herbert von, 32, 33, 59, 74, 75, 89, 91, 96, 101, 125, 135, 139, 153, 160, 243, 253
Kaye, Danny, 35
Keene, Christopher, 32–33
Kertész, István, 49
Kiberg, Tina, 241
Kindertotenlieder (Mahler), 187–88
King, James, 259
King Lear (Shakespeare), 182
Kirchner, Alfred, 236, 237

Kirsten, Dorothy, 31
Kiss Me Kate (Porter), 183
Kleiber, Carlos, 86, 96, 119–20, 160
Klemperer, Otto, 132, 243
Klier, Manfred, 137
Knaben Wunderhorn, Das, 215, 269
Knappertsbusch, Hans, 64, 137, 139
Kober, Arthur, 19
Koenig, Lesley, 197, 201–204
Kolodin, Irving, 31, 41
Koussevitzky, Serge, 63, 93, 94, 96–97,
    101, 153, 159, 184, 185, 266
  assessment of, 195
Kraus, Alfredo, 224, 268
Krips, Josef, 194, 201
Kubelik, Rafael, 35, 36, 37
Kupfer, Harry, 237
Kuyper, George, 38

Lady Macbeth of Mtsensk (Shostakovich),
    109
Lakes, Gary, 82
"Lamento di Federico, Il" (Cilea), 244
Lane, Louis, 29–30
Langenfass, Rolf, 236
Langridge, Philip, 112
LaSalle Quartet, 23–24, 88, 274
Last Savage, The (Menotti), 40
Lee, Larry, *see* Levine, Lawrence
Leech, Richard, 111
Legge, Walter, 160, 243
Leinsdorf, Erich, 32, 37, 45, 54, 105, 125–
    26, 140, 158, 160, 172, 185, 189, 271
  at Bayreuth, 146–47
Leipzig Chorus, 108
Leitner, Ferdinand, 192
Lenya, Lotte, 148
Leoncavallo, Ruggiero:
  Pagliacci, 38
Levi, Hermann, 141, 236
Levin, Evi, 24
Levin, Walter, 23–24, 88
Levine, Helen Goldstein (mother),
    18–19, 21, 22, 30, 58–59, 175

Levine, James:
  on artist's nonmusical life, 55
  art principles of, 54–56, 76–77, 79
  assessment of, 56–59
  baton technique of, 170
  birth of, 20
  childhood of, 21–22
  commercial recordings by, 253–54, 256
  described, 22, 55
  family history of, 18–20
  first opera conducted by, 26
  first piano recital by, 21
  honorary degree of, 36
  musical gift of, 20–21, 23
  as musician, 167–68
  1996 gala tribute to, 216–26
  other artists' relationships with, 27–28
  personality of, 22, 34, 54–55
  preparation of music by, 171
  private life of, 58
  professionalism of, 163
  religion and, 25
  on technical proficiency, 56–57
  toy theater of, 24–25
Levine, Janet (sister), 20
Levine, Lawrence (father), 19, 20, 22
Levine, Tom (brother), 20, 25, 57, 59–60,
    175, 210
Lhévinne, Rosina, 23, 26, 27
Liebeslieder Waltzes (Brahms), 94
Lieutenant Kijé (Prokofiev), 109
Life, 26
Lincoln Center, 32–33, 47, 103, 186, 190
  Alice Tully Hall of, 205
Lind, Jenny, 17
Liszt, Cosima, 136
Liszt, Franz, 101
  Hungarian Rhapsody No. 2, 100
  Piano Concerto No. 1 in E-flat Major,
    69
Live from the Met (TV show), 38
Loewenberg, Alfred, 196
Lohengrin (Wagner), 36, 95, 138, 139, 140,
    259

Lombard, Alain, 32
Lombardi alla prima Crociata, I (Verdi),
  222, 269
London, George, 182
London Philharmonic Society, 157
London Symphony, 74, 112
Lorengar, Pilar, 144
Los Angeles Times, 197
Louise (Charpentier), 112, 224
Louisville Symphony, 177
Ludwig, Christa, 144, 201, 218, 275
Luisa Miller (Verdi), 32, 34, 144, 220–21,
  269
Lully, Jean-Baptiste, 153–54, 156, 157
  Te Deum, 154
Lulu (Berg), 40, 75, 77, 79, 108, 148, 163
Lunt, Alfred, 103, 196–97
Lyriches Intermezzo (Heine), 207
Lyric Opera, 107, 112, 192
  Met compared with, 46–47

Maazel, Lorin, 236
McClintock, Peter, 191
McCormick, Bertie, 67
McCracken, James, 35, 37, 179
MacNeil, Cornell, 144
Madama Butterfly (Puccini), 25, 30, 113, 253
Magic Flute, The (Mozart), 113, 130, 166,
  200, 260, 268, 277
Mahagonny (Weill), 79, 148
Mahler, Gustav, 45, 49, 69, 89, 120–21,
  156, 165, 176, 254, 272, 273
  Kindertotenlieder, 187–88
  in Levine's repertory, 189–90
  Rückert Lieder, 79
  Symphony No. 1 in D Major, 269
  Symphony No. 2 in C Minor ("Resur-
    rection"), 34, 42, 48, 269
  Symphony No. 3 in D Minor, 69, 122,
    125, 187, 209–16
  Symphony No. 4 in G Major, 99, 211,
    269
  Symphony No. 5 in C-sharp Minor,
    188, 209

Symphony No. 6 in A Minor, 121,
    187–89, 190
  Symphony No. 7 in E Minor, 188
  Symphony No. 8 in E-flat Major, 50,
    187, 188, 208, 269
  Symphony No. 9 in D Major, 132
Malfitano, Catherine, 224
Maliponte, Adriana, 34
Mamelles de Tirésias, Les (Poulenc), 40, 79,
  111
Manhattan Center, 264
Manon (Massenet), 111–12
Manon Lescaut (Puccini), 113, 260, 269
Martinon, Jean, 88, 90–91, 133, 158
Marton, Eva, 260
Marx, Karl, 278
Mascagni, Pietro, 223
  Cavalleria Rusticana, 268
  "Cherry Duet," 223–24
Massenet, Jules:
  Manon, 111–12
  Thaïs, 231
  Werther, 111
Mass in D Major (*Missa Solemnis*)
  (Beethoven), 50, 108
Mass No. 9 in C (*Missa in Tempore Belli*)
  (*Paukenmesse*) (Haydn), 272
Mathis der Maler (Hindemith), 109
Matthai (concertmaster), 156
Mattila, Karita, 192
Má Vlast (Smetana), 161
Mavra (Stravinsky), 26
Mayer, Martin, 40, 44, 45, 197–98
May Festival, 36
Mehta, Zarin, 54, 85, 131
Mehta, Zubin, 30, 32, 185, 227
Meier, Waltraud, 144, 214–15, 224, 259
Meistersinger von Nürnberg, Die (Wagner),
  126–27, 139, 142, 191
  Levine's rehearsal of, 192–94, 195
Mendelssohn, Felix, 79, 155
  conducting influenced by, 155, 157
  Piano Concerto No. 2 in D Minor,
    21

Symphony No. 3 in A Minor ("Scottish"), 272–73
Symphony No. 4 in A Major ("Italian"), 273
Mengelberg, Willem, 130
Menotti, Gian Carlo:
The Last Savage, 40
Mentzer, Susanne, 82, 198, 224
Mer, La (Debussy), 195
Merry Wives of Windsor, The (Shakespeare), 182
Met, The (Mayer), 40
Metamorphosen (Strauss), 106, 262, 273
Metropolitan Opera, 24, 31, 37–39, 58, 105, 147, 174, 175–76, 179, 184, 186, 208, 228, 231
  advance planning by, 116–17
  Bing's tenure at, 31–33, 34, 40, 41, 42, 103, 104
  Bliss's tenure at, 38–40, 44, 47
  casting by, 113, 114–15, 118
  centennial of, 41
  Così fan tutte production of, 196–97, 197–99, 200–202, 205
  in early twentieth century, 102–3
  endowment of, 39
  Fidelio production of, 107–8
  financial success of, 43–44
  Levine's debut at, 33
  Levine's first recordings with, 74
  Levine's repertory at, 108–13
  Levine's revitalization of, 40–42
  Levine's schedule at, 118–19
  live events broadcast from, 38–39
  Lyric Opera compared with, 46–47
  National Council Auditions of, 182, 205
  1972–73 season of, 35
  1973–74 season at, 35, 36–37
  1996 gala at, 216–26
  Otello production of, 179–82, 183
  quality of, 103–4
  revivals by, 40
  singers contracted by, 117–18, 258–59
  titles used by, 107, 148, 184, 255
  working season of, 45
Metropolitan Opera Association, 44, 216
Metropolitan Opera Guild, 216
Metropolitan Opera House, 23, 225, 231, 236
  rehearsal room of, 190
Metropolitan Opera Presents, The (TV series), 38, 261
Metropolitan Opera Studio, 33
Milanov, Zinka, 141
Milhand, Darius, 186
Miller, Frank, 76, 96, 99–100, 137
Milnes, Sherrill, 30, 34, 35, 179, 268
"Mi tradì quell'alma ingrata" (Mozart), 221
Mitropoulos, Dimitri, 69, 188, 190
Moffo, Anna, 192
"Mon coeur s'ouvre à ta voix" (Saint-Saëns), 224
Monteux, Pierre, 23, 158
"Moon River" (Mancini and Mercer), 231, 234
Moore, G. E., 128
Moore, Gerald, 164
Morel, Jean, 27, 86, 90–91
Morgana, Nina, 231
Morison, Patricia, 183
Morris, James, 182, 218, 224
Morton, Jelly Roll, 275
Moses und Aron (Schoenberg), 108, 147–48, 165
Moshinsky, Elijah, 182
Mozart, Wolfgang Amadeus, 37, 43, 53, 59, 86, 101, 111, 112, 153, 158, 164, 166, 167, 176, 178, 212, 219, 229–30, 256, 274
  La Clemenza di Tito, 260
  as conductor, 155
  Così fan tutte, 25, 26, 45, 100, 115, 116, 128, 147, 196–202, 204, 224, 260, 269
  Don Giovanni, 30, 100, 120, 144, 166, 187, 196, 221, 260
  Idomeneo, 105, 174, 260, 269

Mozart, Wolfgang Amadeus *(cont.)*
Levine's recordings of, 270–71
in Levine's repertory, 189
The Magic Flute, 113, 130, 166, 200, 260, 268, 279
Le Nozze di Figaro, 36, 166, 174, 183, 200, 203, 260, 262–63, 267, 269, 278–79
Der Schauspieldirektor, 105
symphonies of, 265, 270–71
Symphony No. 36 in C Major ("Linz"), 163
Symphony No. 38 in D Major ("Prague"), 271
Symphony No. 39 in E-flat Major, 129
Symphony No. 40 in G Minor, 69–70, 73, 82, 97, 100, 139, 162, 271
Symphony No. 41 in C Major ("Jupiter"), 82, 271
videodisc recordings of, 260
Mozart's Operas (Dent), 196
Muck, Karl, 137–38, 141, 265
Munch, Charles, 116, 158, 185, 213
Munich Philharmonic, 186
Murray, Ann, 269
Murray Theater, 77, 84
music:
color, texture of, 168
composer's intentions and, 164
conductor's relationship with, 131
and defining art, 149–50
general culture and, 280–81
learning of, 65, 98–99
Levine's preparation of, 171
music unions and, 127–28
opera's domination of, 180
quality performance of, 71–72, 124–26, 147
rest notes in, 94
romantic style of, 156, 158, 159
tempo of, 128–29, 137–38
of twentieth century, 65
see also opera

music criticism, 65–68, 87, 100, 112, 127–28, 168
Music from Ravinia, 48, 274
Music Magazine, 216
Mussorgsky, Modest Petrovich:
Boris Godunov, 131
Pictures at an Exhibition, 132
Muti, Riccardo, 160
"My Man's Gone Now" (Gershwin), 224

Nabokov, Vladimir, 115
Nabucco (Verdi), 113, 166, 224
National Council Auditions, 182, 205
National Endowment for the Arts, 44, 181
National Opera Institute, 203
National Symphony, 134
NBC Symphony, 48, 56, 76, 93, 98, 101, 104, 132, 145, 153, 191, 253, 280
"Nessun dorma" (Puccini), 245
New Amsterdam Singers, 233
New Met in Profile, The (Rubin), 56
"New York, New York" (Bernstein), 233–34
New York City Opera, 33, 184, 203
New York Philharmonic, 89, 93, 101, 121, 135, 160, 161, 184–85, 266, 271, 280
New York Times, 32, 180, 184, 197, 204, 228, 266
Nicolai, Otto, 158
Nietzsche, Friedrich, 214
Nikisch, Arthur, 89, 101, 129
Nilsson, Birgit, 144, 145, 223, 259
Norma (Bellini), 268
Norman, Jessye, 31, 108, 144, 224, 258, 259, 260, 267, 275
Northwestern University, 66
Nose, The (Shostakovich), 109
Nozze di Figaro, Le (Mozart), 36, 166, 174, 183, 200, 203, 260, 267, 269, 278–79
Levine's recording of, 262–63

Oberon (Weber), 156, 242

Oboe Concerto (Strauss), 106, 273–74

Oedipus Rex (Stravinsky), 36, 40, 79, 208, 267

Offenbach, Jacques:
Les Contes d'Hoffmann, 111, 204

Of Mice and Men (Floyd), 110

Of Reminiscences and Reflections (Schuller), 176

On Conducting (Wagner), 156

One Hundred Men and a Girl (film), 58

opera:
bel canto, 115, 140
casting of, 107, 113, 114–5, 143
comic, 110
composer's intentions and, 147
cut vs. complete performances of, 44–45
generational learning of, 143–44
golden age of, 102
Levine's introduction to, 24–25
Levine's recordings of, 267–70
live vs. televised performances of, 222, 223–24
opening night at, 180
recording process and, 174–75
recordings of, 254–56, 267–70
singers of, 144–46
staging of, 141–42, 146–49
as theater, 181
visual elements of, 141–42

Opera, 197

Opera America, 113

Opera Company of Philadelphia, 203

Opera News, 42, 148

Orchestra from Beethoven to Berlioz, The (Carse), 157

Orfeo ed Euridice (Gluck), 165

Ormandy, Eugene, 49, 58, 164, 185, 209, 266

Ortega y Gasset, José, 278

"O sole mio" (Di Capua), 230, 245

Otello (Verdi), 35, 36, 37, 144, 166, 253, 261, 268
Met production of, 179–82, 183

Othello (Shakespeare), 182

Ouzounian, Michael, 43, 178

"Over There" (Cohan), 230

Ozawa, Seiji, 49, 53, 71
at Ravinia, 78–79, 81–82

Pagliacci (Leoncavallo), 38

Paley, William S., 280

Pape, René, 241

Parade (Satie), 40

Parsifal (Wagner), 36, 59, 132, 137, 139, 144, 166, 174, 214, 219, 234, 236, 238, 259, 279–80

Pavarotti, Luciano, 36, 113, 179, 217, 222, 227, 228, 233, 242, 244–45, 256, 260, 268, 269

PBS, 38, 234

Pearl Fishers, The (Bizet), 26

Peduzzi, Richard, 237

Pelléas et Mélisande (Debussy), 102, 111, 114, 174

Perlman, Itzhak, 271

Peter Grimes (Britten), 112, 204

Petrillo, James C., 126

Philadelphia Orchestra, 30, 36, 90, 95, 101, 123–24, 132, 161, 162, 169, 184–85, 208–9, 247
Mahler's Symphony No. 3 performed by, 209–16

Philadelphia Singers Chorale, 215

Philharmonia Orchestra of London, 228

Piano Concerto, Op. 42 (Schoenberg), 52, 53, 79

Piano Concerto No. 1 (Beethoven), 30

Piano Concerto No. 1 in B-flat Major (Tchaikovsky), 28, 80, 229

Piano Concerto No. 1 in D Minor (Bach), 49

Piano Concerto No. 1 in E-flat Major (Liszt), 69

Piano Concerto No. 2 in B-flat Major (Brahms), 68
Piano Concerto No. 2 in D Minor (Mendelssohn), 21
Piano Concerto No. 2 in F Major (Shostakovich), 169, 173, 174
Piano Concerto No. 3 in C Minor (Beethoven), 21
Piano Sonata, Op. 1 (Berg), 65
Pictures at an Exhibition (Mussorgsky), 132
Pines of Rome, The (Respighi), 169, 245, 246
Pinza, Ezio, 262
Plishka, Paul, 33, 34, 260, 268
Polaski, Deborah, 241
Pomp and Circumstance (Elgar), 169, 172–73
Ponnelle, Jean-Pierre, 109, 130, 147, 203, 257, 260, 263
Porgy and Bess (Gershwin), 36, 224
Porter, Cole, 183
Poulenc, Francis:
  Les Dialogues des Carmélites, 79, 111, 148
  Les Mamelles de Tirésias, 40, 79, 111
"Prenderò quel brunettino" (Mozart), 224
Prey, Hermann, 36, 82
Price, Leontyne, 39, 50, 144, 209, 218, 260, 268
Price, Margaret, 82, 180
Principia Ethica (Moore), 128
Prokofiev, Sergei, 273
  The Fiery Angel, 109
  The Gambler, 109
  Lieutenant Kijé, 109
  Sinfonia Concertante, 109
  Symphony No. 5 in B-flat Major, 96, 97, 262
  War and Peace, 109
Puccini, Giacomo, 112
  La Bohème, 35, 46, 96, 113, 166, 192, 260, 268
  La Fanciulla del West, 113, 208
  Madama Butterfly, 25, 30, 113, 253

Manon Lescaut, 113, 260, 269
  stature of, 113–14
  Tosca, 30, 31, 33, 34, 49, 113, 253, 268
  Il Trittico, 113
  Turandot, 245, 260

"Qual voluttà trascorrere" (Verdi), 222
"Quando le sere al placido" (Verdi), 221–22

Rachmaninoff, Sergei, 165
Rake's Progress, The (Stravinsky), 109
Ramey, Samuel, 111, 219, 221, 224
Ran, Shulamit, 274
Ravel, Maurice, 153, 273
  Daphnis et Chloé, 111
  L'Enfant et les sortilèges, 40, 79, 111
  L'Heure Espagnole, 111
Ravinia Festival, 26, 47–54, 123, 134, 205, 246, 267, 274
  Beethoven performed at, 74–75
  Brendel-Levine collaboration and, 52–53
  contemporary music at, 177
  dress at, 73
  Gordon-Levine collaboration and, 49–53, 68, 71, 84
  Levine's art policy and, 76–80
  Levine's debut at, 34
  Levine's enjoyment of, 75–76
  new music at, 77–78
  opening night at, 49
  Ozawa at, 78–79, 81–82
  planning programs for, 68, 80–81
  recordings of, 270, 274–75
  rehearsals at, 64, 69–72, 77–78, 163–64
  repertoire of, 63–64
  site of, 68–69, 74, 83–84
  weather and, 73, 75, 78, 81
RCA, 39, 253
recording(s), 65, 209
  of American music, 274
  of Brahms's symphonies, 72

concert halls for, 263–64
of *Fantasia 2000,* 168–73, 245–49, 281
of French music, 273
Levine's approach to, 263–66
of 1990s, 261–63
of *Nozze di Figaro,* 262–63
of operas, 174, 254–56, 267–70
problems in, 174–75
of Ravinia concerts, 270, 274–75
video, 260
rehearsals, 88
by Battle and Levine, 257–58
at Bayreuth, 140
public perception of, 123–24
at Ravinia, 64, 69–72, 77–78, 163–64
by Solti, 163–64
Stokowski on, 122
Szell's attitude towards, 69–70, 194–95
Toscanini's style of, 92–93, 162–63, 191,
    192–93, 195, 214, 258
Reiner, Fritz, 18, 25, 38, 39, 48, 49, 67,
    72, 88, 89, 90, 96, 97, 101, 105–6, 126,
    133, 138, 171, 172, 175–76, 185, 213,
    265–66, 280
Reinhardt, Max, 103
Rembrandt van Rijn, 115–16
Renard (Stravinsky), 111
Requiem (Berlioz), 52, 79
Requiem (Verdi), 42, 77
Respighi, Ottorino:
    The Pines of Rome, 169, 245, 246
Reszke, Jean de, 179
Rhapsody in Blue (Gershwin), 274
Rheingold, Das (Wagner), 105, 239, 259
Ricca Mandolin Club, 179
Ricciarelli, Katia, 180
Richard Tucker Foundation Award, 205
Richter, Hans, 89, 141
Rigoletto (Verdi), 24, 28, 30, 35, 36, 141,
    253, 260, 269
Ring of the Nibelung, The (Wagner), 45, 54,
    59, 89, 116, 139, 148, 159, 182, 234,
    259

approaches to, 236–38
Bayreuth performances of, 140–43,
    234–36, 238
1996 cycle of, 238–41
Rosalie's designs for, 239–40
staging, 148–49
Robbins, Julien, 221
Rockefeller, William, 38
Rockefeller Foundation, 66, 127
Rodzinski, Artur, 42, 97, 123, 133, 185
Rosalie (set and costume designer), 236,
    237, 239–40
Rosbaud, Hans, 80, 134
Rosenkavalier, Der (Strauss), 106, 107, 120,
    142, 174, 213
Rosenthal, Manuel, 40
Rossignol, Le (Stravinsky), 40
Rossini, Gioacchino, 202
    The Barber of Seville, 30, 35, 36, 201, 268
    La Cenerentola, 110
    William Tell, 110
Rubin, Stephen S., 56, 57
Rückert, Friedrich, 187
Rückert Lieder (Mahler), 79
Rudas, Tibor, 227, 243
Rudolf, Max, 27, 38, 41
Rysanek, Leonie, 144, 219, 259

Sacre du Printemps, Le (Stravinsky), 40,
    108–9, 164, 253, 262, 273
Saint–Saëns, Camille:
    The Carnival of the Animals, 169
    Samson et Dalila, 165, 187, 224, 230, 232
    Symphony No. 3 in C Minor
        ("Organ"), 272
Saks, Jay David, 170, 171, 173, 245–46,
    248, 249
Salome (Strauss), 37, 106, 189
Salzburg Festival, 36, 71, 74, 108, 203,
    205, 269, 274
    Levine's debut at, 96
Samson et Dalila (Saint–Saëns), 165, 187,
    224, 230, 232

San Francisco Opera, 203
Sängerfest, 17–18
Sarnoff, David, 280
Satie, Erik:
  Parade, 40
Schauspieldirektor, Der (Mozart), 105
Schavernoch, Hans, 237
Schenk, Otto, 191, 236, 238
Scherchen, Hermann, 128
Schifrin, Lalo, 227
Schindler, Alma, 188
Schippers, Thomas, 37, 236
Schmidt, Wolfgang, 240
Schnabel, Artur, 52, 100, 101
Schneider, Peter, 236
Schneider-Siemssen, Günther, 191, 236, 238
Schoenberg, Arnold, 52, 53, 108, 131, 147–48, 165, 200, 263, 274
  Erwartung, 267
  Five Orchestral Pieces, 209
  Gurrelieder, 50, 63–64, 75, 79, 208, 270
  Moses und Aron, 108, 147–48, 165
  Piano Concerto, Op. 42, 52, 53, 79
  Verklärte Nacht, 262
schöne Müllerin, Die (Schubert), 275
School for Scandal Overture (Barber), 95
Schubert, Franz, 156, 246
  Die schöne Müllerin, 275
  Symphony No. 8 in B Minor ("Unfinished"), 81, 176, 177
  Symphony No. 9 in C Major ("Great"), 49, 89, 153, 177, 273
  Die Winterreise, 275
Schuler, Duane, 198
Schuller, Gunther, 69, 186, 274
  Of Reminiscences and Reflections, 176
Schumann, Robert, 206, 207, 209, 272
  as conductor, 156
  Dichterliebe, 207
  Symphony No. 2 in C Major, 86
  Symphony No. 3 in E-flat Major ("Rhenish"), 86
Schwanda the Bagpiper (Weinberger), 110

Schwanewilms, Anne, 241
Schwarz, Hanna, 241
Schwarzkopf, Elisabeth, 104, 200–201
Scientific American, 279
Scotto, Renata, 113, 144, 180, 219, 260, 268
Seifert, Gerd, 137
Serkin, Rudolf, 25, 86
Shaw, George Bernard, 183
Shaw, Robert, 30, 36, 97
Shepard, Thomas Z., 269
Shicoff, Neil, 111, 112, 219
Shostakovich, Dmitri, 273
  Lady Macbeth of Mtsensk, 109
  The Nose, 109
  Piano Concerto No. 2 in F Major, 169, 173, 174
  Symphony No. 5 in D Minor, 64
  Symphony No. 10 in E Minor, 91
Sibelius, Jean, 266
  Symphony No. 2 in D Major, 132
  Symphony No. 4 in A Minor, 132, 262, 263
  Symphony No. 5 in E-flat Major, 132
Siegfried (Wagner), 232, 240, 259
Siepi, Cesare, 36
Sills, Beverly, 30, 268
Simon Boccanegra (Verdi), 174, 260
Simoneau, Leopold, 201
Sinfonia Concertante (Prokofiev), 109
Sinfonia Domestica (Strauss), 106
singers, singing, 116, 117–18
  conductor and, 256–57
  for Così fan tutte, 198
  Levine's casting of, 182–83
  Levine's preparation of, 191
  at Met, 117–18, 258–59
  national origin and, 82–83
  at 1996 Met gala, 223–25
  of opera, 144–46
  Toscanini and, 146
  training of, 82–83
Slatkin, Leonard, 134

Smetana, Bedrich, 273
  Má Vlast, 161
Smith, Patrick J., 42
Socrates, 278, 279
Söderström, Elisabeth, 218–19
Solti, Georg, 47, 48, 53–54, 64, 75, 101,
  105, 134, 135, 142, 143, 148, 149, 160,
  172, 176, 192, 220, 236, 239, 247, 259,
  266, 269
  Meistersinger as performed by, 126–27
  rehearsals by, 163–64
Sotin, Hans, 241
Southern, Hugh, 44
Spielberg, Steven, 149
Spohr, Louis, 155
Stanislaus, Leopold, 91
Steinberg, William, 38, 189
Stella, Antonietta, 141
Stern, Isaac, 186
Stevens, Risë, 24
Stiffelio (Verdi), 260
Still, Ray, 96
Stock, Frederick A., 52
Stockhausen, Karlheinz:
  Gruppen, 79
Stokowski, Leopold, 18, 58, 91, 101,
  159–60, 162, 168–69, 172, 184, 195,
  208–9, 214, 247, 249, 253, 263–64,
  265
Stratas, Teresa, 37, 40, 113, 144, 180, 217,
  260
Strauss, Johann:
  Die Fledermaus, 24, 165, 251
Strauss, Richard, 27, 91, 111, 112, 115,
  137, 166, 208, 258
  Alpine Symphony, 106
  Also sprach Zarathustra, 106, 176, 214
  Arabella, 107
  Ariadne auf Naxos, 26, 82, 106, 107, 257,
    259, 269, 280
  Capriccio, 107
  Death and Transfiguration, 105, 274
  Don Juan, 29, 105, 176
  Don Quixote, 105, 176, 178, 274

  Elektra, 106, 189, 259
  Die Frau ohne Schatten, 107
  Ein Heldenleben, 105–6, 176
  Levine on, 105–7
  Levine's recordings of, 273–74
  Metamorphosen, 106, 262, 273
  Oboe Concerto, 106, 273–74
  Der Rosenkavalier, 106, 107, 120, 142,
    174, 212
  Salome, 37, 106, 189
  Sinfonia Domestica, 106
  Till Eulenspiegels lustige Streiche, 105
Stravinsky, Igor, 40, 131, 169, 263
  The Firebird, 245, 248
  Mavra, 26
  Oedipus Rex, 36, 40, 79, 208, 267
  The Rake's Progress, 109
  Renard, 111
  Le Rossignol, 40
  Le Sacre du Printemps, 40, 108–9, 164,
    253, 262, 273
  Symphonies of Wind Instruments, 87
  Symphony of Palms, 270
  Variations for Orchestra, 68, 69
Struckmann, Falk, 241
Susannah (Floyd), 110
Svendén, Birgitta, 241
Swedish Radio Chorus, 108
Swenson, Ruth Ann, 224
Symphonies of Wind Instruments
  (Stravinsky), 87
Symphony No. 1 in C Minor (Brahms),
  131, 167, 194, 262, 272
Symphony No. 1 in D Major (Mahler),
  269
Symphony No. 2 (Ives), 80, 274
Symphony No. 2 in C Major (Schu-
  mann), 86
Symphony No. 2 in C Minor ("Resur-
  rection") (Mahler), 34, 42, 48, 269
Symphony No. 2 in D Major
  (Beethoven), 157
Symphony No. 2 in D Major (Brahms),
  29, 95, 131, 262

Symphony No. 2 in D Major (Sibelius), 132

Symphony No. 3 in A minor ("Scottish") (Mendelssohn), 272–73

Symphony No. 3 in C Minor ("Organ") (Saint–Saëns), 272

Symphony No. 3 in D Minor (Mahler), 69, 121–22, 125, 188, 209–16

Symphony No. 3 in E-flat Major ("Eroica") (Beethoven), 72, 99, 188, 272

Symphony No. 3 in E-flat Major ("Rhenish") (Schumann), 86

Symphony No. 3 in F Major (Brahms), 94, 130, 133, 262

Symphony No. 4 in A Major ("Italian") (Mendelssohn), 273

Symphony No. 4 in A Minor (Sibelius), 132, 262, 263

Symphony No. 4 in B-flat Major (Beethoven), 133

Symphony No. 4 in E Minor (Brahms), 72, 127, 131, 262, 265

Symphony No. 4 in G Major (Mahler), 99, 211, 269

Symphony No. 5 in B-flat Major (Prokofiev), 96, 97, 262

Symphony No. 5 in C Minor (Beethoven), 75, 81, 88, 129, 150, 169, 176

Symphony No. 5 in C-sharp Minor (Mahler), 188, 209

Symphony No. 5 in D Minor (Shostakovich), 64

Symphony No. 5 in E-flat Major (Sibelius), 132

Symphony No. 5 in E Minor (Tchaikovsky), 75

Symphony No. 6 in A Minor (Mahler), 120–21, 187–89, 190

Symphony No. 6 in B-flat ("Pathétique") (Tchaikovsky), 272

Symphony No. 6 in F Major ("Pastoral") (Beethoven), 72, 86, 87–88

Symphony No. 7 in A Major (Beethoven), 133

Symphony No. 7 in E Minor (Mahler), 187

Symphony No. 8 in B Minor ("Unfinished") (Schubert), 81, 176, 177

Symphony No. 8 in E-flat Major (Mahler), 50, 187, 188, 208, 269

Symphony No. 8 in G (Dvořák), 262

Symphony No. 9 in C Major ("Great") (Schubert), 49, 89, 153, 177, 273

Symphony No. 9 in D Major (Mahler), 132

Symphony No. 9 in D Minor ("Choral") (Beethoven), 72–73, 75, 270

Symphony No. 9 in E-flat (*New World*) (Dvořák), 56, 82, 261, 262

Symphony No. 10 in E Minor (Shostakovich), 91

Symphony No. 36 in C Major ("Linz") (Mozart), 163

Symphony No. 38 in D Major ("Prague") (Mozart), 271

Symphony No. 39 in E-flat Major (Mozart), 129

Symphony No. 40 in G Minor (Mozart), 69–70, 73, 82, 97, 100, 139, 162, 271

Symphony No. 41 in C Major ("Jupiter") (Mozart), 82, 271

Symphony No. 53 in D Major ("Imperial," "Festino") (Haydn), 162

Symphony No. 98 in B-flat Major (Haydn), 154

Symphony of Palms (Stravinsky), 270

Szell, George, 12, 29, 30, 33, 41, 43, 48, 53, 55, 58, 65, 66, 72, 75, 87, 88, 92, 96, 97, 100, 101, 106, 118, 120, 126, 127, 139, 153, 158, 160, 162, 163, 167, 168, 170, 175–76, 185, 189, 205, 210, 214, 218, 225, 226, 264, 265, 270, 272, 273

Beethoven's Symphony No. 5 by, 128–29

Brahms's Symphony No. 3 by, 130

Levine's relationship with, 27–28
Mahler's Symphony No. 6 and, 120–21
opera abandoned by, 119–20
rehearsal attitude of, 69–70, 194–95
on rest notes, 94

Taft, Helen Herron, 18
Tamagno, Francesco, 179
Tanglewood, 68–69, 83–84
Tannhäuser (Wagner), 36, 147, 219, 259
Tchaikovsky, Pyotr Ilyich, 27, 162, 169
  1812 Overture, 74
  Eugene Onegin, 224, 269
  Piano Concerto No. 1 in B-flat Major,
    28, 80, 229
  Symphony No. 5 in E Minor, 75
  Symphony No. 6 in B-flat Major
    ("Pathétique"), 272
Tebaldi, Renata, 31, 35, 141, 144, 180
Te Deum (Lully), 154
Te Kanawa, Kiri, 37, 144, 180, 221, 260,
  262, 269
Terfel, Bryn, 186–87, 221
Thaïs (Massenet), 231
Thomas, Jess, 30, 145
Thomas, Michael Tilson, 80, 134
Thomas, Theodore, 17–18
Thomson, Suzanne, 30, 55, 57
Thomson, Virgil, 124, 164, 168, 196
Three Places in New England (Ives), 80
Three Tenors, 226–27
  Munich concert by, 242–45
  preparation for, 231–32
  rehearsals by, 232–33
  repertoire of, 229–30
Tietjen, Heinz, 139
Till Eulenspiegels lustige Streiche (Strauss),
  105
Time, 41
Tippett, Michael, 112
Tomlinson, John, 241
Tommasini, Anthony, 204, 266
Tomowa-Sintow, Anna, 269
"Torna a Sorrento" (De Curtis), 244

Toronto Symphony, 228
Tosca (Puccini), 30, 31, 33, 34, 49, 113,
  253, 268
Toscanini, Arturo, 12, 28, 31, 35, 38, 41,
  44, 48, 55, 56, 59, 69, 72, 75, 76, 88,
  101, 107, 129, 132, 133, 137, 139, 141,
  142, 153, 158, 168, 170, 181, 185, 186,
  208, 210, 220, 221, 226, 236, 241, 243,
  253, 266, 272
  baton used by, 104
  Brahms as performed by, 94
  conducting tradition of, 159–62
  diversity of, 97–98
  Farrar's relationship with, 136
  genius of, 94
  Levine compared with, 161, 270
  Levine influenced by, 159, 254
  Mahler's music disliked by, 161, 212
  memory slips of, 94–95
  Merrill and, 145
  recordings of, 254, 264, 265, 267
  rehearsal style of, 92–93, 162–63, 191,
    192–93, 195, 214, 258
  repertory of, 121
  singers and, 146
Toscanini, Walter, 94–95, 98, 163, 187
Tourel, Jennie, 269
Tovey, Donald Francis, 211
Tragic Overture (Brahms), 95, 262
Transylvania Music Camp, 21
Traviata, La (Verdi), 30, 45, 113, 145,
  269
Tristan und Isolde (Wagner), 24, 45, 138, 139
Trittico, Il (Puccini), 113
Trouble in Tahiti (Bernstein), 31
Trovatore, Il (Verdi), 260, 269
Troyanos, Tatiana, 144, 259, 260, 262,
  268
Troyens, Les (Berlioz), 36, 50, 71, 111,
  259–60
Tucci, Gabriella, 34
Tucker, Richard, 31, 34, 144
Turandot (Puccini), 245, 260
Turin Philharmonic, 228

Index

University Circle Orchestra, 30
Upshaw, Dawn, 82, 223, 224, 262, 275
Utley, Garrick, 220

Valisi Mandolin Orchestra, 179
Vaness, Carol, 198, 224
Vanessa (Barber), 110
"Va pensiero" (Verdi), 224
Varèse, Edgard:
  Arcana, 80
Variations for Orchestra (Carter), 262
Variations for Orchestra (Stravinsky), 68, 69
Varnay, Astrid, 144
Verdi, Giuseppe, 22, 99, 112, 115, 166, 167, 200, 245
  Aida, 24, 30, 31, 102, 113, 141, 209, 261, 269
  Alzira, 113
  Un Ballo in Maschera, 37, 260
  Don Carlo, 24, 45, 46, 119, 166, 260, 269
  Ernani, 260
  Falstaff, 34, 113, 146, 182, 205, 260
  La Forza del Destino, 45, 50, 166, 254, 260, 266, 268
  Giovanna d'Arco, 268
  I due Foscari, 113, 166
  I Lombardi alla prima Crociata, 222, 269
  I Vespri Siciliani, 37, 268
  laserdisc recordings of, 260
  Levine's recordings of, 269
  Luisa Miller, 32, 34, 144, 221–22, 269
  Nabucco, 113, 166, 224
  Otello, 35, 36, 37, 144, 166, 179–82, 183, 253, 261, 268
  Requiem, 42, 77
  Rigoletto, 24, 28, 30, 35, 36, 141, 253, 260, 269
  Shakespearian texts used by, 182
  Simon Boccanegra, 174, 260
  Stiffelio, 260
  La Traviata, 45, 113, 145, 269
  Il Trovatore, 260, 269
Verklärte Nacht (Schoenberg), 262

Vespri Siciliani, I (Verdi), 37, 268
Vickers, Jon, 35, 37, 112, 140, 144, 145, 179
  Levine gala tribute by, 217–18
Vienna Chorus, 108
Vienna Philharmonic, 43, 74, 75, 80, 86, 89, 90, 91, 93, 95, 101, 112, 121, 158, 178, 184–85, 209, 270
Vienna State Opera, 205
Violin Concerto (Berg), 79, 262
Volpe, Joseph, 44, 135, 203, 217
von Stade, Frederica, 218, 221, 224
Voss, Manfred, 236

Wagner, Richard, 87, 112, 115, 136, 153, 156, 166, 167, 176, 190, 200, 208, 256
  as conductor, 157–59
  Der fliegende Holländer, 269
  Götterdämmerung, 149, 224, 231, 240, 259
  Levine influenced by, 158–59
  Levine's recordings of, 259–60
  Lohengrin, 36, 95, 138, 139, 140, 259
  Die Meistersinger von Nürnberg, 126–27, 139, 142, 191, 192–94, 195
  Parsifal, 36, 59, 131, 137, 139, 144, 166, 174, 214, 219, 234, 236, 238, 259, 279–80
  Das Rheingold, 105, 239, 259
  The Ring of the Nibelung, 45, 54, 59, 89, 116, 139, 140–43, 147, 148–49, 159, 182, 234–41, 259
  Siegfried, 232, 240, 259
  Tannhäuser, 36, 147, 219, 259
  Tristan und Isolde, 24, 45, 140, 141
  Die Walküre, 49, 149, 166, 182, 224, 239–40, 241
Wagner, Richard (baton maker), 104
Wagner, Siegfried, 241
Wagner, Wieland, 139
Wagner, Wolfgang, 139, 140, 149, 235
Walküre, Die (Wagner), 49, 149, 166, 182, 224, 239–40, 241
Wallenstein, Alfred, 27
Walter, Bruno, 123, 130, 137, 154, 160, 163, 187–88, 189, 270, 271
War and Peace (Prokofiev), 109

Weber, Carl Maria von, 155
 as conductor, 156–57
 Der Freischütz, 86
 Oberon, 156, 242
Webern, Anton von, 274
 centennial of, 76–77
 Op. 6 of, 67
Wechsler, Gil, 236
Weill, Kurt:
 Mahagonny, 79, 148
Weinberger, Jaromír:
 Schwanda the Bagpiper, 110
Wellington's Victory (Beethoven), 74
Welsh National Opera, 30
Werther (Massenet), 111
Wesendonck, Mathilde, 136
WFMT, 270
William Tell (Rossini), 110

Winterreise, Die (Schubert), 275
Wise, Isaac Meyer, 18
Wlaschiha, Ekkehard, 241
Wolf, Hugo, 229
Wozzeck (Berg), 77, 108, 114, 148, 208

Year at the Met, A (Smith), 42
Yeargan, Michael, 182, 198
Young Artist Development Program, 33,
 83, 205, 223

Zandonai, Riccardo:
 Francesca da Rimini, 259
"Zarathustras Mitternachtlied" (Niet-
 zsche), 214
Zeffirelli, Franco, 179, 182
Zimmermann, Gero, 236
Zipper, Herbert, 190